IN THE SHADOW OF ZION

In the Shadow of Zion

Promised Lands before Israel

Adam Rovner

12 Jan 2015

*To Amy —
Alaska was a real
idea. You could have
been a member of the
tribe!*

NEW YORK UNIVERSITY PRESS
New York and London

NEW YORK UNIVERSITY PRESS
New York and London
www.nyupress.org

References to Internet websites (URLs) were accurate at the time of writing.
Neither the author nor New York University Press is responsible for URLs that
may have expired or changed since the manuscript was prepared.

LIBRARY OF CONGRESS CATALOGING-IN-PUBLICATION DATA
Rovner, Adam, 1970- author.
In the shadow of Zion : promised lands before Israel / Adam Rovner.
pages cm
Includes bibliographical references and index.
ISBN 978-1-4798-1748-1 (hardback)
 1. Jewish diaspora--History--19th century. 2. Jewish diaspora--History--20th century. 3.
Jews--Migrations. 4. Jews--History. 5. Jews--Identity. 6. Zionism--Influence. I. Title.
DS134.R68 2014
909'.049240821--dc23
 2014024562

New York University Press books are printed on acid-free paper,
and their binding materials are chosen for strength and durability.
We strive to use environmentally responsible suppliers and materials
to the greatest extent possible in publishing our books.

Manufactured in the United States of America

10 9 8 7 6 5 4 3 2 1

Also available as an ebook

these extrapolations of territory
are published with an assist from
Jewish Federation of Greater Hartford

In memory of my grandfather, Harvey Rovner z"l, and in honor of my grandmother, Felice Rovner. They told me stories and taught me to be at home in this world, while always trying to make it a little bit better.

And, as imagination bodies forth
The forms of things unknown, the poet's pen
Turns them to shapes, and gives to airy nothing
A local habitation and a name.
—A Midsummer Night's Dream 5.1

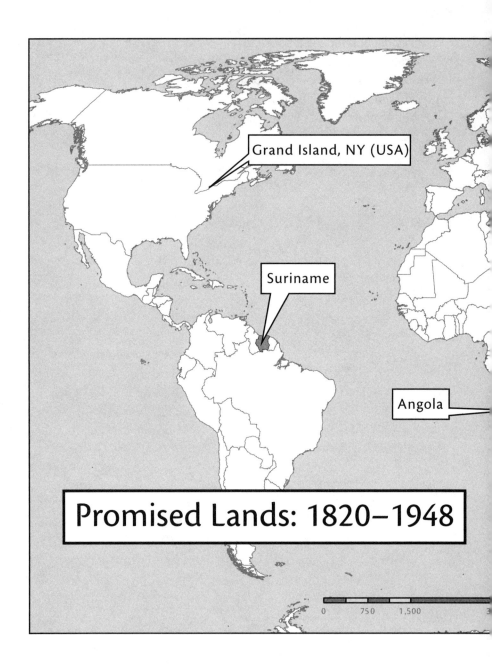

Grand Island, NY (USA)

Suriname

Angola

Promised Lands: 1820–1948

0   750   1,500

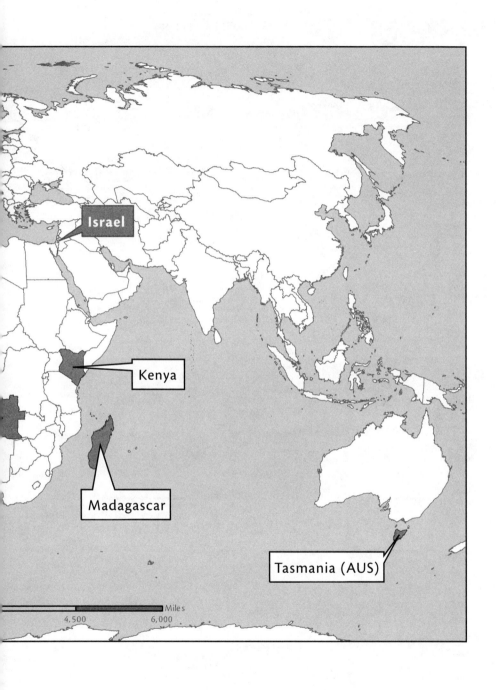

CONTENTS

"Land, Land!—This is the secret to the solution of the Jewish question."
Nathan Birnbaum, "Die Nationale Wiedergeburt des jüdischen Volkes in seinem Lande" (1893)

For generations, Jews and Christians, authors and adventurers, politicians and revolutionaries all sought a territorial solution to the problem of Jewish homelessness. Their searches for a homeland took them beyond the borders of the biblical land of Israel and across the globe to every continent except Antarctica. I have followed in their footsteps to examine first-hand the precise locations of each of these lost visions of Jewish autonomy. Today this little-known history has led me to Angola's second-largest city, Huambo.

It's early morning and the cool air carries the scent of smoke from hundreds of open-air fires. Potholes that could twist a car's axle crater the city streets. Open sewers edge the sidewalks. The façades of most buildings are pocked with bullet holes from Angola's decades-long civil war. Some structures reveal the tell-tale scars of mortar shells: twisted rebar snaking from jagged gashes in concrete walls. A boy, probably not more than ten years old, raises his deformed arms up to me from the pavement. Where his hands should be I see only knuckled humps of scaly-shiny skin. Probably leprosy. You can't travel far in this country without seeing someone on crutches, a pant leg hanging limply beneath the knee. There are millions of land mines buried beneath the country's soil, but leprosy is a new horror to behold. I recoil. So too does my close friend, Michael Kollins. In addition to taking many of the photographs for this book, Mike has tirelessly helped me track down archival sources and once, during a research trip in South America, he came to my rescue after a wild dog sunk its teeth into my leg and pulled me to the ground. "Why are we in Angola again?" he asks.

We're here because a century ago a scientific expedition arrived in the frontier outpost of Huambo to determine whether this region of the Benguela Plateau could be developed into a Jewish state. Angola's master at the time, Portugal, had provisionally approved the plan. The colonial press supported the project. So too did several important Jewish leaders. Yet Angola forever remained a paper state.

Between roughly 1820 and 1948, intellectuals advanced numerous proposals aimed at carving out Jewish territories in remote and often hostile locations. The would-be founding fathers of these imaginary Zions dispatched survey teams to far-flung locales and filed reports on the states they planned to establish. Instead of exporting Jaffa oranges, citizens of these unrealized Israels might have shipped pineapples from the Amazon Basin, stalked lions in East Africa, or hunted whales off the Tasmanian coast. Rather than sweltering under the Mediterranean sun, they might have endured tropical downpours in Madagascar, or felt the chill of the Angolan highlands. The Jewish state might even have been one of the United States.

This book tells the true stories of these fantastic Jewish geographies and the men and women who proposed them. These individuals risked public ridicule, assassination, personal betrayal, financial hardship, the physical dangers posed by a pitiless natural world, and an equally unforgiving political climate. At stake was nothing less than the salvation of European and Russian Jewry. They failed in their rescue efforts, and because they failed, their dreams and schemes have mostly been forgotten. Until now.

Introduction

They Say There Is a Land . . .

Victors and Vanquished

The great Hebrew poet and translator Shaul Tchernichovsky sat aboard an electric tram as it rattled through Berlin's busy streets in 1923. Overhead the wires sent a hum through the crowded car. He stared out the window at the cityscape and smoothed his walrus moustache with his fingers. A child of the countryside, Tchernichovsky first gained renown as a Romantic poet of the natural world. While industrialized Weimar Berlin flickered past him, he was shot through with a longing for another place, for another landscape. Inspiration creased the author's brow and he cast a wild-eyed glance from right to left looking for a scrap of paper. None could be found. His gaze then fell upon the white cuffs of his shirt. He gripped his fountain pen and began to scrawl the words to a new poem on the starched fabric.[1] That smeared verse born in a moment's passion was destined to become one of Tchernichovsky's most famous poems, and also one of his most vexing.

Handsome, barrel-chested, and with a wavy mane of hair, Tchernichovsky was nearly fifty in 1923. He had endured the early twentieth century's upheavals, serving as a medic in World War I and witnessing the Bolshevik Revolution. Tchernichovsky was also a committed Zionist who wrote in praise of Jewish national rebirth. For years he had wandered from place to place, from his native Ukraine across Russia, to Switzerland, to Turkey, and onward to Germany even as he set his heart on living in *Eretz Israel*—the land of Israel. Yet the modern era seemed to offer only dispossession and dislocation. In interwar Germany, Tchernichovsky attempted to eke out a living as a physician while he wrote, but few patients trusted a wordsmith with their health. His poverty grew so extreme that he was forced to walk the freezing winter streets without a coat.[2] At one point he considered emigrating to Madagascar, where the French colonial government offered posts to doctors willing to combat the island's rampant tropical diseases.[3] *Eretz Israel* always beckoned, but Tchernichovsky was frustrated by his efforts to secure a position in the one home he desired. And so he literally wore his heart's desire on his sleeve in the form of the verse to which he gave birth aboard a tram more than eighty years ago.

The resulting eight-stanza poem, "They Say: There Is a Land," reveals the depths of his distress. The final three stanzas read:

> Already
> We have crossed
> Many deserts and seas,
> Long we have walked,
> Our strength is at an end.
>
> How
> have we gone astray?
> When will we be unmolested?
> That land of sun,
> That land never found.
>
> Perhaps—
> the Land no longer exists?
> Surely—its radiance has grown dull!
> To us
> God bequeaths nothing—[4]

The speaker's sense of exclusion from the promised land—the "land of sun"—and of having been forsaken by a God who "bequeaths nothing" reveals a lack of faith in the Jewish future in *Eretz Israel*.

Tchernichovsky recognized that the anguish expressed by his poem would not exactly become a rallying cry for the Zionist pioneers then settling the soil. So he revised the poem that same year, cutting the stanzas above as well as two others. In their place he added eight spirited lines that would serve as a stirring conclusion. The revised, shortened anthem exhorts readers to redeem themselves by redeeming their ancestral land.

The two contrasting versions of "They Say: There Is a Land" continue to rattle through the author's collected works like prisoners joined at their ankles by a chain. Tchernichovsky later indicated that he himself could not decide which he preferred, the pessimistic original or the optimistic revision.[5] His own equivocation is far from surprising. He was well known for his exuberant despair and his desperate exuberance. As Tchernichovsky once declared, he was the poet both of the victors and of the vanquished.[6]

Despite the foregoing discussion, this is not a book devoted to literary criticism. This book traces the history of an idea—the tenaciously held idea of creating a territorial solution for Jewish homelessness *beyond* the biblical land of Israel. The opposing sentiments expressed by Tchernichovsky's two versions of "They Say: There Is a Land" are representative of a struggle that existed at the dawn of modern Jewish nationalism and dogged its development for decades. And because this book presents vivid accounts of individuals who worked to establish a variety of Jewish promised lands, the story of the origin of Tchernichovsky's poem frames the human scale of the dramas that unfold in the chapters to come.

Readers will meet with the fascinating but now obscure figures whose efforts to establish Jewish homelands involved utopian fervor, diplomacy, geographic exploration, catastrophe and perseverance, as well as love and tragic death. Familiar personages such as John Quincy Adams, David Lloyd George, Theodore Roosevelt, Albert Einstein, Eleanor Roosevelt, and Joseph P. Kennedy all played bit parts in these schemes. But I have opted to tell the story of the global search for a Jewish home from the perspective of those typically relegated to footnotes. The effect is to sing what Tchernichovsky called the "song of the vanquished,"[7] and to bear witness in a minor key to their dreams. One of the uses of history, it has been said, is to rescue lost causes from oblivion.[8] To the extent that this book details six proposals for alternate Zions stretching across four continents, it restores these lost causes to the annals of modern Jewish history.

This book further aims to reterritorialize space and place in prevailing conceptions of Jewish nationalism.[9] The narrative this book recounts thus presents a shadow history of Zionism—a history that exposes what has been obscured in the glare cast by both popular and academic histories of Israel's establishment. Many writers tend toward a teleological view of the rise of Israel in the twentieth century, often locating evidence of the nation's inevitable design from among the contingent processes of political evolution. Such narratives assert the supposedly universal significance of a specific brand of Jewish nationalism—Zionism—at the expense of competing nationalist ideologies that once battled "red in tooth and claw."[10]

The echo here of Darwinian discourse is intentional. We may think of Jewish nationalism as a tree with several evolutionary branches, only one of which survived to thrive. One of these vanquished branches possessed a prophetic appeal in certain eras, but may ultimately be seen as a humanitarian program committed to securing a Jewish home in *any* available territory. For the sake of economy, we may term this truncated limb "territorialism"; its mood is that of Tchernichovsky's original version of "They Say: There Is a Land." The victorious branch of nationalism that has flowered and grown may be characterized as idealistic and given to a messianic vision of sacrifice to ensure a Jewish home in one unique location: the biblical land of Israel. This is Zionism as we understand the term today; its tone is that of the revised "They Say: There Is a Land."

Zionism and territorialism, despite considerable differences, share several fundamental ideological principles. Both movements were dedicated to establishing a territorial entity under Jewish control through political means and the process of mass settlement, to a revival of Jewish social and cultural existence through demographic concentration and physical labor, and to a renaissance of national identity through the perpetuation of Jewish language and creative endeavor. They differed, above all, in where that territorial entity should be founded, what forms Jewish socio-cultural life should take, and what language best expressed Jewish national identity. These two rival movements also disagreed on the urgency of finding a solution to Jewish persecution and statelessness. The leaders of mainstream Zionism devoted themselves to an incremental vision of Jewish national rebirth. Territorialists, on the other hand, maintained that a radical and immediate solution to Jewish distress was necessary.[11] Given the fate of European Jewry during the Holocaust, it is difficult to reflect on territorialism without being haunted by the missed opportunities to save hundreds of thousands, perhaps millions, of lives.

Zionism and territorialism made use of similar operative strategies to justify or recommend practical actions based upon their ideological principles.[12] Both movements created formal membership organizations, held international congresses, launched periodicals to disseminate their views, attracted notable intellectuals to their cause, established or sought the creation of financial institutions for colonization, dispatched scientific commissions, negotiated with world leaders, and lobbied to secure agreements for Jewish immigration. In short, Zionist and territorialist leaders both said *there was a land*; they just couldn't agree on where it was located or how it was to be constituted.

Yiddish Policemen, Ostrich Farmers, Turtle-Hunters

Author Michael Chabon's best-selling novel *The Yiddish Policemen's Union* (2007) introduced readers around the world to an altered Jewish state in his depiction of a Yiddish-speaking refugee enclave in America. But the facts surrounding those who sought Jewish homes elsewhere are even more remarkable than Chabon's fiction. These visionaries imagined an island sanctuary for Jews and Native Americans on the edge of Niagara Falls, ostrich farms dotting East Africa, railways connecting Angola to Europe, modern agriculture flourishing on Madagascar's inland plateaus, skyscrapers towering above Tasmania's windswept bush, and turtle-hunting Holocaust survivors in Suriname. I have journeyed to each of these proposed homelands, treading phantom landscapes to explore what historian Simon Schama called the "archive of the feet."[13] But the interconnected stories of these projects have been recovered using traditional archival materials as well: letters, telegrams, internal reports, diaries, FBI dispatches, newspapers, and hundreds of other documents scoured from repositories the world over.

Dozens of other ideas and projects for Jewish settlement were launched during the time period this book discusses. The most familiar of these was the Soviet Union's announcement of the Jewish Autonomous Region in far eastern Siberia (Birobidzhan), though for the most part the organized territorialist movement treated the scheme coolly. While I mention this episode and others in passing, I focus most closely on six examples of what may be termed territorial autonomist projects for promised lands: in upstate New York, East Africa, Angola's Benguela Plateau, the central highlands of Madagascar, extreme southwestern Tasmania, and Suriname's torrid rainforest. These proposals form the core of this book's exploration because they adhere to the following criteria: (1) they were initiated and supported by a Jewish individual or organization; (2) they aspired to sovereignty, or at the very least, to a high degree of cultural and political autonomy; (3) they received the imprimatur of a diplomatic promissory or of legislative consent; and (4) the disparate territories were each the subject of a survey commission, a fact which reveals how a scientific application of settlement ideas aimed to alter Jewish reality and geopolitics. Furthermore, (5) each plan was advanced by a significant author. The connection between the literary imagination and the geographic imagination testifies to the crucial role that writers played in transforming a dispersed Jewry into a nation with territorial ambitions.

Zionist historiography and literary scholarship have long demonstrated the intimate bond between what it is now alliterated as "nation and narration."[14] But insofar as there exist academic studies of territorialism and its leading figures,[15] there has been little attention paid to the exceptional role that authors and journalists played in the many thwarted efforts at Jewish nation-building. As scholar of nationalism Anthony Smith has recognized, intellectuals define national identity and express a community's social and political aspirations through arts and letters.[16] But literary and artistic works have in greater measure failed to create a coherent sense of national identity, or even to chart the course of a given ethnic community's ambitions. A nation may indeed be an "imagined community,"[17] but the contours of some nations remain forever imaginary. Territorialism's author-activists invoked pragmatic doctrines, *realpolitik*, the natural and social sciences, and technocratic principles in support of their state-building projects. Their Zionist antagonists—including Menachem Ussishkin (an engineer), Chaim Weizmann (a chemist), and Stephen Wise (a rabbi and power broker)—often seemed to ground political action for a Jewish state in Palestine in an art of the *im*possible. What these men lacked in terms of the literary, they more than made up for in their mythopoesis of the biblical land of Israel. Ironically, the *literati* who championed territorialism may be seen as having suffered from a deficit of imagination and their Zionist adversaries from its surfeit.

Territorialism, like Zionism, shared a broad mission of cultural and psychological Jewish renewal and a conviction that the Emancipation had failed the masses. Along with various strains of Zionist thinking, territorialism also advocated a land-based solution to the historical problem of Jewish homelessness. Yet unlike mainstream Zionism, territorialism sought a homeland *outside* of the biblical land of Israel. All mainstream forms of Zionism developed to promote Hebrew, encouraged a break with diasporic ways of life, and fostered a sense of continuity with the Jewish history and memory of *Eretz Israel*. Territorialism, at least in its later incarnations, promoted Yiddish and nurtured a sense of continuity with European Jewish folkways, even as its adherents sought to hasten the end of the Diaspora itself. Zionism's leadership was primarily concerned with the fate of the *yishuv*—the Jewish community of pre-state Israel. Territorialist leaders were obsessed by the existential dangers faced by millions of vulnerable Jews in Europe and Russia. They cast off the mythologies of ancient Israel in favor of creating a new Jewish land somewhere—anywhere—else.

The intellectual history of territorialism reveals the first crisis of Zionism. Today Zionism remains the chief Jewish nationalist ideology, often to the point of rendering past and present alternative visions of nationhood invisible. Yet there are clear indications that at least one territorialist movement garnered more popular support on the *yidishe gas*—"the Jewish street"—in the first decades of the twentieth century than Zionism. With the rise of Nazism in the early 1930s and with

Jewish immigration increasingly restricted by the world's nations, territorialism again proved an attractive option for many. Later, as Hitler's grip on Europe tightened, territorialism found influential supporters and presented a resurgent threat to Zionism. If only for the reason that territorialism was considered a viable form of Jewish nationalism by its proponents and sympathizers, and as a danger to Zionist dreams by that rival movement's leadership, a survey of territorialism's most notable leaders and their projects is an important addition to existing historiography.

A number of other modern Jewish political theories developed contemporaneously to territorialism and allow us to clarify the principles of this now mostly forgotten ideology. A useful though far from complete list of competing movements includes: (I) various Zionist incarnations, such as mainstream or Labor Zionism (with its mutually antagonistic parties), religious Zionism (*Mizrahi*), Revisionism (the New Zionist Organization), the binationalist *Ihud* (Union), and the cultural or spiritual Zionism associated with Ahad Ha'am (Asher Ginsberg) and his followers; (II) Diaspora nationalism, incorporating Bundism and other non-Zionist or anti-Zionist socialist streams that sought autonomy in the Diaspora, and (III) "Agudism," a religio-political movement aligned with a metaphysical conception of Jewish nationhood.[18] We may consider territorialism along with these three associated ideologies as chambers in the divided heart of Jewish nationalism, connected though compartmentalized, and together pulsing with life in the modern era. The borders between these positions were, however, permeable, and individual proponents of these schools of thought were capable of remarkable fluidity. Though necessarily reductive, the following schema allows nonspecialists a glimpse of the intellectual agitation of the recent past.

(I) *Zionism vs. territorialism:* Broadly speaking, Labor Zionism championed a socialist oriented, agro-industrial commitment to Jewish national revival in what was first Ottoman Palestine, and later, British Mandate Palestine. Territorialists supported either a bourgeois settler colonialism, or agro-industrial social revolutionary settlements on modest to large areas of land somewhere other than Palestine. Militant nationalist Vladimir (Ze'ev) Jabotinsky and his Revisionists adopted a maximalist position regarding territory in the land of Israel.

Territorialists did not believe a viable Jewish state could arise in the land of Israel no matter what boundaries were established. Adherents of the *Mizrahi* platform attempted to reconcile a secular movement often hostile to Jewish tradition—Zionism writ large—to religious values. Territorialism did not typically express hostility toward Jewish traditions or observance. The *Ihud* and its related forerunner *Brit Shalom* were keenly aware of the Arab population in Palestine and sought to work with them toward binationalist compromise. The territorialists, for all their utopianism, believed that Jewish settlement would create an endless state of war with an Arab population who would never accept mass Jewish immigration. Territorialism was thus opposed to binationalism; the movement's aims were fundamentally separatist. Ahad Ha'am's cultural Zionism demanded a spiritual center in the biblical land of Israel that would revitalize the Diaspora. Territorialists, however, believed that a mass Jewish settlement in some other corner of the globe would rejuvenate Jewish life throughout the world, including in *Eretz Israel*.

(II) *Diaspora nationalism vs. territorialism:* Like Diaspora nationalists—those inspired by historian Simon Dubnov, Bundists, folkists, and others—territorialism sought cultural and some measure of political autonomy for the Jewish people. But unlike Diaspora nationalists, territorialists believed that such autonomy could only be achieved on land acquired through diplomatic means and colonized as the result of mass immigration and rational, planned settlement. Diaspora nationalists called for Jews to reinvigorate themselves in their scattered communities throughout Europe and Russia *where they already lived.* Territorialists called for an in-gathering of Jews on foreign soil that they would settle and then make their own. Though both Diaspora nationalists and territorialists expressed what might generically be termed democratic-socialist visions, the two ideologies were divided as to the role of territorial acquisition and possession. Dubnovian autonomists and Bundists, for example, were committed to the idea of nationhood without statehood. Territorialists dedicated themselves to the idea of a land-based nationalism achieved through cultural and civil autonomy, or even sovereign independence. In today's world we might consider what was once called "third person Zionism"—activism, advocacy, and fundraising on behalf of Israel by Jews who have no intention of leaving their distant homes—as a kind of contemporary Diaspora nationalism in the service of Zionist goals.[19]

(III) *"Agudism" vs. territorialism:* Many Zionist thinkers and pioneers were not only secular, but antireligious. Agudism arose as a reactionary political movement of orthodox Jews who fought modernization and opposed Zionism on theological grounds. While many of the territorialists were secular, they evinced more sympathy for religious tradition than did most mainstream Zionists. Territorialism and Agudism shared an essential belief that the land of Israel was less important than the people of Israel. Agudism promoted Jewish rebirth through a strict adherence to religious practice in places where Jews already lived in significant numbers, though some Agudists did advocate for a Torah-true pioneer movement in pre-state Palestine. Territorialism, as has been stated, wanted to move a large portion of the Jewish body politic elsewhere. Whereas territorialism was originally imperial and bourgeois, and later social revolutionary, Agudism refined an allegiance to rabbinic authority into a political ideology. Similarly, territorialism was materialist where Agudism was metaphysical. Orthodox anti-Zionist political movements have not often been considered part of the history of Jewish nationalism, yet they are a phenomenon of the modern era that can profitably be viewed in this context.

For many Jewish nationalists, the virtues of a mass exodus to Palestine were therefore not self-evident during the first-half century congruent with the rise of Zionism. Today we may take for granted the inevitability of the Jewish state's existence in much of *Eretz Israel.* This common assumption, however, is an "existential illusion,"[20] a conviction that may stem from a transposition of Jewish messianic beliefs to the arena of worldly politics. As welcome as the Jewish assumption of power in the State of Israel may be, we should remember that committed nationalist factions sought their promised lands in many other locations and on the bases of divergent political theories. The contentious past of Jewish nationalist life does not diminish Zionist achievements. On the contrary, it burnishes them by demonstrating Zionism's success over and against the appeal of influential opponents.

To be clear, this book is not a Zionist polemic. I am not a propagandist, though I am attached to Israel through bonds of culture, friendship, family, and citizenship. Neither is this book a territorialist polemic—a ludicrous and anachronistic proposition if ever there was one. True, my sympathies lie with territorialism's proponents who are the heroes of this book; identification with one's subject is a familiar hazard for authors. Zionism's heroes, moreover, already have their books. Nor is this an entry into the crowded field of works by historians, journalists, and literary scholars who "bash" Israel for its shortcomings, real and imagined. The narratives that follow do, however, reveal how some influential Zionists worked to undermine territorialist projects. My purpose in highlighting these episodes is to demonstrate how the Zionist establishment viewed territorialism as a serious competitor for Jewish and non-Jewish support. This fact restores to territorialism some of the significance it once possessed.

Zionism emerged the victor, of course, and responsibility for the defeat of territorialism cannot be attributed solely to the obstructionist campaigns waged by Zionist activists. Territorialist leaders were indeed visionaries, but they were often blinded by a belief in the essential benevolence of the community of Western nation states they were eager to join as equals. So too were they seduced by the internal logic and pragmatism they were certain their expansive schemes possessed. Because they were charismatic, resourceful, and productive people themselves, territorialism's leading figures failed to fully understand that power was vested in the bureaucracies, institutions, and the entrenched interests of the governments with whom they treated, and not the isolated good will of those governments' representatives. The following chapters reveal that the remote areas suggested as Jewish homelands also did not possess a living memory of a collective past—a persuasive ethnoscape[21]—that could attract either the persecuted masses seeking an exit from Europe, or the funding required to resettle them.

Chapter One describes the pioneering work of American playwright and editor Mordecai Manuel Noah, who attempted to establish a Jewish city-state in upstate New York during the first decades of the nineteenth century. Noah is often acknowledged as the first Jew in the modern era to plot the creation of a Jewish state. He originally hoped to establish a sanctuary within the United States, but later argued for the restoration of Jewry to the holy land. Noah may therefore be considered both a territorialist and a proto-Zionist, but in either guise his importance lies in the fact that he recognized that Jewish power is vested in a particular place. A detailed discussion of Noah's plans for homelands in America and Ottoman Palestine allows us to distinguish between these states of the imagination, and to point to an inherent tension in what later came to be known as Zionism. Noah's efforts fascinated Anglo-Jewish author Israel Zangwill, one of Herzl's most intimate collaborators, and Noah's example may have spurred Zangwill to ally himself with Herzl's fledgling Zionist movement.

Chapter Two reveals the extent to which Zangwill and others, especially Eliezer Ben-Yehuda, the man credited with reviving Hebrew as a spoken language, championed settlement in Great Britain's East African Protectorate (now Kenya). The dilemma occasioned by Colonial Secretary Joseph Chamberlain's offer of land to Herzl in East Africa—the "Uganda Plan" of 1903—led to a power struggle in the Zionist Organization. The dispatch of a Zionist Commission to evaluate a large swath of territory in western Kenya nearly ruptured the movement. My research indicates that the findings of this expedition were likely sabotaged from the inside by a member of the Commission. The subsequent rejection of the British land grant in East Africa launched Zangwill's breakaway territorialist movement.

Chapter Three details how Zangwill's Jewish Territorial Organization (ITO)[22] negotiated with the Portuguese government to create a republic in Angola in the second decade of the twentieth century. One of the greatest scientific minds of Zangwill's generation, Dr. John Walter Gregory, traveled through Angola in search of suitable territory for the ITO. The positive report of his expedition, coupled with Portuguese self-interest, almost led to the establishment of a Jewish state there. World War I helped scuttle ITOist colonization efforts in that West African possession, but in the years preceding World War II the refugee crisis in Europe resuscitated interest in Zangwill's territorialist program.

Chapter Four examines how the Freeland League for Jewish Territorial Colonization, the successor to the ITO, and its early ideologue, German author Alfred Döblin, worked to fashion a Jewish colony in French overseas possessions, most notably on the island of Madagascar. This chapter also describes the suspected involvement of right-wing Jewish nationalist Ze'ev Jabotinsky in that territorialist evacuation scheme.

A three-man commission sailed to Madagascar in 1937 to investigate the island's suitability for Jewish colonization. While the findings of the two Jewish members of the expedition were disappointing, for a time the plan held out hope for Jews as conditions worsened across much of Europe.

Chapter Five portrays the work of Melech Ravitch (Zekharye-Khone Bergner), an important Yiddish poet and editor, who helped revive territorialist designs on portions of Australia. The Freeland League's guiding spirit, former Soviet commissar of justice Isaac Nachman Steinberg, struggled to forge a Jewish micronation down under. Steinberg, an editor and author, first looked to the continent's arid northwest as Melech Ravitch had suggested. Later, as war erupted, Steinberg turned his attention to Tasmania. His collaborators, Jewish journalist Caroline Isaacson and Christian gentleman Critchley Parker Junior, pursued the Tasmania option and received the support of influential governmental figures. The story of their relationship and of Parker's doomed survey of southwestern Tasmania reminds readers that the fate of politics often rests on the vagaries of fortune.

Chapter Six chronicles Steinberg's attempt to father a South American freehold for Holocaust survivors in the jungles of Dutch Guiana, now independent Suriname. Steinberg drew inspiration for the Freeland League plan from a semiautonomous eighteenth-century Jewish settlement that once flourished in that country. The favorable reports of two expert commissions sent to Dutch Guiana to prepare for Jewish colonization demonstrate how scientific and rational calculations laid the foundation for this important but little-known plan. An epilogue summarizes the legacy of territorialism and speculates on the continued attraction the movement holds for artists and thinkers.

Before I set off to visit the site of the planned Jewish city-state in Tasmania, Australian novelist and historian Richard Flanagan told me that "the abyss between failure and success is where greatness lies." Territorialism's leaders may not have achieved greatness by this measure, but neither does the fact that they failed indict their efforts. Rather, it is the scope of their aspirations that determines territorialism's value. I hope that the epic sweep of their struggles will inspire readers of this book to reject the shabbiness of reality and to think of better futures wherever they live.

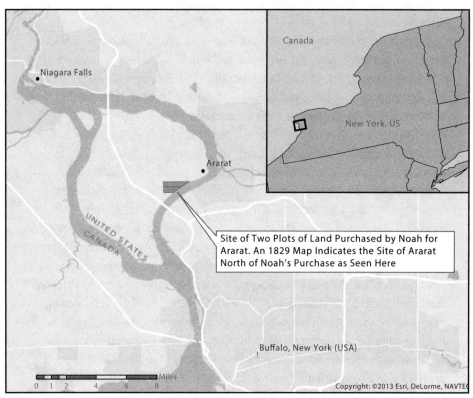

Site of Two Plots of Land Purchased by Noah for Ararat. An 1829 Map Indicates the Site of Ararat North of Noah's Purchase as Seen Here

Niagara Falls

Ararat

UNITED STATES

CANADA

Buffalo, New York (USA)

Miles
0 1 2   4   6   8

Copyright: ©2013 Esri, DeLorme, NAVTE

Canada

New York, US

Grand Island

1

Noah's Ark on the Niagara

Grand Island, New York (1818–1848)

Member of the Hebrew Nation

In the spring of 1818, steamboats ferried passengers from the sleepy village of Brooklyn to Manhattan, the young American republic's largest city and home to approximately one hundred thousand people. Among them were fewer than five hundred Jews.[1] Most of these souls could be accommodated in the city's only Jewish house of worship, Congregation Shearith Israel's Mill Street Synagogue, which was enlarged and dedicated on April 17, 1818. The featured speaker at the ceremonies that Friday was journalist, former diplomat, playwright, and political bulldog Mordecai Manuel Noah. The thirty-two-year-old Noah was a "stout . . . gentleman, with sandy hair, a large Roman nose, and . . . red whiskers."[2] He cut a formidable figure in the first half of the nineteenth century, yet he is remembered not for his many achievements, but for his spectacular failure to create the first Jewish homeland in the modern era. While Noah's ideas may have been ahead of their time, the man himself was most firmly of his time. The remarkable story of his efforts to establish a Jewish state under the protection of the U.S. Constitution emerges from a colorful backdrop featuring a global network of politicians and missionaries, revolutionaries and writers, rabbis and Indians, and a host of utopian settlement schemes.

The published origins of Noah's Jewish nationalism appear in his *Discourse Delivered at the Consecration* (1818) of the Mill Street Synagogue. There he maintained that the "chosen country" for the chosen people was none other than the United States, at least until the Jews could "recover their ancient . . . dominions" in the Near East.[3] In the meantime, he urged his coreligionists to take up "a useful branch of labor" like agriculture in their American dispersion, and to conform themselves to Jeffersonian ideals of yeoman virtue.[4] Noah praised the U.S. as a haven for European Jews who sought "light and liberty"[5] and encouraged them to flock to the New World. But rather than assimilate in the land where all men are created equal, he advocated that his fellow Jews stand fast in their religious traditions and bind themselves to Hebrew, "the language of poets, prophets, and warriors."[6] His historic *Discourse* thus touched on many of the central ideological tenets of what would become known as Zionism more than seventy years later: productive labor, immigration, shared national sentiment, a common Jewish language, and the longed-for physical in-gathering of the Jewish people.[7] The heavy-lidded Noah was, then, a visionary. Certainly, he was a quintessentially American figure who embodied the brash confidence of his day. His pronouncements were both grand and naïve. Grand, because the scope of his aspirations outstripped his abilities to achieve them. Naïve, because he never realized as much.

As a young man, Mordecai eked out a living in a number of cities, including Albany, Philadelphia, and Harrisburg, where he campaigned to elect Simon Snyder as governor of Pennsylvania. Snyder rewarded Noah with the honorific title of "major" in the state's militia once he was inaugurated. Noah further increased his political capital by siding with the War Hawks to support President Madison's successful reelection bid and his declaration of war with Britain in 1812. He soon traveled to Washington and there petitioned America's fourth president for a consulship. After a period of delay, he was duly appointed consul at Tunis, one of the Barbary States.[8]

The Barbary States of North Africa were governed by a loose confederation of strongmen, some owing allegiance to the Ottoman Empire. Their privateers preyed for centuries on non-Muslim ships and raided coastal European towns to replenish slave markets. Successive American governments paid tribute to their leaders even while U.S. vessels were continually harassed and their cargoes and crews captured. Into this world of piracy and state-sponsored terror stepped Noah, an untried twenty-seven-year-old. It may seem surprising today that a Jew could be appointed diplomat to a Muslim nation, but the longstanding enmity between the Christian West and Islamic North Africa meant that Jews were perceived as neutral intermediaries. In fact, Noah petitioned for his consulship based on his religion: "It would be a favourable circumstance in sending a member of the Hebrew nation to the Barbary Powers . . . supported as I should be with the wealth and influence of forty thousand [Jewish] residents."[9] The presence of large Jewish communities across North Africa was thus seen as a natural complement to Noah's diplomacy.

His career ended in disgrace, however, when Secretary of State James Monroe recalled him in 1815. "At the time of your appointment," Monroe claimed, "it was not known that the religion which you profess would form any obstacle to the exercise of your Consular functions. . . . On the receipt of this letter, therefore, you will consider yourself no longer in the public service."[10] Contemporary historians find no evidence that Noah's duties were compromised by his Judaism; his dismissal was likely due to his mishandling of another matter.[11] Once returned to the U.S., Noah struggled to clear his reputation. He exposed the story of his discharge in a public manner, penning an exculpatory pamphlet.[12] His polemic expressed fear that the bigotry manifested by the language of his recall would be used by America's "enemies abroad, to show the little confidence that can be reposed in our . . . institutions."[13] In particular, he worried that Jewish emigration to America would diminish, and that therefore "a numerous and useful people [may] be alienated" from the United States.[14]

Noah also worked to push himself to center stage on the American cultural scene. His financially and critically successful drama, *She Would Be a Soldier, or the Plains of Chippewa*, was produced in June 1819. The patriotic play dealt with an important battle during the recent war and marked Noah's most significant contribution to American theater. The drama featured a dignified Indian chief who defends native territorial rights against the "cruel white men" who "rose like wolves upon us [Indians], fired our dwellings, drove off our cattle, [and] sent us . . . to the wilderness, to seek for shelter."[15] Perhaps Noah's belief, popular at the time, that Native Americans were remnants of the Jewish lost tribes accounted for this sympathetic portrayal. *She Would Be a Soldier* elevated Noah to the self-proclaimed position of "gladiator for . . . American Drama" and helped to forge a national literature by thrusting politics onto the stage.[16]

He next published *Travels in England, France, Spain and the Barbary States* (1819). The book, one of the first travelogues penned by an American, contains a fascinating narrative of Noah's adventures. He reported on the state of London's theaters and Parisian hotels, expressed disgust at the foodways of Spaniards, and described the treatment of women in the Barbary. He devoted considerable space to historical excurses, detailed archaeological ruins, discussed the international trade in ostrich feathers, and advocated launching a modern-day crusade against North Africa's Muslim rulers.[17] Noah also evinced a peculiar interest in the health of people's teeth wherever he roamed. Most notably, the publication of his *Travels* reveals his self-serving streak. Noah's volume offered him a pulpit from which to defend his conduct as consul. "It was not necessary for a citizen of the United States to have his faith stamped on his forehead," Noah railed, "the name of freeman is a sufficient passport, and my government should have supported me."[18] The very faith that Noah had vaunted in his petition to serve as consul had become the official reason for his dismissal. In Noah's published vindication, his treatment by the government emerges as an un-American act that smeared his country's good name. Noah thus set out not only to clear his name, but also that of the U.S. and its democratic institutions.

To that end, he sent the living ex-presidents copies of his *Discourse at the Consecration* of the Mill Street Synagogue and solicited their thoughts on Jewish rights. All three—John Adams, Thomas Jefferson, and James Madison—responded with affirmations of Jewish equality before the law. Noah reprinted their letters in an appendix to his *Travels*.[19] But the damage was irreversible; Noah would never again be granted a federal appointment. Still, these formative experiences in political lobbying and international diplomacy, and his discovery of the power of the press, would coalesce into a grand scheme to ensure Jewish national dignity through territorial acquisition—a plan that borrowed inspiration from Christian restorationism.

During Noah's sojourn in England on the way to Tunis, he had met Reverend John Owen, an influential secretary for the British Bible Society.[20] The Bible Society was a missionary organ of the Clapham Sect, a group of devout Anglicans engaged in proselytizing and social reform. In particular, they were vocal critics of the slave trade. Owen asked Noah in the fall of 1813 to distribute Arabic translations of the Bible among the slave trading Muslims of the Barbary. Noah assented, but quickly recognized the danger in doing so "among the Turks,"[21] and did not fulfill his promise to Owen. Nonetheless, these meetings with Owen likely influenced Noah's view of missionary organizations in general. In his Mill Street *Discourse*, Noah praised the work of bible societies for promoting Jewish and Christian harmony by "teaching each other the benefits and blessings of toleration . . . in view of our common origins."[22] Reverend Owen's colleague and in-law was William Wilberforce, the leading member of the Clapham fellowship.[23] Wilberforce was also Britain's most prominent abolitionist and one of the founders of Freetown, Sierra Leone, a colony established as a sanctuary for freed slaves who had served with the British against American revolutionaries. Noah makes no reference to Wilberforce in his *Travels*, but he was certainly aware of Claphamite notions of collective territorial settlement in Africa as a means to uplift American blacks. In a series of four articles published in October 1817 in *The National Advocate*, then under Noah's editorship, the colonization of Sierra Leone is mentioned with unreserved enthusiasm.[24] The significance of this connection for Noah's future Jewish colonization projects is not merely coincidental. Noah's familiarity with the Freetown experiment in "repatriating" an oppressed diasporic minority may have contributed to his future dreams of a Jewish state in the U.S., and later still, for a reborn nation in Palestine.

The Clapham Sect's Bible Society spawned another ambitious offshoot, the London Society for Promoting Christianity among the Jews.[25] The London Society directed its efforts toward conversion and the ultimate restoration of the Jews to their ancestral land in order to hasten the messianic era. Belief in the physical return of Jews to the promised land was already popular among English, Scottish, and American evangelical groups.[26] During its most active years, the London Society was helmed by an eccentric true believer who boasted a large inheritance, Reverend Lewis Way. The Oxford graduate and lawyer put his scholarly credentials to work by undertaking a self-directed study of Jewish history.[27] What he found was both a tale of woe and a prophetic hope for mankind's future. Reverend Way blamed his fellow Christians for their inadequate display of charity toward God's chosen people.[28] Maltreatment of the Jews, he believed, revealed the depths of Christian hypocrisy. And so the amiable, baby-faced Way devoted the rest of his life to Jewish welfare.[29]

His first step was to welcome sixteen impoverished Jews into his house, baptize them, and instruct them in Christianity. Way's flock proved to be black sheep. They repaid his hospitality by stealing books from his library, as well as the household's silver spoons.[30] In the wake of failure, Way embarked on an even grander scheme. He resolved to travel across Europe to Moscow in order to meet Czar Alexander I, then one of the most powerful world leaders. Reverend Way intended primarily to plead for Jewish emancipation, and secondarily, as Wilberforce's emissary, for an end to slavery.[31] In preparation for his journey, he had a carriage constructed with special springs to mitigate the miseries of the roads, and he commissioned an artist to paint portraits of his beloved family, which he carried with him in a red leather portfolio.[32] He set off from England on August 9, 1817, accompanied by several colleagues, including apostate Benjamin Nehemiah Solomon, a rabbi from Lvov who had turned Christian evangelist under Way's protection.[33] The *Missionary Register* reported that Way planned "to investigate the state . . . of the Jews abroad . . . and to awaken the attention of Christians on the Continent to the conversion of the Jews."[34] His even more grandiose proposal, fired by biblical prophecy, was to seek the gradual emancipation of the Jews as a prelude to their final restoration to the holy land.[35]

In letters home, Way emerges as a guileless gentleman of quixotic tendencies who was convinced the divine guided his efforts. He and his devoted squire, Benjamin Solomon, braved many hardships together on their long journey, often stopping along hazardous roads to pray or preach. Way composed a fervent verse in honor of Solomon's loyalty after they were forced to abandon their carriage and travel by open sledge once winter set in.[36] Solomon, for his part, spoke to crowds of Jews who, at least according to his reports, avidly listened to him as he spread the Good News.[37] The itinerant Way, now wrapped in an "incomparable bear-skin"[38] against the Russian winter, referred to himself as a pilgrim whose "face . . . turned Zionward."[39] He firmly believed that Czar Alexander would support his aims—a belief not without foundation. During this period, the czar found solace in pietism and collaborated with a Russian branch of the Claphamite Bible Society to distribute translations of holy writ to his subjects in the many languages of his empire.[40]

Alexander and Way did indeed meet four times in 1818.[41] After one audience with the czar, Way reported back to Wilberforce that "[i]t was the spirit of God which manifested itself in this memorable interview."[42] The devout emperor who had robbed Napoleon of victory and the evangelist who had been robbed of his silverware proved fast friends. They read the Bible together by candlelight around a small table and discussed the destiny of the Jews literally "tête-à-tête and pied-à-pied," as much because they were in studious sympathy as because Alexander proved to be rather deaf.[43] Like the Clapham Sect's Freetown efforts, the czar also had a plan to colonize territory for the sake of a despised people: the Jews. Czar Alexander proposed to grant his Jews land in the Ukrainian peninsula of Crimea, a plan Way supported.[44] He even traveled to the region to investigate its potential for mass settlement and there he was granted his second audience with Alexander.[45] Though that settlement project was soon abandoned, Way's meetings with the czar did help to publicize the cause of Jewish emancipation.

Alexander, impressed by Way's devotion, asked him to travel to the Congress of Aix-la-Chapelle, which convened in the autumn of 1818 to decide upon the European balance of power in the post-Napoleonic era. The czar further pressed Way to present memoranda on Jewish emancipation to the European statesmen of Austria, Great Britain, and Prussia who were to assemble at the Congress.[46] At the Congress, Way again met with Alexander. There they discussed details of the Jews' planned enfranchisement and agreed that the eternal people should first "be initiated in the principles of civilization & general knowledge" for "if they were restored in their present States they could not cultivate their Land"—*Eretz Israel*.[47] They also determined to collaborate on the publication and dissemination of the New Testament in Yiddish. The convictions Way elaborated in his subsequent report to the delegates at Aix-la-Chapelle rested on the work of some of the leading Enlightenment advocates for Jewish liberty. Influential French Revolutionary cleric Abbé Henri Grégoire and the progressive Prussian man of letters Christian Wilhelm von Dohm are both cited in the "Principles" Way submitted to the Congress in support of Jewish civil and social rights.[48] When Way's proposals for Jewish emancipation were finally signed by the assembled potentates and dignitaries, he praised God, thanking Him for his abundant blessings. He enthused, "it is now not only possible but probable that the *Nation* will be born [into] existence in three years."[49] Here he refers to his certainty that the Jewish nation would soon be granted territory for their physical and spiritual regeneration. His work, he declared, was at an end.[50]

Noah too was familiar with von Dohm's unflagging support of Jewish rights. In his survey of the state of Jewish life in Europe as presented in the Mill Street *Discourse*, Noah cites von Dohm's famous essay "Concerning the Amelioration of the Civil Status of the Jews" as evidence of Christian good will.[51] Noah was connected more directly with another religious reformer singled out by Reverend Way in his "Principles," the aforementioned Abbé Henri Grégoire. The bishop's strident advocacy for humanist causes, especially abolition and Jewish emancipation, garnered him an international reputation. Noah was introduced to Grégoire in Paris. In his *Travels*, Noah reported that the abbé "felt sincere pleasure at my appointment" as consul to Tunis because it demonstrated "the liberality of our [American] institutions."[52] After his dismissal, Grégoire's complaints against the manner of Noah's recall "were no less sincere or powerful."[53] Grégoire was well known in America as the author of a famous abolitionist tract, *Enquiry Concerning the Intellectual and Moral Faculties and Literature of Negroes* (1808). That volume was dedicated to "all those men [who] plead the cause of the unhappy blacks and mulattoes," including Wilberforce and other Claphamites associated with the Freetown colony.[54]

At this point, it may be helpful to summarize Noah's bewildering "social network"—his global connections to notable nineteenth-century reformers and their efforts on behalf of oppressed Jews and blacks. Noah met with Reverend Owen, a leading member of the abolitionist Clapham Sect, and lauded the work of philosemitic bible societies in his Mill Street *Discourse*. He published a long, favorable assessment of African colonization in Sierra Leone as editor of New York's *National Advocate*. One installment praised a black proponent of African colonization for his efforts to purchase an autonomous territory for "people of color" *within* the United States as well.[55] Noah was likewise impressed by the celebrated humanism of von Dohm, recalling his work in his *Discourse*, and he was even more strongly influenced by Abbé Grégoire, whom he praised in both his *Discourse* and his *Travels*. Given the political and diplomatic significance of the Congress of Aix-la-Chappelle, it is not surprising that *The National Advocate* published several dispatches about the proceedings throughout the autumn of 1818.[56] Yet Noah, in his capacity as editor, did not mention the Congress's discussion of Jewish rights or Reverend Way's success in swaying statesmen to approve a protocol designed to improve the Jewish condition in Europe.[57] Nonetheless, Noah must have been familiar with Way's proposals to the Congress, many of which echoed in content and rhetoric those present in his own *Discourse* from earlier that same year.

The only direct linkage between Noah and Way appears to be the result of journalistic error. On July 2, 1819, a newspaper published in the Rhineland city of Koblenz, which had until recently been occupied by Czar Alexander's forces and which Way had visited the year before,[58] reported that the reverend had "affiliated himself with Mr. Noah, a North American, in a plan to gather the scattered Israelites together at some point on Earth and to establish a state for them. For this purpose, they chose ... territory [in] the United States."[59] The paper printed a translation of the proclamation that Noah delivered "to his brothers in faith in the Old World" in support of the venture.[60] In the proclamation, Noah announces that " [f]ree America . . . welcomes the oppressed peoples of the old world."[61] He concludes that a "new Jewish state" that would "equal Palestine in size" would arise in the United States "[u]nder the protection of the great American Union."[62] Though the Koblenz report does appear to reproduce Noah's own views, no extant archival documents unambiguously link Noah to Way. The anonymous Koblenz reporter's connection of Way to Noah probably stems from the former's much publicized travels throughout Europe on behalf of the Jews, and the coincidental nature of Noah's own contemporaneously publicized schemes for Jewish in-gathering.[63]

The presumed collaboration between Way and Noah demonstrates that in the political climate of the time, the kind of settlement scheme the two independently propounded was widespread. Nonetheless, Noah may be regarded as the first Jew in the modern world to advance a practical program for Jewish territorial concentration. Significantly, Way and Noah both hailed from countries in which Jews possessed civic freedoms, thus further revealing how Jewish "ethnic territorialism"—later evolving into Zionism—arose as a response to emancipation and its discontents.

Inner State of the Jews

In August 1819, a series of violent antisemitic attacks erupted in the German principalities, first in Bavaria and then in towns throughout the country and across borders into neighboring nations.[64] Jews were beaten and chased from public places, their property was ransacked, and synagogues and Torah scrolls were desecrated. Rioters chanted "*Hep! Hep! Schlagt die Juden tot!*" (Kill the Jews!) as they cut a swath of destruction through Jewish quarters. The cryptic cry *Hep! Hep!* followed the Jews as they fled for their lives ahead of the mobs. Recent scholarship links these pogroms, known as the Hep Hep Riots, to the ongoing acrimonious debates over German Jewish emancipation.[65] The Congress of Vienna (1814–1815) and its sequel, the recently concluded Congress of Aix-la-Chapelle, had both failed to prod European leaders to grant full civil rights to the Jews, despite Reverend Way's paper success at the latter conclave. Several young German Jewish intellectuals responded to the stalled progress of emancipation and the shock of the Hep Hep Riots by establishing what later became formalized as the *Verein für Cultur und Wissenschaft der Juden* (Society for the Culture and Science of the Jews) in November of that year.

The founders of the *Verein* sought to bring the "inner state of the Jews and their outward position among the nations" into greater equilibrium.[66] More to the point, *Verein* members aimed to advance the cultural status of Jews both in their own estimation and in that of the broader population. In parallel, many of those active in the *Verein* weighed emigration as a response to a German *Volk* that resisted recognizing Jewish rights. Noah was at the time unaware of the *Verein*, but his incipient vision for mass Jewish settlement in America was to resonate with several of the group's notable members, including jurist Eduard Gans, budding poet Heinrich Heine, and the religious reformer and guiding light of modern Jewish studies, Leopold Zunz. A brilliant twenty-one-year-old with hooded eyes and a curly bush of hair, Gans was an ambitious disciple of philosopher Friedrich Hegel. It was the charismatic Gans who later impelled Heine to join the *Verein* and teach in its school.[67] Gans's fellow student, Zunz, was a few years older and resembled a biblical character as sketched by Rembrandt. Zunz already evinced the intensity and scholarly demeanor that would characterize his long life.

While the *Verein* met in Berlin, Noah was busy petitioning the New York State legislature to sell him land as a sanctuary for Europe's Jews. He offered to purchase Grand Island, an unsurveyed wilderness in the Niagara River along the contested borderlands of British Canada.

Majestic Niagara Falls roared only a few miles away. In the War of 1812, British forces had invaded America's frontier through Grand Island, a landmass about six miles wide at its broadest point and offering an area approximately twenty percent larger than Manhattan. The bloody 1814 Battle of Chippewa, romanticized by Noah in *She Would Be a Soldier*, had been fought just west of Grand Island across a narrow channel of the Niagara River. After the war's conclusion, Grand Island was purchased under questionable circumstances by New York State from the Seneca Nation.[68] Red Jacket, a prominent Seneca chief, had negotiated the deal while preserving his people's right to hunt, fish, and camp on their traditional tribal land.[69] Grand Island's strategic location, its rich timber resources, and its proximity to the terminus of the Erie Canal then under construction made its acquisition and settlement a priority for New York State. This combination of factors presented Noah with an opportunity to appeal to convergent interests.

He intended to purchase the island "to cause a town or city to be erected thereon, to be inhabited by a community of Jewish emigrants."[70] His petition of January 16, 1820, noted that he had already "taken preliminary measures to make known to the Jews in Europe the advantages"[71] of emigration—surely a reference to his proclamation from the previous summer published in Koblenz. As extravagant as he was practical, Noah planned to lure Jewish "manufacturers, mechanics, artists, and such persons . . . as may be familiar with agriculture, together with merchants, and enterprising traders of capital" to his colony.[72] His petition revealed that he had been moved by "painful emotions" while witnessing from afar the "spirit of cruelty and persecution" against European Jews, a recognition of the still smoldering Hep Hep Riots.[73] Noah highlighted the shame of those governments who "were unable or unwilling" to grant Jews "that unalienable protection which is due to a citizen," despite the pledges they had adopted in Aix-la-Chapelle.[74] The revival of medieval violence demonstrated that the Jews were in grave need of an asylum in "a country [in] which persecution is unknown"[75]—the U.S.

Christian America would gain in the deal as well. A Jewish colony on Grand Island would mean that "a very important frontier post" could "be defended without cost" from any renewal of British aggression.[76] The land itself was reputed to be fertile, the weather mild. All that prevented the U.S. from realizing a bountiful harvest of "melons, peaches, nectarines, and other delicate fruits" was the presence of Canadian "gypsies and wanderers" who squatted on the land and despoiled its resources.[77] The sale of Grand Island, Noah claimed, would deter these troublesome itinerants and provide a necessary spur to development. The wisdom of Noah's plan also borrowed on the realism of concurrent projects for concentrating white immigrant groups in semiautonomous settlements within U.S. territories, such as programs formulated by German and Irish immigrant aid societies.[78]

The state assembly recognized Noah's request and convened a select committee to examine his proposal.[79] The following day, the *Albany Daily Advertiser* trumpeted, in an article that may reveal the hand of Noah, that the Jews could "have their Jerusalem" and "erect their temple" in peace and security on Grand Island.[80] The committee announced after a brief delay that "the recent persecution of the Jews in various parts of Europe" indeed strengthened Noah's hand, and they further recognized that "the settlement of Grand Island would be a desirable object" for New York.[81] There could "be no objection . . . to the grant . . . to Mr. Noah," they concluded, and prepared a bill allowing for Grand Island's survey and sale.[82] The bill, however, was rejected. Lawmakers opposed to the sale contended that Grand Island "would be of immense value" once the Erie Canal was completed, and furthermore, that Jews ought "to mix with Christians, and not live alone" in a separatist settlement.[83] Noah rejected their charge that immigrant Jews might create an *imperium in imperio*, a state-within-a-state.[84] "I do not wish them to live alone," he insisted. "[T]here will be nothing to prevent Christians, as well as Jews, from inhabiting that spot; and nothing would afford me greater pleasure, than to see churches and synagogues springing up together, their spires towering above the forest."[85] Ever alert to his own real or imagined power, Noah claimed that he had allowed the bill to languish due to unsettled boundary issues with England. Still, he assured skeptics, "*I can have it*"—Grand Island—"*if I want it.*"[86]

Opposition to the plan moved Noah to pursue other proposals for mass Jewish settlement during the course of the year. Even at the time his legislative petition remained active, he foresaw its defeat and the response he would make: "I shall then turn my attention to the possessions of the United States, and make a judicious selection of a tract of fertile land of one hundred square miles. . . . Let the Jews inhabit this territory, and in due time let it be admitted in the Union as an independent state; then . . . with their Senators and members of Congress, they will be restored to as much liberty as they can expect in this world."[87] Major Noah here clearly intended to establish a Jewish state as one of the United States. He followed through on this plan, and in July dispatched a letter to Secretary of State John Quincy Adams requesting a diplomatic position in a European city for the purpose of promoting Jewish immigration to the U.S.[88] Shortly thereafter, Adams acknowledged his letter, noting that Noah had asked to be sent to Vienna in order to promote "great projects for colonizing Jews" in unspecified parts of the Union.[89] The future president served, coincidentally, as an officer of the American Society for Meliorating the Condition of the Jews,[90] a missionizing organization founded by a former acolyte of Reverend Way.[91] The secretary noted in his diary that though Noah "possessed considerable powers" as the editor of a partisan newspaper, the former consul had been recalled from Tunis, and consequently he rejected the Major's Vienna overture.[92] Garbled reports of Noah's efforts to purchase Grand Island had meanwhile appeared in Europe.

The first German-language Jewish periodical, *Sulamith*, described for its intellectual readers Noah's petition for territory on behalf of the Old World's Jews who "vainly seek a homeland."[93] The editor of *Sulamith*, Dr. David Fränkel, was an honorary member of the *Verein*.[94] Fränkel also served as a mentor to one Gerson Adersbach, a physician and contributor of poems to *Sulamith*.[95] Documents from the *Verein* archive reveal that at the group's Sunday meeting on April 30, 1820, Adersbach raised a motion in favor of contacting Noah, "an educated, well reputed and patriotic man," in order to gauge the seriousness of his colonization scheme.[96] Adersbach's enthusiasm failed to rouse the *Verein* at the time, but another member again urged the group to contact Noah in the waning days of 1821; this time the motion was approved unanimously.[97] In the first week of the new year, *Verein* president Eduard Gans and vice president Leopold Zunz penned a letter bestowing on Noah the title of "Extraordinary Member" of the society and "Correspondent General for the United States."[98] The letter highlighted the "sublime comfort" that Noah's territorial proposals had offered during the recent Hep Hep Riots.[99] The *Verein* missive ended with a plea to Noah to "establish a perpetual correspondence . . . about the means of transplanting a vast portion of European Jews to the United States."[100] Now, in addition to the evangelists who supported the creation of a Jewish territory, Noah had found a circle of European Jews to validate his dream.

Noah wasted little time in advertising, and in the process overestimating, the *Verein*'s appeal. He saw to it that Gans's letter was published in the *Commercial Advertiser*, a respected New York daily.[101] A long editorial note lauding Noah's proposal and his "diploma from Berlin" preceded the letter's publication.[102] The unsigned editorial predicted that Noah's project to bring "a colony of Jews to this country to settle in Grand Island" would mean that "the neglected children of Israel . . . can find a home undisturbed—land which they dare call their own" within the U.S.[103] The *Verein*'s support of Noah's territorial initiative, the patriotic desire to prove the freedoms of the New World superior to the shackles of the Old, a contemporary preoccupation with ethnic settlement and repatriation schemes, the fledgling republic's continued anxiety over its border with British Canada, and a recognition that the soon-to-be-completed Erie Canal would enrich New York, all combined to reawaken Noah to the dormant promise of Grand Island.[104]

Had Noah stood on the shores of the Niagara River and peered across the turbid water toward Grand Island at the time, he would have seen a thick white-oak forest and smoke trailing from squatters' shacks. Of course, what really mattered to Noah was not what he saw, but what he envisioned—and that was nothing less than the rescue of his coreligionists from a deluge of antisemitism. Inspired by his biblical namesake, Noah would find his people a patch of solid earth to call their own a few feet above the Niagara's waterline.

City of Refuge

New York State commissioned a survey of Grand Island beginning in 1824 and sold off lots the following June.[105] Reports at the time recalled Noah's effort to induce the state to sell him the land several years earlier, and noted that an investor had purchased on his behalf more than two thousand acres containing the two "most eligible sites for cities on the Island . . . [and] the most . . . commanding positions in the state for a commercial city."[106] Samuel Leggett, a wealthy associate of Noah's, was later identified as having paid $16,985 for the land, an enormous sum at the time for lots already considered to be overvalued.[107] But Leggett likely thought the deal a promising speculation in advance of the Erie Canal's opening. As soon as the sale was complete, newspapers announced that "the foundation stone"[108] of a city to be called "Ararat or Canaan"[109] would be laid close to the time of the canal's official opening in the fall of 1825.

Noah traveled to Buffalo, the nearest town of any size to Grand Island, at the end of the summer to oversee the ceremony. His friend, Abraham Benjamin Seixas, the nephew of Shearith Israel's late religious leader, accompanied him. At the time, about twenty-five hundred people[110] lived in Buffalo, though curious spectators were reported to be "pouring in from all quarters"[111] to witness the much publicized event scheduled for the morning of September 15. According to one contemporary report, a large group of locals and a delegation of Indians massed on the shore across from Grand Island in anticipation.[112] Grand Island's squatters, dressed in frock coats and "armed with rifles," held aloft a staff bearing an emblem of a bald eagle.[113] A reporter maliciously noted that the symbolic eagle bore a "certain *aquiline*-feature" that resembled the "*physiognomy* of the *founder*" of the city" of Ararat.[114] Predictably, Noah's nose received cruel attention while his muscular frame went unnoticed.[115] The cornerstone laying was indeed to have been celebrated on Grand Island and a flagstaff was erected on one of the lots Leggett had purchased for Noah, but it seems that "a sufficient number of boats could not be procured . . . to convey all those to the island who were desirous of witnessing" the ceremony.[116] When the vast crowd who had gathered nearby learned that the event would be held some miles distant in Buffalo's only large edifice, St. Paul's Episcopal Church, they dispersed—the Indians to their canoes,[117] others to their carriages.[118]

The roar of cannon shot booming across Lake Erie shook the ramshackle buildings of Buffalo that morning. Families raced from their homes down the main street, mingling along the way with Seneca tribesmen and their venerable chief, Red Jacket. Together they marched behind a parade of soldiers, clergymen, Masons, and "musicians in Turkish dress" all surging toward St. Paul's.[119] Noah, wearing dignified "robes of crimson silk, trimmed with ermine,"[120] stepped lively amidst the throng. A golden medallion hung around his neck to create a royal

Shoreline of Grand Island, New York, in the vicinity of Noah's proposed city of "Ararat."
Author's collection

effect.[121] His regalia was borrowed from a theater production of Shake-
speare's *Richard III*.[122] The procession entered St. Paul's to the pipe
organ's rendition of "See, the Conqu'ring Hero Comes" from Handel's
Judas Maccabeus. Inside, an eyewitness reported that an "immense
audience"[123] of Christians, Jews, and Native Americans had gathered to
observe an astonishing episode in American history: the laying of the
cornerstone of Ararat, the modern world's first free "City of Refuge for
the Jews."[124]

Ararat's three-hundred-pound sandstone block rested on St. Paul's
communion table along with silver cups brimming with wine, corn, and
oil.[125] Engraved upon the stone was the *Shema*, the central Jewish testament of faith from Deuteronomy (6:4). When the swell of the organ
died down, a service led by the church's reverend commenced including hymns, readings from the prophets, the recitation of Psalms—one
was even read in Hebrew—and a closing benediction.[126] At last, Major
Noah, who had adopted the additional honorific of "Judge of Israel"
for the occasion, took to the pulpit to exhort worshippers.[127] Noah

addressed them for over an hour,[128] presenting them with his "Proclamation to the Jews." His oration trumpeted the "re-establish[ment of] the Government of the Jewish Nation . . . under the auspices and protection of the constitution and laws of the United States of America."[129] His speech remains a significant statement of Jewish nationalism replete with enlightened calls for racial and religious tolerance. Yet its rhetoric cannot fail to strike readers today as arrogant.

He announced to world Jewry that "by the grace of God" he had established an asylum in America's "land of milk and honey" until such time as the people of Israel were qualified "for that great and final restoration to their ancient heritage" in the holy land.[130] With less bombast, he expounded upon the geographic benefits of Grand Island, where his city-state was to arise. He made particular mention of the land's fertility, rich resources, and proximity to Niagara Falls, source of the "greatest water-power in the world for manufacturing purposes," and to the "mouth of the Grand Canal" soon to be inaugurated.[131] Noah well knew that the canal was a scientific marvel that would industrialize the northwestern frontier. Only one week earlier, he had been elected as a member of a committee tasked with organizing the Grand Canal's opening celebration in New York City.[132] Ararat, he explained, was "calculated to become . . . the greatest trading and commercial depot in the new and better world."[133] Such real estate prophecies may have been well-founded, not to mention well-funded by his wealthy associates, but his religious pronouncements lacked the necessary spiritual currency.

Noah enjoined "pious and venerable Rabbis . . . Presidents and Elders of Synagogues . . . and brethren in authority throughout the world, to circulate and make known" his will and rulings as a self-appointed "Judge" over the Jewish people.[134] He then issued a series of instructions which included a demand that a census be taken of world Jewry, the institution of a capitation tax, an edict demanding the perpetual abolishment of Jewish polygamy in North Africa, a decree that "[p]rayer shall forever be said in the Hebrew language," and a grant of equal "rights and religious privileges" not only to the "black Jews of India and Africa," but also to nonrabbinic sects such as the Karaites and Samaritans.[135] Perhaps most remarkable to present-day readers, Noah insisted that the "Indians of the American continent" were "the descendants of the lost tribes of Israel" and should therefore be assimilated to "their brethren the chosen people" in Ararat.[136] This view of Native American origins was supported by numerous writers, scholars, and churchmen at the time—including Reverend Way.[137]

But of all his overreaching pronouncements, the most presumptuous was his appointment of European rabbis and communal leaders as his deputies. These august men were empowered by Judge Noah to "establish Emigration societies" on the basis of instructions said to be forthcoming from him.[138] Those selected for this unsought honor were Rabbi Abraham de Cologna, former head of the Central Consistory set up by Napoleon and a notable member of the Parisian Sanhedrin, as well as the Ashkenazi and Sephardi chief rabbis of London, Solomon Hirschell and Raphael Meldola. He also made sure to elevate his *Verein* correspondents, Eduard Gans and Leopold Zunz, to the status of commissioners, though unbeknownst to him the society had disbanded the year before. Noah had no way of knowing that Gans would undergo baptism within a few months.[139] Heine, once so interested in Noah's settlement plans, had already converted.[140] There is some irony, therefore, that Noah concluded his "Proclamation" with an appeal to his coreligionists to maintain their fidelity to the God of Israel and the laws of Moses.[141] The speech soon appeared in newspapers across the country signed by the authority of the "Judge of Israel" and his secretary, Abraham B. Seixas.

Noah's "Proclamation" was followed by what was later called his "Ararat Address." This "Address" also found its way into print shortly after the cornerstone was laid. The "Address" provides a rationale for Noah's "Proclamation," a document he referred to as a "declaration of Independence" for a revived "Hebrew government."[142] Noah called his listeners to witness that the "nations of the old and new world including the children of Africa" had all had their rights to self-government and territory recognized.[143] Only the Jews, he lamented, had remained homeless. But now he demanded that the Jews' "rights as a nation" be acknowledged.[144] His formulation of national rights in the context of a "declaration of independence" demonstrates his application of American and French republicanism to the problem of Jewish disenfranchisement. To underscore the point, he singled out his "pious friend," the Abbé Grégoire, for espousing the cause of Jewish civic emancipation in revolutionary France.[145]

Noah's solution to the question of Jewish rights harkened back to the earliest origins of America itself. He compared the potential of the

"Hebrew nation" to enrich the Union to that of the "few pilgrims" who had sought religious freedom in America and thus helped to found the nation.[146] His people would play a leading role in expansionism during this age of manifest destiny; they would "increase rapidly and prosperously" to the very edge of the Pacific Ocean.[147] Fittingly, his "Proclamation" and "Address" were issued during America's jubilee year. Fifty years after the Declaration of Independence, Noah too would proclaim Jewish liberty and grant his brethren throughout the world the powers and equal station that the federal government and natural rights entitled them to receive.

But like his Christian counterparts, Noah did not foresee Ararat as Jewry's eternal home. Jews "never should and never will relinquish the just hope of regaining possession of their ancient heritage," he declared, and various world events indicated the imminent fulfillment of this eternal biblical promise.[148] His asylum was only "temporary and provisionary" until the Jewish people's longed-for restoration.[149] America would simply allow them to cultivate those liberal principles that would qualify them to form an "honorable government in the Land of the Patriarchs."[150] Similar invocations of a convergence between Christian and Jewish interests appeared in Noah's earlier *Discourse* and the Koblenz "Proclamation," and would echo in later documents as well. The "Address" reiterated his faith in the God of Israel's unbroken covenant with Abraham, while simultaneously endorsing Jewish self-reliance—both points already present in his *Discourse*. Noah added to this dialectic the admonishment that "we [Jews] have done nothing for ourselves."[151] He maintained that the chosen people must shrug off their supplications for divine intervention, and instead learn to protect themselves and improve their own lot in the world through settlement and agricultural development.[152]

The "Address" draws to a close with an appeal that he be allowed to lead a revival of "the government of the oldest of nations" in America and fulfill "the promises made to the descendants of the Patriarchs."[153] Noah thus saw himself as a vessel of divine will. To this end he asked for God's blessings and repeated his call to form emigration societies throughout Europe in order to launch a systematic colonization of Ararat. Noah took an important step toward what later became known as Zionism when he stated that Jewry should no longer await the messianic era, but instead mobilize for a secular, territorial solution to persecution. But despite these visions, Noah was realist enough to sense that like the biblical prophets', his own dream of a redemptive Jewish future would be treated as chimerical.[154]

American papers rushed to judgment. New York's Jews were said to reject the entire project, deriding it as nothing but a hoax.[155] One prominent paper lampooned Ararat by printing a phony classified advertisement seeking a lunatic asylum to house Noah.[156] Jews were welcome to come to the U.S., an editor in Virginia noted, but Noah's oration was deemed "one of the most *outre* . . . and ridiculous" documents ever reviewed.[157] Ararat was considered even more preposterous than the American Society for Meliorating the Condition of the Jews' conversion schemes—here an intriguing window into how contemporaries linked the two projects.[158] A New England paper referred to Noah as "his rigamarole highness."[159] And a wag in St. Louis published a proclamation to the "Red Skins" that parodied Noah's speech and offered sanctuary on the Missouri plains to refugee "Jews of Ararat."[160] Despite these humiliations, Noah retained the respect of those involved with developing the Erie Canal region. Ararat was referred to as a practicable though unbuilt entity at the time by burghers who witnessed the canal's opening.[161] Noah even chartered a small boat to participate in the celebratory flotilla. Aboard the ship, christened *Noah's Ark*, were a bear, two eagles, two fawns, "two Indian boys, in the dress of their nation," as well as a menagerie of animals, birds, and fish.[162] An eyewitness was "convinced that [Noah's] leading motives were philanthropic and intended to benefit his race" and that "he was not activated by any design or expectation of pecuniary advantage or speculation."[163] Yet press reports continued to portray him as a charlatan.

In one London daily, antisemitic jibes cast doubt on Jews ever becoming capable famers. The "lowing of kine," the journalist suggested, would never "sound more sweetly in the Hebrew ear than the chink of gold or silver."[164] Former *Verein* member Heinrich Heine, by then a nominal Christian, remained aware of developments, too. Heine presented Zunz with a volume of his work and wisecracked that the book should "be transferred to Ararat" when the *Verein* relocated to Grand Island.[165] While Noah's Ararat scheme was much publicized in the press, the formal call he sent to fellow Jews in Europe did not reach its intended audience. A twentieth-century scholar working in Vienna in the interwar period discovered several of these original documents among the papers of the Austrian police. According to a notation found with copies of Noah's call, the chief of police had forbidden their distribution to the Jewish community.[166]

The official Jewish response to Ararat was, in any case, negative. Rabbi de Cologna wrote an indignant letter on behalf of himself and London's chief rabbis, Hirschell and Meldola, to the editor of the *Journal des débats*, the most influential periodical of its day in France. He declined the honor of Noah's appointment of him as "Commissioner of Emigration," and reminded his readers that no Jewish text had ever promised that a "marsh in North America" would become the site of Israel's future redemption.[167] The Rabbi charged Noah with "treason against the Divine Majesty" for daring to restore the Jewish people's "politico-national" rights before the dawn of the messianic era.[168] Another Jewish leader, Judah Jeitteles, criticized Ararat in Hebrew in *Bikkurei Ha'ittim*, an important journal of the Jewish Enlightenment, a reformist movement known as the *Haskalah*. Jeitteles, often cited as having coined the very term *Haskalah*, opened his article with a sly echo of the Book of Esther (2:5), introducing readers to a "Jewish man in the country of North America whose name is Mordecai."[169] The tone thus set for farce, Jeitteles commenced his mockery of Noah's efforts. Though Jeitteles presents an accurate summary of the "Proclamation," he characterizes Ararat as foolhardy. No Jew would leave his home and property for Noah's mad dream, he insists.[170] The entire project of nation-building, Jeitteles further claims, rebels against Jewish law.[171]

Noah's ark sank quickly after being rebuffed by Jewish leaders. So far as is known, not a single individual heeded his call for settlement. There is no record of Noah himself ever having set foot on Grand Island. Despite the ridicule meted out to him in the press, Noah was undaunted. He took a philosophical view, writing to a sympathizer one month after the ceremony: "I . . . stand as the pioneer of the great work, leaving others to complete it, & reap their share of honor & glory, contenting myself with the assurance, that this is the country which the Almighty has blessed. . . . When sneers and mockery shall have had their day . . . then my motives and objects will have been duly estimated & rewarded."[172] The recipient of this letter was Erasmus (Haim) Simon, a Polish convert to Christianity and a former evangelist associated with the American Society for Meliorating the Condition of the Jews. After converting in Scotland, Simon arrived in the U.S. intending to create a communal settlement for Polish Jews and converts in the New World.[173] He soon became an agent for the American Society and fundraised for their proposed colony in New Paltz, and later for a settlement closer to Manhattan in Westchester County.[174] Simon abandoned the latter project for reasons of conscience and then devoted himself to the conversion of the supposedly Jewish tribes of American Indians, whom he and his wife opted to live among.[175]

Noah, too, clung to the notion that the "aborigines of America"[176] were descendants of the lost tribes. In 1837, a year after Erasmus Simon's wife published a tedious book purporting to identify the Jewish origins of native peoples, Noah released his own much shorter tract on the subject, *The Evidences of the American Indians Being the Descendants of the Lost Tribes of Israel*. By the time his *Evidences* appeared in print, Noah had aged as the result of what was likely a stroke,[177] but there are few signs of diminished energy in his advocacy of minority rights. The tract reflects Noah's paternalism toward Indians as well as his esteem of their cultures, an esteem rooted in his belief that they shared a common ancestry with Jews. As proof, Noah presented details from his correspondence with artist George Catlin, whose portraits of Native Americans would later make him famous. Catlin's accounts of life among western tribes assured Noah that numerous indigenous customs reflected Jewish tradition, including the observance of fast days, the practice of animal sacrifice, and the confinement of menstruating women. Catlin observed that ritually unclean native women had a "universal practice" of anointing themselves "with bear's grease," which, he asserted, was "strikingly similar to the Jewish custom."[178] Oddly, Noah did not challenge this claim. He did, however, highlight how the history of cruelty against the Indians was "not unlike those which the chosen people have suffered for the last eighteen centuries."[179] He grieved that the destruction of native life "commenced with the Narragansetts, will extend to the Seminoles, and gradually to the blue waters of the Pacific."[180] This striking passage reverberates even more mournfully today. His rhetoric suggests that the long shadows cast by the dispossession of the Indians influenced his struggle in support of Jewish territorial repossession.

Noah's tendentious identification of Indians as crypto-Jews, like that of Reverend Way, the Simons, and others, was premised on millenialist beliefs in the Jewish restoration to Zion. His conviction that the Indians were long-lost members of the tribe meant that "the final advent of the Jewish nation"[181]—the miraculous return to the promised land—was nigh. Noah's argument for the Israelite origin of native peoples emerges as a defense of a nationalist program for Jewish auto-emancipation in the *Evidence*'s conclusion. "My faith does not rest wholly in miracles," he confesses. "Providence disposes of events, [but] human agency must carry them out."[182] He demanded that "[t]he Jewish people . . . now do something for themselves," and, he continued, "when they DO," God will bless and protect them.[183] Noah further outlined how to adapt his methods for acquiring land on Grand Island to the purchase of land in biblical Israel. He noted the declining power of the Ottomans and recommended that his wealthy brethren form a syndicate to purchase the holy land from the debtor empire with the "cooperation and protection of England and France."[184] Once ransomed with Jewish wealth and safeguarded by Western powers, Palestine would again flourish. Near Eastern commerce would expand with the arrival of European free enterprise to the port of Jaffa. Old World Jews would immigrate to their ancestral homeland to enrich it and themselves. Ukrainian Jews would "revive the former fertility of Palestine" with their agricultural genius, Dutch and German manufacturers would modernize the region, a national army would rise from among the Jewish veterans of Europe's recent wars, and the establishment of a "tolerant and liberal government" would assure justice for all.[185]

At the age of fifty-nine, in the autumn of 1844, Noah once again launched a plan for Jewish territorial autonomy. He delivered two speeches to large audiences at the New York Tabernacle, whose cavernous auditorium boasted a broad stage, an imposing organ, and white marble columns, all brightly illuminated by gas fixtures.[186] These addresses, later published with an accompanying foldout map of the land of Israel, reworked themes familiar from his writings over the preceding quarter century. Yet in its polemic force, its address to a Christian audience, and its programmatic call for Jewish reoccupation of the holy land, Noah's *Discourse on the Restoration* also reveals a striking evolution in his thinking. By 1844, Noah is fully invested in the "return of the Jews to Jerusalem, and the organization of a powerful government in Judea."[187]

His preface opens with a sharp acknowledgement that Christian leaders and those claiming adherence to the message of the Gospels bear a historic responsibility for Jewish persecution. Perhaps in an oblique reference to those associated with philosemitic missionary societies, Noah recalls how "Ministers of the Gospel"[188] have repented of past intolerance, though he reproaches their evangelization of Jewry. He proceeds to outline a clear rationale for a restorationist project and for America's unique role in ensuring its success. He recalls how the U.S. had recently granted "a home to our red brethren beyond the Mississippi"—even then a charitable interpretation of the Indian Removal Act—and had "restored the African to his native land"—a reference to colonization efforts in Sierra Leone and neighboring Liberia.[189] "If these nations were entitled to our sympathies," Noah asks, "how much more powerful . . . are the claims" of the Jews?[190] His invocation of the audience's Christian good will, their patriotic republicanism, and of contemporary precedent were calculated to achieve maximum appeal.

The second half of his address exhibits a prophetic tone. Noah's reading of the geopolitical scene assured him that the Ottomans were in decline, Russia ascendant, and that the British Empire would soon embrace Egypt.[191] Once Egypt fell under Britannia's rule, he insisted that Palestine could again be claimed by "the descendants of Abraham."[192] As he had earlier imagined in his *Evidences*, Jewish control of the holy land would inaugurate a prosperous age of Mediterranean commerce and agricultural fertility. Steam-powered vessels would revive Palestine's trading economy.[193] Jewish farmers from Germany, Poland, and Russia would till the rocky soil and make it bloom.[194] What Noah foresaw, the late nineteenth-century Zionist pioneers accomplished: the modernization of agriculture in scattered collective Zionist settlements and the expansion of port cities, such as Jaffa and Haifa, to speed the economic growth of the *yishuv*—the Jewish community—in Ottoman Palestine.

Noah's plans would not only improve the physical landscape and economic climate, but also elevate the spirit. Christian and Jewish voices would mingle as they sang in harmonious praise to God upon Mount Zion.[195] To achieve these dreams, Noah proposed that "all the Christian societies who take an interest in the fate of Israel . . . assist in their restoration by aiding to colonize the Jews in Judea."[196] The first step toward this goal was to "solicit from the Sultan . . . permission for the Jews to purchase and hold land."[197] Such a charter would later figure as the essential component of political Zionist thinking. Noah was certain that the powers of France and England would support his plan and make his aspiration a reality, but he singled out the land of his birth for a special destiny.

America, the only nation never to have persecuted the Jews, he concluded, was "distinguished in prophecy as *the* nation which . . . shall present to the Lord his chosen and trodden-down people, and pave the way for their restoration to Zion."[198] To the question of which Jews would emigrate to this new Judea, Noah answered that those who are "free and happy" would remain where they were, but those "bowed to the earth by oppression" would flock to the land of their redemption.[199] Zion would be more than a mere sanctuary for the persecuted; possession of the land would insure the Jewish future. "Restoration is not for us alone," he prophesied, "but for millions unborn."[200]

And how did those who gathered at the New York Tabernacle receive his far-reaching vision? The response of one critic of the time remains particularly interesting. Edgar Allan Poe devoted a review to Noah's discourse and found it to be "extraordinary [and] full of novel and cogent thought."[201] The American master maintained that Noah's oration "will be widely circulated and admired."[202] Indeed his ideas were treated seriously, even abroad. England's periodical *The Spectator* thought Noah's proposal feasible and suggested that "a number of Jewish agricultural settlements [be] established at moderate distances from each other" in Palestine under British protection so that the Jews would "inoculate" the Arab inhabitants with "steady industrious habits."[203] Despite support from opinion makers and well-meaning Christians, Noah's imagined new Judea made no progress. Still, he never tired of his vision of the Jewish nation restored.

In 1848, one hundred years before the State of Israel's establishment, Noah, now a double-chinned and corpulent celebrity,[204] delivered a fund-raising appeal to fellow worshipers at Shearith Israel. The cause was a capital campaign to build a synagogue, which Noah referred to as "a Temple," on Mount Zion in Jerusalem.[205] He believed that a cornerstone-laying ceremony for his Temple would attract an enormous crowd of both Jews and gentiles to the holy city, and thus serve to mark the dawn of a new era. "It would be the proudest day of my life, if I could be present at laying the corner-stone of the new Temple of Jerusalem," he said.[206] Noah the impresario seems to have imagined a ceremony in Jerusalem possessed of even greater pageantry than the one he had orchestrated for Ararat nearly a quarter century earlier. But Noah would not live to see his dreams fulfilled. He died after a series of strokes less than two years later, on March 22, 1851.

Contested Legacy

After his death, Noah was eulogized for his many accomplishments. He had helmed or founded a number of influential newspapers, reigned as a grand sachem of Tammany Hall, held public office as sheriff of New York and surveyor of the city's port, signed on as a founding shareholder of New York University, and worked to establish the first Jewish hospital in the city, which later evolved into Mount Sinai Hospital. Though his diplomatic career ended in scandal, Noah long served as an ambassador between Jewish and Christian America. Historian Jonathan Sarna, author of the most comprehensive work on Noah, maintains that he was the first public figure to "confront openly the challenge of American freedom, both as a devoted American and as a Jew."[207] To Christians, Noah explained Jewish traditions and culture. To his coreligionists, he demonstrated compatibility between the ideals of Judaism and the United States.

Nearly two hundred years have passed since Noah failed to establish his new Jerusalem on Grand Island. His legacy in the intervening generations has paralleled that of the Ararat cornerstone—alternately forgotten or celebrated, treated with contempt or dismissed as a curiosity.[208] After Noah's call to create a Jewish polity in America was rejected, the Judge of Israel abandoned the stone against an exterior wall of St. Paul's. A few years later Noah asked his friend Peter B. Porter, a hero of the Battle of Chippewa, to preserve the stone. Porter placed it on the lawn of his riverfront home across the shores from Grand Island. There it remained until 1834, when businessman, legislator, and farmer Lewis F. Allen bought up sixteen thousand acres of Grand Island, including lots first purchased for Noah's Ararat. Allen found the stone abandoned on Porter's property and asked if he could look after it. He then built a six-foot-square, fourteen-foot-high brick obelisk on the site of the unbuilt city of Ararat.[209] The cornerstone was heaved into a niche in the structure on its east side. Niagara Falls had by that time become a major American tourist attraction and regular passenger steamers carried sightseers to the vicinity of the rapids a few miles away. Travelers frequently stopped to view the Ararat stone and sketch its inscription. Several early guidebooks to the falls mention Noah and Ararat, and at least one reproduces an illustration of the original obelisk.[210] But by 1850, the weather-worn monument was torn down and the stone was once again orphaned. A local claimed it for his farm until 1864, when an enterprising businessman removed it to his property on the other side of the island. When his premises burned to the ground, the cornerstone was dumped in an outhouse that had escaped the blaze. Allen once again recovered it from this ignominious resting place in 1865 and deposited the stone at his home, built on another tract of land first purchased for Noah. A few months later, after forty years of wandering, the sole artifact of the City of Ararat was removed to the Buffalo and Erie County Historical Society.[211] There it remains to this day behind glass.

Ararat's cornerstone had become its tombstone. Some of the plots of land purchased for Ararat are today occupied by a Holiday Inn, a golf course, and a small graveyard. As for the would-be savior himself, Noah's own obelisk-shaped grave marker sits crumbling in Congregation Shearith Israel's dilapidated midtown Manhattan cemetery. But Noah's story has lived on in literature, from Anglo-Jewish author Israel Zangwill's tragic-comic treatment of him in his story "Noah's Ark" (1899), to playwright Harry Sackler's depiction of him as a moonstruck dreamer in his play *Messiah—American Style* (1927), to the farcical character he mutated into in Ben Katchor's graphic novel *The Jew of New York* (1998). The Ararat scheme has consistently raised tantalizing what-ifs for writers. Twenty years after publishing his fictional account of Noah, Zangwill maintained that "had the European ghettos to which [Noah] addressed his appeal been sufficiently prepared by propaganda, the great city of Buffalo would by now have been Jewish, with a Jewish majority in New York State."[212] More recently, Pulitzer Prize–winning author Michael Chabon recalled that Ararat served as a model for his counterfactual novel *The Yiddish Policemen's Union*, which depicts a Jewish micronation on an Alaskan island. "I know that the memory of Noah crossed my mind when I was conceiving of the place I would create," Chabon told me, "perhaps most in the sense that I was going to be the Mordecai Noah of my own Ararat."[213] And Israeli author Nava Semel offered a sympathetic appraisal of Ararat in her alternate history *Isra Isle* (2005). That novel imagines what would have happened had Ararat achieved American statehood, thus allowing Grand Island to absorb European Jewish refugees and forestall the Holocaust.

Noah's appeal to Jewish authors is unmistakable, but his relationship to latter-day Zionism remains clouded. Shortly after the first Zionist Congress in 1897, Noah was determined to have been "an enthusiastic Zionist."[214] The Zionist Organization's official mouthpiece, *Die Welt*, depicted Noah in two separate articles as a pioneer in the effort to create a Jewish state (*Judenstaat*) or a Jewish nation (*Judenreich*).[215] The latter article (1902) considered Ararat to have been a signal contribution to Jewish nationalist thinking. Shortly thereafter (1905), a biography of Noah that appeared in Hebrew treated him as a Zionist committed to settling Jews in the biblical land of Israel; the Ararat episode itself was dismissed with apologetics.[216] Influential Zionist leader Nahum Sokolov, however, found no difficulty in claiming Noah as a distinguished precursor to Herzl in his *History of Zionism* (1919).[217] As European antisemitism gathered intensity in 1938, right-wing historian Benzion Netanyahu lamented that Noah was "a lone voice in the wilderness" whose aspirations for achieving Jewish political power in American territory went unheeded.[218]

In the decades following Israel's founding, Noah's pedigree as a Zionist became contentious. One sympathetic scholar maintained that Ararat granted Noah the distinction of being the first Jew to attempt to establish an independent Jewish state.[219] Meanwhile, another judged that Noah should properly be considered the first territorialist.[220] The sentiment was echoed in the 1960s in a polemical Yiddish history of territorialism that insisted that Noah was one of that movement's signal inspirations.[221] Perhaps because Noah was claimed by territorialists, he was dismissed by a leading Israeli historian in the 1970s as merely a "builder of castles in the air."[222] In the 1990s, Hebrew University professor Gideon Shimoni more soberly considered Noah to have been a territorialist during his Ararat phase, and to have presented a Jewish "mirror image of Christian restorationism" in his later appeals to resettle Zion.[223] Noah's connection with both restorationism and territorialist thinking have no doubt tainted his legacy in the contemporary political climate. And the problem of whether to label Noah a Zionist or not is compounded by the divergent definitions of Zionism itself. One suspects the term is useful precisely to the extent that its meaning is malleable.

Noah, like fellow playwright Theodor Herzl several decades later, was more a pragmatist than an ideologue. His efforts to build a territorial ark for beleaguered Jews drifted along several ideological currents and reflected commitments at different times to varieties of what have become known as territorialism and Zionism. My own understanding of Zionism is shaped by scholar Dov Weinryb's concise definition of the movement as committed to "the establishment of a sanctuary, a national home, a territorial center, a Jewish state or some such entity by systematic work of individuals without waiting for heavenly intercession."[224] Noah emerges as a Zionist *avant la lettre* when judged by Weinryb's admittedly broad criteria. His nationalist efforts were not isolated or merely conjectural, as were those of other individuals often considered Zionist precursors.[225] Though Noah's work was in vain, he used his influence and flair for publicity to marshal the support of notable Europeans, both Jewish and non-Jewish. He was apprised of and associated with restorationists, some of whose ideas he adapted to suit Jewish ends. Nor were Noah's schemes inconsequential in terms of their historic import. His adoption and manipulation of restorationist rhetoric presaged the spread and ongoing influence of Christian Zionism in America.

More pointedly, Zangwill, who often invoked Noah and Ararat, was an early supporter of Herzl and the Zionist cause. One biographer of Herzl even suggested that organized Zionism only began after Herzl met Zangwill.[226] Zangwill's connections to powerful figures in Britain proved crucial for the Zionist Organization's first diplomatic successes. Thus Noah's longstanding commitment to Jewish autonomy stands in a causal relationship to the intellectual histories of both Zionism and territorialism. In fact, Zionism *was* territorialism at least until 1903, as the next chapter details.

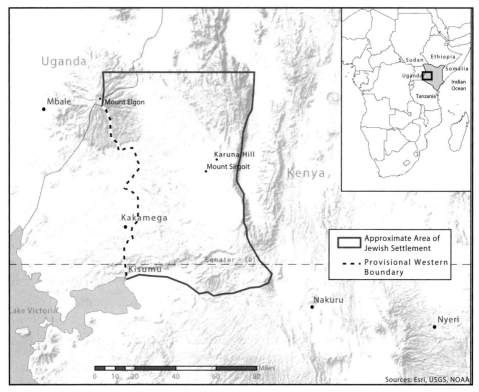

East Africa

2

Greetings from the Promised Land

Uasin Gishu, East Africa (1903–1905)

Dream States

European Jews swayed and prayed for Zion for nearly two millennia, and by the end of the nineteenth century their descendants had transformed liturgical longing into a political movement to create a Jewish national entity somewhere in the world. Zionism's prophet, Theodor Herzl, considered Argentina,[1] Cyprus,[2] Mesopotamia,[3] Mozambique,[4] and the Sinai Peninsula[5] as potential Jewish homelands. It took nearly a decade for Zionism to exclusively concentrate its spiritual yearning on the spatial coordinates of Ottoman Palestine. But even before the early pioneers set foot on Israel's shores, the European lands of their birth had first to be imagined as sites of exile. The Zionists' most radical act of conception was to reterritorialize their homelands as alien, and a foreign landscape—Palestine—as home. This could not have been accomplished without a modern literature that reimagined the ancient biblical promises. Zionist *realpolitik* was born of fiction.

Theodor Herzl himself was a noted journalist, novelist, and playwright. All the world became his stage when he raised the curtain on his greatest production, the Jewish state, amidst the showmanship of the First Zionist Congress held in 1897 in Basel. The medieval Swiss city on the Rhine was the unlikely site of the founding statement of Zionism's modern political program: "The aim of Zionism is to create for the Jewish people a home in Palestine secured by public law."[6] The sober and spare wording of the "Basel Program" stands in contrast to the extravagance of the First Congress's dreams. Herzl later detailed these aspirations in a futuristic vision of the Jews restored to Zion in his 1902 novel *Altneuland* (*Old-New Land*). The technocratic utopia of *Altneuland* consists of a demilitarized Jewish state "evolved out of experiments, books, and dreams,"[7] with airships and high-speed trains uniting the peoples of the Near East. The book was immediately translated into Hebrew under the title *Tel Aviv*, which became the name for Israel's cultural capital soon to rise from Mediterranean sands. Yet only a year after Herzl imagined a communitarian society of Jews rebuilding their old-new land in Palestine, he championed a proposal to create an African Zion:[8] the so-called "Uganda Plan."

The highest echelons of the Zionist leadership backed the idea of an autonomous Jewish colony in East Africa, including the two men who succeeded Herzl[9] as president of the Zionist Organization. Other notable supporters included British author Israel Zangwill and Eliezer Ben-Yehuda, the man whose stubborn drive resurrected Hebrew as a spoken language in Palestine. Herzl's lieutenant, man of letters Max Nordau, also grudgingly endorsed the proposal, though he feared it would lead to "colonial exploitation"[10] and the dissolution of the movement. Instead he envisaged a Jewish settlement in Africa as a *Nachtasyl*[11]—a temporary "night shelter"—until a permanent foothold could be established in Ottoman Palestine.

To fin-de-siècle Europeans, Africa was still the "dark continent"[12] that Henry Morton Stanley had romanticized in accounts of his expeditions through the unmapped interior. Stanley's successful mission to locate Doctor Livingstone, coupled with Victorian-era discoveries in equatorial Africa, sparked both popular fascination and imperial scramble. European obsession with Africa profoundly affected the fledgling Zionist movement. Just as he was first conceiving of a Jewish state in 1895, Theodor Herzl noted on the initial pages of his diary that Stanley's "little travel book"[13] had "enthralled the entire civilized world."[14] Yet Herzl believed that Stanley's work would appear petty in comparison to his own dream of a territorial solution to "the Jewish Question."[15] Herzl's reveries reached a fever pitch a few months later when he imagined the pioneers of a future Jewish state wading ashore in "distinctive cap[s] designed à la Stanley."[16] Here Herzl refers to Stanley's signature mushroom-top hat with its short brim, two bands of ventilation holes, and havelock to protect the neck from sunburn. The playwright could not resist costuming the pivotal scene of national restoration. For Herzl and the early Zionists, the Uganda Plan twinned the adventures of Stanley with the adventurism of the Age of Empire, stagecraft with statecraft.

Next to the publication of Stanley's exploits, the most significant contribution to Africa's popular allure at the time was H. Rider Haggard's best-selling novel of derring-do from 1885, *King Solomon's Mines*. Haggard's widely translated book introduced readers to a trio of stalwart Englishmen who journey into deepest Africa in search of a vanished comrade. There they meet noble black tribesmen who guard a hoard of gold, ivory, and diamonds that had once enriched the biblical king's treasury and allowed Solomon to construct the Temple in Jerusalem. Haggard imagined the ancient Kingdom of Israel as a colonial exploiter of African wealth, but in the early twentieth century, His Majesty's government plotted with Zionist leaders to send Jewish refugees to East Africa in order to consolidate Britain's *own* overseas possessions. Though Haggard said he "had a sentimental hankering to see Palestine re-occupied by the Jews," the celebrity author commented favorably on the proposed African settlement scheme, noting that if an "autonomous Jewish State . . . established in British territory would acknowledge and be obedient to the Crown and Imperial Power [then] I can see no possible objection to its creation."[17] Jews would be used to populate the Empire and render the dark continent a shade lighter.

Despite his vivid fantasies, Haggard proved more practical than another contemporary author, an Austro-Hungarian gentleman whose vision influenced both colonial designs on East Africa and plans for a future Jewish state. That man was an educated, assimilated Jew from Budapest. He wrote for the Viennese newspaper *Neue Freie Presse*. He had penetrating eyes and an impressive beard. He wrote a utopian novel about a socialist society—a novel that inspired readers to leave their European homes, form a settlement collective, and make his dream into reality. His name was Theodor Hertzka. That is not a typo. Improbably, Dr. Theodor Hertzka was a colleague of Dr. Theodor Herzl's and shared with him a parallel background and professional trajectory.

Hertzka, an economist, published his novel, *Freeland: A Social Anticipation*, to massive success in 1890. In his book he describes how a vanguard of European settlers march overland from the port city of Mombasa and along the way awe the local tribes into submission. The Masai and other groups align themselves with the powerful whites who have come to appropriate territory amidst the fertile highland plateaus. Hertzka based his descriptions of the country and its peoples on the detailed writings of Stanley and Livingstone, as well as those of baptized German Jew Eduard Schnitzer, better known as Emin Pasha, the lionized governor of British Equatoria (today, the Republic of South Sudan).[18] Once arrived in their East African "Land of Promise,"[19] Hertzka's settlers erect a communitarian capital to serve the new country they name Freeland. There they domesticate monkeys, zebras, and elephants, establish manufacturing centers, introduce the benighted natives to the latest technology, lay railways across the land, turn a portion of Mount Kenya into a giant ice-skating rink, invent a horseless carriage powered by tightly coiled springs, and disseminate to the world at large the good news that Jesus and his apostles were in fact "Socialists, to some extent Communists."[20]

Like many programmatic novels, *Freeland* manages to be both fatuous and boring at the same time. One contemporary reviewer noted that the novel grafted "the fancy of Mr. Rider Haggard on the theories of John Stuart Mill."[21] Hertzka's decision to pepper the narrative with what amounts to a running balance sheet of income and expenditures doesn't make his novel any more palatable. Yet somehow the book inspired enthusiasm for the author's monetary and social theories, and dozens of Freeland groups soon formed around the world. Hertzka addressed his loyal readers in an afterword, insisting that the fantasy[22] he had "described as really happening *might* happen" if only a "sufficient number of vigorous men"[23] would put his principles into action. Hertzka's exhortation may have inspired one of the most oft-quoted catchphrases in modern Jewish history. In *Altneuland*, Herzl famously challenges his readers in an epilogue that "if you will it, it is no dream."[24]

In June of 1894, well-armed members of the International Freelander Society arrived in East Africa ready to turn Hertzka's dream into reality.[25] European newspapers reported on their progress with a mix of skepticism, ridicule, and admiration. British authorities kept a jaundiced eye on their activities, and with good reason. These were not the vigorous men Hertzka had hoped for. According to confidential reports sent to the commissioner of the East African Protectorate by an eccentric British soldier who "walk[ed] about attended by a tame cheetah,"[26] the twenty or

so members of the Freeland group included: an "exceptionally dangerous German Anarchist, dynamitard, and chemical . . . 'bomb worker'";[27]
a "mentally unsound . . . eccentric"; an "utterly dishonest habitual swin-
dler"; and a pair of "violently anti-British" revolutionaries,[28] all of whom
were led by an ineffective Austrian professor who was dismissed as a
"chicken-hearted cur."[29] The British commissioner, Arthur Hardinge,
believed that the Freeland colonists aspired to create an anarcho-biblical
state where, "like the Israelites under the Judges, [each would] do what
he deemed 'right in his own eyes.'"[30] Hardinge recalled that the settlers
set about renting a building, which they renamed "Freeland House,"[31]
and then proceeded to drink themselves into a stupor and take "liberties,
in the name of 'free love,' with native women."[32] This dissolute bunch of
would-be colonists disbanded by the end of July to scatter far and wide.
To say that Hertzka's Freeland never got off the ground would be inaccu-
rate; in fact, Freeland was always just a castle in the air.

Theodor Herzl's *Judenstaat—A Jewish State: An Attempt at a Modern Solution of the Jewish Question* (1896)—appeared two years after the
Freelanders' abortive effort to put Hertzka's notions into practice. In his
preface, the emergent leader of Zionism recalls his colleague's "interesting book,"[33] but states that Hertzka's Freeland was doomed to forever
remain a "dream State."[34] Herzl maintains that even if Freeland communities were to be established, he "should look on the whole thing as
a joke."[35] Nonetheless, according to Herzl's close friend Israel Zangwill,
"without *Freiland* there would have been no *Judensaat*."[36] To distinguish
his own serious political program from the risible fancies of Freeland,
Herzl noted that the emergence of a new national entity requires a clear
and compelling motivation. And that, he believed, already existed. "The
misery of the Jews," Herzl wrote in his manifesto, will be Zionism's "pro-
pelling force."[37] The need for a territorial solution to Jewish homelessness was pressing, but Herzl was indecisive about where to establish his
state. "Shall we choose Palestine or Argentina?" he asked.[38] The question was one of practicality. By the spring of 1896, approximately seven
thousand Jews had been resettled on about 750,000 acres of land purchased for them in Argentina.[39] Statistics indicate that even seven years
later, in 1903, only about ten thousand Jews had immigrated to Palestine, approximately fifty percent of whom lived on the nearly ninety
thousand acres that had been purchased for agricultural colonization.[40]

Based on numbers alone, Argentina seemed a more attractive option than Palestine. Herzl's *Judenstaat* was the product not of utopianism, but of pragmatic concern, borne within a context of increasing anti-semitism in Europe and Russia, waves of emigration to the west, and a sense that Jewish civic equality could never be achieved.

Of course, the beginnings of modern Zionist ideology had already been established for well over a decade by the time Herzl arrived on the scene, though he was unfamiliar with his predecessors' work. Most notably, Russian physician Judah Leib (Leon) Pinsker's *Auto-emancipation*, originally published in German (1882), demanded the creation of a "Jewish national-ity, of a people living upon its own soil . . . [of] their return to the ranks of the nations by the acquisition of a Jewish homeland."[41] Pinsker patholo-gized gentile society as terminally "Judeophobic";[42] his prescription was to isolate his people from this plague and strengthen Jewry through reter-ritorialization. Like Herzl, Pinsker wrote as a secularist and considered that tracts of land for a self-governing polity might be purchased either in Palestine or, with even greater promise, in the United States.[43] There was justification for Pinsker wavering between the holy land and the American *goldene medina* (golden land). Odessa, Pinsker's hometown, was already the base of operations both for the *Hovevei Zion* (Lovers of Zion) and the *Am Olam* (Eternal People) movements by the time *Auto-emancipation* appeared. The *Hovevei Zion* was a loosely organized nationalist affilia-tion that aimed at agricultural settlement in Palestine. Later, influential members of *Hovevei Zion* would join with the Zionist Organization under Herzl. The *Am Olam* activists set their sights on establishing agricultural colonies in the U.S., some of which aspired to autonomy.[44] Several short-lived communal farms were founded by *Am Olam* pioneers in Louisiana, South Dakota, and Oregon. Pinsker and Herzl offered the two most sig-nificant founding formulations of modern Zionism, and both evinced a pragmatism about where the Jewish question could best be solved.

Eastern European Jews were particularly miserable at the turn of the century. Economic hardship was pervasive in the Pale of Settlement. Pogroms and state-sanctioned antisemitism terrified Jews in Russia and horrified the civilized world. Waves of immigrants fleeing to Western and Central Europe and to America encouraged widespread fears of a mass "alien" influx into these more prosperous regions. Though many in the West recognized the plight of the impoverished newcomers, politicians and social reformers fretted about their impact. These concerns only increased after accounts of the bloody April 1903 outrages in the Moldovan city of Kishinev shocked the conscience of the world. The aftermath of the Kishinev pogrom forced Europe to reckon with a Jewish mass exodus and created an urgent demand for the Zionist leadership to find a territorial solution to Jewish persecution. Herzl looked to the world's superpower, Great Britain, to succor his people.

Early in his effort to attract political and financial support for Zionism, Herzl had traveled to England and met there with a warm reception. The first published draft[45] of his proposal for a *Judenstaat* appeared in London's *Jewish Chronicle*. Thanks to the intercession of Nordau,[46] Herzl was introduced on his visit to Zangwill. Nordau wrote to Zangwill that Herzl was "a great scholar and an author of renown in Germany," who had "written several plays that have achieved considerable success."[47] He felt certain that as men of letters they would find common purpose, though he feared Zangwill would "judge utopian" Herzl's "scheme for resolving the antisemitic question."[48] For his part, Herzl described Zangwill as being of "the long-nosed Negroid type, with very woolly deep-black hair," whose "clean-shaven face displays the steely haughtiness of an honest ambitious man who has made his way after bitter struggles."[49] Indeed, Zangwill had been born to poor and pious immigrant parents[50] and had escaped his humble beginnings as a child of London's East End ghetto thanks to his talent. He was an early adherent of Zionism and used his social capital to provide Herzl with entrée into the salons of those who might support the movement. Zangwill's enthusiasm for the Zionist program, and his devotion to Herzl, owed a great deal to his fascination with Mordecai Manuel Noah. In Zangwill's clearest statement of support for Zionism, he compared Herzl to Noah, and noted that the two men's similarity in temperament and ambition derive from "the playwright's habit of moulding events in the dream-world that leads to . . . attempts to manipulate the tougher material of the real."[51] Zangwill, himself a playwright, recognized this quality in others and indulged in the same alchemical will to transmute dreams into reality.

Thanks in part to Zangwill's efforts,[52] Herzl found himself admitted to the drawing rooms of philanthropic and political power. Most important to the Zionist leader was his introduction to "the great Joe,"[53] Colonial Secretary Joseph Chamberlain. Chamberlain, an influential cabinet member and the most forceful imperialist of his day, was sympathetic to Jewish suffering, though not above making a cutting remark[54] about Jews when it proved politically expedient. In the spring of 1903, the fastidiously dressed sixty-six-year-old secretary was fresh from a trip to British possessions in Africa. Chamberlain had been acquainted with Zionism's aspirations for territorial colonization prior to his departure, and Herzl had been on his mind while in Africa. Chamberlain mused in an official report composed during his travels in the continent, "If Dr. Herzl were at all inclined to transfer his efforts to East Africa there would be no difficulty in finding land suitable for Jewish settlers."[55] Hertzka's *Freeland* may in fact have first inspired Chamberlain's interest in East Africa as a site for Zionist settlement. Chamberlain would surely have been familiar with *Freeland*, which appeared in English translation in 1891 and was widely reviewed at the time. Hertzka was also a major influence on the then-fashionable economic theories of the Manchester School,[56] with which Chamberlain had been associated earlier in his political career.[57] And Chamberlain certainly knew of the ruinous Freeland experiment at colonization.

Whatever the genesis of the idea, Chamberlain received Herzl in his office just weeks after the Kishinev pogroms.[58] He fixed Herzl in his monocle and offered his help. "I have seen a land for you on my travels," Chamberlain told him, "and that's Uganda. It's hot on the coast, but farther inland the climate becomes excellent, even for Europeans . . . [a]nd I thought to myself, that would be a land for Dr. Herzl."[59] The land Chamberlain had actually seen on his travels belonged to the East Africa Protectorate and not the separately administered Uganda Protectorate, which had no coastline. But he had watched this prospective territory pass by while chugging along the Uganda Railway, which stretched from Mombasa to Lake Victoria. The confusion between the name of the railway and the actual region proposed for Jewish colonization meant that the scheme would thereafter be known as the "Uganda Plan."[60]

Chamberlain's journey as far west as mile 521[61] along the nearly six-hundred-mile "iron snake"[62] gave him time to reflect on the vast domain of the British Empire and how best to put it to use. And while memories of the abortive Freeland settlement scheme of 1894 may have given the colonial secretary pause, the methodical Zionist program and the incorporation in England of the movement's central bank[63] must have appealed to

Chamberlain and removed any taint of the Freeland debacle. He described the territory he had seen as being on "very high ground, with an excellent climate suitable for white people."[64] "The whole country bears considerable resemblance to the Sussex Downs, and, in parts, to an English park," he reported, and "English roses bloom profusely, and all English fruits and vegetable can be cultivated."[65] Chamberlain's regard for Herzl and Zionism was no doubt sincere,[66] yet the secretary had selfish reasons to encourage Jewish settlement as well. He had emerged as a vigorous proponent[67] of the construction of the Uganda Railway in the 1890s and believed its inauguration would open East Africa to economic development and reinforce its status as a British possession against a burgeoning German presence to the south. Taxpayers bore the burden of financing the scandal-plagued operation. Skirmishes with local tribes and disease killed hundreds of imported Indian laborers, and more horrible still, a pair of man-eating lions devoured upward of two dozen workers from railway work camps. For all the costs, both financial and human, there was little in the way of commerce for the railway to exploit when it opened in 1903. It looked as if Chamberlain had introduced a white elephant into Africa.

Herzl's desperation therefore offered Chamberlain a neat solution to several colonial dilemmas, and the chance to seize the moral high ground among European powers. If tens of thousands of Jewish immigrants arrived to settle on territory situated close to the Uganda Railway, then Britain's enormous investment might be rescued. Likewise, a substantial colony of grateful Jews in East Africa would mean additional loyal subjects who would pose an obstacle to German expansionism. Perhaps most important, His Majesty's government could at one and the same time vaunt its humanitarian ideals while diverting a Jewish invasion from its own shores. Chamberlain later admitted as much in a speech before "4,000 genuine working men of the East-end."[68] He strode to the stage beneath a banner exhorting his supporters to "Think Imperially."[69] Chamberlain was careful not to mention Jews by name when he denounced the myriad problems an "evil . . . alien immigration"[70] posed to his working-class audience. But he had a solution: "[T]here are thousands and hundreds of thousands of miles of unoccupied territory" where "an asylum for these persecuted people"[71] might be found. Loud cheers[72] erupted throughout the hall. Chamberlain would save the Jews and the Jews would save Chamberlain.

But Herzl was cool to Chamberlain's proposals at first, responding: "Our base must be in or near Palestine."[73] Despite his initial misgivings, Herzl continued negotiations with the secretary for several months through journalist and Zionist activist Leopold Greenberg. Herzl and Greenberg kept up a steady stream of correspondence couched in code: "Brown" indicated Chamberlain, "Window" meant the British government, and "Samson" referred to the Uganda proposal. Just a few days before the opening of the Sixth Zionist Congress, Herzl received a telegram from Greenberg in London following his successful meeting with "Brown": "have everything necessary for present purpose from window re Samson including authorised statement for you."[74] The statement in question was a distillation of a draft charter[75] for an autonomous settlement of Jews in East Africa as agreed upon by Greenberg, Chamberlain, Herzl, and various other officials. Greenberg had hired a solicitor and member of parliament to draw up the charter; his name was David Lloyd George,[76] later to become prime minister.

Herzl complained that his heart was "acting up"[77] on the eve of the Congress. Fatigue, anxiety, and a grueling travel schedule had weakened his health. He foresaw that his announcement of the British offer of a territorial solution to the ongoing victimization in the Russian Empire would be met without "even a smile of thanks."[78] At ten in the morning, Sunday, August 23, 1903, the approximately six hundred delegates[79] in attendance at Basel's Stadt Casino applauded and waved their hats[80] when he took the stage. Herzl commanded attention with his "long black beard and glowing eyes."[81] He began speaking amidst the clamor, but everyone rose to their feet[82] in respectful silence when he invoked the recent horrors of Kishinev. He then launched into a state-of-the-stateless address, cataloguing a host of failures and frustrations. Negotiations for Palestine had collapsed[83] with Ottoman ruler Sultan Abdülhamid II. Protracted efforts to enlist British support for the colonization of the Sinai Peninsula had also come to naught.[84] Yet there was reason to be hopeful, he told them. Unnamed "officials of the British government" had proposed the creation of "an autonomous Jewish settlement in East Africa . . . under the sovereign supervision of Great Britain."[85] Thunderous applause and cries of "three cheers for England"[86] greeted the revelation. But Herzl recognized that the planned "New Palestine"[87] in Africa augured the delegates' dissatisfaction. "It is not and can never be Zion,"[88] he solemnly continued. Still, he urged the delegates to examine the British offer.

The significance of what he announced—the first real achievement of Jewish statecraft in nearly two thousand years—cannot be overstated. The world's most powerful nation had recognized the six-year-old Zionist movement as the instrument of Jewish nationalism and offered its leaders land for mass colonization. Yet within days, delegates would weep openly at Herzl's supposed betrayal, his leadership would be challenged, and the Zionist movement would be divided for years to come. Now, more than a century later, this episode in Jewish history is ignored, misunderstood, or whitewashed. Otherwise well-researched histories often claim that the Sixth Congress voted on whether to accept or reject the Uganda Plan. At the time of the Congress, there was in fact no plan to vote on. The delegates voted solely on whether or not a commission to study the British proposal should be appointed and an expedition be sent to East Africa.

Furthermore, what the British government offered was vague in terms of territory and undefined in terms of specifics. The minutes of the Congress reveal that "no exact territory"[89] had even been discussed at that point. Negotiations with the British over the precise region on offer did not take place until five months later, at the end of the January 1904.[90] However, the authorized statement Greenberg had received, and which he read out at the Congress, did sketch the parameters of autonomy as Lloyd George had hammered them out with officials earlier that summer. A future Jewish colony would include: "the grant of a considerable area of land, the appointment of a Jewish Official as chief of the local administration, and permission to the Colony to have a free hand in regard to municipal legislation and as to the management of religious and purely domestic matters."[91] According to the terms of the British statement, an expedition should be sent to "ascertain personally whether there are any vacant lands suitable for the purposes in question."[92]

The stakes were high. Herzl knew that unless the Congress supported him in pursuing Chamberlain's offer, the entire Zionist movement would lack credibility with the British government and with the masses of suffering Jews. Herzl also believed that even if the East African scheme proved impractical, England's territorial commitment would be honored *somewhere* in its vast empire—perhaps in a revival of an aborted proposal to colonize the Sinai.[93] By his own admission, Herzl had launched political Zionism to create a Jewish state *"n'importe où"*—no matter where—and he had only later become a "Lover of Zion."[94] The bloody news from Kishinev returned him to his conviction that for the "hundreds of thousands [that] need immediate help,"[95] the nowhere of East Africa might just be somewhere safe enough. In contemporary interviews, Herzl held fast to his belief that an autonomous Jewish polity in Africa would "provide material and spiritual assistance to a large portion of our nation's poor,"[96] and at the same time serve "to bring us closer to Zion."[97]

Debate both for and against the formation of a Zionist Commission to investigate the territory raged within the Congress hall and in nearby lobbies and private rooms. Max Nordau gave a stirring speech[98] recognizing the necessity of examining the British offer, though in private correspondence exchanged with Herzl he confided his belief that Jewish settlers would "perish there [in East Africa] more surely even than in Kishinev—less brutally but nonetheless tragically."[99] Zangwill too gave an impassioned address. "The soul is greater than the soil," he told the delegates, "and the Jewish soul can create its Palestine anywhere, without necessarily losing the historic aspiration for the Holy Land."[100] At the Congress, another delegate in favor of the African option unfurled a large map in a tortured effort to demonstrate that the Jordan Valley was a continuation of the Great Rift Valley,[101] which stretched thousands of miles from East Africa north to Syria. Therefore, the delegate argued, the map showed that the British protectorate should be considered a part of greater Israel.

The Russian delegates formed a vocal opposition bloc, this despite antisemitic violence in the motherland. Herzl understood, or misunderstood, the Russian opposition in class terms, explaining that "their delegates for the most part come from well-to-do circles that have not had to suffer as much from the persecution and hatred of the officials. They do not feel so directly and intensely the need to be relieved from their situation."[102] The Russian rejectionist faction's unannointed leader, Menachem Mendel Ussishkin, repeatedly clashed with Herzl. Ussishkin believed that the Kishinev pogrom underscored the urgent need to establish Jewish colonies in Palestine at the expense of working for the welfare of Diaspora Jewry. "The essence of Zionism," he wrote in response to the East Africa proposal, "is to save the Nation of Israel, not our poor brethren in Russia and Romania."[103] Ussishkin was in many ways Herzl's physical opposite as well—stocky, with a round face and a receding hairline. But Ussishkin was not present in Basel in 1903. He had traveled to Palestine to preside over a rival conference meant to embarrass and antagonize Herzl. Ussishkin's fellow Russians apprised him of the Uganda Plan by telegram.[104] It did not take long for him to brand Herzl a "complete Territorialist"[105] who had betrayed Zionism's founding ideals. Part of Ussishkin's rancor was personal and derived from Herzl's portrayal of him in *Altneuland.* There Herzl depicted Ussishkin in the guise of "Mendel,"[106] a sneering, bawling, small-minded peasant who champions a racist demagogue in the newly founded Jewish state. Ussishkin was no Mendel, but his power-hungry self-promotion—his grasping chutzpah—did not endear him to Herzl and the refined Western Zionist leadership cadre.

Days of verbal sparring in Basel degenerated into a near riot. The local police requested angry delegates to observe quiet.[107] Nordau was forced to again ascend the proscenium and defend the pragmatism of sending a commission to East Africa. He dismissed those who feared the creation of a "step-Zion"[108] in East Africa, and insisted that even were a colony to be established there, it would exist for the sake of the true Zion.[109] Finally, the Congress reconvened at five minutes past four[110] on Wednesday, August 26, to vote *ja* or *nein* in an alphabetical roll call. Many of the 295 who voted to appoint and send the Commission were Herzl's allies, including Nordau and Zangwill.[111] Those 178 members voting against the motion included Israel's first president, Chaim Weizmann,[112] who later accused the yea-sayers of "throwing the Kishinev corpses in the scales . . . to turn the balance in favour of Africa."[113] Another future notable who voiced principled opposition to the scheme was young journalist Vladimir (Ze'ev) Jabotinsky,[114] who later fathered the right-wing Revisionist Zionist movement. Rabbi Yitzchak Yaacov Reines, the spiritual godfather of the religious Zionist movement *Mizrahi* (an acronym of the Hebrew *merkaz rukhani*, or "spiritual base"), was one of ninety-nine delegates[115] who abstained and thereby allowed the motion to pass by a wide margin.[116] Reines later wrote to Herzl in support of the East African option, convinced that "the needs of the people are more dear to us than the Land," and that the desperate Jews of Europe "require a safe shelter wherever it may be."[117] As odd as it may seem today, religious leaders among the delegates supported the Commission yea-sayers by a margin of three to one.[118] This apparent paradox can be explained in part by the fact that *Mizrahi* had not yet equated Zionism with the messianic promise of redemption.[119] Therefore, religious Jews granted the Zionist Organization—a secular movement—considerable latitude in its pursuit of a territorial solution to Jewish suffering. Reines also held the conviction that mass immigration to the materialistic United States threatened the Jewish future with spiritual ruination.[120] Russia's Jews required a concentrated area of settlement to preserve their lives and their religion, even if that meant colonization in Africa.

Unyielding members of the Russian delegation stormed out[121] of the hall when the vote was complete. One by one they left in protest until outside "the scene was no other than one of weeping men and women."[122] Herzl tried to appease the breakaway faction. In his closing speech he dramatically raised his right arm and quoted Psalms in Hebrew:[123] "If I forget thee O, Jerusalem, may I forget my right hand." But despite some voices of approval[124] from within the hall, his rivals were not pacified. The exhausted Herzl left the stage while many delegates "remained in their places and sang the Hatikvah, brokenly at first and then all together . . . over and over"[125] in sentimental protest. A weakened Herzl returned to his room with Nordau and Zangwill to share a bottle of mineral water and discuss the future.[126] He recited for them the speech he intended to give at the Seventh Congress, though he doubted whether he'd live to see it. "The ultimate goal [Palestine] has not been reached," he planned to say, "and will not be reached within a foreseeable time. But a temporary result is at hand: this land [East Africa] in which we can settle our suffering masses on a national basis and with the right of self-government. I do not believe that for the sake of a beautiful dream . . . we have a right to withhold this relief from the unfortunate."[127] He informed his friends that he would resign his leadership at the next Congress. Herzl had won his power struggle, but at great cost.

Criminals

The ever-combative Ussishkin published an open letter in Zionist papers claiming in the aftermath of the vote that the decision to send the Commission was tantamount to a renunciation of Palestine and the Basel Program. Ussishkin insisted that "so long as he lived,"[128] he would work against the decision. Later, he publicly denounced Herzl in an ultimatum[129] and insinuated that he was a traitor to the Jewish cause. The charge was an outrage against a leader of remarkable vision and integrity. Yet in the aftermath of the vote, Ussishkin's vociferous propaganda made those who had supported Herzl and "the East African Commission . . . feel that they had assisted at some assassination."[130] By year's end, however, it was an enemy of the Commission who took to arms.

On Saturday night, December 19, 1903, Max Nordau attended a Zionist gala at a private home in Paris with his wife and daughter.[131] A shabbily dressed young man[132] approached him near midnight[133] requesting a private conversation.[134] He handed Nordau a calling card[135] bearing his name, Chaim Selig Louban. Below, in Hebrew characters, were printed the words: "a son of the Hebrews."[136] Nordau was already a well-known and controversial writer accustomed to the attention of fans and foes alike. The flowing moustache and white beard he combed into a part made him instantly recognizable. The eminent Zionist took the stranger's card, and then excused himself to step aside and speak with a friend near a window in the ballroom.[137] They left behind the glittering lights, perfumed air, and dancing[138]—as well as the frustrated student who longed for an audience with Nordau.[139]

Louban followed at their heels, drew a revolver, and shouted in French, "Death to Nordau the East African!"[140] He fired, sending a bullet whizzing past Nordau's ear.[141] Nordau's friend grabbed the assailant, but Louban managed to squeeze off another round, which injured a bystander in the thigh.[142] The acrid smoke of gunpowder[143] filled the air and panicked guests stampeded to escape.[144] Once subdued, the twenty-three-year-old[145] declared himself a Russian revolutionary selected by lot to kill[146] Nordau by adversaries of the Uganda Plan. The police searched Louban for incriminating documents but found just a single ten-*centime* coin[147] among his threadbare clothes.

In the days that followed, scores of telegrams reached Nordau from well-wishers across the globe who congratulated him for escaping Louban's "dastardly attack."[148] Nordau himself felt that the attempt on his life was an "installment payment on the Jewish people's debt of gratitude for my selfless work on their behalf in the form of two revolver bullets which were intended for me but missed their mark."[149] The law student[150] soon recanted his conspiracy claim, insisting that he had acted alone and had tried to fire in the air simply to attract attention to his cause.[151] A judge found Louban to be mentally unbalanced and he was charged with "carelessness in the use of firearms."[152] Herzl, however, continued to maintain that Nordau's would-be assassin had been sent by the Russian rejectionists. In a "highly confidential" and paranoid letter to Nordau, Herzl claimed that "Louban's revolver was loaded in Russia" and that he had already "envisaged the barrel of the gun" after receiving Ussishkin's ultimatum to foreswear allegiance to any territory but Palestine.[153] It probably did not help quiet Herzl's mind that Louban came from a town near Ekatarinoslav,[154] where Ussishkin made his home. Indeed, Herzl had hopes that Louban's trial would reveal "who his correspondents were"[155] in Russia. Though Ussishkin's provocations may have played a part in the attack, Louban confessed that he had targeted Nordau because he had heard his speech at the Sixth Congress[156] and afterward considered him a traitor who would forsake the Land of Israel.[157]

The dramatic attempt against Nordau was condemned, but Ussishkin and his allies continued their struggle to kill[158] the East Africa proposal. In-fighting between Zionist factions jeopardized the Commission's future. No funds had been allocated for the expedition because of Russian obstructionism. Herzl was forced to seek contributions[159] for the journey from outside Zionist institutions. And bureaucratic delays in England meant that the precise territory to be explored remained unknown for several months, thus allowing opponents to sow further doubt about its practicability.

Meanwhile, a forceful letter opposed to the creation of a "semi-independent, foreign Jewish State"[160] in East Africa appeared in *The Times* from the authoritative pen of Sir Harry Johnston. The former special commissioner of the Uganda Protectorate (which once included the East African Protectorate) and one of the key colonial figures involved in the scramble for Africa, Johnston was a tireless explorer and naturalist with literary pretensions. His genial face and weepy eyes belie his strenuous efforts to extend and defend His Britannic Majesty's rule. In print, he inveighed against "Dr. Herzl's plan" because it "resemble[d] so closely Dr. Hertzka's . . . in its geography."[161] He reminded the Foreign

Office and the public at large that the "mad scheme"[162] for a Free-land colony a decade earlier had ended in disaster, adding wryly that the British had been lucky that the worst of the Freeland settlers had been "killed by a well-inspired rhinoceros."[163] Johnston likely resented the notion that indigent Jews would surge into a promising colonial possession. A year earlier, he had published a proposal to set aside a sparsely inhabited territory "as large as Belgium" along the plateau of Uasin Gishu (also known as Guas or Gwas Ngishu) for a "future White Man's Colony."[164] He believed that the region, which possessed "an abso-lutely healthy European climate," would be the natural home of a future administrative center due to its strategic location on the Uganda Rail-way.[165] In a cartographic plate map, he depicted the site of his longed-for European colony, even specifying the location of its capital.[166] Johnston didn't want his carefully laid scheme to benefit those who weren't sub-jects of the Crown.

Public acrimony among the British settlers of the East African Pro-tectorate also threatened the proposal. Antisemitic editorials and letters flooded the pages of the premier newspaper of the colony, *The African Standard*. Journalists sniped that an invasion of "pauper alien Jews"[167] would turn the highlands into "Jewganda"[168] or "The Land of Noses."[169] Other articles feared the "establishment of a new Petticoat Lane in East Africa"[170]—an allusion to Jews in London's rag trade. The paper also graciously suggested that the Jews be granted the "sleeping sickness"[171] regions around Lake Victoria. The "largest meeting of white men"[172] ever held in Nairobi met, ironically, at the Uganda Railway Institute to combat the colonization plan. They later hinted at violence[173] should the scheme be adopted.

Throughout the Jewish world the battle over the Commission moved from the Congress floor to the pages of periodicals. Ahad Ha'am (Asher Ginsberg), the revered father of cultural Zionism, joined Herzl's antag-onists. Ahad Ha'am was an influential intellectual, but also something of a nag who insisted that settlement in Palestine be secondary to the establishment of a spiritual center there that would revivify Jewish life in the Diaspora. He dismissed Herzl's "paper Zionism"[174] and attacked the decision to dispatch the Commission in a bitter polemic. The pointy-chinned tea company manager derided Herzl and his support-ers for their high-handedness, their treachery to Jewish history, and stated, with sour satisfaction, that the Sixth Congress marked nothing less than the death of Zionism. He also scourged those rabbis who had supported the Uganda proposal, writing that though they might fight to keep Zion in their prayer books, it could no longer have a place in their lives.[175]

More trenchant were the criticisms leveled at Ugandism by Ber Borochov. An original thinker and fiery orator, Borochov advanced a synthesis of Marxism and Zionism. Following the Sixth Congress, he served as a traveling mercenary in Ussishkin's employ throughout the Pale of Settlement.[176] He was only in his early twenties when he began delivering speeches against Ugandism that would evolve into a brilliant, if tendentious, essay: "On the Question of Zion and Territory." In that work, Borochov warned supporters to be on their guard against a fetishistic "Palestinomania,"[177] yet he left no doubt that *Eretz Israel* was the proper outlet for Jewish revival. He declared that territorialism had "raised failure to the level of an ideal."[178] The Zionist dream promised the "complete negation of the Diaspora,"[179] while territorialism's willingness to settle for land lacking any Jewish historical claim merely transferred and perpetuated the age-old condition of exile. Zionism, he insisted, was nothing less than a national liberation movement,[180] and "historical necessity"[181] demanded that the Jewish people choose their territory, rather than have one granted by another nation such as England.

He warned that a sudden influx of large numbers of Jewish immigrants to an undeveloped territory in British East Africa or elsewhere at the behest of a European colonial power would undo the fabric of the cultural and economic life of the land.[182] Borochov considered, and then dismissed, the possibility that the Jewish proletariat would brutalize the indigenous peoples as the British had done in Australia because "the eyes of the entire world would look upon our actions in our 'territory,' and the smallest report, even if false, of unjust treatment of the locals" would result not only in antisemitism, but a wave of "horrifying propaganda against us."[183] In a passage that now reads like a tragic joke, Borochov favored *Eretz Israel* because the land's inhabitants were "racially closer to Jews than any other 'Semites,'"[184] a fact which he believed would stave off conflict. He assured readers that the native Palestinian *felaheen* were in fact "the direct descendants of the remnants of

Jewish and Canaanite agriculturists,"[185] and would therefore assimilate more readily among their Jewish blood brothers who had returned to farm their ancient homeland. Borochov concluded his analysis with a stirring promise: "we will return . . . by the sweat of our brow, by the drops of our blood—because this hard exile pushes us forward, because the sublime vision of Zion pulls us onward, because historical necessity, from which there is no escape, is at our side!"[186] These prophetic remarks from more than a century ago have an unsettling resonance today. Borochov was undoubtedly accurate in attacking the weakness of territorialist claims to lands lacking Jewish historical connection. But for all his insistence on a materialist analysis of the Jewish condition, Borochov indulged in wishful thinking no less than his bourgeois territorialist opponents.

Herzl's supporters entered the fray too, often from unexpected quarters. The great Yiddish writer Sholem Aleichem (Salomon Rabinovich), a long-time Russian Zionist, expressed sympathy for the East Africa proposal.[187] Best known as the creator of the Tevye the Dairyman stories, the basis for the musical *Fiddler on the Roof*, Sholem Aleichem was also a noted commentator on Jewish affairs. He composed two plays, really feuilletons not meant for production, during the height of the Uganda controversy. The first, "Doctors in Consultation" (*A Konsilium Fun Doktoyrim* [1903]), features Herzl, Nordau, Ahad Ha'am, and Ussishkin attending a deathly ill patient named Israel. Herzl prescribes the remedy of *Altneuland*, or as it is known pharmacologically, "Zionisticus," to which Nordau assents.[188] Ahad Ha'am demurs and instead insists that to treat Israel's disease, the patient requires a dose of culture and spirit. Ussishkin objects that all Israel needs to recover is "Palestine air and Palestine soil!"[189] The opinion of doctors Herzl and Nordau prevails, but the off-stage pharmacist refuses to fill the prescription and Herzl is forced to substitute another medicine, "Uganda Africanica."[190] The consultants argue and insult one another until finally someone fires a gun at Nordau.[191]

A satiric one-act playlet from 1905, *Ugandiada*, also sides with the plan's supporters. In Sholem Aleichem's hands, a matchmaker introduces "Zionism"—personified as a callow young man—to "Miss Uganda," who is described as an orphaned "black beauty" who had been raised by her "fabulously rich" English aunt.[192] Zionism's family opposes the match, though if they consent, "Aunt England" promises that the bachelor will be "throned and crowned."[193] Still, the Zionist's family stubbornly refuses the offer, and in an echo of the Sixth Congress, they shout down the matchmaker, throw chairs, and the skit ends in chaos.

Eliezer Ben-Yehuda, the influential Hebrew editor, journalist, and lexicographer, decried the Russian assault with far greater force in his newspaper, *Hashkafa*. For Ben-Yehuda, the opposition to autonomy in Africa was evidence that even staunch Zionists suffered from a pathological "Diaspora mentality."[194] In a pamphlet of collected columns from *Hashkafa* entitled *The Jewish State*, Ben-Yehuda identified with the so-called "Ugandists"[195] and berated "Mr. Ussishkin"[196] for threatening to interfere with the Congress's binding vote. He invoked the memory of Mordecai Manuel Noah's failed plan for a Jewish city-state in New York, and begged his readers to avoid "the same foolish mistake, the terrible transgression that we made one hundred years ago, when that great man [Noah] made his plea to throw off the yoke of the Diaspora and become a nation upon the island that he had purchased for that purpose."[197] Africa, he insisted, will "be a New America. Perhaps even more fruitful than America!"[198] Ben-Yehuda maintained that the meager accomplishments of settlement in Palestine over two decades could be duplicated upon Africa's fertile soil in "just one year."[199] He guaranteed that within twenty years, the entire population of the Jewish state in East Africa would be speaking Hebrew.[200] Writing from his Jerusalem apartment, the man responsible for coining thousands of modern Hebrew words could find "no word strong enough in our [Hebrew] language"[201] for those who opposed the establishment of an African Zion. Instead, Ben-Yehuda used Latin characters to denigrate the Russian holdouts' actions as "criminal!"[202]

Ben-Yehuda's vociferous support of Britain's offer may seem incomprehensible today. Indeed, even at the time his support for territorialism unsettled many Zionist partisans, including Borochov, who attempted to rebut Ben-Yehuda and other *yishuv* supporters of Uganda.[203] Israeli historiographers too have tended toward an embarrassed apologetics to explain the eminent linguist's Ugandism. But as Israeli scholar Gur Alroey demonstrates, Ben-Yehuda was a partisan of Herzl and a friend of Zangwill, and was, moreover, ideologically committed to political Zionism because he believed that colonization in Africa held out the hope of saving Jewry from destruction in Eastern Europe and from further deracination in America.[204] Hebrew, he felt, would bind the Jewish nation together wherever they settled. Many in the *yishuv* agreed with him, and viewed territorialism as wholly in concert with Zionist aims.[205]

Zangwill took up his mighty pen for the cause in the English speaking world. Like Herzl and Nordau, he defended the East Africa proposal in terms that did not deny the desired, if unattainable, goal of possessing Palestine. But Zangwill's support for settlement in East Africa revealed an adroit pragmatism that went beyond that of his friends. The origins of Zangwill's Ugandism appear in one of his earliest published statements in support of Herzl. His 1899 essay, "Zionism," favorably compares Herzl to Mordecai Manuel Noah, "the projector of an American Jerusalem."[206] Zangwill, it seems, was the first to propose a link between the American playwright and his Viennese kinsman. He further suggests that the misery of Russian Jews might be alleviated by colonizing available land in Siberia, Canada, Cyprus, Mesopotamia, or the United States, whose "soil still offers the advantages enumerated by Major Noah."[207] Zangwill's proposals may seem fanciful today, but the writer of popular fictions prided himself on realism. Unlike many fervent Zionists, he had first-hand knowledge of Palestine. Prior to the First Zionist Congress, Zangwill had traveled to Jerusalem, a city he described as a "battlefield of contending fanaticisms."[208] The promised land, he recorded, was "a waterless, treeless waste . . . under the primitive rule of the Turk."[209] Based on his impressions, he concluded that "one is tempted to say that Zionism would be practicable but for Zion."[210] Zangwill did acknowledge the limited success of the Rothschild and Baron de Hirsch colonies in Palestine, but criticized the philanthropic model as wasteful.[211] Later, he derided these efforts as toy colonies.[212] Political Zionism appealed to Zangwill because it promoted not scattered settlement but a "legally-secured home," which he believed to be "the only absolute essential" element of Zionism.[213] Thus he maintained that any large, fertile, and sparsely populated tract of land would suffice for Jewish national regeneration so long as Jews would be a demographic majority.

Zangwill's belief that East Africa was preferable to Palestine rested not on an ambivalence about the holy land, but on political and demographic calculus. Nonetheless, he made it clear that "under a Jewish flag," East Africa would be "a rallying point for Zionism, a training school in self-government, a fulcrum of political influence and a nursery of emigrants for Palestine when obtained."[214] He compared the proposed Ugandan *nachtasyl* for the mixed Jewish multitude to the Israelites' forty years spent in the Sinai, a point he underscored with his suggestion to call the proposed East African entity "New Sinai."[215] The Jewish state he envisioned arising there would be one "in which justice shall be better done than in any existing State, in which morality stands higher and crime lower, in which social problems are better solved, in which woman's rights are equal to man's, in which poverty and wealth are not so terribly divided, in which the simple life is the universal ideal."[216] Like Herzl, Zangwill's aspirations for a *Judenstaat* were inspired both by the grandeur he found in the Hebrew Bible and by a democratic humanism.[217] And like Ben-Yehuda, he looked to the example of the new world to persuade his readers. "The Hebraic spirit founded the United States of America," Zangwill wrote, "is it so truly impossible to conceive of its founding the United States of Africa?"[218] Indeed it was not. In 1904, a like-minded British writer imagined a future in which the Jewish East African colony of "Israelia" was so successful that His Majesty would present world Jewry with three further territories.[219] Opponents to the Uganda Plan reacted as fiercely as they did precisely because the colonization of British East Africa seemed *more practicable* and *more promising* at the time than mass settlement in Palestine.[220] Still, the Commission had yet to examine the territory on offer.

Finally, in the summer of 1904, Greenberg managed to secure funding[221] for an expedition to the plateau region of Uasin Gishu—the same territory former Ugandan commissioner Sir Harry Johnston first sought for European colonization in 1902.[222] Most of the money came from a Christian woman sympathetic to the Zionist cause.[223] Soon another non-Jewish friend began to promote the British offer: none other than Sir Harry himself. Previously an enemy of Zionist designs on East Africa, Johnston now supported the plan in print and in public appearances. In a letter to Greenberg written for publication,[224] he claimed to have initially misunderstood the geographic territory on offer to the Zionists. But after reviewing maps of the proposed colony, he confirmed that the Uasin Gishu plateau was indeed "one of the best pieces of unoccupied land which could be found . . . in the British Empire."[225] He believed that agriculture settlements would thrive there, but he hoped that the

Mount Sirgoit rising above fertile fields of Uasin Gishu Plateau, Kenya. Courtesy of
Michael Kollins

would-be Jewish farmers would also see fit to create a "great game
reserve" to protect the majestic animals of the region. Johnston's sudden about-face had nothing to do with geographic error. Likely he had
succumbed to the charm and persuasion of Zangwill, who became his
friend, neighbor, and fellow activist for women's suffrage.[226] Later, while
presiding over a meeting of the Friends for Jewish Freedom, Johnston
went so far as to describe the Uasin Gishu landscape as reminiscent of
a "wild part of England."[227] He looked forward to the Commission setting out to inspect the land tendered for the noble purpose of "shaping
a Jewish State, of building up a healthy physique."[228] His speech to the
Friends for Jewish Freedom was greeted with enthusiastic cheers.

In the Zionist press, Ben-Yehuda hailed the long-delayed dispatch of
the Commission to East Africa as "the greatest event in the annals of
the nation of Israel from the time of our Diaspora until today," and predicted that the date of its departure would be recorded in "golden letters"[229] in future histories of the Jewish nation. Another Hebrew newspaper reminded readers that "only one . . . who held stubbornly, wildly,

and despotically to his opinions" could treat the expedition's embarkation with contempt.[230] Though not named, Ussishkin appears to have been the target of the anonymous journalist's scorn.

Herzl did not live to see the Commission set sail. The psalmist's declaration of loyalty to Jerusalem he had recited in Basel was to be his final public testament. Herzl died on July 3, 1904, of cardiac arrest at the age of forty-four. His friends and supporters blamed the stress of the Uganda controversy, and his public battles with Ussishkin in particular,[231] for his premature death. Ussishkin had told the ailing Herzl before his death that "there is no place for you at the head of the Zionist movement."[232] Yet Herzl remained the movement's inspiration even after his death, despite his position on East Africa. Nordau and Ben-Yehuda also remained central to Zionism, though their roles in the Uganda affair are conveniently forgotten.

Tourists in Jerusalem can now drive down Nordau Street, ask directions to the Ben-Yehuda pedestrian mall, and while wandering in and out of the shops there, buy a T-shirt bearing Herzl's iconic image. True, there's a Ussishkin Street, but the egomaniacal Menachem Mendel insisted on naming the road after himself.[233] (Local lore has it that Ussishkin would leave his nearby home at night to wipe clean the dust that daily accumulated on the road signs bearing his name.) Thirsty travelers tired of souvenir hunting in Israel's capital can also toast Zionism's founding fathers downtown at a countercultural pub called "Uganda." A black-and-white framed portrait of Herzl hangs ironically over the bar. To Israelis, Uganda's three syllables compress a long sigh of existential fatigue. For the hipsters and barefoot anarchists smoking cigarettes inside, the bar's name evokes a desire to be in another time and place. Uganda encapsulates a feeling of belatedness common in Israel today, the sense that young people have arrived on the scene both after the end—the Holocaust—and after the beginning—the heroic efforts of nation-building. Perhaps too there exists a dimly recognized sense that the State of Israel emerged too late for those who needed it most.

A Spy in the Land

On January 13, 1905,[234] Nahum Wilbuschewitz stood on the deck of the steamer S.S. *Africa* at the entrance to Mombasa's Kilindini Harbor. The temperature was a sultry eighty-six degrees.[235] The young man leaned his five-foot, eleven-inch[236] frame over the railing, patted his brow with one of the dozen handkerchiefs[237] he had brought with him, and peered through rimless spectacles[238] at the bustling Indian Ocean port. Mango trees and coconut palms[239] swayed in the meager breeze. Barefoot porters pushed handcarts down gangplanks, across the pier, and up through the city's alleyways that snaked between walls inset with ornate wooden gates. Balconies teetered overhead from whitewashed buildings. Minarets trimmed in green presided over the jumbled chaos. This was Wilbuschewitz's first glimpse of Africa. But the twenty-five-year-old[240] had already covered a lot of ground. He had left his home in White Russia, traveled to Houston, Texas, then gone on to study civil engineering in Germany.[241] After completing his studies there in 1903, he attended the Sixth Zionist Congress as an observer.[242] Soon after, he emigrated to Ottoman Palestine[243] as a Zionist pioneer. There he explored the length and breadth of the holy land[244] on horseback. But now, following a whirlwind trip through Berlin, Basel and Trieste, and after seventeen days at sea[245] traveling no faster than sixteen knots,[246] Wilbuschewitz still had to cross more than five hundred miles of wilderness before reaching the territory the Sixth Zionist Congress had sent him to survey along with two compatriots.

Seasoned adventurer Major Alfred St. Hill Gibbons, a veteran of the Boer War[247] in his forties and the author of several volumes on African exploration, was sent in command of the expedition. The third member of the group, Dr. Alfred Kaiser,[248] was a Swiss naturalist who had lived and traveled throughout northern, eastern, and southern Africa. Their cargo of binoculars, knives, hunting rifles, whistles, rubberized jackets, pith helmets, boots, shoe polish, woolen underwear, pajamas,[249] a voltameter, and a theodolite[250] were carried by dozens of local porters. The caravan's native headman, Feraji, had previously crossed Africa[251] with Henry Morton Stanley in his disastrous mission to rescue the Jewish-born Emin Pasha from jihadists. Gibbons modeled himself on these and other European adventurers of the Victorian era. He was a big game hunter and ardent imperialist with thinning hair and a well-waxed moustache. Dr. Kaiser was short, squat, and spoke both Swahili and Arabic.[252] He had converted to Islam during the years he had lived in the Sinai Peninsula while investigating how the ancient Israelites might have survived their forty years of desert wanderings.[253] Wilbus-chewitz, the sole Jewish representative of the Commission, was by contrast an untested youth.

Though it sounds like the setup to a joke, these three—a Christian, a Muslim, and a Jew—disembarked that Friday morning more than a century ago charged with the serious task of surveying land for a Jewish homeland. Chamberlain and the Foreign Office had earmarked Uasin Gishu for Jewish colonization. Though the exact borders of the proposed territory fluctuated over time, in its largest incarnation it stretched roughly seventy miles east to west, from near the famous flamingo lake of Nakuru to the vicinity of the port of Kisumu on the banks of Lake Victoria, and ninety miles south to north, from the equator to Mount Elgon's volcanic peaks.[254] The total land area was approximately sixty-three hundred square miles,[255] or about the size of Connecticut and Rhode Island together. Most of Uasin Gishu was remote and unexplored, except the regions that stretched along the recently completed Uganda Railway. No one knew what the Commission would discover further inland. Perhaps fertile soil. Perhaps gold. Or they might face hostile tribes. Or have to fight off man-eating lions. Zangwill, for one, relished that idea, exulting that there can be no Judah "without the lion of Judah."[256] Whatever they might find, their official report was of the utmost importance to the territorial aspirations of those who had sided with Herzl in the bitter fight to send the Commission.

Wilbuschewitz, who shortened his name to Wilbusch, understood the importance of his role in the saga. Years later he acknowledged that "all the eyes of Israel [were] watching us and waiting for redemption."[257] But Wilbusch was a double agent who used his position to sabotage the Commission. How he ended up in Africa, his role in torpedoing the Uganda Plan, and his subsequent career make him into a kind of Forrest Gump of Zionism. At the Sixth Congress, Wilbusch witnessed Herzl's pleas[258] for unity from the gallery, but he sided with the Russian rejectionists. His journey on horseback through Palestine on behalf of the Russian Zionist leadership the next year, 1904, resulted in a report[259] on the prospects for industry in the holy land. This report came to the attention of Ussishkin, who recommended the establishment of a factory there under the young engineer's direction.[260] Wilbusch's sister, Manya, went on to become one of the founders of *Hashomer*, the armed

"Watchman" organization in pre-state Palestine and a precursor to the Israeli Defense Forces. Wilbusch himself served in the Ottoman military and was charged with carrying out restorations to the Dome of the Rock mosque.[261] He subsequently became friendly with Chaim Weizmann[262] and once even retained Jabotinsky[263] as his attorney.

But at the time of the Commission's formation in 1904, Wilbusch was still unknown. He was, however, acquainted with esteemed botanist Otto Warburg, future president of the Zionist Organization. Warburg had been asked to go to Africa[264] with the expedition on account of his expertise in tropical agriculture. When he balked, he suggested Wilbusch[265] go in his place. Wilbusch volunteered and departed without seeking any compensation.[266] Correspondence indicates that Wilbusch was not a popular choice. Greenberg did not want to procure insurance for him. Wilbusch's life was ultimately valued at 250 pounds sterling,[267] half that of Kaiser's, and only a quarter of Gibbons'. He seems not to have known—or cared—that the cash-strapped Zionist Commission reckoned his blood so cheaply. A cheerful and perhaps sardonic picture postcard written to Warburg sends "hearty greetings" from "our 'Nachtasyl' on the way to the Promised Land."[268]

Reports of hostile tribes met the Commission when they arrived in the Uasin Gishu district after their 448-mile train journey[269] from Mombasa and a tiring overland march from Nakuru. They learned that bubonic plague and malaria[270] spread through the lowlands near Lake Victoria. Lions remained an ever-present danger. Wilbusch packed a Mauser pistol[271] because he felt the expedition's Schneider rifles were inadequate for protection.[272] He also had little faith in the more than forty native porters, guides, and servants who accompanied them, including several spear-wielding Masai tribesman, who, Wilbusch noted, were said to have Jewish blood.[273] He had even less confidence in Major Gibbons. Almost from the beginning, the expedition was plagued by dissension among the members, undisciplined porters, a scarcity of supplies and numerous delays. Wilbusch suspected that Gibbons was determined to file a positive report no matter what the real conditions in Uasin Gishu might be. The native supply-bearers refused to enter certain regions for fear of enemy tribes. Food stores were inadequate. Luggage and equipment was left behind in Nairobi. Kaiser lamented the loss of his flower-pressing paper.[274] Wilbusch blamed Gibbons for the poor organization. The major in turn singled out Wilbusch as being of "no help" to him "from start to finish."[275] Though when their supplies dwindled and Gibbons shot a hartebeest for dinner, the major archly noted that Wilbusch did at least "help to eat it."[276]

Wilbusch saw "no timber, no pasturage, no game, [and] no people"[277] during the first two days he spent in the region. On the third day, January 30, 1905, he, Kaiser, and Gibbons decided to split up to cover as much ground as possible.[278] They agreed to meet six days later at Mount Sirgoit,[279] an obvious landmark that rises a few hundred feet above the plateau. Wilbusch took ten men with him[280] to carry foodstuffs, weapons, and the green canvas tent and collapsible furniture for his private camp. The weather was "clear and very windy" with comfortable temperatures in the upper seventies. [281] He spent the days collecting mineral samples and measuring water flow in streams and rivulets in the region. Hundreds of antelopes and zebras grazed nearby.[282] He spotted rhinos[283] and hippos,[284] and a single lion that prowled within a thousand paces from his tent.[285] The wild barberries he picked during his short hikes reminded him of his Russian childhood.[286] But after five days of wandering, he had encountered no people whatsoever, only scattered "traces of human habitation."[287]

Then, on day six of his trek, he claimed to have found dozens of bleached human skulls[288] affixed to the branches of a dead acacia tree. His description of this ominous sight was likely nothing but a tall tale, reminiscent of Rider Haggard's *King Solomon's Mines*. But Wilbusch's luck did change for the worse on that day, February 4, when two of his porters absconded with his provisions. He camped for the night about a mile from Mount Sirgoit and hoped they would return. They did, but three days later he had still not found Gibbons or Kaiser. His store of rice had come to an end.[289] One porter killed an antelope whose meat made several others ill.[290] A desperate Wilbusch ate locusts.[291] On February 10, he set off by himself to look for Gibbons and Kaiser. He found no one and even managed to lose his compass in the process.[292] Alone and exhausted, he passed out at the base of Mount Sirgoit. When he came to, he watched a vulture overhead[293] descend in slow circles.

The next day he made contact with Kaiser and soon afterward they joined together and set up their "Promised Land"[294] base camp between Mount Sirgoit and Karuna Hill, and there awaited Gibbons. Wilbusch

View from Karuna Hill with Mount Sirgoit in distance, Uasin Gishu Plateau, Kenya.
Courtesy of Michael Kollins

ascended Karuna's rocky summit during the interval. He found the view of the surrounding countryside "little pleasing."[295] All around he observed poor pastures and few trees. But the daily log Wilbusch kept reveals that he did little actual exploration. For eleven full days[296] he reported that he did nothing but wait at base camp for the others to return from their excursions. The major's extended absence allowed Wilbusch the leisure to draft his report and formulate his negative assessment of the territory, partly in consultation with Kaiser.[297] Wilbusch was convinced that Uasin Gishu held "no population whatever," and therefore future settlers would not be burdened with the "Native Question."[298] But this same conclusion also led him to believe that because the land was unoccupied,[299] it would not be fit for settlement. The only good land, it seems, would be a land already inhabited.

Gibbons drifted into camp on the twenty-fifth of February amidst a light rain.[300] By that time, Wilbusch and Kaiser had spent enough time together to reinforce one another's pessimism. The major's claims that he had traveled through rich, well-watered land to the north were dismissed as exaggerations.[301] Later, Gibbons insisted that he had seen "no healthier country in Africa."[302] Kaiser scoffed, maintaining that a "more promising country"[303] must be found for the Zionist enterprise. Agriculture was sure to fail. Wilbusch, however, did briefly indulge in an idyllic vision of an African Zion. He imagined the rise of a Jewish colony of ostrich farmers and cheese makers[304] drawing power from windmills[305] dotting the highlands. But he checked these fancies and ended his report with a stark and damning conclusion: "Where nothing exists, nothing can be done."[306] Nonetheless, a report published by Professor Warburg and based on updates he had received from the Commission members in the field suggested to him that at least twenty to thirty thousand Jewish immigrants[307] might be settled in Uasin Gishu, where he hoped they could "create a race of tough and useful cattlemen and show the world . . . that it is possible for the Jews to adapt, even under unusual and difficult circumstances, to agricultural life."[308] Though Warburg did not agree with Nordau that the territory could be a suitable "night asylum"[309] for Russia's persecuted millions, he concluded that tens of thousands of Jewish colonists would at least "be able to lead a free, healthy and independent life" in East Africa.[310]

Those who sought a promised land in Uasin Gishu's highlands always discovered a version of the familiar, an image of the home they wanted to find. Hertzka imagined the scene to look something like Europe's Alps. From his railway car, Chamberlain viewed the landscape as akin to the British countryside. Wilbusch tasted the barberries of mother Russia. All three—the utopian, the imperialist, the engineer—projected their memories onto foreign soil and found it to be fertile ground for fantasy.

Today, the area the Commission explored encompasses rolling hills, red soil, and isolated stands of eucalyptus. Gazelles with striped black flanks leap and disappear in the swaying grasslands. Footpaths stretch between scattered mud-daubed homes with thatch roofs. At the precise coordinates of Wilbusch's campsite, women and children wash clothes in a freshwater stream. Nearby a few cows swish their tails at the edge of fields of maize. Birds thrum and sing in thorny thickets. Locusts vibrate unseen. Karuna Hill stands a few miles distant from Mount Sirgoit. The grass at its base is mostly brown and dry. A strong wind rustles the brittle stalks. Stunted trees grow along Karuna's slope. Overhead, a

The author at the site of the Zionist Commission's "Promised Land" campsite in today's Kenya. Courtesy of Michael Kollins

raptor rides the thermals. From atop the rocky summit, a distant lake shimmers to the north. To the east, the land shades to green along the Rift Valley. The peak of Mount Elgon is shrouded in haze to the northwest. The Promised Land campsite lies to the southwest and appears as a lush tributary of the wheat fields surrounding Mount Sirgoit. Today Uasin Gishu is known as Kenya's breadbasket. Had Wilbusch lacked the imagination to see the territory's agricultural potential? Or had he, like the spies sent by Moses to reconnoiter the biblical land of Israel (Numbers 13–14), "brought up an evil report of the land"[311] that condemned the Jewish people to forty years of wandering?

The Plot against Africa

The laconic text of Wilbusch's field notes reveal internal inconsistencies: he sees herds of animals, but claims the region will not support life;

he suggests the establishment of windmills and dairies, and then back-tracks to insist that no development is possible; he finds signs of human habitation, but maintains that the land is totally devoid of inhabit-ants—this even after the Commission convoy is attacked by bandits.[312] At times, he seems to draw conclusions that contradict his own experi-ence. The reason: Wilbusch was serving two masters. A communiqué from Ussishkin leaves no doubt that Wilbusch reported to his patron in distant Russia during the expedition. Ussishkin then forwarded Wil-busch's message to an ally: "I am informing you in *secret* that I have received a letter from Wilbuschewitz *in Uganda* . . . his letter informs me that: 'The children of Ham will inherit the land in Africa, the chil-dren of Shem—the land in Asia.' And so . . . the Uganda question is *over and done with.*"[313] In this dispatch, Wilbusch refers to the notion that black Africans are the "children of Ham" and that Semitic peoples are the "children of Shem," both of whom were among the biblical Noah's sons. This triumphant message coded in biblical rhetoric suggests that Wilbusch played an active role in skewing the Commission's conclu-sions and sabotaging its efforts.

Only a few days after Wilbusch returned to Jaffa, Ussishkin began drafting a letter to his protégé, instructing him "not [to] be scared by the intrigues and insinuations at your expense."[314] He told Wilbusch to ignore gossip about his role in the Commission, and "[d]elve into your machines" and "engineering research" instead.[315] "I want you to know," Ussishkin promised, "that I am going to be always at your dis-posal when it comes to promoting industrial development."[316] But he did ask Wilbusch for one favor in return: to attend the Seventh Zionist Congress later that summer. "Your presence would be very helpful,"[317] he noted. It was at the Seventh Congress that the East Africa proposal would come up for a final vote.

A handful of Jews, mostly from South Africa, did trickle in to Kenya spurred by rumors of a future Jewish settlement.[318] Wilbusch met some of them on his travels, including Abraham Block,[319] a recent arrival from Johannesburg who homesteaded near Nairobi. Block later became one of the richest men in Kenya and the owner of the capital's New Stanley Hotel, a favorite haunt of Ernest Heming-way. Wilbusch too became a wealthy man, thanks to a series of fac-tories he established in Israel that produced vegetable oil. On the strength of Ussishkin's recommendation, he erected his first facility shortly after his return to Palestine from Africa. While he oversaw its completion, he camped in the tent he had slept in during his sojourn in Uasin Gishu.[320] Ussishkin did not settle in Palestine until 1919. There he took over the Jewish National Fund, whose blue charity boxes and tree-planting certificates are familiar to generations of Hebrew-school students. The name of one young Russian delegate who had voted with Ussishkin at the Sixth Congress later became synonymous with maximalist Zionism: Jabotinsky. But even the militant Jabotinsky second-guessed his nay-saying decades later as Nazism spread. In 1938 he flew over East Africa and thought of the millions of Jews trapped in Europe. He told his trusted biographer that he "just couldn't help wondering"[321] whether his rejection of the Uganda scheme had been a mistake.

After the controversy, Greenberg, Herzl's loyal deputy, emerged as one of England's premier Zionist agitators. He helmed London's influential *Jewish Chronicle* from 1907 until his death in 1931. His will requested that his remains be cremated and interred in Palestine. But rabbinic authorities opposed to cremation prevented his burial, and his ashes perched for a time at the edge of the promised land upon a shelf in the port of Haifa's custom's hall.[322] In British government circles, the Uganda Plan died an unlamented death. Former protectorate commissioner Arthur Hardinge recalled that "there was a general relief both in East Africa and the Foreign & Colonial offices . . . when it came to nothing."[323] But the solicitor who had prepared the charter for the Jewish settlement, David Lloyd George, rose to become prime minister in 1916. While in residence at 10 Downing Street, Lloyd George's foreign secretary was Arthur James Balfour, who had been prime minister during Chamberlain's initial negotiations with Herzl more than a decade earlier. In November 1917, Balfour issued his celebrated statement: "His Majesty's Government view with favour the establishment in Palestine of a national home for the Jewish people."[324] The Balfour Declaration encouraged mass Jewish immigration and helped shift the demographic balance in Mandate-era Palestine. Israel, we might say, came out of Africa. But Zangwill and his Jewish Territorial Organization (ITO) tried to keep it there, first in East Africa, then in Libya, and finally with near success in Angola.

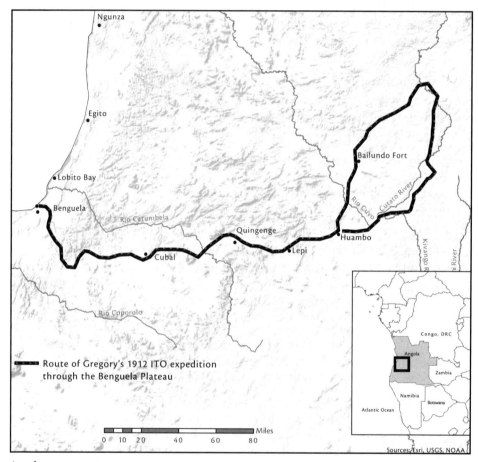

Angola

3

Angolan Zion

Benguela Plateau (1907–1914)

A Land, Any Land

The Seventh Zionist Congress convened in Basel's Stadt Casino on July 27, 1905, in the shadow of Herzl's death. A black band of mourning cut across the edge of the blue-and-white Zionist flag which hung at the front of the hall between imposing marble columns. Herzl's portrait peered down at the assembled delegates as Max Nordau took center stage to open the Congress.[1] On the left of the dais sat those who identified with the territorialists, on the right those who rejected the "Uganda" plan, the *Tzioney Tzion* (Zionists of Zion).[2] Nordau's moving eulogy for Herzl briefly united the delegates in grief during the morning session, but by the afternoon of the first day, the two sides were ready to clash. A report that the few Jews living in British East Africa had formed a Zionist society was greeted with cheers and applause,[3] presumably by the territorialists. Minutes later, Menachem Ussishkin introduced a resolution calling on the Zionist Organization to declare its loyalty solely to settlement in Palestine.[4] When challenged, he urged the "removal of the anti-Zionists from the casino hall."[5] The Congress descended into a tumult of mutual accusations, a prelude to the rowdy emergency session called for the next day to discuss the Expert Commission's report and the future of the East Africa plan.

As Ussishkin had requested, Nahum Wilbusch traveled from Palestine to attend the Congress. He came ready to defend his negative assessment of the Uasin Gishu Plateau. Wilbusch appeared amidst applause after the opening of the emergency session and reiterated his statement that "where nothing exists, nothing can be done"[6]—a kind of photo-negative of Herzl's "if you will it, it is no dream." But Wilbusch then proceeded to backpedal, claiming that several of his other conclusions had been misinterpreted by Major Gibbons. Nordau cut Wilbusch off on the gentlemanly grounds that Gibbons was not there to defend himself, and then acknowledged Israel Zangwill's right to address the Congress. Scarecrow-thin and stoop-shouldered, Zangwill was nonetheless an imposing figure whose haughty bearing lent him dignity. In photographs of the time, he often appears to be staring down his prominent nose, brow furrowed and delicate lips pursed. Zangwill had publicly ridiculed Wilbusch and his report two weeks earlier.[7] Now, befitting the gravity of the Congress, he ignored Wilbusch's apologetics and instead called his fellow Zionists to conscience: "We are more than a parliament of Zionists, we are a parliament of Jews from twenty-three countries from around the world. We have a responsibility not only to Zionists, but to all the people of Israel . . . I mean to our children's children—for we are working for them—for these millions of our children's children."[8] In his appeal to the fate of generations of Jews yet to come, Zangwill duplicated the rhetoric of Mordecai Noah's *Discourse on the Restoration of the Jews*.[9] The precarious existence of Russian Jewry demanded immediate action, Zangwill maintained. His beleaguered people could not wait for *Eretz Israel*.

Zangwill believed that Zionism should be an instrument of pragmatic collective survival, not a romantic nationalist movement. He declared that Herzl had outgrown Ussishkin's proposed path to Palestine, which involved purchasing land to establish small-scale settlements.[10] Ussishkin aimed to create facts on the ground that the sultan would then be forced to recognize. That plan, Zangwill tartly noted, "is based on two premises . . . namely, that General Ussishkin has a large army of Ussishkins behind him, and secondly, that the Sultan of Turkey is a fool."[11] Laughter erupted from the territorialist camp, no doubt humiliating Ussishkin. Zangwill then continued in a serious vein, warning the assembled: "If we decline the East Africa project, we may experience the relief one has after the removal of a painful tooth. But we will recall, too late, that it was our last tooth!"[12] The rancor of the session continued into the following days, each side further entrenching itself and nursing its bitterness.

On the afternoon of the fourth day of the Congress, a weary Nordau brought three resolutions before the delegates: (1) that the Zionist Organization direct all future settlement efforts solely to Palestine; (2) that the Zionist Organization thank the British government for its offer of an autonomous territory in East Africa; and (3) that only those Jews who declare their allegiance to the Basel Program may become members of the Zionist Organization.[13] Zangwill objected. The first resolution, he argued, amounted to a limitation on the actions of the Jewish Colonial Trust, the financial instrument for colonization set up following the Second Zionist Congress in 1898. The Congress did not have the right to limit the scope of the independent company's operations, Zangwill asserted; only the shareholders could do so.[14] The resolution thus overreached the Congress's authority. Zangwill had indeed raised a nettlesome issue. The Jewish Colonial Trust's Articles of Association dictated that the company's objective was to "promote, develop, work, and carry on industries, undertakings and colonization schemes in Palestine, in Syria, *and in any other part of the world* in any manner which may . . . be to the interest of the Jewish race in any country or place."[15] Zangwill correctly saw the Congress's effort to restrict the scope of the Trust's activity as an illegitimate curtailment of its corporate powers.[16] When Nordau insisted on the Congress's right to pass the resolutions regardless, Zangwill was outraged. "You will be charged before the bar of history," he challenged Nordau. The indignant leader responded: "I call you to order for your expression." "I call you to order," Zangwill shouted back, "Herzl told me that the Seventh Congress would be the last Congress and I hope that it will be so."[17] Furious delegates booed Zangwill's outburst before Nordau regained control and instituted what amounted to a loyalty test. From approximately 1:30 p.m. on Sunday, July 30, 1905, a Zionist would henceforth be defined as someone who adhered to the Basel Program, and the only "authentic interpretation" of that program restricted settlement activity exclusively to Palestine.[18]

Zangwill and his supporters could not accept Nordau's "authentic interpretation," which they believed would lead to an abandonment of the Jewish masses and of Herzl's vision. One territorialist claimed that Ussishkin's voting bloc had in fact "buried political Zionism."[19] Zionist-Socialist party leader Dr. Nachman Syrkin, an ally of Zangwill's, announced that the fixation on Palestine hindered "our liberation movement and is in deep conflict with the interests of . . . the broad Jewish masses."[20] He then called on "all truly democratic elements in Judaism and Zionism" to leave the Congress Hall.[21] And so, a heterogeneous group of delegates stormed out in protest amidst a cacophony of catcalls, applause, and verbal abuse. These sixty or so disgruntled Zionists improvised a rival meeting a few hundred meters away from the Stadt's opulence.[22] According to Syrkin, the territorialists too dreamed of settlement in *Eretz Israel*,[23] but dreams could not be the basis for a responsible political movement.[24] Syrkin, with his pugnacious glare, his black beard, and his dark hair swept back atop his head, looked every bit the Russian social revolutionary. He charged that Ussishkin and his allies offered a regressive politics that catered to nostalgic visions of heroic Jewish history in the biblical land of Israel. By contrast, the territorialists promised a "romance for the future"—to create a new, equitable Jewish polity in land offered by Great Britain.[25] "The [Jewish] nation and [its] life," Syrkin contended, "are holier than a sentimental attachment to the past."[26] Syrkin's speech reveals an intriguing distinction between the two camps. Palestinocentric Zionists invented the Jewish future in terms of the mythic past; territorialists jettisoned the land of their fathers in order to pursue a utopian future.

To forge an alternative to the Zionist Organization's exclusive focus on Palestine, Syrkin and others established the Jewish Territorial Organization (ITO). Zangwill emerged as the ITO's reluctant leader after a final speech to the Seventh Congress during which he was jeered with cries of "Go to the Territorialists!"[27] Following the Congress, Zangwill charged Ussishkin and his supporters with vote rigging to defeat the East African proposal. He expressed the hope that others in the Zionist Organization would yet be able "to tame Ussishkin and to continue to pursue the greater political endeavors of Herzl."[28] The combative Russian leader denounced Zangwill's accusations in a private letter. An unusually restrained Zangwill had the letter filed away with the notation "not to be answered"[29] scrawled atop it. Soon the ideologies they represented, Zionism and "ITOism," would become public rivals for Jewish communal support.

In the years 1905 and 1906, nearly seven hundred pogroms erupted in the Russian Pale of Settlement.[30] These vicious attacks against person and property claimed the lives of more than three thousand Jews.[31] The periodic violence and terror helped popularize the ITO and its platform calling for the urgent relocation of vulnerable Russian Jews to any available territory.[32] Zionist organizers, however, continued to propound a gradualist and selective immigration to *Eretz Israel*.[33] Petitions signed by thousands of desperate Jews circulated throughout the Pale expressing their support of the ITO and calling on Zangwill to find them a suitable homeland.[34] By 1911, the ITO had established more than three hundred information offices[35] in the Pale to aid prospective immigrants seeking to flee the Russian Empire. The ITO's administrative presence in the Pale and the work of its numerous agents helped solidify the fledgling movement and gave prestige to Zangwill as its figurehead. The ITO's efforts on behalf of the poor, combined with an official Zionist policy to select only self-sufficient immigrants for Palestine, all but ensured the ITO's popularity among those Jews who most needed assistance.

Zangwill asserted that the ITO remained the rightful heir to Herzl's program and that of his distinguished predecessor, Leon Pinsker, whom Zangwill dubbed "the first Territorialist."[36] Pinsker had indeed suggested the feasibility of mass Jewish settlement in North America in *Auto-Emancipation* (1882). Zangwill, an otherwise mercurial character, consistently believed that rather than being in conflict, ITOism was Zionism's practical manifestation. "[Herzl's] idea was simply to found a Jewish State anywhere," Zangwill maintained, "[b]ut it was natural that he should try first for Palestine."[37] He later came to regard Zionism as "the Palestinian form of Territorialism."[38] Part of Zangwill's territorialist convictions and his criticism of the Zionist Organization stemmed from his recognition that Palestine was already populated. When one of Zangwill's allies took the floor at the Seventh Congress to note that there were more than half a million Arabs already living in Palestine,[39] he was hectored and accused of being a "hater of Zion."[40] Even as early as 1904, Zangwill warned audiences of "a difficulty from which the Zionist dares not avert his eyes, though he rarely likes to face it. Palestine proper has already its inhabitants."[41] Zangwill's refusal to be "hypnotised by the legend that Palestine was empty and derelict" put him at odds with Zionist leaders.[42] He denounced their "airy assumption that the Arabs will obligingly trek out of Palestine."[43] True, after the Balfour Declaration of 1917, Zangwill would endorse his own airy assumption that Palestine's Arabs would voluntarily leave their homes to establish independent states elsewhere.[44] But whatever his later opinions, Zangwill appears to have been the first notable Zionist leader to publicly acknowledge that Zionism's solution to the so-called "Jewish question" called forth a troubling "Arab question."

He foresaw two unpalatable answers to this question in Palestine: "[W]e must be prepared either to drive out by the sword the tribes in possession as our forefathers did, or to grapple with the problem of a large alien population, mostly Mohammedan and accustomed for centuries to despise us."[45] Zangwill's point was rhetorical, a flourish to highlight mainstream Zionism's willful denial of demographics: the six hundred thousand Arabs then thought to be living in Palestine. Zangwill did not in fact advocate violent conquest, which would have been impossible given the Jewish population there of nearly one hundred thousand at the time, not to mention their lack of any military force.[46] He was certain, however, that a sizable "alien"—that is, Arab—minority would impede the establishment of a national home in *Eretz Israel*. A future Jewish state, he believed, necessitated a decisive demographic majority.[47]

No one was more conscious of the difficulties the Jewish minority faced in Palestine than members of the *yishuv* themselves. Territorialism was far from a marginal movement in *Eretz Israel* of the time.[48] And no one lent greater stature to Ugandism in Ottoman Palestine than Eliezer Ben-Yehuda. Ben-Yehuda's journalistic activism on behalf of the plan helped frame the ideological clash between political and practical Zionism. The defeat of Herzlian political Zionism at the Seventh Congress increased his discontent. Ben-Yehuda believed that the real loser at the Congress was Diaspora Jewry itself, which "hovered between life and death."[49] Less than three weeks after the close of the Congress, Ben-Yehuda belittled Ussishkin's victory and indicated that he had misled supporters into believing that Jewish agricultural settlement in Palestine would be quick and easy.[50] The lack of a territorial alternative for mass Jewish colonization tortured Ben-Yehuda "day and night, awake and in dreams."[51] Like others aligned with territorialism, he viewed Jewish misery in Russia and antisemitism in Europe with a sense that time was running out.

The most important Hebrew writer of the era, Yosef Chaim Brenner, also looked upon the contemporary Jewish situation with anxiety. He lent his literary voice to territorialism after the Seventh Congress. Writing from London, the headquarters of the ITO, Brenner wondered how mainstream Zionists could even speak of national regeneration without first attempting to physically rescue the Jewish people.[52] Brenner's comments were in part directed against Ussishkin who, he wrote, would not be able to provide his followers with their desired redemption.[53] In a long essay, the oft-uprooted author cried out for "[a] land! Any land that we can acquire, any land that will allow for the immediate possibility of building our home . . . a land not for today, which is already lost, but a land for tomorrow, for future generations."[54] Brenner's rhetoric here is reminiscent of Zangwill's emotional address at the Seventh Congress, but his assessment of Jewish vulnerability was even bleaker than his fellow author's. "We are not slaughtered for our faith . . . not for our wickedness are we killed, nor for our righteousness are we stabbed," he admonished.[55] No, he continued in a tone of characteristic despair, "[t]he hands of all are raised against us because we are hated, and we are hated for the same reason that all human-wolves hate and are hated, though all other human-wolves are in their own forests, and we alone are dispersed, we are alien."[56] The need for a Jewish in-gathering to achieve a demographic majority in some territory again recalls the urgency felt by Zangwill. But Brenner's flirtation with territorialism was brief, and in 1909 he immigrated to Ottoman Palestine, where he maintained an often jaundiced view of Zionist activity. There, in his "own forest," he was stabbed and beaten to death during an Arab pogrom in Jaffa in 1921.

Whither?

Soon after the close of the initial ITO conference, Zangwill returned to London and began to recruit support for the fledgling international movement. He published a manifesto in *The Jewish Chronicle*—the same organ that had first published Herzl's vision of his *Judenstaat*—to announce the ITO's formation. His appeal began with a famous question in Yiddish: "*Wohin?*" (Whither?)[57] Where could desperate refugees from Russia find shelter as restrictions on immigration took effect in the West? Great Britain instituted an Aliens Act restricting immigration in 1905. In the U.S., the rise of nativist sentiment, which fueled efforts to limit immigration, was another cause for concern. What country would still permit an unregulated flood of poor Jews to congest its cities? Where could they flee to? *Wohin*? Zangwill's answer was at once sanguine and grim: there was no sanctuary, and so, the Jews would have to create their own. He referred to his fantasized paper state as ITOland. "The world still holds . . . vast tracts of comparatively unexploited or neglected territory," Zangwill declared.[58] In such a territory a "publicly-recognized, legally-secured home" for the Jewish people could be established.[59] He vowed, in sharp contrast to the Zionist movement, that "no land whatever is excluded from [ITO] operations provided it be reasonably good and obtainable."[60] Palestine, he indicated, was impracticable: the country could not support mass immigration, and the sultan in any case refused to grant a charter to the Jews.[61] Thus, the "object of the Jewish Territorial Organisation is to procure a territory upon an autonomous basis for those Jews who cannot, or will not, remain in the lands in which they at present live."[62] This succinct formula revises the original Zionist program as formulated by Herzl in advance of the First Zionist Congress in 1897: "To create a legally secured homeland for those Jews who cannot, or will not, assimilate in their current places of residence."[63] The ITO's mission statement demonstrates that Zangwill's organization was philosophically more flexible and politically more pragmatic than its rival, the Zionist Organization.[64]

In a letter written to solicit the support of a distinguished explorer-scientist for his cause, Zangwill explained: "The idea [of the ITO] is to get a Jewish land large enough to receive gradually all the millions of Russian Jews and their posterity. . . . We wish to be placed beyond the possibility of being told at any time in the future that we are not in our own country."[65] These remarks were addressed to John Walter Gregory, a renowned geologist and Fellow of the Royal Society who had coincidentally coined the term "Rift Valley" during explorations in British East Africa.[66] Zangwill likely concluded that J. W. Gregory's first-hand familiarity with East Africa and his international reputation would bolster the fortunes of the ITO. The progressive-minded Gregory had a personal reason to align himself with Zangwill's new organization: his wife and Zangwill's wife, suffragette Edith Ayrton, were cousins who enjoyed a close relationship.[67]

At first, the ITO attempted to revive the East Africa proposal through diplomatic contacts. In November 1905, Zangwill requested that Colonial Secretary Alfred Lyttelton grant two hundred thousand square miles of the protectorate as a "British Judaea."[68] But repeated failures to galvanize the interest of His Majesty's government in the plan led the ITO to negotiate for tracts of land in western Canada in 1906,[69] and for land in northern and western Australia in 1907.[70] Zangwill himself met with Canadian and Australian leaders to discuss immigration matters, but these ITO overtures were rebuffed. Also in 1907, Sir Andrew Wingate, uncle of famed Christian Zionist Orde Wingate, advocated that the ITO colonize Mesopotamia—an idea that Herzl too had promoted.[71] Zangwill supported the proposal both for its feasibility and because he believed it offered a chance to cooperate with Zionists and put an end to "internecine strife."[72] He considered Mesopotamia to be "the future Jewish centre," and noted its historical importance to Judaism as the site of Abraham's birthplace.[73] For a time, the Mesopotamia project attracted de Hirsch's Jewish Colonization Association (ICA), which was hostile to the state-building efforts of both Zionism and territorialism. Because of the ICA's reluctance to endorse Jewish autonomy, Zangwill took a dim view of the organization, accusing its directors of "undertaking"—in the sense of burying—"the Jewish people."[74] In 1909, however, the ICA dispatched an exploratory commission to Mesopotamia. They found the territory unsuitable. The ICA's rejection of the region derailed Zangwill's enthusiasm for the project, though mention of Mesopotamia continued to surface in internal ITO documents for years.

Investigations of Mesopotamia overlapped with the ITO's interest in the colonization of Cyrenaica, the eastern coastal region of today's Libya. Zangwill's attention was first drawn to the region by author-adventurer Sir Harry H. Johnston—the one-time opponent turned supporter of a Jewish East African colony. In 1906, after the ITO failed to gain traction with the British for a revival of the Uasin Gishu proposal, Johnston suggested that Zangwill consider Cyrenaica.[75] Like Palestine, the North African territory was under the rule of the Ottoman sultan. Nonetheless, the ITO had reason to suspect that the sultan might grant autonomy to a Jewish settlement there thanks to back-channel diplomacy conducted with the powerful governor-general of Tripoli, Redjeb Pasha.[76] Dr. Nahum Slousch, a member of the proto-Zionist *Hovevei*

Zion (Lovers of Zion) group who had become an ITOist, sailed to Tripoli "to investigate on the spot the social and economic conditions of the province."[77] While there, Slousch met with Redjeb Pasha to discuss Jewish colonization.[78] It was Slousch who submitted Johnston's proposal for an ITOland to the governor-general, whom he considered to be "a devoted friend of the Jewish people."[79] Redjeb Pasha indeed responded favorably to the idea of mass settlements on large land concessions.[80] Slousch's support for a Jewish home in Cyrenaica emerged from his own detailed academic research.

One of the first scholars of the Hebrew literary renaissance, Slousch was also an archaeologist, historian, translator, and inveterate traveler fascinated by North African Jewry. His journey to ITOism began at the Seventh Congress after he publicly cast doubt on the Zionist Commission's verdict on East Africa. Based on another expert's opinion, he contended that Wilbusch's "report ha[d] no value."[81] He further intimated, over persistent heckling, that the enemies of political Zionism had engineered the report so as to reject Uasin Gishu.[82] Disillusioned, Slousch aligned himself with the territorialists and emerged as a champion of a Libyan ITOland. He claimed that "[n]o country of the Diaspora, with the possible exception of Mesopotamia, has played so leading a *rôle*" in Jewish history as Cyrenaica.[83] Slousch traced Jewish settlement there back to the biblical era and claimed to have uncovered evidence that Jews living in the region possessed "*full autonomy as in the most independent Republics*" even after the Romans had conquered the holy land.[84]

When Zangwill reiterated the ITO's own "demand for 'a species of autonomy'" to Redjeb Pasha, he was heartened by the governor-general's ready assent.[85] Soon the ITO mounted a scientific expedition. Zangwill contracted with J. W. Gregory to lead the mission, which in addition to Slousch, included an engineer, a doctor, an agricultural expert, local escorts and guides, as well as thirteen camels and various pack animals.[86] They followed a crooked route in the summer of 1908, taking nearly three weeks to travel from the eastern city of Derna west to Benghazi. Along the way they reported on the region's soil, climate, hydrology, agricultural resources, minerals, hygiene, and population. Though Cyrenaica was found to be beautiful and healthy, Gregory noted that it was "less fertile" and "not so unoccupied" as the ITO had been led to believe.[87] "All that it seems . . . possible to do at present," he concluded, "would be to establish small colonies."[88] Gregory's disappointing findings brought the ITO Cyrenaica plan to an end. The ITO later issued reports on several other territories to which they turned their attention, including portions of the American states of Idaho and Nevada[89]—the latter inspired by Mormon successes in turning desert regions into agricultural land,[90] the Brazilian State of São Paulo,[91] interior regions of Paraguay,[92] and northern Rhodesia[93] in today's Zimbabwe.

By the end of 1909, Zangwill had failed in all of his much-publicized efforts to find land to house an autonomous Jewish polity. When told that "a politically virgin territory can be found only in the moon," he responded, "Not even there, I fear. For there is a man in the moon, and he is probably an Anti-Semite."[94] But a more terrestrial ITO project than lunar colonization did in fact enjoy modest success: the Galveston Movement. Millionaire American banker and philanthropist Jacob Schiff approached Zangwill with a plan to divert Russian Jewish immigrants away from America's crowded eastern cities to states west of the Mississippi.[95] Schiff's proposal did not conform to the ITO's aims of autonomy, but Zangwill was so concerned about Jewish vulnerability in Russia that he was driven to act. The ITO established an Emigration Regulation Department to distinguish its resettlement work from the ITO's territorial quest. Zangwill presided over the Emigration Regulation Department and cooperated, though not always smoothly, with the Schiff-funded Industrial Removal Office (IRO).[96] Despite its Orwellian name, the IRO was a benevolent society that worked to assimilate Jewish immigrants into America by relocating them to towns distant from eastern population centers. Schiff and Zangwill differed on the importance of autonomy, but found common cause in their goal of rescuing Jews from Russia.[97] Approximately twenty-three hundred Jews had entered the Texas port to disperse throughout the western U.S. by the close of 1909.[98] The number of Jews resettled by the Galveston Movement was small, but the project profoundly affected Zangwill and its legacy continues to shape America's self-image.

Few today have heard of Zangwill, let alone read his many stories, plays, novels, and essays. Yet Zangwill introduced what is perhaps the most common metaphor used to define the social fabric of the United States: the "melting pot." The phrase found its way into the American vernacular after the success of Zangwill's 1908 play of the same name. He began working on the drama, a paean to America as a promised land, while he divided his activism between searching the globe for an ITOland and supporting the incipient Galveston Movement. By August 1908, the manuscript of *The Melting Pot* was complete. The play features a pair of star-crossed lovers, David Quixano and Vera Revendal. A talented musician, the Jewish Quixano escapes Russia after his parents and sisters are murdered in the Kishinev pogroms. He arrives in New York and there meets Vera, a Russian aristocrat turned social revolutionary. She had fled Russia to escape prison, and in the U.S. dedicates herself to the welfare of impoverished immigrants. Soon they confess their love for one another. But David discovers that the Christian Vera is the daughter of the antisemitic Baron who had ordered the massacres that killed his family in Kishinev. Horrified, he breaks off his relationship with Vera and is unable to cross the "river of blood" that separates them.[99] They are reconciled only after David premiers his symphony in praise of America, entitled "The Crucible," on July 4. The harmonies of David's own musical composition compel him to recognize that Old World hatreds must dissolve in the New World. As the symphony resounds, the hero and heroine duly kiss against the backdrop of the Statue of Liberty, symbol of "the glory of America, where all races and nations come to labour and look forward!"[100] Stilted, implausible, sentimental, and at times offensive by contemporary standards, *The Melting Pot* nonetheless dramatizes the affinity between Jewish chosenness and American exceptionalism.

Zangwill invited friends to read through the manuscript at his home prior to its scheduled October 1908 premiere in Washington, D.C. Though he was unable to attend, his neighbor Harry Johnston did offer mild criticism of the play's conclusion. He implored Zangwill to cut the lovers' final kiss, "as there is a growing belief that [kisses] are insanitary."[101] Zangwill knew better than to take literary advice from Johnston, who was a first-rate explorer but a second-rate novelist. The playwright did, however, seek approval from another celebrity outdoorsman: President Theodore Roosevelt. Zangwill invited the president to the premiere of *The Melting Pot*, promising to regale him with tales of the "strange adventures" his "quest for a land" had led him to as head of the ITO.[102] Roosevelt attended opening night at the Columbia Theatre and was reported to have exclaimed from his box when the curtain went down, "It is a great play, Mr. Zangwill."[103] Later, Zangwill dedicated the published version of his play to the president. Roosevelt, for his part, continued to count the play "among the very strong and real influences upon my thought and my life."[104] *The Melting Pot* clearly made an impact on Roosevelt, but it was Zangwill's ITO work that gave rise to the play in the first place. He related that *The Melting Pot* "sprang directly from . . . [my] concrete experience as President of the Emigration Regulation Department of the Jewish Territorial Organisation."[105] So the familiar idiom used to describe America's assimilatory power was coined by a British author in the midst of his frustrated efforts to establish a Jewish homeland.

The ITO produced nothing more than negotiations for a Jewish home in its initial years. Yet these failures should not be the test of territorialist ideology. The Zionist Organization, having synthesized political and practical Zionism, could demonstrate no diplomatic success with the Ottoman rulers of Palestine during this period either. Nor were the Zionists much interested in—or capable of—coping with the phenomenon of mass emigration. They well knew that the ITO was correct in judging that Palestine could not receive hundreds of thousands of desperate Jews, even if the sultan were to allow them entry and some degree of autonomy. Thus the ITO declared itself to be "the only existing Jewish organisation which corresponds with the actual conditions and needs of the time."[106] Zangwill denigrated Zionism as "a poem, not a plan" for this reason.[107] Yet pragmatism was also ITOism's great weakness. The movement's failure to bring forth a Jewish polity was, paradoxically, a failure of imagination. Zangwill simply could not envision *Eretz Israel* as a viable territorial solution to Jewish homelessness.

Russian Zionists, who influenced the work of the movement at large, recognized their own shortcomings. They revised their tactics in 1906 to attend to work "which can be carried out already in the present"— that is, in the Diaspora.[108] This program, known as *Gegenwartsarbeit* (work in the present), was an explicit acknowledgment both of the collapse of Herzlian political Zionism and of the limits of the piecemeal settlement program espoused by Ussishkin.[109] The *Gegenwartsarbeit* resolution implicitly recognized that other ideologies competed for mass Jewish support, such as Bundism, which sought Jewish cultural autonomy on Russian soil, various strains of communism, which held out universalist appeal to persecuted Jews, and of course, territorialism, which promised a swift resolution to Russian Jewry's woes.

An estimated thirty-five to forty thousand Jews,[110] mostly from Russia,[111] did arrive in Palestine during the tumultuous decade between 1904 and 1914. Approximately half of this immigration wave,[112] known as the Second Aliyah, left the *yishuv* in the ensuing years, many for North America. By comparison, the latest scholarship shows that Zangwill's Emigration Regulation Department diverted nearly seventy-four hundred Russian Jews to the American west by 1914.[113] Given the demographic data, the settlement activities of both Zionism and the ITO Emigration Regulation Department were modest in these years. The Galveston Movement should not be seen as having diverted Jewish immigration from Palestine. On the contrary, the ITO's work in the Pale encouraged the emigration of those who either did not want to leave for Palestine, or those who were discouraged by Zionist criteria from ever coming to *Eretz Israel* in the first place. Nor did the Galveston Movement come at the expense of the ITO's own pursuit of its territorial mission. The ITO's Emigration Regulation work was a practical means to establish the trust of beleaguered Jews and to demonstrate the efficacy of the organization should a future ITOland ever be located.

Zangwill continued to assiduously seek an ITOland throughout the years of the Galveston Movement. He recruited powerful Jewish figures in Europe and North America to serve on the ITO's international Geographic Commission, which played a nominal role in studying and approving territories for planned settlement. The Geographic Commission was a means for Zangwill to borrow equity on the strength of the names of the luminaries he had appointed as commissioners: American industrialist Daniel Guggenheim, Roosevelt's cabinet secretary Oscar S. Straus, and the esteemed judge Mayer Sulzberger, the British banking family magnate Lord Rothschild and diplomat Matthew Nathan, and the German industrialist James Simon and communal leader Paul Nathan.[114] Thanks to Zangwill's leveraging of social clout and financial backers, the ITO very nearly succeeded in establishing a "Portuguese Palestine"[115] in Angola in the years leading up to World War I.

At the End of the World

In late 1907, Zangwill's agitation for the ITO cause came to the attention of engineer and Boer War veteran John Norton-Griffiths,[116] a feisty character known as "Empire Jack." Norton-Griffiths held a contract to construct a railway that would stretch from the Angolan harbor of Lobito up through the highlands of the Benguela Plateau, eastward toward the desolate edge of what the Portuguese termed *o fim do mundo*—the end of the world—and then northward to exploit rich copper fields. Empire Jack notified ITO representatives that he "knew the whole of Africa, N. S. E. & W. and that the finest part and most suitable" for an ITO-land was Angola.[117] He encouraged Zangwill to abandon the pursuit of British East Africa, which he insisted was on the way to becoming "a black man's country."[118] Portugal, however, would continue to put "the interests of the white settlers" first.[119] Zangwill shelved the idea, preferring to concentrate on other ITO efforts such as Australia, Canada, and Cyrenaica.[120]

In 1911, a prominent rabbi in Rhodesia wrote to Zangwill to suggest a covert infiltration of Angola. "[I]f a few thousand Jewish farmers were settled in Angola, they could do as they pleased," Rabbi M. I. Cohen wrote, "[s]ecrecy seems to me essential. Colonists must be settled down steadily without talk. . . . Once the foundation is laid, nothing can stop progress."[121] Zangwill dismissed the plot, fearing that the "four million blacks" he thought to be living in Angola would "prevent any real colonization by doing all the dirty work."[122] For Zangwill, Jewish agricultural and industrial settlement—whether in Palestine, Angola, or elsewhere—was geared toward self-reliance, not exploitation of a native population.[123] Zangwill's views on race were complicated, however.[124] He remained an imperialist like Harry Johnston, and similar to his friend, Zangwill held paternalistic views toward African peoples. But he was also a progressive for his time who defended native rights. In one speech, Zangwill decried the treatment of black Africans at the hands of the European powers: "They say the devil is not so black as he is painted. . . . I can even believe his predominant hue is white."[125] Such a strong statement makes it clear that the rhetoric of Empire Jack and Rabbi Cohen would not have appealed to Zangwill. To his credit,

Zangwill retained a Herzlian conviction that only a publicly and legally assured charter would ensure Jewish territorial rights.

Angola resurfaced yet again in March 1912, when the ITO received a letter written in French by a Russian Jew working for the Portuguese Ministry of Agriculture. The unknown correspondent, Wolf Terló, was a balding, paunchy civil servant of about forty.[126] When the Jews were expelled from Moscow in 1891, he traveled to Jaffa and enrolled in an agricultural school. Later, he studied wine making in Bordeaux, and after much wandering, settled in Lisbon in 1904. There he organized an oenological council and found employment in the Agricultural Ministry.[127] Shortly after the First Republic replaced Portugal's monarchy in 1910, Terló approached the provisional government's minister of finance and other politicians to advance a plan to settle Jews in the country's colonial possessions in Africa.[128] His letter to the ITO detailed a proposal to settle "our miserable brothers" on the healthy highlands of Angola, where each family of colonists would receive, free of charge, five hundred hectares (approximately two square miles) of land.[129] Terló claimed that his idea had support from distinguished parliamentarians in the young republic.

In a subsequent letter, he begged the ITO to send someone to Lisbon to pursue negotiations.[130] The ITO's Executive Committee responded by resolving to dispatch a deputy to meet with Terló in order to further examine the scheme.[131] Zangwill hedged, but nonetheless reversed his earlier blanket objections to Angolan colonization. He made it clear to Terló that the minimal ITO conditions for proceeding with the project were an agreement to "concentrate all colonists within a given area" and a guarantee that "the colony should not be interfered with" if and when it began to flourish.[132] Terló's promise of Portuguese governmental support intrigued the ITO, but they were wary about working with a mysterious individual whose motives were in doubt.[133] For his part, Terló was confused about the conflicting aims of Zionism and ITOism, and seemingly ignorant of the two movements' mutual antagonism.

Terló had originally approached the Zionist Central Bureau in Berlin about his Angola scheme in January of 1912.[134] In a long letter similar to the one he later wrote to the ITO, he described his peripatetic background, noted his governmental connections, and outlined his plan "to colonize . . . a healthy plateau in Africa with Russian Jews, and those

from other countries."[135] The Zionists responded that while colonization in Africa was not their goal, the Angolan plan "has a certain interest to our organization if the climatic and agricultural conditions were
favorable," and if appropriate settlers could be found.[136] Berlin's tentative
support for Terló's efforts remains surprising given the Zionist Organization's principled rejection of other territorialist ventures. Perhaps the
ITO's support among Russian Jews clamoring for escape, and the influx
of Russian Jews to Germany itself, had softened the position of at least
some in Berlin.

Encouraged by their response, Terló sent notice to the Bureau that the
Portuguese parliament's lower house, the Chamber of Deputies, would
soon consider a bill to allow for mass settlement of Jews in his country's
distant African colony. He also sent his correspondents a clipping of an
interview that had appeared in Lisbon's newspaper of record, *O Seculo*
(*The Century*). The article invoked the writings of Pinsker and Herzl,
and then quoted Terló as explaining that while the resettlement of Zion
was yet far off, in the meantime there was a need to send Jewish emigrants "to other countries that offered more economic advantages than
Palestine."[137] Terló also indicated to readers that Jewish arrivals would
pose no danger to Portugal's sovereignty and would have the requisite
international financial backing to establish agricultural settlements.[138]
He suggested that a commission of experts be sent to study various Portuguese holdings in Africa, citing the Benguela Plateau, which cuts east
to west across the middle of Angola, as especially promising.[139]

As Terló claimed, the Chamber of Deputies convened an earnest
debate over the admission of Jewish refugees to Angola beginning in
February 1912. One representative highlighted Portugal's security interest in the scheme. "[T]he colonization of the highlands of Angola is
an absolute necessity to maintain our dominance in those regions," he
declared.[140] Furthermore, the speaker continued, the Republic would
benefit economically by diverting to Angola "the stream of Russian
Jewish immigrants" who were then enriching Palestine and America.[141]
Another speaker invoked the Republic's enlightened ideals and presented a humanitarian justification for the legislation. The Jews "seek
to flee the countries wherein they are persecuted to settle in a country
that will allow them to live according to their faith, and this is only possible in countries like our own."[142] The anticlerical First Republic was

indeed more liberal than the monarchy and accorded full rights to Portugal's Jewish community for the first time since their expulsion had been ordered in 1496.

Terló, who had helped establish a Zionist group in Lisbon in 1911,[143] maintained his correspondence with the Berlin Central Bureau even after Zangwill and the ITO's Executive Committee had offered him their cooperation. In late April 1912, he sent a flurry of letters to Berlin. Terló and his associates had translated Herzl's *Der Judenstaat* into Portuguese,[144] he informed them, and "all of the reports in the press are in favor" of Angola.[145] The next day he wrote with evident satisfaction to notify the Central Bureau that language for a bill in support of Jewish colonization in Angola had been provisionally approved by lawmakers: "It is a true pleasure to see that no other project has been ascribed as much importance as this one. . . . As you see, the bill was accepted by all of the parties that have an interest in this matter, and without the slightest objection."[146] But Terló's report to Berlin's Zionists was misleading. In fact, two competing Angolan colonization bills had been put forward to the Chamber of Deputies in early 1912 and debate on their relative merits continued well into June. The first bill favored Portuguese and foreign immigrants with concessions along the Benguela highlands. The second, bill number 159, also promoted settlement in Benguela, but was worded specifically to attract Jews to the region and called for the naturalization of these Jewish immigrants.[147]

The Zionist office responded to Terló's report on Bill 159's progress with cautious encouragement. They maintained that "it is not of minor political significance when a European parliament seriously discusses the question of Jewish colonization . . . [but] we know too little about the plateaus of Angola at this point to be able to evaluate whether or not the approval of the bill would result in any sort of practical consequences."[148] After a lapse in correspondence of more than a month, the Central Bureau sent an anxious letter to Terló awaiting details of the progress of Bill 159 through parliament, noting that "some 'ITO' conferences have taken place, in which you probably also have participated."[149] The Berlin-based correspondent continued, "we would be grateful if you would provide details about the [ITO] conferences themselves and their outcome, in particular with regard to the Angola project."[150] There is no record of Terló having provided inside information about the work of his ITO confederates to Berlin's Zionists. Terló had by this point firmly aligned himself with Zangwill's goals thanks to the ITO's intense diplomatic efforts in Lisbon.

In early May, as debates continued in the Chamber of Deputies, the ITO sent Russian jurist Jacob Teitel as its representative to Portugal. Teitel was a vigorous man in his early sixties with bushy brows and a thick white moustache. A brilliant man of many contradictions, Teitel was the last remaining Jewish judge under czarist rule, yet a friend of radicals such as Vladimir Lenin and author Maxim Gorky. Teitel's son had met Terló in Lisbon and discovered that the families were distantly related.[151] Terló subsequently invited his distinguished relative to visit.[152] When the Kiev branch of the ITO learned of Teitel's connection to Terló, they asked him to assess the man's character, the extent of his governmental contacts, and the seriousness of his proposal.[153] Teitel was not affiliated with the Zionist Organization or with the ITO, yet he agreed to undertake the mission.[154] Before he left for Portugal, he traveled to his boyhood home in the Pale of Settlement where he was outraged at the treatment of Jews confined there by czarist sanction.[155] The miseries he witnessed on his trip into the past no doubt sharpened his commitment to ensuring a collective Jewish future.

After traveling through Vienna, Paris, and Madrid, Teitel arrived in Lisbon in early May.[156] He stepped off a third-class rail carriage to find Terló awaiting him, dressed in a top hat and gloves.[157] The next day, Teitel arrived at Terló's wine export office, where he studied a large map of Angola that his eager host had hung on a wall.[158] There the jurist also met with a physician who had vast experience in the colony, and later with Terló's partner in advancing the proposal, Dr. Alfredo Bensaúde.[159] The middle-aged Bensaúde was a patriot, a leading scientist, the founder and director of Lisbon's Instituto Superior Técnico, a former minister for development,[160] and the scion of a distinguished Jewish family from the Azores. Bensaúde was well aware of the dangers of antisemitism—his son had suffered a dueling injury sparked by some antisemitic slight—and had belatedly rallied to the cause of Jewish national revival.[161] Teitel learned that the energetic Terló and the well-connected Bensaúde had first initiated efforts to sway Portuguese politicians to the cause of Jewish settlement in Angola in 1911, soon after the monarchy was deposed. Teitel examined Terló's and Bensaúde's latest

Landscape along the Benguela Plateau, Angola. Courtesy of Michael Kollins

proposal and became its strong supporter.[162] He arrived at the conclusion that "five or six hundred thousand" Jews could settle Angola's Benguela province.[163] Teitel believed that Portugal was motivated to aid the ITO by *realpolitik*—the need to populate their colony and head off

German expansionism—and romance—the desire on the part of many leading Portuguese citizens descended from converted Jews to redress their country's ignoble history.[164]

In mid-May, the London ITO office received a memorandum from Teitel assessing the plan.[165] The communiqué announced that the ITO was offered territory stretching along the 45,000-square-mile Benguela Plateau. The land was reported to be well watered, possess fertile soil, and boast a "mild and healthy" climate.[166] Moreover, several Jews were already known to be living in the region.[167] "I would be happy," Teitel told interested journalists, "if the last years of my life were dedicated to this cause."[168] Despite his envoy's optimism, Zangwill moved with deliberation. He engaged the services of a law firm to determine whether the ITO could in fact legally treat with the Portuguese Republic. His attorneys ruled that his organization was "quite competent to enter into negotiations with various persons or Governments and as you well know it has already done so with the British and other Governments."[169] While the ITO considered its next step, debate pressed on in the Chamber of Deputies.

Two competing settlement bills were discussed over the course of many legislative sessions. Ramado Curto, a supporter of Bill 159 who was said to have Jewish ancestry,[170] proclaimed that the "Jewish Territorial Organisation in London . . . pledges to settle 2,000 Jews in the highlands of Angola within two years."[171] He argued that these pioneers would improve the infrastructure and create population centers at no cost to Portugal. All the ITO demanded was to be free of hindrance so Jewish immigrants could follow their faith. Curto made it clear to fellow lawmakers that Portugal lacked the resources to pacify and exploit their vast Angolan colony. However, the offer of territory to the Jews would allow for a "peaceful conquest" that might prefigure a "colonial resurgence" for their weakened country.[172] He emphasized to opponents that the prospective settlers were a dispersed people who could not challenge Portuguese sovereignty.[173] Finally, Curto blamed the fifteenth-century expulsion of the Jews for Portugal's decadence and decline as a world power.[174] The establishment of a Jewish territory in Angola would right a historic wrong and return Portugal to glory.

Other supporters similarly invoked Portugal's self-interest, often in bio-racial terms. One believed that Jews, who had resisted assimilation, would serve as an example of how to avoid miscegenation in Angola and thereby preserve Portuguese colonists from the danger of imitating the "indolence of the African populations."[175] Another believed it would be a "crime to abandon or hand over" to indigenous people the Benguela territory, which was "destined to become one of the richest" of Portugal's extensive holdings.[176] Still another suggested that the success of a Jewish pioneer vanguard would show prospective Portuguese emigrants that "the white race" can "live and thrive" in Angola.[177]

Developments in the Chamber of Deputies at the end of May forced Zangwill to travel to Lisbon. There he met with Teitel, Terló, and other ITO officials. A photograph from a popular weekly depicts the unsmiling men dressed in dark overcoats with hats in hand. Zangwill, taller than the others, leans on his umbrella and turns in three-quarter profile from the camera.[178] In Lisbon, a careworn Zangwill arranged two long interviews with Sir Arthur Hardinge, Great Britain's minister to Portugal.[179] Zangwill knew that Hardinge had served as commissioner of the East African Protectorate just prior to Chamberlain's offer of territory there to Herzl. The career diplomat was thus well acquainted with Hertzka's Freeland efforts and with Herzl's support for Jewish colonization in Africa. He was accordingly skeptical of the ITO's plans.[180] Hardinge reported to his superior, Foreign Secretary Sir Edward Grey, to apprise him of the latest effort to achieve "the 'Zionist' ideal of a territory mainly inhabited and administered by Jews" where they could "develop the latent capacities of the race for agricultural and industrial as distinct from merely mercantile pursuits."[181] He noted that he was "surprised that the scheme should be revived" in Angola, "[b]ut the previous discussions"—referring to the East African proposal—"showed that Mr. Zangwill and his friends were quite impractical people."[182]

At one point, an impolitic Zangwill questioned Hardinge directly about "secret Anglo-German arrangements . . . respecting the Portuguese colonies in Africa," but the canny minister reported to Grey that he "thought it best not to discuss these contingencies."[183] Zangwill alluded here to a clandestine agreement from 1898 to divide Portuguese colonies between England and Germany.[184] The two powers sought a reconciliation in the years leading up to World War I and their efforts centered on a mutually beneficial renegotiation of the 1898 accord.[185] Zangwill reasoned that the Portuguese Republic, debt laden and in disarray, looked to maintain its hold on Angola with the help of Jewish settlers, who would then protect the colony's integrity from both British and Prussian imperialism. Yet he feared that should Portuguese rule be undermined, his Angolan ITOland would fall into German hands under the terms of the secret conventions then being discussed.[186] Zangwill's longed-for African Zion thus held out political peril, as well as potential.

On June 20, 1912, shortly after Zangwill had returned to England, the Chamber of Deputies passed the final version of Bill 159 to authorize concessions to Jewish settlers.[187] Just as Curto and others had argued for, its articles reveal both charitable sympathy for the Jewish plight and the republic's desire to use Jewish immigration to consolidate its hold over Angola. Colonists wishing to settle the Benguela Plateau would become naturalized Portuguese citizens at their port of entry upon payment of a nominal fee.[188] Each head of household would receive between 100 to 250 hectares (approximately 250 to 600 acres) of land, which would be doubled when the settler had utilized seventy-five percent of his original plot.[189] Any schools, hospitals, or public buildings that might be erected on the territorial concessions would remain the property of the organization heading the settlement project.[190] And while these aspects of the bill would no doubt have appealed to impoverished Jewish refugees, other articles seemed designed to discourage immigration. No "benevolent society" in charge of colonization—like the ITO—could have a "religious character," and Portuguese was to be the exclusive language of instruction in any schools the Jewish colonists might build.[191]

Part of the text of Bill 159 appeared in the important Russian Hebrew newspaper *HaZman* (*The Times*), whose reporter and literary critic, S. L. Zitron, informed readers about the status of ITO negotiations for Angola.[192] The leading Hebrew paper in Russia at the time, *HaZfira* (*The Clarion*), also covered territorialist efforts under the editorship of Nahum Sokolov, who in later years served as president of the Zionist Organization. Sokolov himself wrote a scathing critique of the Angola Plan.[193] Both *HaZfira* and *HaZman* devoted many column inches to the opening of the ITO conference in Vienna just days after the final approval of the bill in Portugal. Meanwhile, in England, the *Jewish Chronicle* published long descriptions of the ITO proceedings, reporting that eighty delegates and five hundred additional people attended the conference.[194] Even the *New York Times* announced developments under the headline "Angola Is Offered for Zionist Colony," thus demonstrating that contemporary observers often saw the aims of the ITO and the Zionist Organization as identical.[195]

HaZfira chose to emphasize Zangwill's moving speech delivered at Herzl's graveside in Vienna's Döbling cemetery.[196] Almost exactly eight years after the great leader's death, the assembled ITOists recited the traditional funerary prayer, *El Malei Rachamim* (God full of mercy).[197] Zangwill hoped that Herzl's memory would prove to be a unifying force that would bring the ITO and the Zionists together.[198] Yet he also railed against his rivals, charging that "[a]fter the death of Dr. Herzl, the Palestinian faction took the [Zionist] movement hostage."[199] *HaZman's* Zitron recorded that news of the Angola plan had spread around the world and aroused passionate interest.[200] But he took a critical tone, noting the ITO's internal division over the proposal.[201] Elsewhere Zitron mocked Terló for his diplomatic pretensions and his imperfect French, and doubted whether the Portuguese offer would profit Jewry.[202]

Enthusiasm for Portugal's offer nonetheless found voice in the English, German, Russian, and Yiddish press. One individual who read of the plan in Rhodesia volunteered for the cause: "I am [as] ready as I was then when the Uganda Scheme was under discussion to go out to Angola with . . . men who can ride and shoot . . . [and] contribute some energy to the making of a future colony, where our people can find an asylum and escape from the clutches of the Russian barbarities, under a Southern African sky and a Jewish Home Rule."[203] Still, Zangwill worried that Bill 159's restrictive clauses would prevent the establishment of a distinctly Jewish colony. In a speech made to ITO delegates, Zangwill did not hide his concern over the bill's wording, though he believed that "[a]ll that matters is—does Angola provide the possibility of a Jewish home-land?"[204] He responded to his own question, announcing that "the answer should be in the affirmative."[205] The ITO leader did, however, present the objections of Sir Harry Johnston, who was one of the few Europeans to have traveled through Angola. Johnston, Zangwill told his audience, did not believe that there was a "sufficient continuous tract of white man's country" in the colony for the creation of an autonomous ITOland.[206]

After much discussion, the ITO cabled its respectful rejection of the offer to the Chamber of Deputies, while holding out the possibility of continued negotiations.[207] The delegates thanked the deputies for their "offer which softens the memory" of the expulsion of the Jews from Portugal, but stressed that the present agreement did not grant the ITO "the necessary powers and guarantees" to colonize an "unsettled, unsurveyed, and even dangerous" country.[208] The telegram was read before the assembled lawmakers of the Portuguese Senate on July 2.[209] Angry supporters of the plan in Lisbon considered Zangwill and his organization to have acted impertinently and ungratefully.[210] The suggestion that Portuguese colonial power was tenuous in Angola was met with particular vehemence. Dr. Slousch, the ITO activist who had previously traveled to Cyrenaica, set off for Lisbon on a mission to minimize the damage that the ITO telegram had caused.[211] When Hardinge learned of the ITO decision, he wrote to Secretary Grey that "unless—which is most unlikely to happen—the Portuguese Government were to give very large political powers to the new Jewish Colony, Mr. Zangwill and his friends do not think its offer worth entertaining."[212] He neglected to mention to his superior, or was unaware, that the ITO had nonetheless unanimously voted to send an expedition to Angola to examine the region proposed for Jewish colonization.[213]

A New Judea

Zangwill learned from Bensaúde that despite the ITO's slight, governmental ministers and lawmakers were still willing to amend Bill 159 in future parliamentary sessions.[214] From Zangwill's central London ITO office in, of all places, Portugal Street, he pressed on with his plan to dispatch a commission to the Benguela Plateau with the full consent of Angola's governor-general.[215] Once again he contracted with his trusted friend J. W. Gregory to lead the expedition. The product of a Victorian upbringing, Gregory remained a model of rectitude and industriousness throughout his life. He was a free-thinking,[216] tee-totaling,[217] gentleman-explorer who had published numerous scientific tomes and academic papers by 1912. His wide-ranging intellect and physical endurance were legendary. He lived on four to five hours of sleep[218] and could sustain a remarkable foot pace of four and a half miles per hour over rough terrain.[219] In photographs, Gregory's penetrating gaze lends him a restless appearance, as if he is ready to cast off his high-collared shirt and thrust his body out of the frame. Gregory in turn enlisted his colleague, Dr. Charles J. Martin, head of London's Lister Institute for Preventative Medicine, to join him on their trek to a largely unknown region.

On the night of July 16, 1912, Gregory formalized his agreement with Zangwill and the next morning wrote to a contact at the Colonial Office to enquire: "(1) whether there are any political considerations which would be liable to stop the establishment of a Jewish colony in the highlands of Southern Angola. (2) whether there is any special area we should avoid or which we could not more safely select."[220] Gregory's letter was redirected to the Foreign Office, where he met with the undersecretary and provided him with a description of plans to "form a large colony of Jews who could live together and preserve their own religious and social rites in freedom."[221] At that meeting, Gregory requested letters of introduction to Hardinge in Lisbon, and to British consular officers in Angola. In return, he offered—in a nod to imperialist aspirations—to "secure any information that might be useful" to H. M. government during his travels.[222] But Secretary Grey blocked Gregory's request for letters of introduction, indicating that the Angola plan was strictly an internal matter for the Portuguese government.[223]

The Foreign Office was understandably reluctant to involve itself in Portuguese colonial affairs. While the ITO focused its efforts on Angola, the Foreign Office had become embroiled in a public dispute with the British Anti-Slavery Society, which charged that Angolans were subjected to forced labor.[224] These indentured laborers—serviçais—toiled under miserable conditions on cocoa plantations in the Portuguese island of São Tomé in Africa's Gulf of Guinea. British officials were aware of abuses and of Portugal's inability to stop them, but a series of books, pamphlets, and exposés revealed the misery of the serviçais to the public and created a diplomatic scandal.[225] Zangwill knew of Portugal's shameful record on slavery, and promised a concerned ITO confidante that "if we came in [to Angola] we should just hope to do away with those conditions."[226] He also wrote to Bensaúde to indicate that a successful ITO venture would help dispel the negative publicity Portugal was receiving in the British press at the time.[227] Zangwill had come to rely on Bensaúde as his negotiator, fearing that Terló's outspoken support in the press and his clumsy behind-the-scenes agitation for the scheme damaged the ITO cause.[228] He further hoped that Bensaúde's gravitas would provide the momentum to submit a more attractive settlement bill for parliamentary approval.

Angolans were kept informed of plans to populate their colony with Jews. A series of articles penned by Angola's foremost writer of the day, native son Augusto Bastos, ran in the weekly *Jornal de Benguela* for more than a year.[229] The newspaper appeared in the region's coastal capital, also called Benguela. The city, with its grand Portuguese architecture and palm- and eucalyptus-lined boulevards, was home to an elite who welcomed the prospect of Jews thronging to the province. Benguela appears prosperous even today. Whitewashed homes with small plots of trimmed grass and pruned shrubs border the well-maintained old commercial district and the nearby town plaza. A few stucco colonial-era buildings boast their original decorative tiles. Along the beachfront promenade, children run back and forth; some dart and plunge into the waves. Small fishing boats bob near a ruined dock, the only remaining artifact of the once-thriving slave trade that had enriched the town.

Bastos's columns reassured readers that Jewish colonists would not threaten Portuguese sovereignty because they were dispossessed, and therefore would not have "cannons or an army behind them."[230] He urged Portuguese lawmakers to alter the terms of the colonization bill so that it would be more attractive to the Jews,[231] and hailed the arrival of Gregory and Martin. Bastos was certain that the scientists "would soon be convinced" that there was no place better than the Benguela Plateau to establish a home for "the persecuted [Jews] in Russia."[232] But the Benguela region struggled with administrative instability. There were four governors of the district in 1912 alone,[233] and it remained unclear what local conditions might exist if and when Jewish immigrants arrived. Gregory and Martin were tasked with finding out.

The ITO expedition was both more intensive and extensive than the Zionist Commission that had explored Uasin Gishu seven years earlier. Soon after Gregory and Martin landed in the dusty port city of Lobito, the terminus of the Benguela Railway, on August 22, 1912, they set off for the interior.[234] Their caravan consisted of thirty-two natives— a headman, a cook, twenty-five porters, a "tent boy," and another four aides.[235] In all they spent five weeks surveying the plateau, traveling more than one thousand miles by rail, wagon, and on foot.[236] The party traversed a ragged course that began at sea level and reached a height of over six thousand feet.[237] Gregory met with no "warlike tribes," found "few dangerous animals, snakes or insect pests," and believed the country "should make a very comfortable and pleasant home."[238] He noted in his ITO report that the plateau was "first-rate as regards public health" and possessed "scenery [that] is often beautiful and picturesque."[239] Gregory also indicated that "the land in Angola is decidedly superior to the average of Palestine."[240] Dr. Martin too considered the highlands to be "remarkably free from tropical diseases" and to possess "a fine climate" in which the "average European" would maintain a "healthy and comfortable life."[241] His one concern were the tsetse flies that fed on the crocodiles that infested waterways at lower elevations.[242] Gregory found that oranges, bananas, corn, and coffee flourished, and that "European vegetables grow luxuriantly."[243] Though he believed the country would be expensive to develop, he thought that "settlers would have no difficulty in raising an adequate and excellent supply of food for their own use."[244] He also located "ample timber for building, for the manufacture of furniture" and for fuel.[245] And with the completion of the Benguela Railway, there would be no reason that crops could not be exported in the future.[246]

Gregory made demographic estimates as well, hazarding a guess that there were only about one hundred thousand natives living along the vast plateau.[247] "It would be only fair to the natives," he wrote, "to insert in any concession provisions securing them the land they already occupy and a reasonable reserve" for future population growth.[248] He found no evidence of European participation in slavery, contrary to rumors in England, though he did suspect that slavery was still practiced by tribespeople.[249] The abstemious scientist was also pleased to discover that the colonial administration had "suppressed the liquor traffic with the natives."[250] Gregory summarized his findings: "In view of its healthiness, fertility and attractiveness, and the ease with which the land could be acquired and developed, there seems no reason, if the Portuguese Government would grant a suitable concession, why successful European colonies should not be established" along the Benguela Plateau.[251] "I cannot think of any area which offers better prospects . . . as would satisfy the aspirations of the ITO," he concluded.[252] Gregory's published report remained intentionally vague as to the precise region to be colonized. But in a confidential shipboard memo written as he steamed toward England fresh from his Angolan adventure, he recommended that Zangwill petition for five thousand square miles of land encompassing the village of Bailundo and the Cutato River valley northeast of the town of Huambo.[253]

Today the region Gregory selected for a Jewish homeland is one of Angola's richest agricultural zones. The road from the port of Lobito, where he and Martin landed, ascends east toward Huambo through the plateau. For much of the time, the route still travels within sight of the Benguela Railway. A victim of repeated bombings during Angola's nearly thirty-year civil war (1975–2002), the railroad track and numerous bridges are now being rebuilt with Chinese labor and capital. Near one river crossing, a battered tank rusts in the mud. Baobabs disappear as one heads eastward and upward, replaced by otherworldly black tors that rise above scrubland as the road climbs to the railway junction at Cubal. The uneven road through the plateau is treacherous. Burnt-out hulks of cars and trucks rest one upon the other in the gullies at the crook of sharp turns. Further inland, the route twists its way more than a mile above sea level to offer a view of irrigated fields and the watershed below, much as Gregory had described.

In Huambo, the toll of war is again apparent. Concrete apartment blocks are scarred by bullets and mortars. Dazed young petrol sniffers squat in empty lots amidst trash and the stink of human waste. Closer to Bailundo, sorghum, pineapples, banana trees, and sturdy firs grow in incongruous proximity. But the fires of slash-and-burn agriculture give the countryside a hellish tinge. Flames flare up and crackle from the dry brush, wafting a sharp heat across the road. Subsistence farmers live in red-brick homes with corrugated tin roofs held down by heavy stones. Skinny dogs with sores bark at the few vehicles that pass by. Further north and east, the vegetation grows more lush in the Cutato River Valley recommended by Gregory. Flowers and vines twist around wild coffee plants in an ocean of mist as the sun sets, and for the first time, the Benguela Plateau looks like a promised land.

Zangwill met with Gregory and Martin on October 22, 1912, five days after they disembarked in Southampton.[254] Once convinced of the

Road through the "Portuguese Palestine" north of Huambo, Angola. Courtesy of Michael Kollins

practicability of founding an Angolan ITOland, he wrote to prominent banker and Jewish communal leader Leopold de Rothschild. Zangwill floated the idea of establishing an Angola Development Company that, he maintained, would attract twice as much capital "as [Cecil] Rhodes began Rhodesia on."²⁵⁵ He also suggested that the ITO, with Rothschild's help, might bring about a long-desired rapprochement between England and Germany. One of the ITO's geographical commissioners, business-man and arts patron James Simon, was an intimate of the kaiser, Zang-will informed Rothschild, "and there thus seems to be an instrument to our hands . . . to bring England and Germany publicly together."²⁵⁶ A Jewish homeland in Africa, Zangwill believed, would serve the cause of peace in Europe. Rothschild, however, was unimpressed.²⁵⁷

So too was his fellow ITO geographic commissioner Sir Matthew Nathan. The Jewish former governor of Natal in South Africa and the Gold Coast (now Ghana), Nathan studied a draft of Gregory's report. His verdict was unequivocal: "The Angola project does not seem to me to offer the big solution . . . which you are looking for."²⁵⁸ Another geographic commissioner, Dr. Paul Nathan, founder of the *Hilfsverein der Deutschen Juden* (Aid Association of German Jews), had appar-ently resigned altogether.²⁵⁹ Yet despite defections and a lack of sup-port, Zangwill promoted the scheme throughout the spring of 1913 with a growing apprehension for Jewish safety. In one apocalyptic public address he insisted that his "ITOland is a preparation for the deluge."²⁶⁰ Only in a "New Judea" could " a sturdier and manlier breed" of Jews arise and thereby ward off the coming disaster.²⁶¹

Sholem Aleichem, though a supporter of Zionist causes, seems to have been sympathetic to ITOist arguments, at least insofar as the Yid-dish writer's *luftmensch*, Menachem-Mendl, can be said to represent the author's views. Sholem Aleichem serialized epistolary adventures of Menachem-Mendl in Warsaw's Yiddish daily *Haynt* (*Today*) in 1913. These satiric letters deal primarily with Jewish politics and current events as reported by Menachem-Mendl, who has forsaken financial speculation for a career in journalism, much like his real-life creator. In his letters, Menachem-Mendl portrays Zangwill as an advocate for European Jewry and a canny negotiator for Angola. Zangwill emerges as a kind of market trader who outwits the Portuguese to conclude an agreement in which colonizing Jews "will maintain [their] own army . . . will speak [their] own language, institute [their] own laws, [and] have [their] own schools and synagogues."²⁶² The often bewil-dered Menachem-Mendl manages to get many details of the plan right, including the involvement of Rothschild and Teitel, the dispatch of an expert commission, Portugal's fears that it would lose Angola to competing European nations, the division of land into large parcels to facilitate the establishment of agriculture, and the proposal to float a land development company that would issue shares and dividends.[263] Menachem-Mendl's provincial wife, Sheyne-Sheyndl, scolds him for his Angolan advocacy in the name of their townsfolk who angrily believe he has been converted to ITOism.[264] His response is telling: "I never was either a Zionist or a territorialist . . . [but] Angola is being offered to us almost free and as of now I don't see any other land anywhere for Jews. There isn't one . . . if tomorrow they find another land for us, I will write in favor of that land . . . so long as *it is a land*, because *we are eager and ready, and if you are eager and ready, you take what you can get.*"[265] Despite this heartfelt defense of the territorialist rationale, Menachem-Mendl's final letters relate his return to the Zionist fold. The importance of this late work by Sholem Aleichem lies in its acknowledgment of the foment the Angola plan engendered, and the widespread publicity Zangwill's efforts aroused.

By May 1913, Zangwill had begun circulating a draft of his introduction to Gregory's forthcoming report. He placed special emphasis on the fact that an Angolan Zion would serve Portugal's interests: "A Jewish colony in Angola under the Portuguese flag may be the only way of keeping the flag flying there."[266] He informed Bensaúde that he hoped his introduction would coax the Republic to adopt a "policy of trusting 'the State within the State'" proposal in order to benefit both the Jews and Portugal.[267] However, the Portuguese worried that a Jewish *imperium in imperio* would challenge their state sovereignty, much as the British had feared in East Africa and Americans had fretted in Noah's time. Terló tried to mitigate such concerns in Lisbon, denying that the ITO sought to create a Jewish fatherland. "This is most absurd," he claimed, "there are 1,125,000 Jews in New York. Do they ever think of creating such a movement?"[268] Even in Palestine, he continued, Jews loyally serve in the Turkish military.[269]

Lawmakers debating the bill in the Portuguese Senate were not placated. Critics suspected that an independent Jewish state would arise in Benguela.[270] Others resented making laws to benefit foreigners.[271] At least one senator aware of the 1898 partition accords claimed that Jewish immigrants were a fifth column serving the interests of British and

German imperialism, and were lying in wait to undermine Portuguese sovereignty.[272] Supporters emphasized the benefits Portugal would reap from the project. One advocate saw Jewish settlements in Benguela as the "beginning of a new era" for Angola, a project that would safeguard national interests and prevent denationalization of the colony by other European powers.[273] Another foresaw that the enterprise would be highly profitable for the metropole.[274] Explicit biopolitical considerations entered the debates when one advocate insisted that all Angola required to flourish was an influx of industrious white labor—and Jews were, apparently, just white enough.[275] Other senators took to the floor to persuade colleagues that passage of the bill would be "an act of justice and reparation" for the fifteenth-century expulsion of the Jews from Portugal.[276]

At times, the rambling debate turned nasty. Senators interrupted one another. Heated exchanges degenerated into charges of antisemitism and indignant claims to the contrary.[277] One senator insinuated that an anonymous representative of the Jewish community had bribed his fellow lawmakers to vote in support of the colonization scheme.[278] His colleague then confirmed that the unnamed Jew was none other than Terló, whom he referred to as a "Russian Jewish agent."[279] When the senator proved hostile to the ITO scheme, Terló was said to have muttered that he "had already spent too much money."[280] Terló's words—if he even uttered them—were open to various interpretations, perhaps referring to the costs of legitimate lobbying efforts. Still, the ITO's reputation had been harmed. Zangwill expressed frustration at the turn of events. He redoubled his efforts, informing Bensaúde that Portugal must abandon "suspicions of our plans" and permit the establishment of a "Portuguese Palestine."[281] Days later, on June 29, 1913, the Senate did indeed revise and approve concessions for Jewish settlement.[282]

After the bill's passage, Zangwill told the Hebrew press that Angola presented the best chance to achieve Herzl's ambitions of a Jewish state "because [Angola] has no Christian influence, as does Palestine, nor does it have an Arab population, as does Palestine."[283] Gregory, too, remained optimistic. He predicted that the Benguela Railway would eventually link up with the projected Cape to Cairo Railway, thus "connect[ing] Angola to Europe."[284] As for Bensaúde, he maintained pressure on governmental insiders, giving Zangwill to understand that the Portuguese "[g]overnment is ready to go over the heads of Parliament and make a concession in accordance with Professor Gregory's views, provided [the ITO] can show an adequate capital."[285] But no funds were forthcoming and Bensaúde expressed "infinite regret that the Societies which devote themselves to Jewish colonization cannot or will not conduct this Angola affair as it should be conducted."[286] Zangwill too was distraught at the short-sightedness of Jewish financiers who refused to form a land-development company for Benguela, a territory that he believed "could provide thousands and ultimately millions of Jewish people with a home of their own."[287] Without territory, the ITO could not obtain capital, and without it, it could not obtain territory.[288] Zangwill was left to howl and run in futile circles, like a dog cast in a well. Momentum stalled for lack of finances and the required final vote on the plan by both chambers of Portugal's parliament never materialized.[289]

Unpopular Causes

In October 1913, a day after the Jewish New Year, Zangwill vented his exasperation with Jewish communal leaders and mainstream Zionism. He reminded the ITO's London Council that territorialism was determined to bring an end to suffering in the Diaspora, whereas Zionist efforts to settle "a few thousand Jewish agriculturists in an all-swamping Arab environment is no longer even put forward as an ending of the Exile."[290] On the contrary, Zionism had merely become a means to "unify and uplift the Exile" and distract it from its miseries.[291] He insisted that Zionism had betrayed its mandate and that the ITO remained "the *only* Jewish organization aiming at the creation of a Jewish land."[292] Zangwill thus pressed for a reinvigoration of negotiations with Portugal, confessing to his audience that "[o]utside Angola, I personally see no possibility of the rise of an ITOland."[293] Many of his followers had begun to turn against the proposal, however. A former ally wrote to Zangwill arguing that "the future Jewish Nation is more likely to be a worthy successor of the one which produced the Law and the Prophets if it is evolved in . . . Palestine, than if it arises from a melting pot in Angola."[294] The cutting reference to the author's famous play was worthy of Zangwill's own wit, though it is doubtful he appreciated the swipe. Another blow came from Robert M. Sebag-Montefiore, an influential Anglo-Jewish leader, when he resigned from the ITO after Zangwill's address.[295] Yet the ITO leader obstinately insisted that "[i]f our results should prove negative, negative results have also their value. If they do not show the way for our people to go, they show the ways in which it *cannot* go."[296]

In the face of defeat, Zangwill turned to a strategy he often employed: he upped the ante. Zangwill submitted a cranky memorandum to his London Council that attacked Lord Rothschild for his ambivalence and laid blame on him for the lack of financial support. "The rejection of Angola," he wrote, "seems to me no less tragic a blunder" than the refusal of land in East Africa nearly a decade earlier.[297] "[I]t shows that the Jews *prefer* to be landless and powerless," he concluded.[298] Privately, however, Zangwill expressed the "gravest doubts" about Angola.[299] Contact with Bensaúde nonetheless limped on into the summer of 1914. Bensaúde's last letter to Zangwill before the eruption of World War I indicated that the Portuguese government had "lost confidence with *the Jews*."[300] On the same day that the first clouds of poison gas wafted over allied lines, April 22, 1915, a despondent Zangwill confided to Gregory that the ITO had effectively come to an end: "I cannot pretend that much hope of an ITOland prevails in a planet so sundered from Reason and Love."[301] Perhaps only the moon would do after all.

The Angola scheme had been the ITO's last and best chance to establish a territorial solution for Jewish homelessness. Following the Balfour Declaration, Zangwill reconciled for a time with Zionist aims.[302] A short-lived spirit of cooperation moved him to write to Winston Churchill to campaign for "heroic measures of race-distribution," whereby Palestine's Arabs would be "gradually emigrated, with full compensation from the Jews, towards the new Arab Kingdom" to be established nearby.[303] Without such a population transfer, Zangwill insisted, "no Jewish state worth the name could possibly arise, but only a state of perpetual friction."[304] The refusal of Zionist leaders and the British government to pay heed to demographics soured Zangwill on the Balfour Declaration. He resumed a defense of the ITO's work in speeches and essays. Two years after the Declaration, he lamented the failure to establish a Jewish polity outside of Palestine. He declared that Jewish history was nothing less than "a story of lost opportunities."[305] Later, Zangwill decried Zionism's "mirage of the Jewish state," and asserted that greater autonomy had been agreed to in Uasin Gishu "than that with which Dr. Weizmann has now been fobbed off in Palestine."[306] Gregory maintained the faith with Zangwill. The erstwhile ITOist parsed the Balfour Declaration with a legalistic fervor, declaring in 1920 that its "promise was for permission to establish a national home *in* Palestine, and not Palestine *as* a national home."[307] He went so far as to suggest that if the ITO had "achieved its purpose and established a strong autonomous Jewish colony" in Africa, then Zangwill's "practical expression of Zionism" might have sped the development of a more substantial Jewish home in Palestine.[308]

The ITO—moribund for a decade—was dissolved in July of 1925. Zangwill's followers presented him with a leather-bound album at a ceremony to mark the occasion. At the time, the sixty-one-year-old Zangwill was known to suffer from bouts of insomnia, depression, and nervous exhaustion.[309] The album bears a poignant inscription to the ailing Zangwill in calligraphic script: "We dreamt with you of a new effort to solve the tragic problem of Jewish . . . homelessness and, under your gallant captaincy, we set forth . . . to find a territory in which . . . our kindred might live their own lives as a free and independent people. It was an act of high faith . . . which will assuredly yet find its vindication, if not in literal fulfillment, in the magic of eternal justice."[310] A year later, Zangwill died of pneumonia.[311] His remains were cremated and interred in London's Liberal Jewish cemetery. The inscription on his columbarium reads: "A Man of Letters and a Fighter for Unpopular Causes." After his death, Edith sent one of Zangwill's cherished possessions—a mezuzah—to one of her husband's friends and collaborators on the Galveston Movement. Zangwill never placed this mezuzah on his doorpost; instead he had always carried it with him on his travels.[312] Symbolically, at least, Zangwill made his home wherever he went.

Zangwill's instrumental contributions to Zionism's early years were eclipsed by his bitter criticisms of the movement's direction, and by his tenacious fight for the ITO vision. Oddly, right-wing historian Benzion Netanyahu remains one of the few to have praised Zangwill, even including him in his pantheon of Zionism's founding fathers.[313] Zangwill's literary reputation suffered in the era of Modernism too. Now his sly and sentimental works are rarely read, or are considered curious relics of a faded imperial era. Even Zangwill's hearty "melting pot" has been emptied of its cultural import in favor of the politically correct, albeit less fulfilling, metaphor of the "salad bowl." But the memory of Zangwill would inspire a successor territorialist movement as European Jewry faced an uncertain future in the 1930s.

Madagascar

4

The Lost Jewish Continent

Madagascar (1933–1942)

Freelanders

One warm spring evening in 1913, the Galician-born agronomist Salomon (Shlomo) Dyk sat on the porch of his wooden shack in Merchavia, the struggling Zionist cooperative he managed in the Jezreel Valley.[1] Before he had time to relax from the day's labor, a shot rang out over the nearby fields.[2] Dyk dashed inside to grab his Mauser pistol, shoved a Browning automatic into his belt, pocketed several loaded magazines, and raced in the direction of the gunshot, firing his pistol as he ran.[3] A witness who had just changed into his nightclothes recorded the scene and later hailed Dyk as a hero for protecting the settlement from a band of Arab thieves.[4] Twenty-four years later, Dyk, the man who had helped the Zionist movement establish one of the first modern farms in Ottoman Palestine, found himself slogging through Madagascar in an effort to determine whether Jewish colonists might turn the distant Indian Ocean island into a tropical Zion. The convoluted history of how a former pioneer of the *yishuv* found himself investigating possible sites for mass colonization on a remote African island the size of Texas involves pirate fantasies and Victorian scholars, antisemites and philosemites, Frenchmen and Poles, a famed German novelist of the interwar period, a militant Jewish nationalist, and one of Zionism's leading technocrats: Franz Oppenheimer.

The son of a Reform rabbi and educator in Berlin, Oppenheimer trained as a physician and later became a prominent political economist in the closing years of the nineteenth century. He was known for his vigorous intellect, and his duel-scarred visage testified to his physical daring.[5] Oppenheimer was a combative participant in the salon culture of the era too, and during this time came into the orbit of Theodor Hertzka.[6] Hertzka's celebrated novel *Freeland* had captivated Oppenheimer,[7] who sought to structure a just, model society while treating patients plagued by urban violence, prostitution, and degradation in Berlin.[8] Hertzka's programmatic fantasy had of course also influenced Herzl's own vision of the Jewish future both in his manifesto *The Jewish State* and his novel *Old-New Land* (*Altneuland*). But Oppenheimer was even more indebted than Herzl to Hertzka, going so far as to publish a critical revision of *Freeland* entitled *Freiland in Deutschland* (1895), which promoted a system of economically rational settlements in Germany rather than in East Africa.

On the strength of Oppenheimer's socio-economic theories, Herzl invited him to participate in the 1903 Zionist expedition to El Arish in Sinai, an offer he declined.[9] Later that year, Herzl asked Oppenheimer to address the Sixth Zionist Congress as an expert on emigration and resettlement. He hoped Oppenheimer's speech would reinforce among the delegates the practical nature of the so-called Uganda Plan, which critics found to contain warmed-over aspects of Hertzka's ill-starred East African Freeland settlement.[10] Oppenheimer's blueprint for cooperative settlement would not bear fruit until 1911, when his system formed the basis for the establishment of Merchavia. And it was none other than a pajama-clad Oppenheimer who had watched his trusted disciple Shlomo Dyk race off pistols blazing into the Jezreel Valley that spring night in 1913.

Oppenheimer maintained his commitment to Jewish colonization efforts throughout his long career. By the early 1930s, he had achieved an international reputation and was asked to review a plan to settle one million Eastern European Jews in Peruvian land concessions.[11] Jewish emigration organizations met with Oppenheimer and others in Berlin to consider the proposal, but the colonization of Peru failed to gather momentum. The project only developed in earnest late that summer after a military coup d'état in Peru. Albert Einstein, whose support for Zionism was often equivocal, was acquainted with Oppenheimer and trusted the eminent professor's contention that further exploration of the region in Peru proposed for colonization should be conducted.[12] Einstein wrote to the Jewish Colonization Association (ICA) in Paris to advance the scheme, but his entreaties were rebuffed. "I almost have the impression," Einstein reported, that the ICA "aim[ed] at making it appear Jewish colonization is not advisable."[13] Some months later, in February 1931, Julius Brutzkus, a physician, scholar, former minister for Jewish affairs in Lithuania, and sometime ally of Ze'ev Jabotinsky, revived the Peruvian proposal. Brutzkus declared that the soil and climate of Peru's interior was "splendidly adapted for Jewish settlement."[14] He noted with frustration that while he and Oppenheimer had collaborated to send a fact-finding commission to Peru, "the responsible Jewish organisations took up a negative stand . . . to any organized measures for . . . a regulated Jewish immigration movement to Peru."[15] The Peruvian affair, though abortive, had one significant outcome: it catalyzed the founding of the Freeland League for Jewish Territorial Colonization (*Frayland-lige far Yidisher Teritoryalistisher Kolonizatsye*).[16] The Freeland League, of course, owed its name[17] to Hertzka's utopian novel.

The movement coalesced in Warsaw in the early 1930s as an organization dedicated to providing a territorial solution to Jewish homelessness in the wake of rising antisemitism in Poland and the growing belligerence of Nazism on its borders. The League's founders also saw their movement as a challenge to another quasi-territorialist project then underway in the Soviet Union: Birobidzhan. Perhaps the best known of all the many alternative Zions, Birobidzhan has been the subject of several scholarly works in recent years.[18] Communist party leaders announced initiatives in the 1920s to settle Jews in Birobidzhan, an area in the Far Eastern Territory of the USSR that abuts Manchuria. A sparsely populated region, Birobidzhan was rich in natural resources, but devoid of infrastructure. The Jewish Autonomous Region (J.A.R.) of Birobidzhan was formally established in May 1934. Soon the J.A.R. garnered the support of Jewish Communists and sympathizers in America, Canada, and elsewhere throughout the world. On the surface, the J.A.R. promised harried Jews a national existence, an organized mass settlement effort, agro-industrial employment, and a subsidized Yiddish cultural life. In practice, however, the J.A.R. never reached the threshold of Jewish population necessary to achieve autonomy, and expressions of Jewish nationalism were in any case curtailed under Stalin. Resettlement programs were mismanaged, poverty and despair were widespread, and Yiddish, though it endured, was overtaken by Russian as the language of those aspiring toward upward mobility and the protection, or largesse, of the Party.

The history of the establishment of the J.A.R. reveals a parallel but different political evolution from that represented by the Jewish Territorial Organization (ITO) and Freeland League. The J.A.R. existed outside the political philosophy, organizational structure, and key ideological commitments of territorial autonomism as proclaimed by the ITO and Freeland League. These Jewish organizations emerged from humanitarian contexts and were indebted to the practices of settler colonialism and theories of liberal nationalism. By contrast, the J.A.R. was centralized under a dictatorial Communist regime hostile to authentic Jewish cultural expression and enamored of forced population transfer. The ITO and the Freeland League, while critical of Zionism, typically viewed territorialism as complementary to settlement in Palestine. Stalin, however, employed Birobidzhan as a cynical anti-Zionist tool. Scholars have concluded that the creation of the J.A.R. owed more to non-Jewish apparatchiks concerned with Soviet economic and security interests than to a sincere concern with Jewish welfare.[19]

True, Israel Zangwill did support the creation of a Jewish enclave somewhere in the vast lands of Siberia, where the J.A.R. was later established. In his capacity as ITO president he suggested as early as 1915 that "the Jews, instead of being cooped up in stinking poverty in the towns of the Pale, should . . . be invited to carve out a province with the ploughshare from these vast neglected territories."[20] Two years later, in the wake of the Revolution, he voiced the opinion that in a free "United States of Russia" a Jewish state might arise.[21] He identified Siberia—the "mighty land of the future"—as the most promising locale for Jewish self-government.[22] His early enthusiasm for a Jewish state in Siberia led one close friend and collaborator to proclaim Zangwill the prophet of Birobidzhan.[23] Zangwill's focus on Siberia stemmed from his acquaintance with anarchist theoretician Prince Petr Kropotkin. Kropotkin had mentioned eastern Siberia's potential to the ITO head as early as 1906.[24] Before the years of his long exile in England, Kropotkin gained fame as a geographer and geologist who had conducted pioneering surveys of the land and resources in the region of Birobidzhan.[25] Zangwill's enthusiasm for the Revolution waned in the years after the Bolsheviks consolidated power, yet he voiced support for Birobidzhan in his final public appearance before his death.[26]

Adherents of the Freeland League remained more ambivalent about the J.A.R. One of the leading intellectuals of the day, social revolutionary and Yiddishist Chaim Zhitlowski, contributed an article to the first official Freeland League publication in 1934 in which he expressed skepticism as to whether Birobidzhan would truly become a Jewish republic. Economic factors would limit Jewish immigration to the J.A.R. from beyond the Soviet Union, indicating to Zhitlowski that Birobidzhan would never provide a solution to Jewish wandering and persecution. "For the millions of Jews in Eastern Europe," Zhitlowski claimed, "Birobidzhan is not an answer."[27] By 1936, the Freeland League had established a political branch in London. Members there also felt that Birobidzhan "was not enough, and that something more must be done elsewhere."[28] A later assessment of Birobidzhan by a Freeland League activist noted that while the organization "had no formal and factual part in Birobidzhan, [the League] never denied that in essence Birobidzhan represents a Soviet, Communist variation of the basic tenet of Territorialism."[29] Nonetheless, the writer emphasized, Jewish territorialists always "regarded and interpreted this phenomenon"—the J.A.R. experiment—from an "equivocal viewpoint."[30]

A heterogeneous group of Jewish intellectuals, scholars, belletrists, and political activists formed the core of the Freeland League. They sought to provide Jews with an alternative to Zionism, Diaspora nationalism, and assimilationist trends. The two central objects of the League were to (1) locate a territory and establish settlements there "where Jews can live a normal life unmolested," and (2) to cooperate or join with other organizations having similar goals.[31] This disunited cadre conceived of the Freeland League as a reincarnation of Israel Zangwill's defunct and bourgeois ITO, crossed with the agrarian commitments of left-labor socialism.[32] At one point, the British branch of the Freeland League entertained the possibility of adopting the ITO name and platform,[33] and even considered reviving the plan to colonize Angola.[34] But before chartering their organization at a London conference in 1935, Freeland supporters—*Fraylandistn* in Yiddish—had already published two volumes of a short-lived periodical in Warsaw. Contributors to the journal, *Frayland*, included Zhitlowski, socialist leader Ben-Adir (Avrom Rozin), demographer Jakob (Yankev) Lestschinsky, poet Melech Ravitch (Zekharye-Khone Bergner), and—in both issues—the famous novelist, physician, and exile from Nazi Germany, Alfred Döblin.[35]

In the Hands of Others

On November 5, 1923, three days before Hitler's failed Munich Beer Hall Putsch, mobs of unemployed men and nationalist thugs descended on the Scheunenviertel, a poor Jewish immigrant neighborhood of Berlin. They looted stores and beat and humiliated anyone who looked Jewish.[36] Döblin, who later chronicled the neighborhood in his Modernist masterpiece *Berlin Alexanderplatz* (1929), called the pogrom Nazism's "first shriek."[37] In the wake of the antisemitic riots against the mostly Polish Jews living in the Scheunenviertel, the assimilated Döblin, who had his medical office nearby—in the same Berlin district where Oppenheimer had practiced—was forced to reckon with his own religious identity.[38] He realized he knew nothing about Jews or Judaism and began to attend Zionist meetings.[39] A year later, in the autumn of 1924, he left his beloved Berlin in order to "get [his] bearings about the Jews"; authentic Jews, he was told, could readily be found in Poland.[40] What began as one man's intellectual investigation into his origins would soon turn into a spiritual quest to ensure the collective Jewish future in France's overseas possessions.

When he set off for Poland, the forty-six-year-old Döblin looked the part of a bookish writer. He favored tweedy suits, wore eyeglasses that gave him a fishbowl stare, and had a pronounced crease in his brow that only deepened with age. His two-month tour of Poland[41] brought him into contact with religious Jews, wonder-working rabbis, Zionists, and Yiddishist intellectuals. And though Döblin traveled by train through modern Europe, his railway journey brought him into the heart of an "ancient national feeling."[42] His revelation that the Jewish "nation remained whole" despite having been "thrown out of Palestine . . . two thousand years ago" roused Döblin.[43] He contemplated Jewish rebirth through Zionism, wondering: "What if history were turned backward and the Jews were really given Zion?"[44] But his flirtation with the movement was short lived. He ultimately sided with a Yiddish writer he met in Lodz who concluded that Zionism is "not where the future of the world lies"; first "the world has to be humanized."[45]

Following his return from Poland, Döblin began to frequent Berlin's Sholem Aleichem Club. There he came in contact with a number of émigré Jewish intellectuals whose socialist vision of the Jewish future suited his political temperament.[46] Soon they would draw the author into their circle. As Germany descended into barbarism, Döblin dedicated himself to a humanist vision of Jewish redemption. He was influenced in large part by his Polish journey and his subsequent encounters with the émigré writers and activists he met in Berlin. Formerly an alienated and indifferent Jew, he now emerged as an uncompromising Jewish nationalist.

Döblin fled Nazi Germany in February 1933 ahead of the Gestapo and arrived in Zurich. There he was said by a colleague to have "discovered Herzl" and taken a particular interest in the failed Uganda Plan.[47] From Switzerland he made his way to France, where he settled. While his books were being burned in Berlin, in Paris he wrote two volumes of meditations on the question of Jewish collective renewal.[48] He presented Jewish Emancipation as a total failure, railing against assimilated Jewry's "canine devotion" to European culture, and dismissing his contemporaries as a "generation of degeneration."[49] Instead of a European "mis-emancipation,"[50] he exhorted a "renewal of the Jews . . . pledged to a mass colonization."[51] In his work, he advocated a reconsideration of ITO designs on "the Portuguese colony of Angola in West Africa,"[52] a plan he also revealed in letters from this period.[53] Döblin envisioned a territorialist organization spearheaded by Jewish "proletarian and intellectual masses" that would be even "farther-reaching than Zionism."[54] Indeed, he believed that his proposed movement would supercede Zionism as means to rescue the millions of Jews "who live as a slave-people, near, on, or over the verge of destruction."[55] His vituperative rejection of assimilation, his enthusiasm for Zangwill's efforts, and his hazy socialist agenda caught the attention of the *Fraylandistn.*

By November 1933 he had become a founder of the *Ligue Juive pour Colonisation* (League for Jewish Colonization), later to become the Paris branch of the nascent Freeland League.[56] Suddenly the frustrations and fantasies of a small but influential circle of Warsaw-based Yiddishists had found powerful expression in the writings of an internationally celebrated author, a Jewish atheist who had first reconnected to his religious heritage in Poland.[57] The Freelanders translated some of Döblin's polemics to bring them to the Yiddish-reading public.[58] Döblin himself began learning Yiddish under the influence of Freeland leaders.[59]

The first of Döblin's essays to appear in *Frayland* in 1934, "The Tragic Fate of West European Jewry,"[60] presented a grim assessment of Jewish homelessness: "Since Jews lost their land and state, they sit . . . locked up in a cage like a pack of trapped animals . . . because there is no security or law for Jews in the world, because behind the law there must be the sword, and the sword, as we know, is in the hands of others."[61] He believed that assimilated Jewry stood at a crossroads, one marked by the bent-armed shadow of the swastika. Jewish "lovers of Goethe and Schiller are on trial," he wrote, tested by an atavistic antisemitism.[62] Döblin felt certain that without knowledge of "their own history" and without "one shred of Jewish content," his Westernized coreligionists would fail to save themselves.[63] He scorned these "ruins of the Jewish people, these end results of Western Emancipation," who persist in a "one-sided love" of European culture.[64] Though not observant of Jewish law himself, Döblin respected orthodox Jewry, calling the religious community "powerful bearers of a great, ancient history."[65] The author's sensitivity to tradition is due to the influence of his friend and correspondent Nathan Birnbaum.[66]

Birnbaum had been a Jewish nationalist before Herzl arrived on the scene, became the first general-secretary of the Zionist movement,[67] and is credited with coining the very term "Zionism" in 1890.[68] Shortly after the 1903 Zionist Congress, Birnbaum attacked the methods of both the supporters of Herzl's charterism and his opponents' piecemeal settlement tactics. Even were the illusions of Herzl to be gratified by international recognition, and even were the naïve "nay-sayers" to purchase large portions of Palestine, Birnbaum indicated that the whole Zionist movement was characterized by elitism, and its claims to Palestine remained a "ridiculous farce" without the support of the Jewish masses in the Diaspora.[69] He went on to theorize a brand of Diaspora nationalism that he termed Pan-Judaism (*Alljudentum*). Although Birnbaum experienced numerous ideological shifts, he long claimed that the people of "Israel come before Zion."[70] Like Zangwill, Birnbaum was one of the few early Zionist leaders to warn that the Arab inhabitants of Ottoman Palestine would not allow their dispossession at the hands of future Jewish immigrants who waved paper deeds of land tenure in their faces. No, he continued, "the surprised Palestinians will not accept this quietly."[71] Thus Birnbaum became the first individual to use the term "Palestinian" in its modern sense to refer to the indigenous Arabs then residing in *Eretz Israel*. He did so, notably, in the wake of the Uganda crisis. Later, the restless Birnbaum broke from Zionism entirely, ran unsuccessfully for political office, championed Yiddish, and ultimately became an orthodox religious penitent—a *baal tshuva*. He then reemerged as an activist in the first successful political party of orthodox Jewry, *Agudas Yisroel* (Union of Israel). In the interwar period, the fiery Birnbaum agitated within the *Agudas Yisroel* for a religious pioneering movement and the establishment of Torah-true agricultural colonies in Palestine.[72] Under Birnbaum's influence,[73] Döblin concluded that it was secular Jews who must undergo a spiritual and social renewal to become "New Judeans."[74]

Döblin's second article for *Frayland*, "Territorialism and New Judea," appeared at the end of 1934 and expanded his earlier vision. In this apocalyptic essay, he focused not on the original Zionist and territorialist question—"How can we get a land for the Jews?"—but on the more fundamental question—"How can we get Jews for a land?"[75] Döblin believed that Herzl's "wavering between Palestine and Argentina" and his readiness "to come out in favor of Uganda" were symptomatic of a weakness inherent in both Zionism and "the old territorialism" of Zangwill.[76] In their narrow pursuit of land, both leaders had failed to consider the spiritual dimensions of the Jewish condition.[77] While Herzl and Zangwill hoped to create a Europeanized sanctuary for Jews on foreign soil, Döblin believed that the struggle to ape Western civilization had already "spiritually killed off half the Jewish community."[78] He insisted that Jews "must stop . . . turning toward the 'West.'"[79] Instead, Jews must "gather themselves together, define their own identity, restore themselves once again, and only then, acquire a land."[80] How they were to do this in practice remained undefined, but Döblin drew on his contact with Birnbaum and his study of Jewish history to suggest a path forward.

He compared Judaism's "battle with assimilation" to the Jewish "situation after the destruction of the Temple."[81] As the people of the Land of Israel, Jews once had an "organic national structure,"[82] and to endure as the Diaspora people, their identity had to change. "Now," he declared, "a new form is needed [to] ensure the survival of Judaism, which is being threatened with catastrophe."[83] Territory was not enough; Döblin sought nothing less than a complete revivification of Judaism. Döblin's rhetoric turned metaphysical in his depiction of a New Judea. Jewish life would be *new* to the extent it would "turn away . . . from Western civilization" and "safeguard its own spiritual base."[84] And Jewish life would be *Judea*-ized when it acknowledged its relationship "to an ancient people formed not through a belligerent or political act, but through a lofty *spiritual* one."[85] He explained further that New Judea "will be Jewish precisely in that *it will carry out a task for humankind.* . . . For that reason—and not so as to be an ordinary people living within its own borders—was the Jewish people formed thousands of years ago."[86] Here the jab at Zionism's normalizing mission is unmistakable, and familiar from religious critics of the movement from Birnbaum to his successors helming contemporary Israel's non-Zionist *Agudat Yisrael* party, which has had representatives in every Knesset since Israel's founding. Still, it is remarkable that Döblin, despite being every bit as assimilated as Herzl and Zangwill, here sounds more like a messianic prophet than a secular political activist.

Döblin's reach extended beyond German intellectuals and Yiddishists. Excerpts of his writing on the Jewish condition appeared in Hebrew translation in a nine-part essay, "Jewish Revival," published in the *yishuv*'s most influential cultural journal, *Turim* (*Columns*), a weekly edited by the most important poet of the day, Avraham Shlonsky. His reflections on the failure of the emancipation appeared from November 1933 through February 1934 in *Turim*'s pages alongside poetry by now canonical Hebrew authors.[87] Döblin even penned a special introduction to his work for Hebrew readers in which he charged that little had changed for Westernized Jews since Herzl, a claim that must have puzzled many in the *yishuv*.[88] In the penultimate installment of "Jewish Revival," Döblin lectured his Hebrew readership about the importance of establishing a mass settlement to absorb the majority of world Jewry in some underpopulated region; he particularly considered resurrecting Zangwill's Angola plans.[89] Surely such a suggestion would have stunned and outraged those reading his words in Tel Aviv and elsewhere throughout the British Mandate who were struggling to establish a Jewish national home.

The following year, Döblin coedited a German edition of *Frayland*[90] and published a summary of the Freeland League's actions in Birnbaum's journal *Der Ruf* (*The Call*). In the latter, he noted that Angola was under consideration for possible mass settlement.[91] Döblin also wrote to Thomas Mann in the spring of 1935 in an effort to interest him in the Freeland League's colonization agenda.[92] That summer, he traveled from Paris to attend the London conference that formalized the Freeland League. He presented the opening lecture on the "aims and character of the Freeland movement"[93] to delegates assembled at the Russell Hotel on Sunday, July 21, 1935.[94] Notables who lent their name to the cause included philosopher Bertrand Russell, author J. B. Priestley, Jewish communal leader and scholar Dr. Moses Gaster, politician and labor activist Arthur Creech Jones, and Israel Zangwill's widow, Edith.[95] Though the meetings of the Preparatory International Conference of the League for Jewish Colonization were ignored by the mainstream British press, coverage in London's *Jewish Chronicle* focused on the gathering's "realist attitude."[96] The *yishuv* newspaper *Davar* (*The Word*) devoted a long article to the "new territorialism" and highlighted Döblin's role as the movement's "spiritual leader."[97]

At the conference, Döblin stated his fervent belief that Jews "stand at the end, at the catastrophic aftermath of the lost battle for emancipation."[98] The "central and essential task" of the League, he wrote, "is to enlighten and awaken the Jewish masses, for this is indeed a matter of establishing their own 'Freeland.'"[99] But Döblin believed that prior to any territorial settlement, the Freelanders must "build-up the people,"[100] a labor both spiritual and "political-diplomatic in character."[101] His speech recognized Zionism's contribution to Jewish life and the eternal holiness of the land of Israel, while echoing Birnbaum's sense that "the Jewish people are greater than the land."[102] Thus Döblin declared that "the definitive impulse of the [Freeland] movement" should be the "formation of a new Jewish people."[103] He concluded his address by stating that "Hitler is the reckoning that history presents to us."[104] At the time it was still possible to believe that Nazism could be countered by Jewish rebirth. Before the close of the conference, many of the delegates paid their respects to Israel Zangwill by laying a wreath at his columbarium.[105] Following the ceremony, attendees assembled for the conference's closing session at the Royal Hotel.[106] There Döblin reiterated that Hitler's rise demonstrated that Jews "could only live in peace in their own land."[107] "The greatest joy in my life now," Döblin maintained, "is that I have resolved to give my life and energy to the new 'Free Land' movement, whose aim is to obtain a free territory for the oppressed Jews, who cannot go to Palestine."[108]

The author served on the board of the Paris branch of the Freeland League until 1936,[109] the year in which he became a French citizen and Léon Blum became France's first Jewish prime minister. He continued to take an active role in the organization through 1937, and was considered by the Freelanders to be something of a diplomat in the early months of that year, able to "bridge the gulf" between the group's various factions.[110] In mid-November 1937, Döblin attended the Second General Freeland Conference in Paris,[111] where fundamental questions of the Freeland platform were debated.[112] Wearied by infighting, Döblin abandoned the movement a few months later.[113] By that time, his stirring meditations on the Jewish question coupled with his vocal support for a spiritually inflected territorialism had made him the most well known Freeland advocate. The Freeland League, never a popular movement, owed a great deal of its ideology and early legitimacy to Döblin. The author's vigorous response, both in word and deed, to the growing persecution of European Jewry have long since been overshadowed by his eventual conversion to Catholicism.[114] And though he died a Christian, Döblin lived his life during perilous years as a very public Jew.

In late 1936, when the author was still active in the organization, the Parisian Freelanders and the *Société d'émigration et de Colonisation Juive* (EMCOL) joined forces to create a Political-Geographic Committee in order to explore the possibilities of Jewish settlement in French territories.[115] The committee met on November 20 and 21 in Paris.[116] Their agenda listed discussion of New Caledonia and French Guiana as possible sites for mass emigration.[117] The committee did not include Döblin, but he later informed his son that a Freeland expedition would be sent to these same two French colonies.[118] The Freelanders also knew that Blum's colonial minister, Marius Moutet, was keen to populate Madagascar with agricultural settlements, though they remained skeptical of the island's promise.[119] The president of the Parisian Freeland League wrote to the central branch in Warsaw stating his group's determination "to devote in-depth studies" to all three French territories.[120]

The Freeland League and EMCOL directly approached Moutet on December 16, 1936, to seek his support for Jewish colonization in some French overseas territory.[121] Their aim, they explained to Moutet in a memorandum, was "the establishment of a new Jewish Center" for those "Jews from Central and Eastern Europe who are compelled to leave the countries of their birth to settle in some corner of the immense [French] colonies which are so greatly underpopulated. Our preliminary investigations have drawn our attention more particularly to New Caledonia, Madagascar and French Guiana."[122] Moutet not only had the proper administrative authority to enter into such negotiations, but he was also seen as sympathetic to the Jewish plight,[123] perhaps because his late wife had herself been a Russian Jewish immigrant to France.[124] Those involved in drafting the letter included Léonard Rosenthal, the millionaire "Pearl King," and Julius Brutzkus, who had been active in advancing the Peruvian settlement scheme with Franz Oppenheimer. They met with Moutet a few weeks later, on January 14, 1937, to follow up.[125] The powerful Rosenthal provided the Freeland-EMCOL delegation with direct access to Moutet, with whom he was well acquainted.[126]

Two days after their meeting, and exactly one month after receiving the Freeland-EMCOL letter, Moutet publicly announced that he was "very sympathetic to the idea of the eventual establishment of Jews in our colonies. . . . Madagascar, for example, presents a favorable opportunity if there is appropriate organization and financial backing."[127] He went on to presume that "upon the high plateaus of that great island suitable land might be found" for Jewish settlements.[128] At the same time, Moutet sent the Freeland-EMCOL representatives a private letter similar in tone and content to his public declaration. In his letter, he reiterates his interest in the project and notes that the issue "is now being studied both by my officials and by the respective local authorities."[129] Freeland efforts had clearly swayed Moutet to their cause. His pronouncement in January 1937 was hailed by territorialists as a French version of the Balfour Declaration. A well-informed Paris correspondent for the yishuv's Davar newspaper noted the Freeland League's role in obtaining what it referred to the "Moutet Declaration."[130] The diplomatic Moutet, however, had made no mention of a "national home" for the Jews in his pronouncements as Lord Balfour had done.

Still, Moutet's assistant was forced to issue a hasty clarification to Jewish organizations, stipulating that colonization of French colonies "could not constitute a solution of the world Jewish problem."[131] While Minister Moutet would "offer all administrative facilities to grant the

Terraced farmland in central highlands, Madagascar. Courtesy of Michael Kollins

colonists land in healthful regions permitting immediate cultivation and, if possible, cattle raising," his assistant warned that "the experiment cannot be on a large scale, but only for a few hundred persons."[132] Despite this backpedaling, there is little doubt that the French minister sincerely believed, as he himself stated, that he could help Jewish "victims of political passions and religious and racial prejudice"[133] by resettling them in Madagascar. He also thought he knew where the Jews would come from who would populate the island possession: Poland.[134]

The so-called "Jewish problem" dominated internal Polish politics across the political spectrum in the 1930s as the world economic crisis battered Europe. Jews represented approximately ten percent of the country's population, and were perceived as an alien element whose numbers stood in the way of gentile economic advancement. Nationalist politicians at the time agitated to relocate the country's Jews, even as more refugees arrived from Hitler's Reich. In 1935, responsibility for Jewish policy[135] shifted from the Polish interior ministry to the foreign ministry. This transfer demonstrates how the Polish government made the mass resettlement of the country's Jewish population a cornerstone of its foreign policy. Colonel Józef Beck, the minister of foreign affairs, emerged as the central figure in negotiations for Jewish emigration. Beck, no friend of the Jews, was a career politico in his early forties who had to balance his government's desire to assert itself as a European power with increasing German bellicosity, and the demands of reactionary elements in Poland with a Jewish parliamentary voting bloc and a skeptical press. The impossible task is told in photographs from the era in which Beck appears weary, his lower lip protruding in a pout. Much like Great Britain's Joseph Chamberlain more than thirty years earlier, Beck viewed the Jewish "problem" as a means to achieve political ends. If he could broker a deal to transfer tens of thousands, or even hundreds of thousands,[136] of Jews from Polish soil to an overseas colony, nationalists would hail him as a hero and other European states could close their borders to Jewish refugees with a clean conscience. There were only two obstacles to putting this plan into effect: most Jews did not want to leave Poland,[137] and the Poles did not possess any colonies.

As to the first difficulty, the revocation of Jewish minority rights in Poland and restrictions on Jewish admission to universities, economic boycotts, attempts to outlaw kosher slaughtering, and outbreaks of mob violence all helped to encourage some Jews to emigrate. Still, the vast majority of Jews remained committed to the belief that their place was in Poland. This attitude, *doikeit*, or "hereness," extended even to those Jews who sympathized with Zionism.[138] But one man, Ze'ev Jabotinsky, had been urging a Jewish "evacuation" from Poland for years.[139] Jabotinsky had a prominent lower jaw that thrust forward like the prow of a ship. As a young man he favored thick round glasses that gave him the pop-eyed appearance of silent film star Harold Lloyd. And though he was partial to British tailoring, photographs often make it seem as if he is wearing someone else's suit jacket. A skilled journalist and forceful orator, Jabotinsky propagandized for mass emigration both in person and in print in the years preceding World War II.

In June 1936, he provided Beck with a memorandum describing his plans for a "mass Exodus" of "several million Jews over the course of two or three decades" to Mandate Palestine.[140] His willingness to meet with antisemitic leaders like Beck often put him at odds with the Jewish establishment. And his scorn for the elitist "Zionism de luxe"[141] of men like World Zionist Organization leader Chaim Weizmann didn't help matters. Jabotinsky saw himself as the rightful heir of Theodor Herzl and his lieutenant, Max Nordau.[142] Like these men, Jabotinsky was a successful author and ideologue. His literary work lent him considerable credibility in both the Jewish and gentile world, and perhaps most importantly, contributed to his far-reaching political imagination.

By the early 1920s, Jabotinsky had made a name for himself as a skilled translator, rendering Edgar Allan Poe's "The Raven" into Hebrew. Even today his translation of Poe's gothic verse is considered a masterpiece. Soon Jabotinsky became editor in chief of a publishing house dedicated to printing books in Hebrew for young readers.[143] He intended to publish Hebrew translations of some of the most popular books of the time, including works by Daniel Defoe and H. Rider Haggard.[144] Adventure literature, he believed, would allow Jewish children to "dream 'royal dreams'"[145] and give them the courage to pursue their aspirations. But his most significant educational project remains the first geographical atlas written in Hebrew. The *Atlas* was much celebrated at the time of its publication in 1925 for its accessibility and its many attractive color plates. Jabotinsky's volume emphasized the size of Jewish communities throughout the Diaspora, and made special mention of Chamberlain's offer of Jewish autonomy in East Africa as well as the ITO scheme to create a Jewish "national home" in Angola.[146] Jabotinsky's *Atlas* was less a *theatrum orbis terrarum*—a "theater of the world"—than a theater for Jewish empire. The *Atlas* testified to its editor's lifelong obsession with demographics and territory. The volume's maps laid out a new projection of the continents, a world where Jewish population became the central axis of its readers' imagination.

Later, Jabotinsky broke with mainstream Zionism to form his New Zionist Organization (NZO), whose followers were called Revisionists. The Revisionists laid out a ten-year plan to forge the Jewish state that they believed Weizmann had dithered over establishing. The main platform of the plan involved the evacuation of 750,000 Jews from Poland to Palestine.[147] Jabotinsky thus shared common cause with Beck and soon approached the foreign minister directly. But Poland's lack of any colonial possessions complicated Beck's intention to export his Jews. And Great Britain's restrictions on Jewish immigration to Palestine stood in the way both of Jabotinsky's royal dreams and Beck's more pedestrian ones. Still, Jabotinsky met with Beck and the Polish prime minister himself to press them to seek an accord with Great Britain.[148] The British, however, were reluctant to provoke Arab nationalists in Palestine. Weizmann claimed that as a compromise Jabotinsky had gone so far as to suggest to Beck "a mass evacuation . . . partly to Palestine, partly to other places—Madagascar for instance."[149] Weizmann's record of a conversation between his antagonist, Jabotinsky, and Beck is suspect, but the British ambassador to Poland's detailed dispatches from Warsaw corroborate Weizmann's account.

In a report on the Polish government's pursuit of a policy of mass Jewish emigration to Madagascar, Ambassador Hugh Kennard wrote that the Poles "have given some countenance" to Jabotinsky's NZO, and that Jabotinsky himself advocated that Jewish emigration should only "so far as possible" be directed to Palestine.[150] The context of Kennard's report—Madagascar as a site of colonization—and his careful choice of words—"so far as possible"—reveal that Jabotinsky may indeed have expressed a willingness to accept limited Jewish emigration to the French colony. An article in the widely circulated Berlin Zionist paper *Judische Rundschau* (*Jewish Review*) also linked Jabotinsky's evacuation plans to the Madagascar project in 1937.[151] What is certain is that Jabotinsky recognized that Jews needed to "evacuate the ruin"[152] that he believed Poland and east-central Europe was about to become.

The notion that Jabotinsky, a tireless proponent of maximalist Jewish statehood in Palestine, might support colonization in Madagascar is not as surprising as might be expected. For Jabotinsky, the organized rescue of as many Jews as possible would head off the destruction he foresaw. Both he and the *Fraylandistn* shared this sense of impending catastrophe, though from opposing political perspectives. Jabotinsky's concern for Jewish life and culture—despite his own estrangement from tradition—mirrors that of Döblin. Whatever his position in 1936, it is clear that by 1938 Jabotinsky feared a "resurrection of Territorialist illusions."[153] Still, his relationship to the Freeland League remained friendly for the rest of his life. Taking stock of the situation just a few months before his death in 1940, Jabotinsky wrote that the Freeland League's quest for large-scale Jewish settlement *outside* of Palestine should "be treated with the fullest respect, even by the most zealous and uncompromising Zionists."[154] He took seriously their efforts to colonize remote lands, even permitting himself to rhapsodize on a future in which "radio and television will permit a dweller of Central Africa to attend first nights of the New York Metropolitan Opera."[155] Yet despite this apparent optimism, he concluded that territorialist aims were doomed to failure in the here and now.

Members of the Zionist establishment also recognized the gathering dangers and negotiated with Polish government officials around Madagascar. Dr. Nahum Goldmann, a cosmopolitan and idiosyncratic figure who cofounded the World Jewish Congress (WJC) with Rabbi Stephen Wise, the most powerful American Jew in the prewar era, considered the island a possible refuge. In a "strictly confidential" telegram to Wise, Goldmann reported that Beck himself had asked the WJC to "intervene [with the] French government" regarding "Polish Jewish immigration [to] Madagaskar [sic]."[156] Goldmann informed Wise that the "French government [is] not opposed in principle" to the idea, and requested "five-thousand dollars" from WJC coffers to fund an "experts commission" to the island.[157] In tandem, he encouraged the Poles to establish "a governmental level study committee and be ready to present the French Government with a concrete plan" for Jewish resettlement there.[158] He wrote to the governor general of Madagascar that Jewish artisans, tailors, cobblers, masons, carpenters, and merchants might represent the vanguard of Jewish settlers.[159] Goldmann's plan rested on shrewd political calculus: Blum's government worried about an influx of impoverished Jewish immigrants to France and looked for a way of diverting a potential flood elsewhere. Goldmann also acknowledged that successful resettlement of Polish Jews in Madagascar would give his fledgling WJC "much prestige [and] importance" on the world stage.[160]

Not wanting to be left out, other Jewish organizations, including the American Joint Distribution Committee (JDC), considered relocating refugees to the island. The JDC's two main decision makers in Europe met with Moutet's assistant and other officials in June 1937 and came away convinced of France's "desire to make a fair trial in opening some of the French colonial possessions for Jewish immigration."[161] Though the JDC officials were wary of endorsing "the so-called 'Beck plan' of Jewish evacuation from Poland" to Madagascar, they concluded that "it would be a great mistake for the responsible Jewish organizations to sidetrack the proposition. It fully merits at least a thorough competent investigation."[162] The JDC likewise considered contributing to the costs of resettling Jewish emigrants there.[163]

Official inquiries made by Jewish interests represented by the Freeland League, Goldmann's WJC, and the JDC, coupled with Jabotinsky's fiery rhetoric and internal political forces in Poland and France, continued to mount. Colonel Beck himself broached the topic of Madagascar with Léon Blum.[164] But the roots of the various Madagascar plans are to be found in myth as much as in *realpolitik*.[165]

Oy, Madagascar

Persistent legends claim that the island's inhabitants are descended from the lost tribes of Israel. As early as 1658 Madagascar's governor affirmed the Malagasy's Jewish origins in part because he witnessed tribes practicing circumcision, a custom that remains nearly universal there today. The evidence was flimsy, but the idea caught on. Daniel Defoe, best known as the author of *Robinson Crusoe* (1719), helped popularize the connection between Jews and Madagascar in his tales of Libertalia. The legend of this pirate utopia survives thanks to Defoe's story about Captain Mission, the brigand who founded a settlement on the island and dedicated himself to smashing European capitalism, colonialism, and slavery. Captain Mission regarded with curiosity the connection between Jews and Africans in their parallel practice of circumcision, "said to be the Sign of the Covenant made between God and this People."[166] Later, as the ghostwriter for the popular *Madagascar: Or, Robert Drury's Journal, During Fifteen Years' Captivity on that Island*, Defoe (or Drury) suggested that the Malagasy preceded the Israelites, suspecting that "the Jews derived a great deal from [the Malagasy], instead of they from the Jews."[167] He even went so far as to claim that the priestly garments used in Solomon's Temple were merely improvements on more ancient Malagasy customs.[168]

Defoe's legends may have helped fuel a fascination with Madagascar during the twilight of the nineteenth century. Scholars of the day sought the lost "El Dorado of the Ancients"[169]—King Solomon's mines—in the pages of crumbling texts, in archaeological ruins, and through speculative philology. The Hebrew Bible (I Kings 10 and II Chronicles 9) refers to Ophir as the source of the gold, precious stones, and coral used for the construction of the Temple of Solomon. Augustus Henry Keane, a linguist and ethnologist believed that Madagascar was the true source of the "gold of Ophir."[170] According to Keane, "Israelitish crews of David's gold-fleet" first encountered the great island, and later mined its mineral wealth for Solomon, all the while importing Jewish customs and loaning Semitic words to the Malagasy.[171] Keane even claimed that the continent of Africa derives its very name from the Hebrew root of the biblical Ophir: *aleph* (A), *fey* (F), *reysh* (R).[172] British and French scholars maintained throughout the nineteenth and into the twentieth century that the Malagasy descended from biblical-era seafaring Jews.[173] The fact that the *Grand Île* had a Jewish colonial governor in the second decade of the twentieth century may have added to the mystique.[174] Others were interested in Madagascar for purely antisemitic reasons. The notorious German scholar and Jew-hater Paul de Lagarde suggested the expulsion of Jews to the island as early as 1885.[175] If the Malagasy are crypto-Jews, the reasoning went, then Madagascar itself should be either a promised land, or an island prison. Had the interwar Polish government had its way, it might have been.

In the late 1930s, Jewish evacuation to the island seemed at one and the same time preposterous and imminent.[176] Polish nationalists marched and cried out, "Jews to Madagascar!"[177] A novel appeared fantasizing that all but a hundred thousand Polish Jews would be exiled to the island.[178] Jewish journalists reported that anxious members of the community "purchased maps and sought out the location" of Madagascar.[179] A Warsaw theater performed a comic political play, "We're Off to Madagascar . . . or, a gay voyage to the Promised Land."[180] The satirical magazine *Szpilki* (*Pins*) featured cartoons of "everyday life in Madagascar" superimposed on a map of the island drawn to resemble a bearded, big-nosed Jew.[181] And cabaret performers sang a popular Polish satiric number, "Madagascar," whose lyrics include the lines: "Oy, Madagascar! / beloved country, / long live the dark continent!"[182] In France, a Jewish newspaper published a cartoon depicting an evacuee—a caftan-clad, hook-nosed Jew from Kishinev—surrounded by half-naked natives wielding spears.[183] An article decorated with swastikas that appeared in a pro-Nazi Arab nationalist magazine advocated Madagascar as a national home for Jews, Jehovah's Witnesses, nudists, Marxists, and jazz musicians.[184] Elsewhere, a skeptical American Zionist commentator noted bitterly that "even if the native population consisted of a handful of cannibals," the African island could not "digest Jews except in small, imperceptible quantities."[185] So long as Madagascar was a sight unseen, it remained a locus of antisemitic dreams, Jewish anxieties, and colonial obsession.

Finally, at the instigation of Beck and the Polish Foreign Ministry, and with the agreement of Moutet,[186] an expedition to Madagascar was organized. While this development presented an opportunity for the Freeland League to publicize its political influence, the movement's leaders recognized the danger of seeming to cooperate with antisemitic elements in the Polish government.[187] French Freeland leaders were well aware that the Polish expedition was viewed negatively by many Jews, and they agonized over their official stance toward it.[188]

Moutet had expressed his own doubts about the character of the expedition to the Parisian *Fraylandistn*, and they therefore considered sending their own separate commission of inquiry.[189] Their compatriots in Warsaw were similarly divided. They believed that Moutet's declaration held "historic significance," a fact seemingly confirmed by Zionist resistance to the expedition, of which they took note.[190] Nonetheless, the *Fraylandistn* worried that as productive as the expedition might prove to be, it "may get in the way of other work."[191] And so, despite having been in large part responsible for advancing the scheme, the Freeland League looked on from the sidelines when a three-man Commission of Experts departed on a fact-finding mission to Madagascar in the spring of 1937.

The delegates consisted of Leon Alter, director of a Jewish emigrant aid society based in Warsaw; Mieczysław Lepecki, a non-Jewish military officer and vice president of Poland's International Colonization Society; and Dr. Shlomo Dyk, the trigger-happy *yishuv* agronomist who had since left Merchavia to take up residence in Tel Aviv. They met in Paris on May 4 with Moutet,[192] who reiterated his support for Jewish colonization, though now with greater hesitation. He discouraged any illusions about the project, and warned that opening the gates to a sudden flood of immigrants would be premature.[193] Tempered by this announcement, the Commission left Marseille the next day aboard the French vessel *Compiègne* for a twenty-six-day voyage to Africa.[194]

The Commission's ten-week[195] odyssey through possible sites of settlement on the island was an arduous one. The members bounced along rutted roads and endured exhausting overland marches across rough terrain. At times they were "carried on the shoulders of natives" while seated in a *filanza*, a kind of sedan-chair.[196] A photograph of their slow progress depicts Lepecki, who wears a long white coat, peering with amused interest at the four bare-footed natives who struggle to carry him down a muddy slope.[197] A caravan of fifty-five local porters[198] accompanied the Commission, their figures trailing into the brush behind Lepecki's *filanza*. In another image, Alter, Dyk, and Lepecki stand together on a bridge.[199] All three wear pith helmets paired with stiff suit jackets that look out of place against the lush backdrop. Alter, his eyes shaded by the brim of his hat, hangs his arm over the shoulder of the shorter, stiffly posed Dyk. Both men wear ties and hold cigarettes in their right hands. Lepecki stands apart—the width of half of the river in the background between them—and stares in profile at the two Jews. The pictures were likely taken by Polish journalist and adventurer Arkady Fiedler, who accompanied the Commission and filed glowing reports on their progress in Poland's governmental mouthpiece, *Gazeta Polska* (*Polish Gazette*).[200]

In the capital, Antananarivo, they met with the governor of the island and other officials, including the colonial directors of health services and agriculture, to review settlement possibilities.[201] Then, as now, smoke from tens of thousands of wood fires suffused the thin air of Antananarivo, known as Tana for short. In the dilapidated city center lies a filthy lake, Anosy, dominated by a memorial to French and colonial soldiers who fell in World War I. Tana's streets, some paved, some cobblestone, some cratered, disappear uphill from Lake Anosy at crazy angles. The city is built on a series of hills split by a ridge of rocky cliffs from which Christian martyrs were thrown to their deaths by bloodthirsty Queen Ranavalona during the mid-nineteenth century. A few decades later steeples spread across the cityscape, and today church bells ring out on Sundays. No synagogue has ever graced Tana's skyline.

The Commission undertook several trips around the country from their base in the capital, four thousand feet above sea level. They traveled south through the highlands by way of the spa town of Antsirabe and the island's intellectual capital, Fianarantsoa, whose name means "place of good learning."[202] From there they continued on to the scrublands of the dry south, then made their way northwest up to the

Landscape of central highlands near Fianarantsoa, Madagascar. Courtesy of Michael Kollins

deepwater port named after the Portuguese explorer Diego Suarez. But Alter, Dyk and Lepecki concentrated their investigation on the promising central plateau region.[203] An official communiqué from the Polish Political Information Office based on the Commission's study indicated that parts of "central Madagascar, lying 800 metres above sea level" were "suitable for white settlement" and "peasant labor."[204]

Today this majestic region features bouldered hillsides and terraced fields that stretch out in every direction. White plumed cattle egrets swoop and soar over brilliant green rice paddies. Wagons pulled by zebu, muscular oxen with humped backs and long horns, shamble along ancient trails. Mud-daubed homes with thatched roofs sag at odd, exhausted angles. Built from the same red soil on which they sit, the homes look temporary and elemental, as if at any moment they'll fall back to dirt. The tombs that dot these same highlands, however, are made of solid gray stone and concrete. Houses are for the living, so they don't need to last, but death, well, death is forever. These eternal homes contain the bones of ancestors, revered by some Malagasy tribes who perform the custom of *famadihana*, "the turning of the bones." Families reunite several years after a loved one's death to ceremonially exhume the body: the family tomb is unsealed, the ancestor's bones are carried forth, and the assembled family members parade with the skeletal remains before wrapping the bones in new shrouds.

After nearly three months spent considering whether the strange terrain of Madagascar might afford Jews a provisional home, the Commission returned to Paris. They arrived in September, just as Beck reached the metropole on his way to a League of Nations meeting.[205] Lepecki met with Beck to debrief him,[206] and later returned to Poland to prepare an official report. The Commission's report, submitted to the Polish government by Lepecki, expressed a supposedly unanimous optimism for the venture.[207] According to Lepecki, four important conclusions were reached by the members: (1) large areas of the island were suitable for colonization, (2) appropriate terrain allowed for the immediate commencement of work, (3) investment opportunities existed for development, and (4) the information they had gathered would allow those of "different social milieu"—read "Jews"—to learn more about the island.[208] Lepecki's pointed refusal to mention Jews highlights the biased nature of the report. His enthusiastic assessment further indicated that between ten and fifteen thousand families, or between fifty and seventy thousand Jewish settlers, could be absorbed there.[209]

The Jewish delegates were less encouraged, despite Lepecki's claims of unanimity. They believed that settling Madagascar would be difficult due to the inhospitable climate, widespread malarial swamps, and astronomical expense involved in relocating immigrants. But the JDC's internal report on Alter's and Dyk's opinions noted that the two "did not deny that there are possibilities for group settlement."[210] The JDC document indicates that the central plateau would allow for the cultivation of rice, sweet potatoes, peanuts, tobacco, coffee, and fruit and almond trees.[211] The report further claims that "nearly all vegetables and flowers which are cultivated in Europe and especially in France" can be found in the central region.[212] The climate is described as "not absolutely tropical," but more "similar to that in Asia Minor, the [South African] Cape and California" and "could well serve as a colony for Europeans."[213] Recommendations that future settlements "ought to comprise at least 50 families" and that agro-industrial cooperatives be established appear to be drawn from Dyk's own views.[214] According to the JDC, "Jewish colonization in Madagascar may be possible in the form of a large colony to the South or to the North of the Central region."[215] Dyk's personal report from October 1937 suggests that the central plateau region could indeed support small numbers of European colonists.[216] He concludes, albeit inconclusively, that "all pertinent questions are still subject to investigation and many observations are still to be made."[217] Dyk also reported his findings to the director of *yishuv* land settlement efforts, sociologist Arthur Ruppin, who encouraged his colonization research.[218] While it may seem fanciful today to think that a Jewish colony might ever have flourished in Madagascar, Dyk, thanks to his efforts in Merchavia, knew that pioneers in Palestine had overcome equally daunting hardships in their settlement work.

Alter was more dismissive of the scheme than Dyk and the JDC. He recorded his indignant response to Lepecki's views in an independent Polish newspaper following his return because no government-aligned paper would allow him to give "the other side of the picture."[219] While Alter praised the "noble French utopian projects of resettlement," he railed against the "reactionary press"—in the form of Arkady Fiedler—who accompanied the Commission to beat the drum for Jewish emigration.[220] He sympathized with those Zionist groups who "saw a revival of Herzl's ideas regarding Uganda [and] Angola" in the evacuation plan to the "mysterious island"[221] of Madagascar. He also pointed to the fact that "[e]ven those groups that promoted Jewish territorialism"—presumably a reference to the Freeland League—"remained aloofly silent."[222] Alter conceded that "there are conditions for potential colonization in the [central] area located between 800–1000 meters above sea level,"[223] but that native elements would oppose Jewish settlement in this well-populated district. However, he grudgingly admitted that the northern plateau region "may be possible for colonization" if swamps were drained and a "road or railroad" could be built between the coast and the interior.[224] His calculations indicated that at most twenty-five hundred people could be resettled on island.[225] He believed that it would be "[e]specially difficult to convince the 'shtetl' Jews . . . to settle on the soil."[226] And in a private memorandum, Alter worried that the indigenous peoples' opposition would be "greater even than that of the Arabs against the Jews in Palestine."[227]

The Commission did indeed provoke fears in Tana's newspapers that "Jewish settlement would give rise to exploitation and unrest."[228] *La Voix de Madagascar* (*The Voice of Madagascar*) proclaimed that a "semitic invasion" would devour the colony, comparing the Jews to the plague of locusts visited upon the Egyptians.[229] *Le Journal de Madagascar* published an alarmist map indicating a massive area of proposed settlement.[230] Despite the Commission's mostly negative conclusions and the increasingly vocal opposition within Madagascar, Moutet continued to insist that Jewish immigration to the *Grand Île* remained "the object of favourable study."[231] But support waned among officials in France as criticism mounted.

Former governor general of Madagascar Marcel Olivier echoed Alter's pessimism, pronouncing the island no "land of asylum."[232] In the Parisian weekly *L'Illustration*, he recalled the frenzy in which "every party in Poland, with Mr. Jabotinsky, took hold of the idea: 'Evacuate the Jews.'"[233] Olivier pleaded with Jewish leaders not to allow themselves to "be seduced by the mirage" of Madagascar.[234] Drawing on his years of experience there, he cautioned against authorizing a "flood of immigration" to Madagascar, and warned that the inevitable high fatality rate of colonists would make Poland and France party to slaughter.[235] (As it turned out, both countries would soon have their Jews slaughtered nearer to home.) The French colony, Olivier continued, offers the "eternal wanderers of Israel . . . no such Canaan."[236] The article closes on a damning note: "exile on a high plateau of Madagascar . . . is nothing but a dream."[237] Warsaw's leading Yiddish newspaper, *Haynt* (*Today*), also tried to dampen enthusiasm. In an interview, a JDC powerbroker who had previously supported the plan now expressed the opinion that mass emigration to Madagascar or other French colonies was an impossibility.[238] Nonetheless, the notion continued to draw adherents, and French embassies were besieged by Jews desperate to emigrate to the island.[239]

The British followed these developments closely throughout 1937 and 1938. A long dispatch from the British ambassador to Poland describes the Lepecki mission and its controversial findings.[240] Press reports indicated that "several hundred young Polish Jews have expressed their readiness to leave for Madagascar to begin the pioneer work."[241] Colonial Secretary William Ormsby-Gore also sought to pressure the French to cede the "large, healthy, undeveloped and sparsely populated" colony of Madagascar for the benefit of the "wretched [and] hunted" Jewish people.[242] He believed that His Majesty's government's effort to "placate the Arabs" by limiting Jewish immigration to Palestine violated England's legal and ethical commitments as laid out in the Balfour Declaration.[243] "Now that the gates of Palestine are so very closed against them," he wrote, "Madagascar seems to me a chance."[244] Representatives of the British, French, and Dutch governments convened in London in December 1938 for a subcommittee of the Evian Conference, which had failed several months earlier to find sanctuaries for Jewish refugees fleeing Nazism. An official from the Netherlands discussed settlement possibilities in Dutch Guiana (Suriname). The British again raised East Africa as a potential destination. The French suggested that as many as ten thousand Jews might be relocated to the "central part of Madagascar."[245] But once more, the nations of the world failed to act.

Soon European Jewry was trapped by the Nazis and their collaborators. Europe became a land of smoking chimneys, a lost Jewish continent. So too was the "eighth continent" of Madagascar lost as a potential sanctuary. It is tantalizing to imagine that had Dyk and Alter been able to draw more sanguine conclusions from their expedition, Jewish organizations and European leaders might have mobilized to create a safe haven for Jews, who then might have survived the war in greater numbers. Perhaps some Jews could have waited out the war in tropical exile, homesteading in a strange land where comet moths unfold their nine-inch wings atop silver cocoons and lemurs dance in the treetops. As for Alter and Dyk, they both managed to escape the Nazis' net by fleeing to unoccupied France, though Dyk was later arrested by Vichy police.[246] Alfred Döblin too survived the war. His mathematician son, Wolfgang, enlisted in the French military and when his position was overrun by the Wehrmacht, he shot himself rather than be captured by the Nazis.[247] Döblin's spiritual mentor, Nathan Birnbaum, died before the Final Solution was implemented, but one of his sons was deported from the Netherlands and murdered in Auschwitz.[248]

In a perversion of the concept of Jewish rebirth and territorial autonomy,[249] the Nazis took up the abandoned Madagascar plan. Madagascar was to become, in Adolf Hitler's diplomatic parlance, a "reservation,"[250] or, as scholars have termed it, a "super-ghetto."[251] There was to be no autonomy for the Jews; Nazi ideologue Alfred Rosenberg feared that "the Jews would use it only as a world center in which to carry on machinations."[252] The proposal,[253] endorsed at various stages by Heinrich

Himmler and then by Hitler himself, called for Europe's deported Jews to become "residents of the Mandate of Madagascar."[254] Hitler noted his interest in Madagascar both to Mussolini and his grand admiral, Erich Raeder, just days before the formal French surrender. Raeder recorded in his diary that the "Führer wants to use Madagascar for the placement of Jews under French jurisdiction."[255] The Nazi leadership's head of "Jewish affairs," Franz Rademacher, worked out details of the plan in the summer of 1940. He called for a kind of reservation to be established on the island, where "the Jews will have their own administration . . . their own mayors, police, postal and railroad."[256] But, he was clear, the Jews of Madagascar would be subject to the whims of the "German Police Governor, who will be under the administration of the *Reichsführer SS*."[257] Later, Adolf Eichmann was tasked with sketching out the plan's logistics, leading to his outrageous claim at his postwar trial in Israel that he had always been a Zionist sympathizer who desperately wanted to provide Jews with "soil under their feet."[258] He submitted a detailed report to his superiors in 1940 describing the "Madagaskar-Projekt." At first, Jews from Austria and Germany would be forced to emigrate,[259] but four million Jews were ultimately to be resettled there over the course of four years.[260] According to Eichmann's report, "The overall administration of the Jewish State will be in the hands of the Chief of the Security Police and the Security Service."[261] The island's interior would be turned into a vast prison for the deported.[262]

How did the Nazis plan to ship millions of Jews halfway around the world to their tropical police state? By forcing a defeated Britain to open sea routes and turn over the Royal Navy for transport.[263] And American Jewish organizations, it seems, were to foot the bill. The Gestapo sent a German Jewish academic to the United States to solicit funds to support the plan in 1940; wisely, he didn't return to the Reich.[264] Once the Jews were interned on the island far from Western eyes, the Nazis would be free to do as they pleased with them—perhaps as a prelude to their extermination. The Madagascar Plan was to be the Nazis' "penultimate solution."[265] Until the winter of 1941–1942, at least some in the Nazi hierarchy seriously pursued it. But no Jews ever arrived. The British invasion of the island in 1942, code-named Operation Ironclad, rendered the scheme permanently unworkable. The linchpin of the British assault was the capture of Madagascar's northernmost city, Diego

Suarez, whose deepwater port the Nazis had hoped to turn into a strategic naval base.[266]

Turning of the Bones

Diego Suarez is humid and smells of the sea. The humdrum reality of the city belies its fantastic past. In Defoe's tales of Libertalia, the port becomes the pirate redoubt of Captain Mission, who settles there "to fortify and raise a small Town" where his brigand-socialists might retire to "enjoy the Fruits of their Labour, and go to their Graves in Peace."[267] The battered concrete portal to the city's airport still bears the French Air Force insignia from its colonial past. Just beyond the terminal, the rusted ribs of a World War II–era hangar rise over rows of palm trees. Squatters string their laundry up beneath the hangar's skeletal shell. Along the side of the rutted main road to the city center, women dressed in cheerful printed fabrics sell sticky vanilla beans at ramshackle stands. Blooms of bougainvillea spill over fences along Diego's boulevards. At night, the city is often plunged into darkness when the power cuts out. Crowds then wander through the dark streets and enjoy the briny breeze sweeping in from the harbor. On clear nights, the Southern Cross hangs overhead and you can watch the lights of distant ships blink along the bay's horizon.

In the early morning hours of May 5, 1942, Royal Navy vessels cruised into this same channel, taking the French forces by surprise and dealing Vichy a strategic blow.[268] A few kilometers southeast of Diego, a British war cemetery holds the remains of 314 combatants who died in Operation Ironclad and the subsequent occupation of Madagascar. The caretaker, a spry, gray-haired man, shoos away a chicken scratching for food on the trim lawn. The Commonwealth War Graves Commission keeps the grounds in immaculate condition. Ruler-straight rows of graves stretch out between manicured flower beds and the shade of tamarind trees. The order and symmetry are jarring amidst the haphazard poverty that encroaches on the cemetery. Markers for fallen British soldiers are carved with crosses, but the many tombstones with East African names are otherwise blank. Some are chiseled with Arabic, a few soldiers appear to have been Hindu. Amidst the hardened grief of these headstones, several rows from the front and shadowed by a stunted baobab, stands a single grave with a Jewish star. The inscription records the final resting place of Captain Israel S. Genussow, age twenty-eight, who died July 30, 1944. I happened upon his grave precisely sixty-three years later. The worn Hebrew inscription indicates that Genussow "fell on the battlefield to liberate his people and his land." But which people? The Malagasy? Which land? England? Wherever home was for Captain Genussow, it was far away from this quiet patch of green on the out-skirts of a town at the end of the world.

More than three thousand miles away, Israel Genussow's youngest brother, Herzl, still lives in a sleepy neighborhood of the coastal Israeli city of Netanya. Multistory white apartment blocks spring from the sandy soil surrounded by palm trees and tidy gardens. The climate is not that much different from Diego Suarez's. The shaded stairwell up to Herzl's apartment stays cool even on the stickiest of summer days. A tall man with a broad chest and a shock of white hair, Herzl moves with a vigor that belies his more than eighty years. His wife, Rachel, boils water for tea and serves a slice of apple cake with a dainty fork to the stranger who shows up on their doorstep asking to pry open memories sealed for more than six decades. My meeting with them is a kind of *famadihana*.

"What can I say?" Herzl asks, switching from Hebrew into a sharp South African English undulled by lack of use. He clasps an album of black-and-white snapshots as he narrates the story of Israel's life. "My brother was an excellent student, brilliant, an athlete, handsome." Let-ters from those who knew him all attest to Israel's generosity and intel-ligence. His army buddies called him "Spinach" because of his physical strength.[269] But I want to know more about his brother. I want to know how he came to take part in Operation Ironclad, and thus played a role in denying the Nazis their Jewish reservation on the island.

"Our father was a Zionist in South Africa," Herzl explains, his clear voice booming like a thump on a hollow wall. "He grew wealthy from diamond mining. Where we lived we played with diamonds the way other kids played with marbles. And people would come for miles to hear us speak Hebrew. We were curiosities from the Bible." Later, the family moved to Palestine, where their mother, the niece of Solomon Schechter, had grown up. So not only was Captain Genussow Jewish, he was also a member of the *yishuv*. When World War II broke out,

Israel was a student in England. He volunteered for the British military, a decision Jabotinsky would surely have approved of. Soon the young Genussow found himself shipped out to India, then Kenya, and ultimately to Madagascar. There he drilled East African troops during the British occupation. A single stray bullet squeezed off during a training exercise on Tisha B'Av, the traditional day of Jewish mourning, ended his life. His last letter home recorded that his only regret had been that he had not played a "more active role in the war against the enemy."[270]

"Do you think your brother knew about the Nazi plans for Madagascar?"

"I don't know," Herzl responds with melancholy, "all I know is that he wanted to fight for his country."

Which country?

"Ours!" Herzl is frustrated by the question and a gulf opens between us.

Rachel clears crumbs from the table with the edge of her hand. "I grew up in Poland," she interjects to fill the silence. "As a girl I had to keep my voice down, be polite everywhere, on the bus or in the park, so people wouldn't point at the 'noisy Jew.'" Her eyes mist over, her voice shakes and trails off. "And you know what happened there . . . "

Herzl, his voice grown softer, picks up her story. "But here we're like everybody else, here we can be just as bad as every other country."

Is that what his brother fought and died for, to protect his old-new homeland so it could be just like every other place? They both turn to look at each other, stunned by the impertinence of the question. Then they answer at the same time: "No."

Herzl sighs and fiddles with his hearing aid. The photo album rests open at a picture of Israel in uniform, his moustache neatly trimmed, round spectacles slimming his youthful face. Herzl shakes his head at the loss of his brother so long ago, his brother who forever remains a young man. He shakes his head at the history that never was, his brother's lost future, and stares out the window toward the Mediterranean and beyond, off to his brother's tomb an ocean away, a Crusoe marooned on an island without Jews.

"But here at least," Herzl says, and raps his knuckles on the table, "here, here is home."

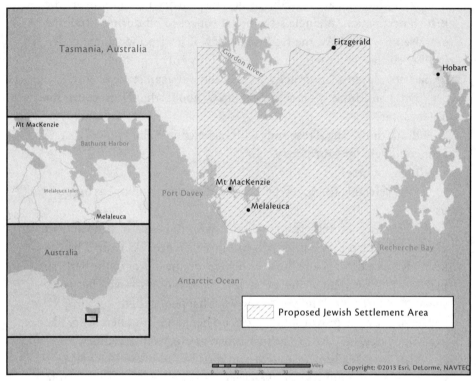

Tasmania

5

New Jerusalem, Down Under

Port Davey, Tasmania (1940–1945)

Kangaroo Messiah

In 1933, a clean-shaven forty-year-old Yiddish writer left his home in Poland to travel alone through the Australian continent's vast emptiness.[1] His wife and two young children remained behind in Warsaw. In the outback, the urbane author wore his trousers held high above his waist by suspenders, a pith helmet tilted rakishly against the sun, and kangaroo-skin boots.[2] He kicked his way through the dusty lanes of an Aboriginal reserve one morning and there encountered a "full-blooded black boy"[3] who begged him for candy. Perhaps thinking of his own son a world away, the man swept the child up in his arms. "Your murderer is holding you," he wrote, "and the lolly he has given you and which you are sucking with such pleasure is your poison."[4] The author of these words was poet, editor, and journalist Melech Ravitch (Zekharye-Khone Bergner).

Ravitch stood at the center of Jewish literary life in interwar Poland. His deeply personal yet socially engaged verse had made him one of the most important voices of Yiddish Modernism in the 1920s. As executive secretary of the Association of Jewish Writers and Journalists, Melech Ravitch saw his influence grow thanks to his tireless advocacy on behalf of Yiddish authors, nearly all of whom found their way to the Association's Warsaw headquarters on 13 Tłomackie Street for moral or financial support. But as antisemitism in Poland intensified, Ravitch lost faith in a Jewish future in Europe. He repeatedly advised his fellow

writers: "Listen to me—get out of here!"[5] His former literary collaborator, poet Uri Zvi Greenberg, believed the future lay in Palestine writing Hebrew verse in support of Ze'ev Jabotinsky's Revisionist Zionism,
while Ravitch's political commitments expressed themselves in the form
of a romantic attachment to the "idea or ideal"[6] of territorialism.

Ravitch sailed for Australia in the summer of 1933, ostensibly on a
fundraising mission for beleaguered Jewish schools in Poland.[7] His real
intention, however, was to find in that far-flung land of "Jules Verne–
legend"[8] free territory for mass Jewish immigration.[9] Referencing biblical tales of agents sent by Moses and Joshua to reconnoiter Israel,
Ravitch considered himself a spy reporting back to his distant Yiddish
readers on colonization possibilities in Australia's Northern Territory.[10]
Ravitch traveled by train from Australia's south coast through outback
wilderness to the desert town of Alice Springs, the geographic center of
the island continent: the middle of nowhere. Despite the bleak scenery
and privations, he seemed to enjoy himself. In a photograph taken during his journey he grins as he poses with an Aboriginal woman. She
stands stiffly next to him as he leans against a corrugated metal shack.
Ravitch's bow tie is askew and he looks ludicrously out of place beside
the barefoot woman in her threadbare dress.[11] When the railroad tracks
ended, he bounced north for several days in an open mail truck along
dirt roads. He proceeded to the sleepy territorial capital of Darwin and
there acquainted himself with unemployed locals, union leaders, and
government officials. They offered the curious Polish stranger business
deals—a "shipload of mother of pearl, the establishment of an ice factory, the financing of a goldmine"[12]—but he was interested in a slice of
the Northern Territory's half million square miles, a land that could
"flow with milk and honey," he wrote.[13]

He knew that Australian leaders had long wanted to populate the
region, and that Australia's "whites only" immigration policy[14] meant
that Jews had a chance to secure immigration visas. Ravitch thought
the tropical climate bearable and he learned that with proper water
management agriculture could flourish in the hot, dry north.[15] He concluded that a settlement of as many as one hundred thousand refugees
might thrive there.[16] Furthermore, in an apparent jab at Zionist activity in Palestine, he believed that "[t]he Northern Territory is a land
which will not be taken from any original population whatever; in that

respect one's conscience can be quite peaceful."[17] Of course, the Aborigines had already been driven from their land, a fact of which Ravitch was certainly aware after he had visited their miserable compound near Darwin.[18]

Ravitch's optimistic reports from Australia's distant shores echoed in Poland's Yiddish press. He filed feature stories about his expedition, which appeared between 1933 and 1934 in Warsaw's *Naye Folkstsaytung* (*New People's Paper*).[19] At the end of 1934, while he was completing his travels, he published an article in the second issue of *Frayland*, the organ of the nascent Freeland League. His article argued that there was nothing fantastic about Jewish colonization schemes, whether they aimed to create a "Jewish-Uganda," a "Jewish-Angola," or a settlement in Australia.[20] The *Frayland* journal enjoyed only a small circulation among Yiddishist intellectuals, and Ravitch's ideas seemed to garner little attention.[21] But by 1936, he was writing vehement letters to his literary colleagues, announcing with finality: "All Jews should leave Poland and pull up the very stones from the graves and bring them with them."[22] A young Isaac Bashevis Singer credited Ravitch with coaxing him[23] to emigrate, though he left Warsaw for New York.

In 1937, Ravitch's newspaper dispatches were collected in a modest travelogue, *Iber Oystralye* (*Across Australia*), which contained the outline for his dream of a Jewish sanctuary in the Northern Territory. His readers enjoyed cheerful descriptions of "the land being proposed with great seriousness for large-scale Jewish mass immigration."[24] However, by the time of that volume's appearance, Ravitch seems to have abandoned any grand schemes for a mass exodus in favor of personal survival. He wisely arranged for his teenage son, and later his wife and daughter, to join him in Melbourne as war loomed. His son, Yosl Bergner, went on to become a major figure in the Australian and Israeli art scenes. During his initial tour of Australia in 1933, Ravitch wrote "Aborigines—A Ballad of Doom" (*Aboridgin—Untergang-Balad*),[25] surely the first, and perhaps only, Yiddish verse about Australia's native people. His son, Yosl, later claimed to have been "the first painter in Australia to depict Aborigines" because he believed they had been "persecuted exactly like the Jews."[26] The fates of these two persecuted and dispossessed peoples—Aborigines and Jews—were to echo one another in even more remarkable ways as Europe prepared to plunge into war.

While Ravitch made his way across the great "Australian endless-ness,"[27] the situation for the Reich's Jews grew more and more unten-able. Officials in Poland called for a method of ridding the country of its "excess" Jewish population.[28] Jews fleeing these antisemitic diktats sought sanctuary wherever they could. The Freeland League focused on Australia as a destination for refugees from the Reich and beyond. Israel Zangwill's ITO had discussed settling Jews in Western Australia as early as 1906.[29] The origin of Zangwill's Australia plans was Dr. Rich-ard Arthur, president of the Immigration League of Australia. Arthur urged the ITO to consider "a Jewish colony somewhere in the vast Aus-tralian continent rather than in East Africa."[30] A published version of his proposal made its way to England, and the two men soon began a correspondence directed at leveraging their political contacts.[31] After years of little progress, a prominent half-page advertisement touting the resources of Western Australia and its massive size—equal to "eight Englands, eight Scotlands, eight Irelands, and eight Wales"—appeared in the *Times* and provoked Zangwill to further action.[32] He wrote to Australian prime minister Newton J. Moore reproaching him that "the development of one of these thirty-two countries by an industrious persecuted people could do no harm to the other thirty-one!"[33] When Moore and Western Australia's premier came to London in 1911, they met with Zangwill[34] but no agreement was forthcoming and Zangwill, as we know, turned the ITO's attentions to Angola.

But Melech Ravitch's enthusiasm over Australia as a possible site for mass Jewish settlement helped rekindle the *Fraylandistn's* interest in an antipodean colony. The London office of the Freeland League received dispatches from Ravitch, who assured members that "there were excel-lent possibilities" to obtain "considerable tracts" in the Northern Ter-ritory.[35] Freeland leaders soon directed their energy to acquiring the privately held lease to a 10,800-square-mile[36] territory—equivalent to seven million acres—in the Kimberley region of northwestern Austra-lia.[37] The extensive holdings were being sold by Michael Patrick Durack, a rancher who had lived in the region for more than a half century.[38] He wrote to the Freelanders to assure them that the Kimberley, "with its soil, its assured rainfall and large natural river water supplies, is capable of the fullest development and will reasonably respond in proportion to the energy and efficiency of labour exercised in its development."[39]

Durack offered his land, approximately fifty thousand head of cattle, as well as two homesteads and several additional buildings for the sum of 180,000 pounds sterling (approximately twelve million dollars in 2012).[40] Unfortunately, the *Fraylandistn's* finances were in the red, and they recognized that they "remained an esoteric group of thirty or forty people" who were not "taken seriously."[41] Yet somehow the Freeland League—a young, poorly understood, and cash-strapped organiza-tion—found itself conducting high-level negotiations for a vast swathe of territory nearly the size of Belgium.

A central plank in the Freeland platform was the organized mass colonization of an area other than Palestine that was "uninhabited or scarcely populated so as to avoid competition with the native popula-tion."[42] The Kimberley was indeed sparsely populated, with the best estimates recording a "total white population" under seven thousand in 1938; as an afterthought it was noted that "[t]here is also a black popula-tion."[43] The Paris Freeland branch had successfully lobbied the minister of overseas France, Marius Moutet, to support Jewish immigration to Madagascar and other underpopulated French territories in 1936;[44] two years later the League's London office hoped they could duplicate this diplomatic achievement with ministers in Whitehall. The British Jewish establishment, however, distrusted the Freelanders. The president of the Anglo-Jewish Association feared that the League's interest in Australia would become another failed "Madagascar scheme."[45] Nonetheless, the Freeland League had managed to attract a host of British notables to its cause, including several members of parliament, one of whom was David Lloyd George's son.[46] With powerful names lending gravity to their movement, the Freelanders were able to meet with Australian offi-cials visiting London in 1938 to discuss chartering a settlement on the Durack family holdings.[47]

In the run-up to the International Refugees Conference held at Evian in July 1938, a score of organizations, including the Freeland League, prepared to represent Jewish interests to the more than thirty nations who were to convene in France. The aim of the Evian Conference was to find sanctuaries for Jews displaced by Nazism. Some Zionist leaders, like Menachem Ussishkin and Zionist Organization president Chaim Weizmann, fretted that the powers assembled at Evian would treat Pal-estine as only one possible destination for refugees.[48] They were right;

neither man attended the conference. Freeland leaders, taking advantage of the absence of influential Zionists, pushed their agenda to the British. Later, Weizmann would attack the territorialists as anti-Zionist "advocates of . . . utopias who gathered on the fringe of the Conference."[49] The *Fraylandistn*, however, drafted a well-reasoned memorandum aimed at defusing Whitehall's anxieties over Jewish demands for Palestine. "The immediate possibilities of Palestine . . . fall far short of the pressing needs for emigration," the authors lectured Evian's delegates, but "[e]mpty spaces suitable for colonisation on a large scale still exist within the British Empire."[50] Australia, then still a dominion of the United Kingdom, was not mentioned by name. But given the high-level contact between the Freelanders and various Australian representatives in the preceding months, the distant continent must have been near to their thoughts.[51] In the failed aftermath of Evian—of all the countries attending, only the Dominican Republic agreed to accept Jewish emigrants in any significant number—the Freelanders resolved to send an emissary to investigate the Kimberley region of Western Australia. There they hoped to establish political contacts and launch a public relations campaign in support of their colonization program.[52] International Freeland League Council and London Executive Committee member Dr. Isaac Nachman Steinberg got the job.[53]

Steinberg is one of the most important Jewish figures of the twentieth century you've probably never heard of. He was a Russian-born social revolutionary, intellectual, Yiddishist, author, and orthodox Jew. Virtually no one remembers him today, but until his death in 1957, he was revered by his loyal partisans and reviled by just about everyone else, especially those in the Zionist establishment who attacked him in print and plotted against him behind his back. They objected to Steinberg's tireless efforts on behalf of the Freeland League to rescue European Jews and resettle them somewhere beyond *Eretz Israel*. For his part, Steinberg protested the "state-fanaticism" that he felt was "characteristic for Zionists."[54] One of Steinberg's few Zionist defenders was Jabotinsky, who praised Steinberg's dogged work on behalf of European Jewry in his final published testament, *The Jewish War Front* (1940). Steinberg himself was astonished by the ultra-nationalist leader's praise.[55] And though Jabotinsky believed that Steinberg's efforts were doomed to failure, the Revisionist leader lauded him for his "calm obstinacy"[56] and "timely common sense"[57] in exploring Australia as a sanctuary for Jewish refugees from Hitler's Europe. The right-wing Jabotinsky and the leftist Steinberg shared a common adversary, Labor Zionism, and a common aim: to save Jewish lives.

Steinberg stood five feet, eight inches in height,[58] had a broad forehead, wavy hair, and rheumy brown eyes,[59] and sported a well-groomed, ginger-colored[60] beard. His son, the late art historian Leo Steinberg, recalled: "When I was a child and would draw, I would look up at [my father's] face at the dinner table and think it the most beautiful face in the world."[61] Noted psychologist Erich Fromm hailed him as a visionary realist.[62] Two Nobel laureates, Norman Angell and Thomas Mann, publicly supported his work.[63] His own Freeland colleagues compared him to Theodor Herzl.[64] And like Herzl, Steinberg was a journalist, playwright, and publicist.

During the period of instability that followed the abortive Russian revolution of 1905, Steinberg was arrested in Moscow for anticzarist activities. When offered early release from a Russian prison, he refused to sign his name on a Jewish holy day and so remained behind bars.[65] He was exiled to Germany for three years, and in Heidelberg received a doctorate for his study of criminal law in the Talmud.[66] Steinberg returned to Russia in 1910 armed with a legal degree and rose to become a leading figure in the non-Marxist Left-Social Revolutionary Party. In 1911, he was groomed to take a role in the defense of Menachem Beilis, a Jewish man accused of the "ritual murder" of a Ukrainian youth.[67] Following the 1917 Revolution, Steinberg became Lenin's first commissar of justice. He remained religiously observant during this period and would pray in the middle of cabinet meetings called by Lenin. "He had very discreet ways of doing it," his son remembered. "He would get up as if to stretch his legs, lean, and cover his head with his hand. But you knew he was silently running through the prayers, which he knew by heart. He never missed it."[68] Steinberg "took it for granted that Judaism would not be in conflict" with his brand of ethical socialism.[69] But he failed in his bid to reform the Bolsheviks and resigned in March 1918.[70] He also failed to prevent Lenin's political terror and his butchery of the regime's critics, and was himself twice arrested.[71]

Steinberg fled Soviet Russia for Berlin in 1923 with his wife and two children. There he claimed, not entirely accurately, that he "withdrew from all political activities" and turned his attention to history, philosophy, and literature.[72] He was instrumental in establishing the YIVO Institute for Jewish Research in Berlin during this time, and he lectured at 13 Tłomackie Street, where Melech Ravitch held court in Warsaw.[73] Steinberg's German-language play *Der Dornenweg* (*The Thorny Path*) won the city of Bremen's Goethe Prize in 1927.[74] The play dramatized the dilemmas Steinberg had faced under Lenin through the quasi-autobiographical character of Alexander Ivanovitch. Ivanovitch, a lawyer, naïvely believes that as a revolutionary commissar he will "give justice to the world."[75] He grows impatient when his ideals are called utopian,[76] and fumes when others cannot see a better future as within reach.[77] Ultimately, he becomes complicit in state-sanctioned terror. Steinberg himself maintained a passionate commitment to nonviolence, but his first-hand knowledge of the abuses of power left him with few illusions. He wrote another play on the theme, *Du hast gesiegt, Mochnatschow!* (*You Have Triumphed, Mochntaschow!*), in 1928.[78] That drama depicted the October Revolution and the descent of Lenin (Mochnatschow) into totalitarian rule. Steinberg's "facto-montage"— a rebuke of autocracy—had its premiere in Barcelona in July 1937, on the evening of the one-year anniversary of the outbreak of the Spanish Civil War.[79]

After the Nazis consolidated their hold over Germany, they targeted intellectuals for arrest and intimidation. Steinberg was among those they sought, but he was in London presenting a series of lectures when they came for him.[80] His family fled under cover of night and made their way to England to join him.[81] Once resettled in London, Steinberg's vitality, organizational skills, and charisma launched him into his new role as a pivotal member of the Freeland League, with which he and Melech Ravitch had been associated from the group's very first publications in 1934.[82] It was Steinberg who had drafted Alfred Döblin into the Freeland ranks and had his work translated into Yiddish.[83] And like Ravitch, Steinberg continued to function as an advocate for Yiddish culture. In 1937, he served as the Yiddish-language representative to the Fifteenth PEN Congress. Steinberg warned his PEN colleagues that Poland's poisonous antisemitic atmosphere would spell an end to that country's independence.[84] One of the PEN representatives from Palestine, poet Shaul Tchernichovsky, considered it a brave oration.[85]

Steinberg, for his part, dismissed Tchernichovsky as sounding like a Hebrew-speaking *goy*.[86]

At the first meeting of the Freeland League Central Committee for Great Britain in 1935, Steinberg was appointed to the group's propaganda committee.[87] Later, he reported on Freeland activities in Warsaw and Paris, and noted that the Portuguese government had no interest in reviving a version of Zangwill's ITO plan for Angola.[88] In early 1939, the British Freelanders informed the League's Central Committee that negotiations were proceeding for the Durack property, and urged the dispatch of "a delegation to Australia for political negotiations and to investigate the areas suggested by experts."[89] Steinberg was the natural choice to represent Freeland interests. His fellow *Fraylandistn* believed that his leftist pedigree, cosmopolitan background, and charm would sway the powerful leaders of Australia's labor unions to support a mass colonization project in the remote and forbidding Kimberley. As for Steinberg, he sought a Jewish Freeland down under in part to rescue his brethren from the Nazi menace, and in part to redeem the crushed ideals of the Soviet Revolution.

He docked in Perth on Australia's west coast in May 1939[90] and set off in early June on a trip of more than two thousand miles to the "magic land of Kimberley" in the tropical northwest.[91] The thermometer read ninety degrees Fahrenheit[92] when he and agricultural scientist G. F. Melville arrived in the midst of the antipodean autumn. He described passing through "thickets of trees, plants and grass so fragrant and cheerful" that he imagined himself "on some exquisitely cultivated English estate."[93] He rested in the shady "tabernacles . . . [of] ageless, broadbellied bottle-trees" and marveled at the "mile upon mile" of fertile soil that reminded him of the coveted "Russian *chernoziom*, 'black earth.'"[94] Kangaroos bounded past.[95] Tens of thousands of white cockatoos circled overhead.[96] A photo of Steinberg taken during the expedition depicts him dressed in a light-colored suit and tie, his face shaded by a white sun hat.[97] Behind him flows the Ord River, which excited prophetic reverie: "No need here to resort to the miracle of Moses and strike water from a stone for an unbelieving flock. . . . Let but the hands of science and experience . . . and [the] determination of Jewish labour . . . awaken this dormant earth."[98] He gazed out at the landscape burning beneath a "fiery sun" and imagined that the Kimberley would "transform the

European Jew physically" and even diminish Jewish "nervousness and anxiety."[99] The future immigrant poets of Australia would "write Jewish poems about the kangaroo or the laughing kookaburra . . . [y]et their voice would be the voice of Israel."[100] To Steinberg, the Kimberley offered a combination of English stately garden and Russian peasant homestead, mixed with a heady dose of biblical *Eretz Israel.*

Steinberg and Melville prepared a detailed report for the government of Western Australia after their return from the Kimberley.[101] The authors suggested that future crops include maize, rice, jute, hemp, mango, and passion fruit.[102] They proposed establishing cattle ranches[103] as well as tanneries, workshops to weave carpets from angora goat wool, dairies, and canneries.[104] Steinberg imagined a privately funded settlement of between fifty and seventy-five thousand refugees to be organized and implemented by the Freeland League.[105] The magnetic Freeland emissary had meanwhile attracted the support of politicians, publishers, clergymen, and union bosses.[106] And on August 25, Western Australia's once-skeptical premier approved the Freeland proposal subject to certain conditions.[107] But Steinberg's stunning diplomatic victory was short lived. Exactly one week later, the Nazi blitzkrieg decimated Poland and Europe plunged into war. Though more urgent than ever, the Freeland proposal for a Jewish sanctuary in the Kimberley was put on hold. Steinberg was trapped while the war raged, a stateless man pursuing a phantom Zion for his *landsmen* being annihilated on the other side of the globe.

Steinberg's efforts to rally Jewish Australians to the Freeland cause introduced him to a remarkable young journalist, Caroline Isaacson. She edited the "Women's Page" of the left-leaning Melbourne daily *The Age*, and was active in the resettlement and education of Jewish refugees. Born in 1900 in Vienna, the vivacious Isaacson spoke French and German, and was given a pet name, Lynka, by a governess as a child.[108] In London after World War I, Isaacson married an Australian soldier almost twenty years her senior. She and her husband, Arnold, went on to have two children. A woman of self-confessed "mercurial temperament,"[109] Isaacson felt her husband belittled her volunteer work and professional aspirations.[110] Her impersonal marriage was a "great grief" to her, though she took solace in the "complete bond of understanding" she had with her children, Peter and Joan.[111]

In March 1940, she wrote to Steinberg to ask him the provocative question: "Would it be possible to change from Kimberley?"[112] Isaacson soon met Steinberg in her small office in Melbourne's central business district to discuss the future of the now stalled Kimberley Plan.[113] The journalist offered Steinberg a scoop, confiding to him that another corner of Australia was ripe for settlement, a paradise with a "wonderful climate" and "few people": Tasmania.[114]

Even though Tasmania had been suggested for colonization during the course of the Durack negotiations,[115] the idea still came as a surprise to Steinberg,[116] who worried about diverting attention from his activities in the northwest. But the slender, attractive, blue-eyed Isaacson charmed him, and he agreed to learn more about the history and potential of Tasmania.

Fatal Shore

Tasmania is the land down under the land down under. The smallest of Australia's six states, the island is about the size of Ireland and lies 150 miles from the mainland. Tasmania's meager population and lack of industrial development make it a relatively unspoiled Eden. But Tassie, as locals call it, also possesses a lurid past as a brutal penal colony, and it was the site of what some consider to be a genocide against its Aboriginal inhabitants. Dutch explorer Abel Tasman set out to find *terra australis incognita*—the unknown southern land—in 1642. At the time, many believed in the existence of a mythical temperate continent rich in gold located at the bottom of the known world. Abel Tasman couldn't find what didn't exist, but he did discover a forested island he named Van Diemen's Land, after a Dutch official. Great Britain claimed Van Diemen's Land in 1803, and focused a host of settlement schemes on the territory. Various groups and individuals put forward proposals to establish progressive collectives there throughout the nineteenth century.[117] All ended in failure.

Like many utopian dreams, the reality of Van Diemen's Land descended into nightmare. Abel's sylvan island became a dumping ground for those bearing the mark of Cain. Until 1853, Van Diemen's Land served as a penal colony for criminals transported from England. The first miserable vessels sailing to the island spent from three to four months at sea.[118] Slave ships that had once made the Middle Passage now carried British prisoners in chains[119] to Van Diemen's Land's "fatal shore."[120] Inmates faced a grim life of servitude, dank cells, and corporal punishment when they arrived in the police state. Those who reformed themselves through good behavior could be granted a ticket of leave enabling them to make a new life in the colony. Through the first half of the nineteenth century, a majority of the islanders were or had been transported convicts.[121]

One Londoner who was not a convict, George Augustus Robinson, arrived in Tasmania in 1824 and soon established himself as a "hard-working and public-spirited man."[122] Robinson, a builder, was of average height for his day,[123] wore a wavy-haired wig,[124] and had a doughy face and a prominent nose.[125] He lacked formal education but was an avid reader of travelogues and novels.[126] The most significant literary influence on his character was surely the Bible. There are few hints in the first years of his residency in Hobart that Robinson would soon vault himself into the position of the Aborigines' savior. But after years of skirmishes between tribesmen and the white settlers, the devout Robinson applied to the colony's equally devout lieutenant governor, George Arthur, to "ameliorate the condition of the aboriginal inhabitants."[127] He was a sensitive man, unusual in his day for recognizing that the Aborigines were human beings "made after the express image of God."[128] At one point, Robinson records that he "imagined himself an aborigine"[129] and broke down and wept in the grip of his humanist vision: "God has made of one blood all nations of people and I am not ashamed to call them brothers. . . . [Yet] [w]e have imported into this land, which . . . flows with milk and honey, the wickedness of three kingdoms."[130] For Robinson, Tasmania was a promised land despoiled by Christian hypocrisy.

He was an astute critic of colonialism as well, decrying the fact that "the leading principle in founding colonies, not only by the English but by every civilized nation on the face of the globe" meant that "the rights of the original inhabitants were never thought of."[131] At the time, Aborigines were kidnapped, enslaved, raped, sold into prostitution, forced to eat their own flesh,[132] shot out of trees for sport,[133] had their fingers cut off and made into tobacco stoppers,[134] and after death were dismembered for "scientific" study.[135] Robinson wanted to abolish what he considered to be Tasmania's "African slave trade in miniature" [136] and rescue the Aborigines from the sadistic injustices they suffered at the hands of whites. His journals reveal his conviction that God had sent him to save his "sable companions," as he often referred to them, "for their moral, religious and material improvement."[137] Between 1830 and 1834, Robinson undertook six grueling missions to tribes in all corners of Tasmania as the Aborigines' appointed "conciliator." His expedition parties mostly consisted of Aborigines whose trust he had gained and who guided him to tribal grounds across the island.

In February 1830, Robinson's first mission took him to Port Davey. His goal: to pacify a local tribe suspected of mounting raids against white settlers. He looked over the inhospitable southwest and saw "mountains rising upon mountains to a great altitude," valleys covered with "impenetrable thickets,"[138] and "immense chasms through which the water was heard to gush with frightful roar, mountain tops hid in the clouds."[139] After more than a month of strenuous efforts, he had still failed to contact the Port Davey natives. Finally, after six weeks of wandering, several tribesmen approached him.

"They were fine looking men," Robinson recorded, "about five feet nine inches in height and several of them six feet, well proportioned, broad shouldered, their features resembling that of the European, intelligent countenances, and the beard like that of the Poland Jew, growing long and to a point."[140] Robinson had come to find Edenic man, but instead he came face to face with a visage that reminded him of the rag-trade Jews he must have seen in London's street markets. Convict artist William Buelow Gould drew a contemporary portrait of one of the kangaroo-skin clad Port Davey men Robinson described. The pencil portrait of the chief, Towterer, depicts him as a thin man in a loose-fitting robe with a scraggly beard.[141] His broad, furrowed brow recedes from oversized eyes. Towterer's wooly hair is styled in a kind of tonsure that at first glance does make it seem as if he is wearing a yarmulke. Otherwise, Robinson's description of the Aborigines' supposed Polish Jewish features seems exaggerated.

The Aborigines protected their protector in his wanderings across the unmapped wilderness from coast to coast, over snowy peaks, along jagged coastline, and through dense forest. Robinson kept detailed journals while in the bush that preserve some of the few trustworthy accounts of native life, language, song, dance, and beliefs. He continued to crisscross the island to contact the various tribes and succeeded in gaining their confidence, though he increasingly used deceit to do so.[142] His aim was twofold: to convince the tribes to end their raids against the colonists of Van Diemen's Land, and to force the settlers to cease their rampages against the Aborigines. Once he had convinced a tribe that he was a "good white man,"[143] they would introduce him to other tribes, and he worked systematically in this way to remove the island's hunter-gatherers to a sedentary settlement away from hostile white populations. He believed that by transforming their culture, he would redeem their lives and their souls.

Robinson set out to become the Aborigines' Moses, but ended as their Pharaoh. He led them from their homelands into bondage. After he completed the resettlement of the Aborigines to a reservation on Flinders Island off the northeastern coast of Tasmania, his charges succumbed to tuberculosis, influenza, pneumonia, and other diseases to which they had little resistance.[144] They began to die in such large numbers at the Flinders Island settlement that Robinson's Aboriginal friends asked whether he intended "to stay till all the black men are dead."[145] A little over forty years after their forced exodus had come to an end, the last full-blooded Tasmanian Aboriginal died in 1876.[146] Her name was Trugernanna. As a teenager, she had accompanied Robinson on his first Port Davey expedition and had remained loyal to him throughout his career, though she herself had been called a traitor by the last remnants of her people.[147]

That Aboriginal hunting grounds in Tasmania were proposed as a refuge for Europe's Jews during the Holocaust is a cruel irony. For most Tasmanians today, Aborigines are an absent presence. Their memory is debased in Hobart's craft market where stalls hawk rag doll "golliwogs" that caricature Aboriginal features with googly eyes, thick red lips, black fabric skin, and coiled string hair. Similarly, in Polish towns where Jewish life has been all but blotted out of existence, hand-carved wooden figurines of big-nosed, caftan-clad, money-grubbing Jews sell briskly as totems of prosperity.[148] The Aboriginal ways of life that Robinson recorded have vanished; the vibrant Yiddish culture that Steinberg had hoped to preserve on Aboriginal lands has all but disappeared as well. The pasts of both peoples have become memorialized as tourist gimcracks.

Refugees as Pioneers

Isaacson arranged for Steinberg to meet with the moving force behind the Tasmania scheme, a young Christian gentleman named Critchley Parker Junior, whom she had befriended. Critchley, the only child of a wealthy Melbourne family, was a brooding twenty-nine-year-old. In the single extant photo of Critchley as an adult, a sepia-toned portrait, he wears a three-piece suit and a checked tie.[149] He peers off into the distance, his eyes shadowed by dark brows. His arms are resolutely crossed, as if resentful of the camera's intrusion. Critchley has an aquiline nose and a pronounced chin dimple. His parted hair is slicked down and appears wet. Though not conventionally handsome, the photograph reveals him to have possessed an alluring, melancholic intensity.

Critchley's father, Frank Critchley Parker, had built his fortune as the publisher of the *Industrial Australian and Mining Standard*. A formal man conscious of his civic standing, F. C. Parker was a staunch Australian patriot who had penned several anti-German pamphlets and was fiercely pro-conscription during World War I.[150] A column praising Steinberg and the Freeland League for suggesting the use of "refugees as pioneers" in the Kimberley had appeared in Parker's paper soon after Isaacson first approached Steinberg about Tasmania. The editorial noted that "the Jew is not a foreigner . . . [h]e is . . . the most desirable end of all nations, an internationalist."[151] Racist biopolitics played a role in the *Mining Standard*'s unequivocal endorsement of "group settlement";[152] the author insisted that European Jewish immigrants would allow Australia to remain "white *owned*."[153] Whether F. C. Parker approved the editorial is unknown, but he certainly helped influence the shift in focus from the Kimberley to Tasmania. The elder Parker was an avid fly-fisherman who had published inventories of his catches. His many angling trips to Tasmania made him one of the state's most vocal boosters. In 1937, he coauthored a travelogue-cum-investment prospectus entitled *Tasmania, Jewel of the Commonwealth*. This illustrated volume lavished praise on the island's hydroelectric potential and timber resources. Thanks to his business connections and support for industrial development, F. C. Parker counted Tasmania's premier among his friends.

Critchley, born in 1911 when his successful father was on the cusp of fifty, lacked for nothing save direction and affection. According to

Isaacson, his parents "loved him, but in an undemonstrative way."[154] They "never understood him," she wrote, "and never pretended to."[155] His mother, Kathleen Kerr Parker, was unemotional.[156] Critchley spent long days with his governess, Lizzie Baldwin.[157] As a student at the prestigious Geelong Grammar School modeled on Eton, Critchley was a misfit, too delicate to play sports.[158] He excelled in his studies, winning prizes in divinity, classics, and French.[159] Later, he lived in France and returned to his aging parents in Australia with reluctance.[160] He had become a devoted walker during his years abroad. Critchley once undertook a strenuous trek across Lapland "250 miles north of the Arctic Circle" and reveled in his experiences eating preserved reindeer meat with Lapp tribesmen.[161] Despite his outward vigor, the evidence suggests that he suffered from tuberculosis. His custom-built home, La Mabelleion,[162] in the forested hills outside of Melbourne featured a detachable, screened porch on skids that could be moved from damp shade to sunlight.[163] And had Critchley not had a chronic condition, he would have been pressed into military service during World War II, especially given his domineering father's anti-German stance. Instead, the fragile, high-cheekboned young man had the leisure to dream of settling Europe's Jews on the island his father referred to as the "Land of Promise."[164]

Steinberg recalled that at their first meeting Critchley spoke "in drawn-out, confused phrases" and "uttered his words with difficulty, as if he lacked breath."[165] The son echoed his father's boosterism for Tasmania, enthusing over the island's forests, rich fishing waters, and untapped mineral wealth.[166] He was convinced that Tasmania could become a "new Jerusalem" for the "Jewish homeless who seek a land."[167] His assurances were soon supported by a letter from the powerful Tasmanian premier, Robert Cosgrove, who wrote that the "anticipated difficulties" of settling "migrants from Europe" in his state could be surmounted, "so far as my Government is concerned."[168] Steinberg at first questioned the young man's motives.[169] But the studious young Christian used his familiarity with the Hebrew Bible to urge Steinberg onward: "[L]ike the ancient prophets, it is your mission to lead your people into the wilderness."[170] With the Kimberley Plan at an impasse, Steinberg reconsidered Critchley's offer.

Isaacson assured Steinberg that Critchley's father was "almost pathetically anxious" for a Jewish settlement in Tasmania to "come into being in his life-time [and] will leave no stone unturned to help us."[171] Steinberg found himself visiting the "old and ailing"[172] publisher in the wealthy district of South Yarra. His patrician home was lined with bookshelves packed with volumes on coal, minerals, metals, and fishing.[173] Over tea, F. C. Parker echoed his newspaper's enthusiasm for Jewish colonization, confirming Isaacson's initial report. He offered Steinberg his political contacts with the premier, and assured him that his son, "young Critchley," would accompany him to Tasmania as a guide and fixer.[174] Soon Premier Cosgrove's under-secretary, Edward Parkes, formally invited Critchley, Steinberg, and Isaacson to visit Tasmania. "[T]he Government would provide free transport facilities within the State," he wrote, and "full information of an authoritative nature" would be made available to the delegation.[175]

Steinberg consented to the trip, much to Critchley's delight. He assured Steinberg that "in the west and south-west of Tasmania you will find your 'promised land' for a great part of your people."[176] On Sunday, January 12, 1941, the two men set off together by plane to Hobart.[177] Critchley became ill during the flight, and after their arrival on *terra firma*, the ferry trip from the aerodrome to the city made him even sicker.[178] Steinberg had to call a doctor who set Critchley on his feet by morning.[179] Once recovered, Critchley bustled from office to office in his black coat and stiff hat.[180] His serious manner impressed Steinberg, who thought he resembled a "Jewish hermit."[181] They spent the first few days meeting with government authorities, including the surveyor-general, the secretary for agriculture, the conservator of forests, the director of mines, and the hydroelectric commissioner.[182] Isaacson arrived with photographer and agricultural scientist Bertie Pearl a few days later.[183]

By then, Steinberg was anxious to leave Hobart, a city founded by jailers, convicts, whalers, and whores. Beyond the capital's harbor lies Stormy Bay, whose sea-reach stretches unbroken to Antarctica more than two thousand miles away. Crisp, salt-heavy air rolls in with the tide. The hilly downtown backs up against Mount Wellington's four-thousand-foot-high table. Fog shrouds the mountain on damp mornings, rendering it invisible. Despite the rugged beauty that surrounded him, Steinberg wanted to see the "unsettled parts of the country that longed for colonization."[184] Under-Secretary Parkes supplied them with cars, a boat, and horses for their journey.[185] Once outside of Hobart, they passed apple plantations, scanned hills and valleys, and scrambled up mountains.[186] The regions they traveled through were already flourishing with "small saw-mills, dairy farms, poultry farms and cattle runs."[187] Steinberg knew they had yet to see the untamed bush of the southwest that had been identified as suitable for mass Jewish colonization.[188] Critchley served as "tireless guide, pathfinder, rider and mountaineer," and briefly led Isaacson and Pearl into the interior.[189] Steinberg, meanwhile, returned to the capital to meet with Cosgrove and present him with the informal commission's initial impressions.

Cosgrove, a short man with gray hair and ruddy cheeks,[190] received Steinberg "like an old friend."[191] The premier reaffirmed his interest in colonization, despite a report from his own secretary for lands that the southwest was "not in any way suitable for the purpose proposed by Dr. Steinberg."[192] The land, the secretary reported, was "practically worthless" owing to the vast moors of button grass, a primitive plant species that grows in peaty, nutrient-poor soil.[193] Nonetheless, Cosgrove assured Steinberg in a signed memorandum that "my Government accepts in principle . . . the proposal that a settlement of Jewish migrants should be established in Tasmania."[194] Now two premiers had lent their support to the establishment of Steinberg's Australian Freeland. Steinberg recalled celebrating his latest diplomatic coup with a stroll through downtown Hobart. He visited the Tasmanian Museum to learn more about the history of the island he soon hoped to turn into a Jewish sanctuary. Inside the museum's brick walls he came face to face with a diminutive Aboriginal skeleton on display for gawking tourists. He gazed at the bones and sadly reflected that "[t]here are to-day no natives left."[195] The human remains[196] he inspected through the glass case[197] were those of Trugernanna, faithful friend to that other Tasmanian Moses, George Augustus Robinson.

A Model for the Whole World

Steinberg returned to the Australian mainland at the end of January 1941.[198] Shortly after, the federal government faced fears of a Japanese invasion in the northwest, and so the Kimberley Plan was suspended. But the indefatigable Steinberg continued to speak on behalf of the Freeland vision to anyone who would listen: chambers of commerce, women's organizations, a society dedicated to increasing Australia's population, socialists, trade representatives, labor leaders, student clubs, and both Jewish and Christian groups.[199] Meanwhile, Critchley and Isaacson advanced the cause for Tasmania, meeting together many weeknights to strategize.[200] Isaacson, however, was soon preoccupied with anxiety over the safety of her twenty-year-old son, Peter, who shipped out in May 1941 to Canada for advanced flying training. She felt exceptionally close to Peter and considered him one of the few people who understood her.[201]

After she bade Peter farewell at the station, Isaacson spent the evening with Critchley and "sobbed [her] heart out."[202] Her son's absence, she wrote to Steinberg, spurred "the secret beginning of my friendship with Critchley,"[203] who was eleven years younger than she was. While Isaacson longed for her son, she gave Critchley "an affection he had not known before."[204] Critchley pined for a maternal surrogate, finding in Isaacson "the warmth and beauty and motherly devotion of all Jewish women through the ages."[205] Grateful for her attentions, he "wanted to do something for [her] no one else could do."[206] "In Tasmania," Isaacson wrote, "he felt he had found the answer."[207] And so, impatient, he determined to push the scheme through single-handedly, leaving Melbourne again for Hobart in March 1942, the beginning of autumn in the southern hemisphere.

Before he left on his mission, Isaacson presented her knight errant with a leather-bound diary. She wished Critchley a "Happy and Successful Year"[208] on the inside cover and signed her pet name—Lynka—with a flourish. Critchley provisioned in Hobart with the intention of heading into the southwestern bush to survey the land. He phoned Lynka before setting off. "You'll think of me," he promised her, "all the time."[209] Then he sailed south out of Storm Bay and likely tacked west toward the sheltered, broad inlet of Cox Bight more than one hundred miles away. There he could pick up a trail and head further inland by foot to see firsthand the region proposed for Jewish colonization. Based on his discussions with Under-Secretary Parkes, Critchley believed that the future Jewish territory should stretch from Recherche Bay in the east to Port Davey's deep water harbor in the west, and from the Antarctic Ocean in the south to the banks of the Gordon River in the north.[210] Though the precise borders he had in mind are uncertain, the general area of the settlement was to be about the size of Puerto Rico.

Critchley trudged his way across a muddy, undulating track to Melaleuca, an isolated tin mining camp. Charles King, a hardy Boer War veteran and the only resident of Melaleuca, hosted him in the comfortable cabin he had built with an eaveless roof so that the winds of the Roaring Forties would not peel it back like the top of an anchovy tin. King's snug home still stands amidst a copse of trees that is home to forest-dwelling wallabies. Critchley confided his vision to King, who was surprisingly "most enthusiastic" [211] about turning his backyard into a Jewish micronation. On Saturday, March 28, 1942, King even insisted on rowing Critchley in his small wooden boat to the vicinity of Port Davey, though the aging miner "suffer[ed] from a bad rupture & a worse cough." [212] They navigated the shallows of Melaleuca Inlet and glided into Bathurst Harbor. Critchley perched on the rowboat's thwart and observed a "sheet of water studded with green islands & beyond hills & massive mountain ranges." [213] From the harbor, they bucked the waves pulsing through the narrows of Bathurst Channel and headed west toward Port Davey.

Critchley intended to hike an old prospector's trail, Marsden's Track, from Port Davey northeast to Fitzgerald, approximately sixty miles distant. Along the way he would catalogue the resources the first Jewish colonists might exploit. The walk was to take no more than a week despite having to cross the gullies and peaks of the Arthur Range, so named by George Augustus Robinson, who had first traversed them on his own mission to Port Davey. [214] Critchley, an experienced bushwalker, knew that changeable weather might force him to extend his trek. So he carried extra provisions, including nearly fifteen pounds of oatmeal, eleven pounds of bacon, eight pounds of cheese, six pounds of self-rising flour, two pounds of dates, and three quarters of a pound of cocoa. [215] In addition to his food stores, he carried a sleeping bag and tent, and stuffed his rucksack with extra clothes, matches, game snares, and aspirin. He also carried the slim brown diary Lynka had given him as a token of her affection.

King landed Critchley at a brambled cove near Mount MacKenzie and told the young explorer that should he get in any trouble, to light a fire of flammable button grass from the mountain's slopes and he

Mount MacKenzie from Bathurst Channel near Port Davey, Tasmania. Author's collection

would return to collect him.[216] Critchley swung his heavy pack on his back, waved farewell, and set off alone into the wild.[217] He made his way up the brush-covered banks to camp for the night. The next day was unseasonably warm[218] and Critchley had to rest frequently and so made little progress along Marsden's Track. He bathed at noon in an "ice cold stream"[219] and watched a score of black swans[220] feeding along the estuarial rivulets whose waters ran the color of strong tea. Critchley camped nearby and awoke the following morning to find the weather had taken a sudden turn for the worse. He returned to the foot of Mount MacKenzie and there hunkered down through days of unremitting "hail, rain, and violent gales."[221] Critchley knew that the autumn storms might continue into winter, and so he prudently ascended Mount MacKenzie to fire "2 smoke columns"[222] to summon King as they had arranged.

Three times he made the miserable climb up the steep, slippery incline to light the fires, but there was, he wrote, "no response."[223] The fierce weather did not abate and Critchley began to panic. He discovered that he had only two boxes of matches, not the four he thought he had packed.[224] Dampness ruined one box and he wasted half of another trying to light his final rescue fire.[225] "I knew so well the importance of the smoke signals," he recorded, "that thinking of nothing save the one in reply, I forgot about the matches left beside a turrock I had lit."[226] His last few matches went up in smoke at his feet while he scanned the gray horizon for a sign from King. Now he could neither cook nor light a fire for warmth, and though the country was full of game, without matches his snares were useless.[227] Had the tubercular Critchley been a smoker, a cigarette lighter might have rescued him from his predicament. Now without a means to light a fire, the damp affected his lungs already "weakened by pleurisy."[228] His food supplies dwindled. Wet, ill, and short of breath, a depleted Critchley despaired of reaching Fitzgerald over the now flood-swollen rivers plunging down the quartzite peaks of the Arthurs. Melaleuca was a mere twelve miles away by water, but Critchley had no boat and he was too weak to walk the circuitous fifty-mile shoreline route back to King's outpost.[229] Nor, presumably, was he strong enough to swim the hundred or so meters across the frigid narrows of Bathurst Channel to shorten the overland journey. Twelve days after setting out, he made a "comfortable camp" surrounded by a brush-wood windbreak near the shores of Port Davey.[230] There, weak and lonely, he crawled into his tent to compose a blueprint for the "Paris of Australasia"[231] he hoped to establish for Jewish refugees.

Critchley presented his feverish considerations on the Jewish settle-ment[232] as a gift to Lynka, written in a cramped hand in the journal she had given him. The deep waters of Port Davey would become the "natu-ral centre"[233] of the settlement, he wrote, because immigrants could dis-embark there from ocean-going vessels. In a suggestion that discloses Critchley's generous sympathies, he advocated that Port Davey revert to its "original name," Poynduk, "as a tribute to the Tasmanian aboriginal" culture that had been uprooted from the region.[234] He further hoped that Jewish refugees would fulfill Tasmania's "moral obligation" to "look to the welfare" of the "half-caste descendants" of the displaced Aborigi-nes.[235] Here he echoed his father's regret, and Robinson's sorrow, that the first white settlers had not treated the island's "sable natives"[236] more charitably. In a sense, Critchley believed that Jewish immigrants from Hitler's Europe would help redeem Tasmania's haunted genocidal past. He adopted his father's program for industrial development, foreseeing large-scale hydroelectric plants supplying the settlement's power.[237] Canneries would process the local crayfish and "excellent eels"[238] for food, and a "furniture industry could be developed"[239] to exploit the stands of hardwood timber.

Critchley also imagined a planned economy[240] for the settlement inspired by Soviet collectives—something his capitalist father would surely have despised, and which Critchley feared Steinberg would balk at considering. Settlers would establish mining operations with an "enlightened administration,"[241] thirty-five-hour work weeks, and a month's paid holiday each year. The "finest pre-natal medical service"[242] would be provided for women. Kindergartens, parks, playgrounds, and schools would be established at the community's expense.[243] He envisioned the founding of a university that would become "the finest seat of learning"[244] in Oceania. In order to "uphold the principles of racial tolerance & international brotherhood,"[245] scholarships would be offered to Japanese, Arabs, "African negroes,"[246] and native peoples of the Pacific and Indian oceans. The liberal, technocratic society he foresaw would send scientists "to study [the] statues at Easter Island" and fund expeditions to the South Pole.[247]

Not only would the Jewish settlers export justice, higher learning, and science, they would also import the treasures of the globe to Poynduk. Critchley imagined a kind of Epcot Center of world architecture.[248] He instructed that "entire buildings [and] castles" should be purchased, moved to the settlement, and then be "reconstituted in identical surroundings."[249] He drew on his knowledge of ancient history[250] to propose an annual celebration of physical prowess, literary talent, and craft. These competitions, the "Tasmian Games," would be modeled on the Olympics.[251] In addition to athletics and yacht races, he suggested there be readings of plays and poetry, musical performances, art exhibitions, as well as displays of weaving and pottery making.[252]

Critchley's utopian Poynduk was to arise along the flat land that extended from the shallows of Bathurst Harbor south through Melaleuca and on to Cox Bight.[253] The city-state would become a center for Antarctic whaling and a shipyard for the construction of steamers[254] to take passengers on cruises to the polar ice shelf. Streams flowing through the region resembled those of Scotland, he thought, and so local whisky could be distilled for export.[255] Wool and cotton would be produced to rival English "serges and worsteds."[256] The colder reaches of Poynduk would house seal, wallaby, and silver fox fur farms.[257] French Jews would turn the settlement into a "centre of fashion" and "articles de luxe."[258] Dutch Jews would help reclaim land from the sea and increase agricultural yields.[259] Tourists would arrive to take advantage of the area's natural beauty, and so chalets and youth hostels would employ settlers as guides and ski instructors.[260] Highways "constructed like the Germanautobahnen"[261] would speed travelers to the region. Electric railways[262] would encircle the capital, which "should be so planned that it will be a model for the whole world."[263] He concluded by calling on renowned architect Le Corbusier to design "the outward aspect of the settlement" which would provide the "spiritual meaning of the whole project."[264]

There is no doubt that Critchley selflessly aimed to aid Europe's persecuted Jews. He used all his familial connections, considerable energy, and political capital to do so. But the foundation of Poynduk—its spiritual meaning—was inseparable from his love for the unattainable Lynka. "We had planned so much & each had brought something to the life of the other," he wrote to her from the solitude of his Camp Davey bunker, "but if this joint existence cannot be in the flesh let it be in the spirit."[265] Critchley sought to rescue the Jews, and in so doing, to woo Lynka from her emotionally distant husband.

Alone in the World

Today the region surrounding Port Davey exists as a protected marine reserve, an untouched panorama of tannic waterways, wind-scoured moorlands, and stony peaks. Storm fronts race over the distant Arthur Range. More than seven feet of rain falls there each year. The boggy banks of Melaleuca Inlet, where Critchley expected a Jewish city-state to arise, offer a stark and desolate vision. Brush tumbles down to the edges of the brown water. Knotted tufts of button grass, some several feet high, pock the moors. Robinson's descriptions of the area from 180 years ago remain accurate—marshes, stunted stands of trees, [266] cheerless mud flats,[267] and "lofty barren mountains"[268] mark the landscape. Contemporary charts of the area yield place names like Mount Misery and Lost World Plateau. Gale-force winds commonly sweep across

Looking east from area of Critchley Parker Junior's final campsite near Port Davey, Tasmania. Author's collection

Bathurst Harbor. Westward toward Mount MacKenzie, Bathurst Channel tapers between rocky spits that reach their flinty fingers across the rough tidal water and nearly touch. The site around Critchley's camp, on the shores of present-day Parker Bay, is a morass of hillocks and channels crowded with melaleucas, celery-top pines, and bottlebrush trees. A mucilaginous algae clings to the many rocks. In this mournful wilderness, amidst meandering wombat trails and beneath an endless sky of gray clouds chasing blue chasing gray, Critchley lay sheltered from the howling wind and dreamed his dreams of a Jewish city state.

Days went by without a break in the weather while Critchley waited out the storms. By Wednesday, April 8, twelve days after landing, he began to despair of rescue and composed what he believed to be the last letter he would ever write to Lynka: "I do not feel that there will be anything more than a gradual loss of the senses & a final sinking into unconsciousness."[269] He hoped she would fulfill his ambitious plans for development "knowing that I mean something to you."[270] Critchley managed to draw comfort from his vista despite his predicament: "You must come Lynka to this country & see the mountains of Port Davey as I have seen them now clear & shining . . . now enshrouded with mist & snow. You must . . . climb Mt. MacKenzie at whose foot I camped & from whose summit I scanned the waters for a boat. You will realize what a magnificent centre this will be for the settlement."[271] But even in summer, Mount MacKenzie's slope can be sodden and treacherous, and the weather near its summit diabolical. There's little chance that King could have discerned Critchley's smoke signals had the weather been as blustery as he recorded it to be.

In a last testament written to Steinberg, Critchley gave his address at the top of his letter as "Mt. MacKenzie, Port Davey":

Dear Dr. Steinberg,

It is at Port Davey that I hope the Jewish Settlement will start not far from where I sever all earthly connection with it.

I came to this magnificent harbour some weeks ago . . . [but] bad weather and my consequent failure to get in touch with my base make my fate certain.

To die in the service of so noble a cause is to me a great satisfaction, and if as I hope the settlement brings happiness to many refugees and in so doing serves the State of Tasmania, I die happy.

May your abilities and those of Mrs. Isaacson bring these schemes to fruition.[272]

Critchley lay weak, alone, and tortured by "visions of tables piled with food,"[273] but he never abandoned his dream of rescuing those men, women, and children whom the world had forsaken. Unbeknownst to Critchley, the killing center of Auschwitz-Birkenau began the large-scale gassing of Jews from across Europe at the very moment he sought a sanctuary for them.

Critchley longed for Lynka as he felt death's approach. He instructed her: "I should like my body to lie at the southern side of the entrance to Port Davey, close to the edge of the yellow cliff that stands there so that I shall see all the vessels that go in & out of the Harbour from our settlement. When you join me there a column could be erected so that all will see it."[274] The city-state of Poynduk was to be a gift to Lynka, the joint tomb he imagined an eternal monument to their thwarted love. Some familiar with the story believe that Critchley had gone to Port Davey to die, pining away for an unattainable woman like a latter-day Romantic.[275] Yet in his final letter from April 21, 1942, Critchley writes lucidly to Lynka: "I exist better than I had hoped on the aspirin & water diet so that I may yet be saved. Though resigned to die, the desire to live ever & anon, surges within me. . . . Oh that I could live on to guide and help you with the wisdom acquired here in the last fortnight!"[276] Critchley did not die for love: if anything, he died for hope. Hope that he could succeed where his father had failed in domesticating Tasmania's wilds. Hope that he could grasp a measure of immortality as a communard Moses leading Europe's Jews to a windswept Canaan. Hope that the weather would break, that his signals might be seen, that he'd recover enough strength to escape the solitary, cold death of a sick man in the wild.

Search parties fanned out across the area looking for Critchley; they found only a single discarded biscuit tin.[277] By June, Under-Secretary Parkes called his parents and Caroline Isaacson to inform them that "there is no trace of Critchley . . . all hope [is] abandoned."[278] Isaacson described her reaction to Steinberg in a letter: "I was so stunned, almost as though I had been dealt a physical blow . . . and I was all alone . . . and not just alone in my house, but it seemed alone in the world."[279] While she waited for news of Critchley's fate, she met with his mother, Kathleen, who could not "understand Critchley's obsession and determination to get to Port Davey."[280] Isaacson had difficulty explaining his single-mindedness to her. She could not tell Mrs. Parker that her son had been in love with her—a respectable married woman—and that she had loved Critchley in her way as well. But Kathleen Parker did not blame Isaacson, and in fact sent her snapshots of her son as keepsakes.[281] To Steinberg, Isaacson unburdened herself in a letter he presumably destroyed out of discretion. All that remains in his archive is a sensitive response to Caroline's absent confession: "Yes, my friend, I guessed many things, in Melbourne and later in Hobart but never wanted to bring them into a coherent story. Nor could I do it out of respect for you."[282] Agonizing months followed Critchley's disappearance, during which Isaacson continued to write heart-rending letters to the sympathetic Steinberg.

On September 4, fishermen buffeted by storms at Port Davey took shelter in a cove near Mount Mackenzie. They went ashore with their dog and found a cloth bag tied to a stick with the word "Help" written on it.[283] The dog took off into the bush. His barking led the sailors to the remains of a tent, the scattered traces of a campsite, a water-logged leather journal, and a green sleeping-bag.[284] Inside, they found Critchley's moldering corpse. One of those who stumbled upon the body, tough cray-fisherman Clyde Clayton, was so horrified by the grisly discovery that it's said he never again slept in a sleeping bag.[285] A formal coroner's inquest held in October concluded that Critchley had died "some time about the month of May . . . the cause of death being starvation & exposure."[286] Though he had wanted to be buried on the south side of Port Davey so that he could watch immigrants enter his fantasized Jewish homeland, Under-Secretary Parkes had Critchley's body interred near his final campsite in the button-grass moors at the base of Mount Mackenzie.

Critchley Parker's simple concrete and stone gravesite still lies there hidden from view in thick bush. The maze of animal tracks that double as pathways through the tangle of grass and brush can make finding the site next to impossible. Wombat dung smears the foot of his grave. Aggressive jack jumper ants whose venom can cause anaphylactic shock have built a nest nearby. The black-streaked marble of the headstone bears the inscription: "In Memory of Critchley Parker Junior who lost his life on a walking tour from Port Davey and rests peacefully here where he was found on 4th September 1942, aged 31 years." The area around Port Davey, with its bald hills, moraines, endless waves, and long horizon, is a fitting final resting place for a man of Critchley's boundless vision. And his burial plot's desolation is appropriate for his brief life of frustration and failure.

Steinberg eulogized Critchley as a "martyr for the cause of human dignity and for the Jewish people."[287] He even compared Critchley's febrile visions of Poynduk to the prophecies of Herzl's *Altneuland*.[288] In summing up his legacy, Steinberg proclaimed that Critchley's "name is closely linked, for all time, with the Jewish people."[289] But his sacrifice has been almost entirely forgotten. Israel's Yad Vashem Holocaust museum and research center boasts a memorial to another righteous Australian gentile, William Cooper, whose Aboriginals League marched through Melbourne following *Kristallnacht* to protest the persecution of Jews.[290] Yet there is no memorial for Critchley, the only non-Jewish Australian to die in the service of a Jewish cause.[291] For want of a cigarette lighter, Parker might have lived. For want of a lighter, southwest Tasmania might today be a Jewish city-state.

Caroline Isaacson was devastated by Critchley's death, but according to her children, she never once spoke of her feelings for him.[292] Her daughter remembers the telephone call informing her mother of Critchley's death and her mother's stricken silence.[293] Isaacson blamed herself for not having done enough to save him: "I, the woman to whom he gave all his faith and trust and love failed him."[294] For nearly a year she struggled to "regain something of the old serenity of spirit . . . thought lost . . . forever with Critchley's passing."[295] Isaacson volunteered for army service to distract herself from her anguish and to feel closer to her war hero son, Peter.[296] Critchley possessed a remarkable empathy for the sufferings of strangers a world away, yet was blind to how his actions would affect those closest to him. His sacrifice embittered and perplexed his parents, and continued to haunt his beloved Lynka.

Even a decade after his death—on the tenth anniversary of her presenting Critchley with his diary—Isaacson confessed that the "past still lives within me as vividly as though it were present. I think it will always be thus. . . . I cannot get it all sorted out: cannot quite reconcile myself to Critchley's death which I always feel might not have been had he never met me."[297] Though Isaacson remained active in journalism and Jewish affairs, she ever after felt bereft. "Critchley, who really understood me, isn't here," she wrote, "so I have learnt to live within myself."[298] To console herself, she worked to perpetuate his memory. She tried to convince members of the Australian Jewish community and Critchley's elderly mother to fund the establishment of a "Children's Memorial Centre"[299] in his name. She even offered to donate her vacation home in the rural hamlet of Sassafras for that purpose. Isaacson imagined creating "a small home where children that had been ill could go to become well. A home in the bush that [Critchley] loved so much: where they could learn bush lore, see bush birds, fern gullies, go for tramps . . . [and] have a library and learn the joys of reading; learn handcrafts . . . learn the beautiful Hebrew songs . . . and sing them around a camp fire at night."[300] But even this scaled-down version of

Critchley's would-be Jewish state—a convalescent home in the country for sickly Jewish children—was not to be. Isaacson died in 1962, and with her passing Critchley's memory faded into oblivion.

Unfulfilled Wishes

Steinberg continued to press the Tasmanian government for a colonization agreement without mentioning his young friend's tragic death. Barely six weeks after Critchley's body had been recovered, Steinberg wrote a confidential letter to Parkes suggesting the dispatch of an expert commission to the region.[301] Cosgrove remained encouraging. He sent three separate letters to Steinberg reiterating his government's interest in and support for the Freeland League proposal.[302] But in June 1943, Steinberg sailed from Melbourne to Canada aboard the Swedish vessel *Mirrabooka*.[303]

While in transit to North America, his movements were followed by the U.S. Military Intelligence Service[304] and the Federal Bureau of Investigation.[305] Two years earlier, Steinberg had applied for an American visa in order to fundraise,[306] and as an FBI agent noted at the time, to "report at New York and Washington on a project for the establishment of a Jewish settlement."[307] Powerful Zionist leader Rabbi Stephen Wise, a friend and advisor to President Franklin Roosevelt, supported Steinberg's application with a personal letter of recommendation. Wise was in his late sixties at the time and at the height of his influence, a familiar fixture in Washington who lowered his pugnacious glare at those who crossed him. He hailed Steinberg as a "man of fine character and a person of moral and political integrity"[308] in a letter to the Department of State. Despite Wise's kind words, Steinberg's application was "unanimously disapproved"[309] on two occasions[310] because of the "serious[ly] derogatory"[311] dossier the FBI had compiled. They classified Steinberg among the "more odious" of the "potentially dangerous"[312] aliens seeking admission into the United States. The FBI believed that the now stateless[313] Steinberg still retained Bolshevik or anarchist[314] tendencies. Worse, they had information indicating that he had served with the "German General Staff as chief espionage organizer against the Russians"[315] in World War I. The notion that Steinberg had not only offered himself to America's enemy in the Great War, but had also acted as "an espionage agent against his own country"³¹⁶ particularly troubled the State Department's Visa Control Committee.

Instead of reuniting with Freeland League activists and establishing a base of operations in the U.S., Steinberg was forced to remain in Canada with his daughter, Ada, who worked as a magazine editor. She struggled to help her father legally resume his life's work in America, and used her publishing contacts to secure an introduction to Eleanor Roosevelt. In August 1943, she traveled to Washington to meet with State Department officials and the first lady, who happened to be out of town.³¹⁷ But Eleanor Roosevelt's personal secretary wrote on her behalf to Under Secretary of State Sumner Welles, who had familiarity with territorialist schemes, asking for his consideration in the matter of "Dr. Steinberg [who] has been devoting his life to find a homeland for Jewish refugees."³¹⁸ As a result of Roosevelt's advocacy, Steinberg received a visitor's visa and entered the U.S. a little more than two weeks later.³¹⁹

The FBI frowned on the decision, blaming Steinberg's admission on "the intervention of Mrs. Eleanor Roosevelt."³²⁰ Once in the U.S., he redoubled his efforts for the Freeland League and signed a lease for a new headquarters on the third floor of the Manufacturers Trust Building³²¹ that once stood along the northwest arc of Columbus Circle. Steinberg then set about applying for immigration visas for himself and for his wife and children still in England.³²² He had been separated from them for nearly five years. Steinberg petitioned the Visa Review Committee in a statement indicating that he "would be most grateful for the opportunity to settle with my family in this country where we can find assured a democratic way of life and the spirit of freedom and justice."³²³ His application was again denied unanimously.³²⁴ Steinberg had to wait until July 1944 for a Board of Appeals to reverse the decision.³²⁵ For months afterward, FBI agents monitored Steinberg's activities through confidential informants.³²⁶ They ultimately concluded that nothing "indicate[d] any un-American tendencies on the part of the Freeland League nor its present directing agent, Dr. Steinberg."³²⁷

As the FBI wrapped up its investigation, the first English edition of the League's magazine, *Freeland*, appeared in December 1944 edited by Steinberg. A clear statement of the Freeland program appeared above the masthead: "We aim to create a Jewish Settlement in some unoccupied area for all those who seek a new home . . . [and] . . . to acquaint

Americans with the possibilities for Jewish settlements in sparsely populated areas of the World."³²⁸ Contributions to the inaugural issue included an essay by Nobel Peace Prize–winner Sir Norman Angell, a brief letter of support from violinist Yehudi Menuhin, and what may be the first published translation into English of a dispatch from Emanuel Ringelblum, the martyred scholar who initiated the Warsaw ghetto's *Oyneg Shabes* archives.

The destruction of European Jewry—and the missed opportunities to save lives before the war—haunted the *Fraylandistn*. Steinberg's own mother likely perished in Auschwitz.³²⁹ To its members, the Freeland League "represent[ed] the unfulfilled wishes and frustrated efforts of the millions of Jews, who did not succeed in escaping in time and who perished in the catastrophe of Nazism and war."³³⁰ Before the war, Freeland supporters such as Alfred Döblin, Melech Ravitch, and Steinberg foresaw the dangers of Nazism and sought to provide European Jewry with a territorial ark as exterminationist antisemitism flooded the so-called civilized world. After the war, bereaved Freelanders longed to resettle their brethren in order to preserve the surviving remnants of Yiddish-speaking European culture.³³¹

Support for an Australian refuge had been strong enough even during the war itself to attract the worried attention of the Jewish Agency's *Keren Hayesod* (Palestine Foundation Fund). In May 1944, Foundation Fund executive member Nahum Goldmann wrote a letter of introduction on behalf of Ida Marcia Silverman, a wealthy American who was dispatched to Australia on a fundraising mission.³³² Silverman, who had already helped scuttle the settlement of displaced Jews in the Dominican Republic after the Evian Conference, was a volunteer Jewish Agency operative who dedicated herself to torpedoing efforts to resettle Jewish refugees anywhere but British Mandate Palestine.³³³ She criticized Steinberg's efforts in Australia in a snarky article in the *Jewish Frontier*, an American Zionist periodical. Her attack accused Steinberg of fomenting antisemitism in Australia and claimed that "persons (or organizations) behind Dr. Steinberg" worked against Jewish interests.³³⁴ She upbraided "these self-appointed 'bosses'" for condemning fellow Jews "to the doom that has befallen so many others."³³⁵ In response to her outrageous accusations, the *Fraylandistn* charged Silverman with "character assassination."[336] But the damage to their cause had been done both in America and Australia.

Nonetheless, Cosgrove put forward yet another revised plan to encourage Jewish immigration to Tasmania as 1945 drew to a close. In a letter to the head of the United Jewish Overseas Relief Fund, the organization responsible for resettling Holocaust survivors in Australia, the premier suggested that the Fund purchase "about 3,000 acres"[337] for Jewish settlement on Flinders Island off the northeastern coast of Tasmania. Flinders Island had been the site of the notorious Aboriginal settlement that had led to the deaths of nearly all of George Augustus Robinson's charges, including those whom he and Trugernanna had worked to relocate from Port Davey more than a century before. That cursed place held out little promise for Jewish resettlement endeavors, and the idea of colonizing Tasmania soon disappeared from the Australian political horizon. Today researchers in Hobart can request the heavy, leather-bound folio of the Tasmanian state register on immigration from the early 1940s. Its pages remain completely blank.

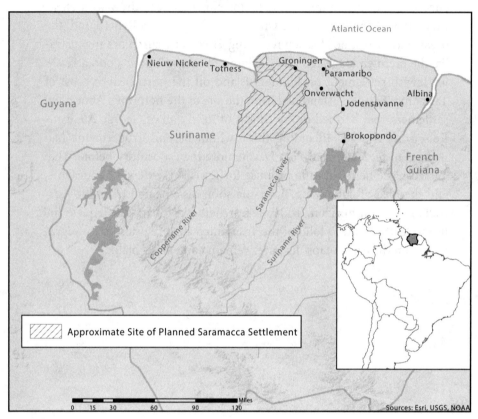

Suriname

6

Welcome to the Jungle

Suriname (1938–1948)

New Palestines across the Sea

Representatives from fifty nations attended the 1945 San Francisco conference that formally established the United Nations. Now in the U.S., Steinberg presented a memorandum that recounted territorialism's failed efforts to these delegates. He recalled Zangwill's support for a Jewish state in East Africa, French minister Marius Moutet's endorsement of mass settlement in Madagascar, and the Freeland League's own recent negotiations for colonization in the Kimberley and southwest Tasmania.[1] The document explained that the League's principal mission was to "preserve for the future the Jewish *community*, the historic continuity of its ideals and beliefs."[2] This noble purpose, he declared, "requires a planned, regulated, concentrated emigration, that is, colonization."[3] Any land offered to the Jewish people that was both large enough to absorb mass immigration and scarcely populated would help redress the world's silence during the Holocaust, which the League termed a "disgrace to the conscience of humanity."[4] Despite the diplomatic language of the memorandum, it is clear where responsibility for justice lay: "There is sufficient room in the world for a Jewish *Freeland* within the framework of the British Empire . . . or in the French Empire."[5] The Freeland League was careful to note that they were willing to consider other lands as well, including those in South America.[6]

The linkage of Great Britain and France to mention of South America was not coincidental. The northeastern rump of the continent contained several European territories at the time. British Guiana (now independent Guyana) was a reasonably prosperous Crown colony. French Guiana was then, and remains today, a department of the *Métropole* and is the site of the notorious Devil's Island penitentiary where Alfred Dreyfus had been unjustly imprisoned. In between these two colonies sat Dutch Guiana, now known as Suriname. All three Guianas were considered, separately and together, as potential lands of refuge for European Jewry in the years leading up to World War II. Zangwill originally proposed Dutch Guiana as a possible site for mass settlement. Shortly after the East Africa proposal was rejected in 1905, the ITO studied colonization possibilities in that most nether possession of the Kingdom of the Netherlands.[7] Decades elapsed before the region again became the focus of serious territorialist ambitions. Freeland League activists next considered French Guiana in 1936.[8] After Madagascar had been declared unsuitable for Jewish settlement, the Freelanders pressed for a comprehensive investigation of French Guiana, which Moutet had singled out in his 1937 declaration.[9] In 1938, even as Steinberg promoted the establishment of a Freeland colony in Australia, he urged his fellow Freelanders to keep French Guiana on the agenda.[10] British Guiana emerged as a significant possibility during this same era.

On November 12, 1938, just days after the Nazi pogrom of *Kristallnacht*—the "Night of Broken Glass" on the ninth and tenth of November 1938—America's ambassador in London, Joseph P. Kennedy, met with British prime minister Neville Chamberlain at Downing Street to discuss the Jewish refugee crisis.[11] Contemporary press accounts and subsequent scholarship indicate that the initiative to find a safe haven in British Guiana originated with the ambassador, who felt that the U.S. and U.K. needed to cooperate to evacuate Jews from the Reich in order to salvage the recently concluded Munich Agreement and avert war with Hitler.[12] The Kennedy family patriarch and stalwart Roosevelt campaigner had been appointed to the Court of St. James by the president nine months earlier. A wealthy and distinguished fifty-year-old political insider, Kennedy was an intemperate diplomat. With his slick, combed-back gray hair and toothy grin, he looked the part of an eager, can-do American, but was an outsider to the pedigrees and protocols that regulated Whitehall. Kennedy had a number of close Jewish friends, despite the open secret of his paranoid antisemitism. Nonetheless, he played a leading role in promoting the quasi-territorialist resettlement scheme in British Guiana. Chamberlain, for his part, was the thin, dour son of former prime minister Joseph Chamberlain, who had first suggested territory in East Africa to Herzl. His appeasement policy toward Hitler had put him under political attack at home, on the continent, and in the United States. Kennedy felt that he offered the weary Chamberlain a chance to secure his much-vaunted pronouncement that he had indeed negotiated "peace in our time." Kennedy also believed that he was serving American interests in doing so; Roosevelt and his advisors had spent months discussing territories suitable for settling the Reich's Jewish refugees.[13]

Five days after *Kristallnacht*, President Roosevelt held a press conference in which he remarked that he "could scarcely believe that such things could occur in a twentieth century civilization."[14] A grave Roosevelt told reporters that a "great deal of thought" had been given to finding a sanctuary for Jewish refugees from the Reich.[15] He held off further questions, maintaining that "the time . . . [is] not ripe for an answer" as to possible locales.[16] Prominent Britons, meanwhile, were moved by the cause of Jewish welfare. One member of the House of Lords pressed the British government to remove all immigration restrictions on Jewish refugees. "Let us not wait until a plan is agreed upon . . . ," he warned. "If we do that then the Jews will all be dead before the time comes."[17] Front-page news in Poland's *Haynt* (*Today*) announced to its desperate Yiddish readership that British Guiana and Australia had both been discussed by cabinet ministers as outlets for persecuted Jews.[18] The British government, it reported, was ready to absorb fifty thousand Jews in Guiana.[19] The *New York Times*, however, warned that immigrants to Guiana would be forced to contend with giant anacondas, venomous bushmaster snakes, and caiman—a voracious crocodile species.[20]

By contrast, Mandate Palestine, even with its provincialism, deserts, malarial swamps, and hostile Arab nationalists, seemed a more comfortable destination for the Reich's Jews. British government ministers did consider increasing the flow of immigration to Palestine, where thousands of German Jews had already found refuge. But due to Palestine's size and lack of absorptive capacity, officials came to the realization that "new Palestines must be found across the seas."[21] The *New York Times*' London bureau chief to whom Kennedy leaked information wrote that the "the atlas is being searched" to find a place where "Jewish settlers might repeat the triumphs of pioneering that they have achieved in the Holy Land."[22] Ironically, Zionist agricultural successes in *Eretz Israel* had come to testify to the practicality of ambitions for a tropical Freeland. Unlike the racialist debates regarding settlement in East Africa, Angola, and Madagascar, there was now no question that Jews could perform the physical labor of pioneers.

A debate in the House of Commons ensued, and Chamberlain addressed concerned members of parliament. The prime minister told his listeners that he had instructed the colonial governor of Guiana to investigate "whether without detriment to native interests land could be made available . . . for the purpose of large-scale settlement."[23] British Guiana, he continued, contains "extensive tracts of sparsely occupied land consisting of mainly forest and savannah" that might be suitable for Jewish settlement.[24] The *New York Times* treated Chamberlain's statement to MPs as a virtual guarantee that his government had in fact "offered new homelands in distant colonies" to those hounded by Nazism.[25] Kennedy remained skeptical, and responded to the news with the kind of crude bluster that would eventually end his diplomatic career: "The first job was to find places to put the Jews. Now we will see how sorry the world is for them. It's a case of getting money now."[26] To that end, Chamberlain's and Roosevelt's governments sought financial and diplomatic support for the Anglo-American Guiana initiative from European leaders and private charities.[27] Chamberlain could take solace in the fact that the Dutch premier backed his multilateral approach to finding a sanctuary for threatened Jews.[28] Only a week after making public his designs on British Guiana, the prime minister traveled to Paris to discuss the refugee crisis with officials at the French Ministry of Foreign Affairs. There he again highlighted the suitability of Guiana.[29]

American pressure to find an outlet for Jewish refugees continued all the while. In December 1938, Roosevelt's key advisor on migration issues, Dr. Isaiah Bowman, who was instrumental in swaying the president against Zionist designs on Palestine, suggested carving out a Jewish entity from Portuguese Angola.[30] Bowman later became an ally of Steinberg and offered his expert opinion to the Freeland League on several occasions.[31] But Bowman's advice on pioneering and immigration was not disinterested. He was "*profoundly* anti-Semitic," according to one colleague, and his hostility toward increasing Jewish immigration quotas to the U.S. or to Mandate Palestine made him one of the individuals in the American government most responsible for the Roosevelt administration's wartime failures.[32]

Under Secretary of State Sumner Welles, who would later intercede to help Steinberg enter the U.S., promoted the Angola option in consort with Bowman. Welles deemed the scheme so critical, he informed the president, "as to warrant heroic efforts to overcome political obstacles."[33] Roosevelt himself cabled Chamberlain to pursue the matter in no uncertain terms: "I cannot emphasize too strongly the importance which I attach to the creation of a supplemental Jewish homeland . . . or my belief that Angola offers the most favorable facilities for its creation."[34] Despite repeated overtures to Chamberlain's government to pressure Angola's masters in Portugal, the project never advanced.[35] Another contemporary British inquiry into settlement in Kenya concluded that the East African colony was suitable only for "a comparatively small number of Jews of nordic type on individual holdings."[36] The pace and intensity of these collaborative investigations by the American and British governments, not to mention the interest in resettlement voiced by French and Dutch officials, threatened contemporaneous Zionist efforts to increase quotas to Palestine.

In late January 1939, Chaim Weizmann authored a sharply worded letter to London's *Times* lamenting the myriad proposals "put forward for dealing with the problem of Jewish refugees."[37] He named British Guiana as one of those potential dumping grounds, and warned that such undeveloped territories "cannot satisfy the dire and immediate need of German Jews."[38] Weizmann invoked the failures of mass settlement in Birobidzhan as evidence against the Guiana proposal. By contrast, he attributed successes in Palestine to the belief that "every furrow ploughed, every tree planted, [has been] sanctified into an act of national redemption."[39] His public pronouncements against the Anglo-American project in British Guiana roused the Freeland League to action. Steinberg penned an indignant response to Weizmann in the *Jewish Chronicle* a few days later. He accused Weizmann of refusing to acknowledge that "the catastrophe of European Jewry . . . is greater and more pressing today that at any other period in Jewish history."[40] Chamberlain's "very important proposals of British Guiana," Steinberg wrote, would forestall the "political and economic extermination" of Jews in Eastern and Central Europe.[41] He could not, of course, fully imagine his people's physical extermination. Steinberg closed with a plea to Weizmann and his allies not to "repeat the fatal policy of 1903, when England's offer to the Jews of Uganda was rejected by them."[42] His letter appeared in print the same day as news that France's colonial minister, Georges Mandel, himself Jewish, had approved the establishment of small settlements by Jewish refugees from the Reich in French Guiana.[43]

The United States soon pressured Chamberlain's government to dispatch a fact-finding mission to British Guiana.[44] The Anglo-American expedition was launched in February 1939 and was tasked with submitting a comprehensive report on the suitability of the territory to President Roosevelt's Advisory Committee on Political Refugees.[45] The eight-man expedition included the former colonial secretary of British Guiana as well as agronomist Dr. Joseph Rosen, the head of the American Jewish Joint Agricultural Corporation (Agro-Joint), who had been a vocal proponent of mass settlement in Birobidzhan and in Madagascar.[46] Dedicated Italian physician Dr. George Giglioli, who first identified the mosquito species responsible for spreading malaria in British Guiana, served as a consultant to the expedition during its eight weeks of work.[47]

The expedition examined three regions, two in Guiana's southernmost areas along the Brazilian border and one in the northwest.[48] On Sunday, February 19, Rosen and three others took off from Georgetown, the colony's capital, in a flying boat to survey the Potaro River, which snakes through the thick rainforest blanketing the interior.[49] There they visited gold mines, took soil samples, examined the medical condition of the Amerindian populations, collected mosquito larvae, and viewed thunderous Kaieteur Falls. Rosen fell ill several days later and had to be evacuated back to Georgetown.[50] He rejoined his colleagues a few days after visiting the one district proposed for Jewish settlement in the northwest, which he deemed "capable of some development."[51] (Decades later, a semiautonomous, utopian socialist farming settlement would in fact rise in this same northwest region that Rosen surveyed: the Peoples Temple Agricultural Project—Jonestown, now a byword for mass suicide.) Rosen and his fellow explorers composed a careful report on their findings in mid-April, a month after Hitler's conquest of Czechoslovakia. Their conclusions were both sober and encouraging. "While the territory offered for settlement in British Guiana is not an ideal place for refugees from middle European countries," they wrote, "it undoubtedly possesses potential possibilities" for a large-scale settlement.[52]

An advance copy of the report circulated to British officials after its completion.[53] Chamberlain's government presented the cautiously optimistic conclusions of the report as a sop to Jewish organizations in order to divert Zionist criticism from the pending white paper, which was to limit Jewish immigration to Palestine in order to placate—perhaps the better term is appease—Arab nationalists.[54] The timing of the Guiana report's release was no accident. It was published in the U.K. and the U.S. on May 10; the Palestine white paper was officially announced on May 17.[55] Proposals for settlement in British Guiana must therefore be understood as a joint Anglo-American initiative in which both governments made common cause, first, to redeem Chamberlain's discredited Munich Agreement, second, to limit the number of Jewish refugees entering the U.S., the British Isles, and Mandate Palestine, and third, to redirect Britain's legal and ethical obligations under the Balfour Declaration to another territory. Like Zionists worldwide, the Freeland League opposed the white paper, even while they continued to pursue the Guiana plan.

A week after the white paper's release, the Freeland executive board members in Warsaw wrote to their counterparts in London advocating for a role in Dr. Rosen's plan to send thousands of young colonists to Guiana. They noted that Rosen was anxious to attract *halutzim*—a Hebrew word typically reserved for pioneers in Palestine—to a pilot settlement program in the distant Crown colony.[56] In July, demographer and territorialist sympathizer Jakob Lestschinsky published an article in favor of Guiana in the influential Zionist-oriented *Parizer Haynt* (*Paris Today*) newspaper. He proclaimed that "Guiana can become a Jewish country . . . [and] we must send our homeless there."[57] Like so many others who despaired of the fate of Jewry as Nazism raged and Palestine remained closed, he concluded that the "rejection of Uganda was a great crime."[58] And while individuals and charitable institutions did at times support the creation of an autonomous Jewish entity in British Guiana, no significant funds were forthcoming.[59]

As we know, the Freeland League subsequently turned its attention to Australia, but settlement possibilities in the Guianas long intrigued the *Fraylandistn*. In the postwar years, Steinberg's effort to establish a Jewish colony in Dutch Guiana became the Freeland League's most serious and most nearly successful project. In part, Steinberg's enthusiasm developed from his reading of an account of "the glorious past of the Jews in Suriname."[60] He then "had a vision": the Freeland League would establish a colony in Suriname and help that land "regain its old glory."[61]

The Wild Coast

Rainforest covers most of Suriname, and though the size of Georgia, it is only as populous as Atlanta. The country is green, humid, and hot. Hot like sitting in a car with the windows rolled up on a sticky summer's day. Until the sky takes on the color of steel wool and the rains beat down. Then, an afternoon there feels like sitting in a car on a summer's day with the windows down while going through a carwash. In addition to being one of the world's least densely populated countries, it remains one of the least visited. They don't make it easy. No English guidebooks exist. One baffling poster touting Suriname as a tourist destination actually features scenes of llamas in Peru's Machu Picchu. Maps are hard to come by and are more aspirational than accurate. Roads that may one day in the future slice through thick forests already cut across the map's green shading.

Suriname suffers confusion even about its name, which is officially spelled since achieving bloodless independence in 1975 with an "e" on the end, except when it isn't—as in the national air carrier, Surinam Airways. And when your plane touches down at Johan Adolf Pengel Airport, there's nowhere much to go but back up in a single-engine charter: there are precious few roads, and those that exist are poor. Upon arrival, the customs official flipped through my Israeli passport and asked me a single question: "How did you hear about our country?" This was not interrogation; this was astonishment. Israelis don't need a visa for Suriname, but even the hordes of adventure-craving young men and women who wander the world after their military service haven't made it there. Perhaps more would come if they knew that Suriname's Saramacca District almost became a Jewish homeland in the 1940s. The proposal to settle tens of thousands of Jews in Saramacca had full governmental approval, local support, and historical precedent. Suriname once contained the only officially sanctioned autonomous Jewish settlement from Roman times until the founding of modern-day Israel.

Today the country's capital, Paramaribo, is a sleepy city in the tropics where only dogs go out in the midday sun. But Paramaribo—called Parbo for short—was once the seat of power for valuable Dutch possessions along the "Wilde Kust"[62] of South America. The city stretches inland along the broad Suriname River, which empties into the Atlantic about ten miles distant. Trade winds blow in over the mud flats and mangrove swamps that line the coast. Colonists constructed their homes to catch the breeze, and many of the white clapboard houses still stand, their broad porches trimmed in peeling black, red, or green paint. This port of palm trees and faded grandeur is the site of the oldest enduring Jewish community in the New World. Documents trace an unbroken Jewish presence here back to at least 1643.[63] By the middle of the next century, Jews made up more than one half of the white population of Paramaribo.[64] The first fully emancipated Jews of the modern era traveled along a dusty road that still bears testimony to their influence: Jodenbreestraat, the "wide street of the Jews."

Castaways, thrice exiled, the first Jews of Suriname were a mixed breed, at home everywhere and nowhere. These Sephardi Jews came from several regions, spoke a variety of languages, and maintained familial and economic ties around the world. The Inquisition in Spain and Portugal set their exodus in motion. Large numbers fled to the Netherlands, or to Brazil, where they established themselves as "New Christians" under laxer colonial rule. Many who traveled to the New World remained crypto-Jews who prayed in sandy cellars and secretly lit Shabbat candles in cupboards or earthenware jars. When the Dutch held dominion over Brazil for a brief period in the 1630s, some Jews there emerged from hiding. But the Portuguese reconquered their territory with a vengeance and the Catholic Church put torch to tinder in the New World. This time the Jews fled the *auto da fé* with their Dutch protectors for what is now French Guiana. Then French forces captured that settlement in 1664, and many Jews decamped to Suriname, at the time a British possession. There too the Jews were caught between warring powers. In the turbulent seventeenth century, England and Holland repeatedly clashed in the Americas. The Treaty of Breda in 1667 brought a temporary end to the hostilities. As part of the peace, a defeated King

Charles II ceded to the Netherlands the prosperous sugar cane territory of Suriname. In return, Britain was deeded the backwater of the New Netherlands—today's New York. If you're living in Manhattan and not Paramaribo, you have sugar to thank for it.

Under Dutch rule, many of Suriname's Jews became wealthy merchants, globalizing trade just a century after the globe had first been trotted. Others were peasant farmers, plantation lords, soldiers, physicians, shopkeepers, or industrious fortune seekers. Some were impoverished refugees, *despechados*[65]—"the dispatched"—sent by their Jewish brethren across the Atlantic with only a few florins in their pockets. Most remarkably, the Jews of Suriname were free. Starting in 1665, when the British still held sway along the Wild Coast, the Jewish community enjoyed equality under the law. This was only a decade after England repealed its nearly 375-year-old Edict of Expulsion. The Dutch confirmed and extended these "Privileges Granted to the People of the Hebrew Nation."[66] Doctor David de Isaac Cohen Nassy, the leader of Suriname's Jewish regents, could claim in 1788 that for more than a century his coreligionists had enjoyed freedoms unknown to Jews since antiquity.[67] Ample records testify that the Jews of Suriname had indeed settled in the Amazon Basin "on a happier and more favorable basis than in any other place in the universe."[68]

The centerpiece of their security and prosperity was land. At a time when their counterparts in Europe were often forbidden to own property or were crowded into ghettos, the Jews of Suriname built an enclave that came to be called Jodensavanne, the "Jewish Savannah." The territory lies about forty miles upriver from Parbo in thick jungle on the edge of a sandy plain that gives the site its name. In 1682, pioneer Samuel Nassy, one of Doctor Nassy's forebears, deeded twenty-five acres of land to a grateful Portuguese Jewish community. Within a decade the colonial governor had enlarged the grant by one hundred acres.[69] A low hill rising over the river dominates Jodensavanne. Plantations spread around it made the most of the region's clayey soil and exploited the Suriname River waterway to the capital's harbor. The Portuguese Jews in the Savanne educated, governed, and defended themselves "with the right of autonomy anciently known of them in the time of the Romans."[70] Jodensavanne was referred to by its residents as the "village on the hill,"[71] a reference to the settlement's symbolic role as a new Jerusalem and an accurate topographical description. Suriname's Jerusalem in the jungle can be seen as more than just an agrarian settlement free from gentile meddling. The Savanne embodied a self-conscious sense of Suriname as a promised land. The improbable freedom and good fortune these Jews enjoyed must truly have seemed a sign of divine favor.

Writing just after Jodensavanne's centennial, Doctor Nassy confirmed as much in his description of the settlement: "The place where regularly built houses are to be found forms a rectangle 450 feet long by 300 wide, divided by four cross streets. The houses built at the corners of the rectangle are large and commodious. . . . The houses whose rears face the two valleys . . . present a view that is very agreeable. . . . In the middle of this rectangle is to be found the synagogue . . . [which is of] indescribable majesty."[72] Scholar Aviva Ben-Ur explains that the idealized layout of Jodensavanne corresponds to God's commandment (Numbers 2:1–31) that the Twelve Tribes encamp beneath their respective banners positioned at each of the four cardinal points.[73] In the center of this biblical encampment stood the Tent of Meeting; in the center of the Savanne's broad plaza stood the synagogue, Beracha ve Shalom (Blessing and Peace). The geometric symbolism of the village suggests that the wandering Sephardim felt they had found a home at last on a paradisaical patch of earth. By the rivers of Suriname they remembered Zion, and there they rebuilt it according to the blueprint they found in the Torah.

Life was sweet, literally. Sugar fueled the economy. Plantation lords boasted majestic homes, sumptuous clothes, and all the luxuries of Europe. While they ate from silver plates, their slaves endured a bitter lot. Most arrived in chains from West Africa and soon bent their backs beneath the broiling sun to thresh cane along the malarial rivers and cola-colored creeks. The exact number of slaves remains in dispute, but recent estimates suggest that Jews purchased about one quarter of the slaves in the colony.[74] Voltaire's Candide travels to Suriname during the apogee of slavery and there meets a nearly naked black slave writhing on the ground. The slave has lost his right hand to an accident, and his left leg as punishment for attempting escape. Candide asks the wretched man why he is treated so cruelly. "That's the price of your eating sugar in Europe," he answers.[75]

The Old World's despised Jews prospered in the New World thanks to Europe's sweet tooth. By the 1730s, Jews in Suriname not only enjoyed equal protection under Dutch law, they also owned more than twenty-five percent of the agricultural settlements, "most of them in sugar, and without a penny of debt."[76] Their influence grew under the Jewish board of regents, whose governance over communal affairs was recognized and confirmed by Princess Anne of the House of Orange.[77] The Jewish population increased, and community members participated in the wider cultural life of the colony. They even donated funds to erect the first purpose-built synagogue for their poor cousins in North America, Manhattan's Shearith Israel,[78] now one of America's wealthiest congregations. Mordecai Noah had been a leading member of the congregation and was aware of the Jodensavanne's Jews, even mentioning them in one of his published books.[79] Despite this clear connection, no evidence so far uncovered indicates that the Jodensavanne model influenced Noah's own quest for Jewish autonomy in North America.

As one eighteenth-century observer recorded, Suriname was indeed a "land that flowed with milk and honey"[80] for its Jewish residents. The main thing that troubled them were the slaves who escaped, many of whom later returned to wreak vengeance on their former masters. African slaves began to slip away from the plantations and flee into the trackless jungle almost simultaneously with their tortured arrival in the New World. These fugitives, called Maroons or *Bosnegros*—"bush negroes"—organized themselves into villages and made raids against the neighboring settlements, killing land owners, freeing their compatriots, and carrying off anything of value. One of the largest of these guerrilla republics was in the vicinity of the Saramacca River. But Maroons settled along all the major waterways and repeatedly skirmished with colonists. Jodensavanne was targeted, too. In the 1770s, the Dutch established a military cordon that extended eastward from the Savanne and provided security for the settlement and its economic interests. John Gabriel Stedman, an English mercenary who arrived to quell the revolts, participated in patrols in the vicinity. He described Jodensavanne as a place where Jews "possess particular rights and privileges . . . I never knew Jews to possess in any other part of the world whatever."[81] Stedman also reported on Maroon superstitions against eating certain animals, which they called "*treff*."[82] The word clearly derives from the Hebrew term for forbidden foods, *tareif*, a concept the Maroons likely assimilated during their servitude in Jewish households.

To demonstrate their loyalty to Holland and to avenge private losses, the Jewish community organized military expeditions against the runaways. Captain David C. Nassy, another member of Doctor Nassy's clan, led more than thirty of these bloody campaigns.[83] In a particularly atrocious episode, the captain attacked a Maroon village "on the day of *Kippur, or of Atonement of the Jews*, and without any regard for this sacred day, he pursued the enemies, set fire to their cabins, utterly ruined the village, tore out of the ground the roots of their victuals, took fourteen prisoners, and killed a large number."[84] His exploits were celebrated in a lost panegyric written by the eighteenth-century British Sephardi poetess Bienvenida Cohen Belmonte. Today it is difficult to accept that those who had been victimized by the Inquisition would hunt down and murder escaped slaves. Yet because the Jews were granted the same rights and privileges as Protestant subjects under Dutch law, they were free to create themselves in the image of the gentiles who admitted them to society. These Jews were eager to show their unprecedented equality and their superiority to another class: the *Bosnegros*. Suriname may be where the Jews first became white. But Suriname is also where the Jewish and African diasporas grew most interconnected.

Author Cynthia McLeod, a coffee-complected woman in her seventies, is the daughter of independent Suriname's first president, Dr. Johan Ferrier. She remains best known for her popular historical novel *The Cost of Sugar* (*Hoe duur was de suiker?* [1987]). Based on years of research, her book treats the history of Jewish sugar cane planters during the slave revolts. McLeod traces her own heritage back to Jewish ancestry. "Every Surinamese has Jewish blood," she likes to say, "shake a family tree, and a Jew falls out."[85] McLeod explains that some Jewish plantation owners kept slave mistresses with whom they had children, who were termed mulattos. Free mulatto women often lived with Jewish men in a quasi-legal, socially acceptable concubinage system called "marriage Surinam-style."[86] The children of these unions were sometimes raised according to Jewish tradition, giving rise to a class of mulatto Jews whose status greatly troubled Nassy's board of regents in the eighteenth century. McLeod continues, "There is a responsibility to acknowledge this history of slavery. American Jews don't want to speak of this, but [Jews] did [have slaves] in Suriname, we can prove that."[87] Despite this shameful history, she notes with affection that "Jews are the first Surinamers. Other colonists came to get rich, while Jews came to make Suriname their home."[88] Three of McLeod's own grandparents had Jewish fathers.

Generations of mixed-race relationships mean that Afro-Creole women still wear Star of David pendants. Few Surinamese know that the national treat, *pom*, a kind of tuber mashed with chicken, originated with a dish Jews ate on Passover. Ancient Hebrew echoes in contemporary Sranan Tongo, the local language. To this day, the word *treffu* refers to taboo foods and behaviors. And Saramacca's Ndjuka tribe of Maroons speaks a dialect known as Dju Tongo[89] ("Jew language"). Even the churches in Suriname are Jewish. The famed Petrus en Paulus Kathedraal, one of the largest wooden structures in the Americas, repurposed Parbo's defunct Jewish theater, De Verrezene Phoenix (The Risen Phoenix). These Jewish traces have long been obscured, but the legacy of Suriname's first Jewish settlers persists, especially in the Jodensavanne.

The notorious red dirt road to Jodensavanne is dusty when dry. Bauxite trucks lumbering to and from the mines stir up road grit that cuts visibility to nil. In the rain, the dirt turns to mud and the route becomes treacherous. A 4x4 is necessary to maneuver between the potholes and to skirt around slower tucks and broken-down vehicles. Red dirt spatters everything. Fine dust seeps its way into the car even with the windows closed. Loose rocks thud against the undercarriage. At the Suriname River's edge, a span of concrete lies half-submerged alongside the hulk of the barge that destroyed the recently completed bridge to Jodensavanne. The incomplete arch of the bridge deck yawns overhead like a gap-toothed smile. The only way across is via a ferry, really more a metal dock on pontoons that holds three vehicles and however many villagers are willing to clamber aboard. The river looks languid, but cast a twig into the water and it rapidly disappears downstream. The ferry barely has enough horsepower to fight the current to reach the other shore. Once across, a mile or so from the river, a weather-beaten metal sign sticks out of a white sand hillock to mark the Savanne. No one guards the overgrown entrance, though a barrier stops anyone from driving into the site itself. A paved path winds beneath a canopy of dense forest. Birds thrash overhead, frogs croak. Somewhere a hive buzzes. Not far from the entrance, the root-buckled tombstones of the Jewish cemetery spread across a clearing. Wet grass steams in the afternoon sun. The tombstones are flat slabs the size of a person, or in the case of the many children's graves, achingly small. Centuries of rain and neglect have worn away most of the Hebrew and Portuguese inscriptions. Beyond the cemetery, the jungle falls away at either side to reveal the foundations of Beracha ve Shalom, one of the earliest synagogues in the Americas. The synagogue sits on the crest of the hill with a commanding view of the Suriname River, just as Doctor Nassy described more than two centuries ago.

Jodensavanne boasted an active Jewish community for about a hundred years, but by the turn of the nineteenth century, the village was all but abandoned. Sugar markets had dissolved, and the slow bleed of the slave revolts shifted the population to Paramaribo. Worshippers continued to gather here until 1832, when Beracha ve Shalom was burned down, probably by vandals. Like the Israelite tribes whose biblical encampment Jodensavanne imitated, the settlers scattered along chaotic geometries. Then the jungle reclaimed their untended New Jerusalem. Ironically, the Dutch colonial administration used the area as an internment camp for German nationals and Nazi sympathizers in World War II. Prisoners were put to work clearing the site and hacking back the jungle. Today, despite preservationists' best efforts, tropical brush still threatens to overwhelm the excavated remains of the village on the hill.

A Graveyard for Europeans

Both Jews and antisemites considered the Wild Coast a potential dumping ground for Europe's Jews in the years leading up to the Holocaust. Ten days after *Kristallnacht*, wealthy Dutch Jew Daniel Wolf underwrote the foundation of the International Refugee Colonization Society (IRCS).[90] The organization's goals were "first to finance wholesale emigration of Jews . . . and, second, to find out which countries would offer the best opportunities for settlement."[91] Within weeks, two million dollars had been pledged to the IRCS by private individuals in Belgium, France, Switzerland, and the Netherlands.[92] Steinberg wrote to Wolf from London to tout Freeland efforts in the Kimberley.[93] Later, the IRCS considered the League's Australia plan as "perhaps the only possibility of great importance" to the organization.[94] Wolf's initiative to create a haven for millions of Jews also received the support of relief organizations in several countries and drew the attention of the British and American governments.[95] The *New York Times* hailed the announcement as a "great step forward . . . in the matter of the settlement of Jewish refugees."[96] But the IRCS plan and its rapid momentum drew quick condemnation from Zionist leaders[97] who doubted Wolf's assurance that "Palestine will remain the organizational center and cultural heart"[98] of Jewish resettlement efforts. Chaim Weizmann warned that the IRCS might raise "illusory hopes,"[99] though he recognized that the dire Jewish situation in Germany required immediate action.

Nearly simultaneous with the IRCS's formation, Anton Adriaan Mussert, the leader of the Dutch National Socialist Movement, began publishing articles later collected in a pamphlet, *United States of Guiana—The Jewish National Home*. This booklet, replete with maps and tables, proposed that the Jews of Europe be forcibly resettled in the South American colonies then belonging to Britain, the Netherlands, and France. Mussert insisted that "the Jews will have to be given a national home of their own,"[100] one "large enough and fertile enough to reunite the Jewish people within its borders."[101] Despite the antisemitism he espoused, the fleshy-faced fascist conceded that "even the Jews have the right to exist,"[102] and he justified his scheme on the basis of the historical Jewish presence in Suriname. Nothing came of what opponents called Mussert's "Jewish home of horrors."[103] But in March 1939, Wolf's IRCS did send a three-man commission to investigate whether Dutch Guiana could support voluntary, large-scale Jewish colonization.

The expedition's members included Dr. N. H. Swellengrebel, an eminent professor of parasitology, G. J. Vink, a retired agricultural inspector, and one Jewish member, Shlomo Dyk, the *yishuv* agronomist who had previously been sent to Madagascar to explore colonization possibilities there. Once again, this time from Paramaribo, Dyk wrote to Arthur Ruppin, who had recently served as a member of the Jewish Agency's executive board. Dyk scribbled greetings and an update on his research on the back of a picture postcard of a cooperative palm plantation.[104] The restless Dyk had traveled the world from his birthplace in the Ukraine to Germany, to Austria, to London, to Prague, to Palestine, to Madagascar, to Suriname and points in between, and finally to France, where he was arrested by the Vichy police.[105] Though he was released after two weeks,[106] Dyk succumbed to disease[107] in occupied Grenoble in May 1944,[108] a few months before liberation. What must he have thought of all his wanderings while he lay dying in 1944 as Jews deported from Paris chuffed their way into ash? Perhaps he wished he had stayed in Palestine. Or gone to Madagascar. Or remained in Suriname. The only plot of land he may have found was a grave, and perhaps not even that.

Dyk and Vink spent just over three months in Suriname, while Swellengrebel stayed on longer to complete his research.[109] Swellengrebel published an official report on the expedition in 1940 as the Nazis overran Europe. The war prevented Dyk's observations from finding their way into Swellengrebel's study, but according to Vink, he was in agreement with the findings.[110] The resulting book, *Health of White Settlers in Surinam*, is a classic of colonial biopolitics. In order to determine whether Jews could settle in a country reputed to be "a graveyard for Europeans,"[111] Swellengrebel presents a detailed "history of white settlement in Surinam."[112] Discussions of racial impurity[113] and European degeneration[114] are interspersed with a horror-logue of tropical diseases, including malaria, leprosy, yellow fever, and elephantiasis. He maintains—in what now reads as a chilling choice of words— that a "holocaust" of Jewish colonists in the tropics "can be avoided by judiciously locating the settlement"[115] away from areas of disease. The good doctor asserts that Maroons "have been one of the main causes of sickness among Europeans"[116] because of their so-called primitive condition and consequent high rate of malarial infection. And so, he advocates their "rigorous segregation"[117] from future Jewish colonists. If this advice is followed, the report concludes, then "hygiene has no objection to offer to the plan of settling whites in Surinam."[118] Swellengrebel refrained from selecting a particular region for colonization, though he mentions that "the coast of Surinam is unique" because of "unbelievably favorable rural health conditions."[119] The story of refugee colonization in Suriname might have ended with this promise, entombed on a shelf in the Colonial Institute at Amsterdam's Department of Tropical Hygiene. But after World War II, with survivors in displaced persons (D.P.) camps clambering for a new life away from the bloodlands of Europe, the IRCS report came to the attention of the Freeland League. According to Steinberg, Swellengrebel's "book became the leading and encouraging light"[120] as the *Fraylandistn* considered sites for mass emigration.

The revival of the proposal was in large measure due to Henri van Leeuwen, an opera-loving, religiously observant sausage-casing maker who was a disciple of Nathan Birnbaum.[121] Van Leeuwen helped Birnbaum, the former Zionist turned orthodox ideologue, escape from Berlin to Holland in 1933.[122] In the interwar period, van Leeuwen made frequent trips to the League of Nations in Geneva to meet with the organization's Intergovernmental Committee on Refugees (IGCR).[123] His work on behalf of refugee Jews was supported by the fortune of his wife, the daughter of one of the founders of the multinational Unilever company.[124] Van Leeuwen was also a cousin through marriage to Daniel Wolf and had served as the secretary for Wolf's IRCS.[125] His experiences working with the IRCS and his negotiations with the IGCR left him pessimistic about the Jewish future in Europe. He urged family and friends to leave the Netherlands, but his prophecies of impending disaster were largely ignored. However, he did succeed in sending his wife and five of his six children to the United States in 1939.[126] After their escape, van Leeuwen joined the underground Dutch resistance and was said to have dressed as a priest in order to recruit sympathizers to the cause.[127] He was eventually captured and sent to Bergen-Belsen but managed to survive until freed in a prisoner swap.[128] Van Leeuwen arrived in the U.S. at the end of 1945[129] determined to continue Wolf's IRCS work from America.[130]

He established contact with the Freeland League in New York and encouraged Steinberg to resurrect the prewar scheme and open negotiations with Dutch authorities to bring Jewish refugees to rural areas of Suriname. Van Leeuwen also connected Steinberg to his friend, Amsterdam-based historian Dr. Boris Raptschinsky. According to Steinberg, it was Raptschinsky who had "conceived and developed the scheme of a Jewish home in Suriname . . . during the last terrible years in Holland under Nazi domination."[131] In fact, even before the Nazi invasion of the Netherlands, Raptschinsky published a book, *The Jewish World Problem* (*Het Joodsche Wereldprobleem* [1941]), that called upon the British,

Dutch, and French to open the Guianas to Jewish colonization.[132] He believed the region to be far superior to Palestine. [133] Although his plan seemed to draw inspiration from that of Mussert, Raptschinsky was motivated by the plight of his coreligionists and his certainty that their situation was about to get even worse. He managed to survive the war in occupied Holland thanks to a loophole in Nazi law[134] that allowed him and his wife to be registered as having no religion; he was born in the Ukraine, and because no birth certificate could be produced to demonstrate his Jewishness, he was spared. His Dutch-born daughter, however, was deported and murdered at Auschwitz.[135] The horrors he witnessed and the grief he bore led him to resurrect plans for the colonization of Dutch Guiana after the war, despite the unseemly connection to Mussert's own antisemitic machinations.

Disappointment over the Kimberley and Tasmania projects continued to nag at Steinberg[136] after arriving in the United States. His proposals aimed not simply at "survival but revival"[137] of the Jewish people. However, Steinberg blurred his political vision with a sentimentality in his support for what he termed "family colonization."[138] The father—often all too absent from his own family—believed that "[o]ur people need the warmth and the atmosphere of a family and a home,"[139] not just a state, as in Palestine. So he resolved to advance van Leeuwen and Raptschinsky's territorialist proposal, even as support for Zionism swelled. He sent a letter to Suriname's governor, Dr. J. C. Brons, in March 1946 hoping to begin a dialogue concerning "the possibilities of Jewish colonization in Dutch Guiana."[140] Brons responded that the Freeland League proposal "met with sufficient interest" to discuss the matter further.[141] Brons raised questions about the "state in the state" aspect of the resettlement plan, a familiar objection faced by Noah and Zangwill earlier.[142] Communication between the two lagged until later that spring, when Steinberg sailed aboard the Cunard White Star line's flagship R.M.S. *Queen Mary* to England. While at sea Steinberg received a marine service radiogram in his A-deck stateroom from Freeland associates: "HIS EXCELLENCY BRONS IS ON QUEEN-MARY ON WAY TO HAGUE KINDLY CONTACT HIM."[143] The stunning coincidence meant that Steinberg had as a captive audience the one man who could help him achieve his vision of Suriname's renewed glory. Steinberg and Brons soon met in a corner of the starboard lounge, and there they discussed "the Jewish problem as far as Surinam can be concerned."[144]

No details of their conversation were recorded, but the charismatic Steinberg must have made a favorable impression. In May, he traveled to the Hague and was reunited with Brons to present his colonization plans to the Dutch minister of the Department of Overseas Parts.[145] Raptschinsky, now the Freeland League's official Dutch representative,[146] had already met with Brons[147] to present a revised draft of his earlier scheme from 1941. He urged the New York *Fraylandistn* to revive "the old and neglected plantations" of Jodensavanne where he believed "colonization could begin immediately and develop swiftly."[148] Minutes of the subsequent meeting between Brons and Steinberg describe a proposed self-governing agro-industrial[149] settlement. Their summit resulted in the submission of a confidential memorandum to Dutch authorities outlining the contours of a future Jewish colony and assuring officials that "the Jewish Settlement is not intended to become a separate political entity."[150] In keeping with Raptschinsky's expansive vision,[151] Steinberg maintained contact with both British and French colonial authorities in his ongoing "search for a land for our homeless"[152] in the Guianas. French colonial minister Marius Moutet—the same Moutet who had earlier considered opening Madagascar to Jewish colonization—expressed particular interest[153] in Steinberg's postwar project.

Brons circulated a version of Steinberg's proposal to Suriname's parliament, the Staten. By February 1947, representatives informed the governor that following "two closed meetings . . . the Staten have no objection to the establishment of Jewish colonization in Surinam."[154] In fact, of the twelve voting committee members only one opposed the plan.[155] Some representatives, like the leader of the powerful Moslem Party, recommended the resettlement of thirty thousand Jewish refugees, while others preferred a lower ceiling of ten thousand.[156] Telegrams between Brons and Steinberg indicate they negotiated back and forth for the admission of between five thousand to as many as fifty thousand Jewish colonists.[157] The *New York Times* soon reported the pending investigation of Dutch Guiana.[158] The news even reached survivors languishing in the Bergen-Belsen D.P. camp. Many wrote letters to the Freeland League promising to "undertake pioneer work"[159] on a future settlement. Refugee Freelanders organized themselves in the camps, and within months claimed more than five hundred enthusiastic D.P.s as members.[160] As time dragged on, others wrote in despair, lamenting the Allies' reluctance to speed immigration: "A little wisecrack has been making the rounds in our camp lately: 'So where are we going? To the moon—it's the only place where there is room for us.'"[161] Desperate for relief, a Freeland Conference of D.P.s representing twenty-five camps demanded the dispatch of two thousand survivors as soon as possible.[162]

An upbeat Steinberg hoped to maintain his plan's momentum and arrived in Suriname on April 10, 1947,[163] accompanied by Van Leeuwen and another stalwart Freelander. The delegation planned to tour regions of possible colonization, especially the Saramacca district west of the capital, and they hoped to impress Dutch officials with their settlement proposal. A grainy eleven-minute silent movie[164] documenting the trip reveals Steinberg's optimism. The handheld camera shows him smiling, his unruly hair blowing in the wind while palm trees sway in the distance. He stops by a local's wood-and-straw hut, his tie flaps in the breeze, chickens and a stray dog scurry around him. Then the frame jumps to Steinberg walking briskly down a rutted dirt street, absentmindedly crushing the brim of a black hat in his hand. Another shot finds him climbing a rickety wooden ladder with his sleeves rolled up. He pauses, removes his glasses, and flashes a fleeting grin half-obscured by his grizzled beard. Title cards explain that the delegates were "accompanied by officials of the Surinam government," that they traveled to Saramacca to visit an "experimental fruit plantation,"[165] that they saw the jungle villages of the Djuka—the Maroon tribe that claims Jewish ancestry—and that they surveyed vast sugar cane fields. The final image of the delegates shows them riding a railway handcar operated by two muscular men who propel them down the tracks, past agricultural fields, and off into the horizon. Ten days after the Freeland delegation had arrived they signed a joint statement with Suriname's Governmental Advisory Commission proposing the "immediate immigration of 30,000 Jews to be selected by the Freeland League."[166] The Governmental Advisory Commission included the future president of the Staten, the director of social affairs and immigration—Dr. M. de Groot (a Jew)—and several other important officials.[167]

After what he had seen, Steinberg was confident that Suriname could absorb "communities of Jewish colonists who occupy themselves with agriculture and industry."[168] Whenever he spoke to locals, he emphasized that the refugees would arrive to "do pioneer work, to develop the land with shovel and spade" and would most definitely not be "Jewish dentists, [because] there are more Jewish dentists than there are teeth in Jewish mouths."[169] Steinberg also angled for cultural autonomy within the colony, insisting that "assurance must be given of a free development of Jewish culture, including the religion, the language, and the customs."[170] During one speech in Paramaribo, Steinberg asked his audience: "If there was a cultural center here in 1788, why could this not come to pass again?"[171] His rhetoric was convincing.

On April 21, 1947, the day after the Freelanders departed, Governor Brons signed an agreement that provided for Jewish colonists to possess "rights of autonomy in local government."[172] The "Jewish language"— Yiddish—would be used in schools as the "initial medium of instruction."[173] The announcement made the *New York Times* under the headline "Haven for Homeless Is Offered By Dutch."[174] Dr. de Groot praised Steinberg's efforts, writing that his visit swayed "many more people . . . in favour of Jewish Colonization than before."[175] A month after returning to the U.S., Steinberg received the telegram he had been waiting for: the Staten "ACCEPTED THIRTYTHOUSAND SCHEME."[176] By the close of the year, Governor Brons reconfirmed the agreement for an autonomous settlement, which again stipulated that the Dutch would "admit 30,000 Jews into Surinam for colonization."[177] The governor's main concern prior to the commencement of immigration was that the Freeland League had not yet presented a detailed budget for resettlement costs.[178] He also insisted, in contrast to his Advisory Commission's position, that "the selection of immigrants should ultimately be decided upon by the Surinam Government."[179]

Despite the work yet to be done, Steinberg must have felt immensely satisfied with his diplomatic achievements. The much-celebrated Balfour Declaration of thirty years earlier was in essence a vaguely worded statement of sympathy for Jewish national aspirations in Palestine, whereas the Freelanders had secured a charter for an autonomous sanctuary for tens of thousands of their stateless brethren interned in European camps. At that historical moment, the British authorities in Mandate Palestine prevented Holocaust survivors from landing on Israel's shores in an effort to appease Arab nationalists. The Surinamese people, for their part, offered help and encouragement to the Freelanders. One correspondent from Saramacca submitted a recipe for an invigorating soy-groat cake with onions that "requires no refrigeration" and "will be useful to the Jewish pioneers building Surinam."[180] An engineer representing the Independency Party guaranteed Steinberg success and urged: "Freeland has been given to you and yours, make use of it as quick as possible."[181] Beloved folk poet L. E. "Goedoe Goedoe" Thijm, a fixture on Paramaribo's streets, wrote verses in favor of Jewish immigration, predicting: "If we open our gates / Just as America did / Then our country will prosper."[182] In another poem he chastised those who opposed the plan: "If the Jews come, / they will not be lazy. / If a horse wants to run, / do not hold his lead."[183] As for the people of Saramacca, the numerous Javanese residents "heartily welcomed" the "Orang Jehudi"—the Jewish people.[184]

But Steinberg was frustrated[185] that concrete plans had stalled after his departure. By September, he wrote to beg the once-enthusiastic Dr. de Groot to provide him with material for public relations purposes.[186] The Freeland cause received a boost in November when E. M. J. Sassen, the Dutch representative to the U.N., addressed a General Assembly meeting on the Palestine partition plan. He noted that his government had been working to provide a solution to Jewish homelessness, declaring that "an agreement was concluded" between Suriname and the Freeland League to admit thirty thousand Jews to the territory as part of a "large scale resettlement" effort.[187] The U.N. voted in favor of Palestine's partition three days later. Despite the dramatic events unfolding in the Middle East, public diplomacy helped the Freeland League gain the support of wealthy American Jews and other notables, including director George Cukor (*The Philadelphia Story*), cosmetics magnate Max Firestein (of Max Factor), screenwriter Herman Mankiewicz (*Citizen Kane*), Nobel laureate Thomas Mann, and the once popular author Robert Nathan, whose intriguing novel *Road of Ages* (1935) imagined world Jewry exiled to a territorial refuge in the Gobi desert.[188]

Despite recent success, the Freelanders feared a further loss of momentum. And so by December 1947, a Commission of Experts appointed by the Freeland League arrived to determine "the prospects of Surinam as a future home for the Jews."[189] The personnel included a civil engineer; a soil scientist; an authority on tropical agriculture who had participated in a 1939 expedition to survey the Dominican Republic for Jewish settlement in Sosúa; Dr. George Giglioli, the malariologist and DDT pioneer who had served *ex officio* for the Commission to British Guiana; and a former staffer of the U.S. Department of Commerce, Nathaniel Weyl.[190] In a group photo, Weyl appears younger than his distinguished colleagues. His dark hair is combed high on his head, he slouches forward and smiles, and unlike his coworkers, he sports an open collar and casually dangles a cigarette.[191] An ex-Communist, the Jewish Weyl achieved notoriety a few years later when he testified against Alger Hiss. (Coincidentally, Hiss happened to have presided over the San Francisco United Nations conference that had ignored Freeland League pleas for settlement in British and French dominions.) Steinberg too returned to Suriname. He attended a "scientific dinner"[192] in Paramaribo and there dined on traditional Surinamese-Jewish dishes such as peanut soup and *pom*. A few weeks later, Steinberg himself was made a meal of. He developed a "small hole"[193] in his abdomen that became infected. A doctor had to lance the boil-like lesion to release squirming, creamy-white botfly larvae that had begun feeding on his flesh.

The Commission's experts spent months gathering data and exploring the region, traveling more than 200 kilometers by foot and more than 650 by boat.[194] The proposed size of the settlement was to be 250,000 hectares[195] (about one thousand square miles), or two thirds the size of Rhode Island. Land would be leased for seventy-five years, with a renewal option for another seventy-five.[196] The first settlement would be founded west of Groningen and south of the Saramacca River where it begins to follow an east-west course.[197] Future expansions would continue south and west on a contiguous swathe of territory.[198] This area of the Saramacca District offered a number of advantages, including a healthy climate, well-drained sites for settlement, fertile soil, ample water supply, a suitable location for the transport of goods, and a local population totaling only 10,087 people, of whom exactly nine were "Europeans."[199] The Commission's report runs to nearly 150 pages and treats many aspects of the proposed colonization scheme.

The Commission's agricultural expert saw potential for sugar export to the Benelux nations, just as the Jodensavanne plantations had done

Shores of the Coppename River along site of planned Saramacca settlement, Suriname.
Courtesy of Michael Kollins

centuries before. He discussed at length the future settlement's ability to exploit the "world pineapple situation,"[200] and recommended that Jewish colonists cultivate "pork and its products"[201]—an oddly insensitive suggestion. The civil engineer drew up an estimate of how many professionals per thousand families would be necessary for the settlement project. He foresaw bustling hamlets of "milkmen" (five), "shoemakers" (four), "fishermen" (ten), "cinema operators" (three), "undergarment makers" (two), one "banana handler," and one "rabbi."[202] (Only one rabbi per thousand Jewish families was perhaps the most fantastic of the Commission's suggestions; as the joke has it, even a Jewish Robinson Crusoe would have built at least two synagogues.) Notwithstanding Steinberg's "no dentists allowed" policy, the report maintained that four dentists would be required, a reasonable conclusion given that the Commission anticipated that at least one "candy man"[203] would also be necessary.

Weyl composed one of the more fascinating chapters of the report, noting that only about 150 square miles of land was under cultivation[204] in Suriname at the time. The Freeland settlement would therefore exponentially raise the Dutch colony's agricultural output. Weyl also recommended the establishment of specific industries, including dairies, canneries, oil presses, and fisheries. And "in view of the world protein shortage" of the postwar period, he added, "exploration should be made of utilizing turtle meat."[205] What sort of Jewish nation would arise on the labored backs of Yiddish-speaking pineapple growers, pig farmers, and turtle hunters? Would such Jewish settlers have created a viable, alternate Israel? The Expert Commission's unanimous[206] conclusion was loud and clear and shouted in all-caps: "THE CALCULATED RISKS INDICATE THAT THE FREELAND SURINAME SETTLEMENT CAN ACHIEVE ECONOMIC SUCCESS."[207] The American Jewish Committee's own Committee on Immigration recommended financial and operational collaboration with the Freeland League, noting with some urgency that "[t]the Surinam plan should be put into effect; everything must be done towards its realization. . . . Our active support for the initiation and development of the Surinam plan must be given without much delay."[208] The acting director of the United Nations Food and Agricultural Organization also endorsed the Commission's findings after conducting a review. He presented some further thoughts, including suggestions for phased colonization and the establishment of cooperatives in Saramacca.[209]

A second detailed document describing the pace of colonization, the living conditions, and the projected costs of implementing the Saramacca Plan was submitted to Brons at his request by Weyl and another member of the Commission of Experts.[210] Their supplementary report describes the incremental immigration of thirty thousand Jews over the course of four years at a total cost of $35,048,500, or $1,168 per person.[211] They envisioned establishing a tent city to house the first one hundred D.P.s and administrators,[212] who would then clear land and begin building the settlement's infrastructure of roadways, drainage, irrigation, and dikes.[213] Shortly thereafter, two buildings, each containing fifty "one-room-with-porch apartments,"[214] would house the next batch of immigrants. These were to be followed by the construction of four hundred semidetached houses for families and ten "village centers."[215] The latter are described as akin to the communal buildings on *kibbutzim* and were to include a large kitchen and dining room, school rooms, commissary, lending library, first aid station, workshop,

A road in Saramacca, Suriname. Courtesy of Michael Kollins

and meeting hall.[216] A power plant, telephone exchange, agricultural research station, printing plant, and hospital were also planned [217] The first twenty-four hundred settlers would tend garden farms, commence rice planting, dairy, hog, and poultry farming,[218] and begin the operation of a saw mill, brick plant, furniture factory, and machine shop.[219] Smaller enterprises were to focus on the production of ice cream, textiles, cigarettes, beer, rum, molasses, and batik printing for the hospitable Javanese inhabitants of Saramacca.[220]

Would uprooted European Jews have fared better among the Javanese and descendants of their coreligionists' former slaves, the Maroons, than they did among the Palestinians? Or, as Cynthia McLeod suggests, would the Maroons have just "thrown stones on the other side of the Saramacca River, [creating] Suriname's own intifada"?[221] Though it's impossible to answer such what-if questions, today's Saramacca suggests an optimistic answer. The terrain varies from savannah to marshland to jungle. Few signs of commerce or large-scale agriculture exist along the routes through Saramacca and the proposed sites of settlement. The capital, Groningen, consists of scattered buildings that appear empty too, except for the ever-present stray dog sniffing its way toward something invisible and probably long gone. A lazy stretch of the Saramacca River cuts through town. Speckled lizards lumber along the grassy riverbank. A Chinese man casts a line into the shallows. Creole children play around a gazebo. A black woman comforts a crying child. An Amerindian girl dozes in a hammock behind a makeshift stand selling dried fish. Saramacca's lack of development, its superabundant vegetation, and its sparse and heterogeneous population make it look like a utopian social revolutionary's dream.

Suriname Nightmare

For a while, it looked as if Steinberg would realize his planned colony in Saramacca. The *New York Times* reported on developments throughout 1947 and into 1948. The leftist daily *PM* devoted a long column to the plan and printed a detailed map of the region.[222] Suriname's Jewish community paper, *Teroenga* (*Teruah*, or *Clarion*), provided Steinberg and the Freelanders' Commission of Experts with positive press during their visits. In the December 1947 issue, a 1,400-word article described the Commission's progress and extolled the scheme. In the same issue, a mere sixty words are devoted to "the joyful news that the United Nations Organization has approved the partition of Palestine into a Jewish and an Arab state."[223] Steinberg himself seemed to ignore the dramatic developments in Palestine. He enthused in a farewell address to his local supporters several months after the U.N. partition vote: "A grand venture will be established here. The focus and the capacities of all the Jews of Suriname for this effort will be needed."[224]

After his return to the U.S., Steinberg tracked down Professor Swellengrebel, author of the favorable 1939 IRCS expedition report commissioned by Wolf. He asked the professor to endorse the Freeland Commission's own findings. In response, a letter signed by Swellengrebel and four other experts announced that "[t]he new project of settling D.P.s from Europe undertaken by the Freeland League . . . is heartily endorsed . . . as far as health possibilities are concerned."[225] The letter is dated Friday, May 14, 1948—the day the State of Israel declared its independence. Just one day later, 166 Freelanders trapped in a D.P. camp in Vienna pleaded to be allowed to "assist this great cause" in Suriname.[226] "We, the desperately determined remnants," their letter continues, "will in spite of all obstacles start the journey which promises us a brighter future."[227] What future did the refugee Freelanders imagine for themselves in South America? "The creation of a new and healthy Jewish community in Surinam," they wrote, "means the rebuilding of the destroyed and decimated Jewish community in Poland."[228] Eighteenth-century Jews in the Jodensavanne re-created a vision of ancient Jerusalem; the Freelanders proposed the re-creation of interbellum Jewish Warsaw. Steinberg's followers sought nothing less than to import the "ways of life and the language"[229] of Eastern European Jewry to the Amazon Basin region.

To that end, Freeland League organizers in D.P. camps registered willing pioneers, men and women like Fanica S., a twenty-six-year-old hairdresser and the only survivor of thirty-eight family members; Sigi H., a forty-year-old radio technician, and his son, Hugo; and Hayim Z., a thirty-six-year-old furrier who was the only member of his family left alive at the war's end.[230] Survivors in Romania pleaded in an open letter to American Jews, writing: "From this death valley, surrounded by the graves of our kin, we call to you to give the Freeland plan for saving 30,000 Jewish souls your utmost cooperation."[231] Their call went unheeded.

American Zionists weren't about to let such people go. They reasonably feared that success in Suriname would weaken support for the nascent State of Israel. At stake were the fates of hundreds of thousands of potential Israeli citizens waiting to leave Europe. These survivors, so the thinking went, would provide the demographic wave necessary to secure Israel's future when they washed up on its shores. But the antagonism between Zionist and Freeland leaders was personal as well as ideological. Steinberg's testimony before the Anglo-American Committee on Palestine, a joint effort to deal both with instability in Palestine and with the fate of Holocaust survivors, had rendered him suspect in early 1946. Though he supported the "immediate abolishment"[232] of white-paper restrictions on Jewish immigration to Mandate Palestine, he voiced skepticism about the project of nation-building itself. In the name of the Freeland League, he told American and British officials that his organization was "not very interested in the establishment of a Jewish State in Palestine, because we don't believe that the world . . . is very much in need of a new State."[233] He went on to explain: "I am afraid not of the fight for the establishing of the State; I am afraid of the consequences of the fight [because] our people would be militarized from the start. I am afraid under these conditions the moral and spiritual and economic development of the country might be crippled."[234] Such remarks contained more than a dose of defeatism and were nothing short of blasphemy to the Zionist establishment.

Stephen S. Wise, still one of the most influential Jewish leaders in the United States, played a role in scuttling the Saramacca Plan. Although he had written a letter on Steinberg's behalf when he first sought entry to the U.S. in 1941,[235] Wise turned on him as the Freeland League scored diplomatic and public relations successes. In a telegram sent in the midst of the Saramacca controversy, Wise cabled: "I personally believe that Steinberg should be lynched or hanged in quarters, if that would make his lamented demise more certain. He represents a combination of a Messiah complex and anti-Zionism, that appeals, understandably, to many Jews."[236] For Wise, one of the founders of the NAACP, "lynching" was not an empty image.

The recipient of this vicious missive was sixty-six-year-old[237] Ida Marcia Silverman, who had previously traveled to Australia to attack

Freeland plans there. A jeweler's wife fond of charm bracelets,[238] she crisscrossed the world as a fundraiser and publicist for Zionism and wrote articles under her *nom de plume*, Mrs. Archibald Silverman. She repeatedly worked to defeat large-scale Jewish emigration to anywhere other than Palestine. "I became alarmed and intrigued every time a counter-colonization scheme was foisted upon an anti-Zionist, hence gullible, Jewish public," she later explained.[239] In the first years of World War II, her vituperative articles in Jewish periodicals helped diminish enthusiasm for the resettlement of Jews in Sosúa[240] in the Dominican Republic, then underway. "When in 1940, Jews were being settled by the Joint Distribution Committee, in an isolated corner of the Dominican Republic . . . among the blacks, I made it my business to investigate this new plan for a Jewish autonomous state," she recalled. "My published findings prevented a nationwide money-campaign. . . . So, another colonization chimera came to an end."[241] In 1944, she arrived in Australia to oppose Steinberg's plans in that country. "[I]t was my lot," Silverman wrote, "to study the plan . . . to settle Jews in Kimberley (among the head-hunting aboriginals close to the Equator) and again I may have had something to do with the final abandonment of this outrageous plan."[242] Steinberg's nemesis dogged his heels in Suriname, too.

She sent a telegram to Jerusalem to her nominal handlers at the *Keren Hayesod* (Palestine Foundation Fund), the central fundraising body of Zionism, to inform them she was headed to Paramaribo in order to "investigate Steinberg's colonization scheme."[243] "I decided to go and see for myself what sort of a hoax the Freeland League was plotting," Silverman recollected. "Yes, Steinberg was following his usual procedure. He was promising a backward and bankrupt government a minimum of $35,000,000 for permission to settle Jews in the disease-infested jungles along the Surinam River."[244] Boastful histrionics, appeals to racist sentiment, and a penchant for misrepresentation and outright lies characterized her long battle against territorialist efforts. So when the Freelanders in New York learned of her trip, they telegrammed associates in Suriname: "Mrs. Silverman, Zionist speaker arriving . . . [s]upposedly to investigate Freeland colonization project, but really to discredit it. War[n] Dr. de Groot and counteract her propaganda quietly."[245] The combative Silverman managed to split opinion in Paramaribo's Jewish community during her whirlwind three-day sojourn there in March

1948. When asked about the Saramacca project during a town-hall meeting in the capital, she reportedly responded: "I will not allow any discussion on that point. This is a Zionist meeting. . . . Let us sing the Hatikvah!"[246] She was equally high-handed in her treatment of Paramaribo's Jewish community who, she claimed falsely, "huddle[d] close together in fear and trepidation."[247]

Soon after her return, Silverman reported back to *Keren Hayesod* officials in Jerusalem that she had compiled enough evidence to "kill the whole [Saramacca] plan."[248] Yet she felt leaders in Jerusalem remained ungrateful for her sacrifices, maintaining that "someone should not only thank me for it, but should actually pay my expenses."[249] Silverman next penned a vitriolic article called "The Surinam Nightmare."[250] Her exposé described "diabolical plans" to abandon Jewish "guinea pigs" to "terrifying tropical diseases" all because of Steinberg's "jungle pipe dreams."[251] Though she claimed to "tell the world at large the truth"[252] about the scheme, her article misspells the name of the district under consideration ("Saramassa"), misrepresents its size, and suggests that "anti-Semitism has sprung up" in Suriname as a result of Steinberg's efforts.

One leader of Suriname's now divided Jewish community wrote to Steinberg to complain of Silverman's damaging lies.[253] De Groot worked from Paramaribo to reassure Steinberg that neither he nor the governor had given Silverman any ammunition against the plan.[254] In Europe, meanwhile, D.P.s who continued to support the Freelanders faced retribution. One activist complained: "I was called to the local Zionist federation in Camp Steyr to make a public declaration that I dissociate myself from the entire Surinam 'affair'; that we disband our organization and stop our work and join the fight for Palestine. As a beginning I was dismissed from my post. . . . I had been working as director of camp registration. . . . The Zionists might force us to leave the camps and . . . in that way we will be confronted by the hard problem of sustenance."[255] Still that informant and other refugee *Fraylandistn* were committed "to wait for the emigration to Surinam" rather than be sent to Palestine.[256]

Steinberg fought back against Silverman's assault. He wrote to supporters in Paramaribo decrying her "criminal attack" in the press, and he was certain that an enemy in the Staten had leaked confidential information to her. [257] When the Second Freeland Conference convened in New York, attendees resolved "to continue negotiations with Surinam and Holland" and to "strik[e] back at the attacks made on the Freeland movement."[258] In an open "Call to the Jewish People," the Freelanders pleaded: "Do not permit the repetition of the fatal historic mistake of 40 years ago when, because of national shortsightedness, the offer of a Jewish land in Uganda was rejected. Surinam dare not become a second Uganda in the history of the Jewish people."[259] But the Saramacca Plan was indeed to become a "second Uganda" of sorts—anachronistic, misunderstood, maligned, and finally forgotten.

Although Silverman's screed did damage support for the proposal, the fate of the Freeland plan had already been decided. One week after her article saw the light of day, the State of Israel was established and then recognized by the United States. Freeland D.P.s in Europe remained faithful to the plan, insisting that "Surinam is a positive solution. . . . The jungle will 'step aside' before the forward march of the new generation of pioneers."[260] But shortly after Israel declared its independence, the Staten suspended all discussion of mass Jewish immigration. One of the experts who had explored Saramacca for the Freeland League informed Steinberg that while in Paramaribo in July 1948 he had learned that external "pressure has been put on the Netherlands Government to call off this colonization scheme and that this pressure comes from one of two sources—either our own State Department or from the Zionist group."[261] This intelligence received confirmation from Raptschinsky in Holland the same week: "What I heard from reliable sources is very alarming. I am told that the Zionists put a very heavy pressure upon the Dutch Government to reject our proposals."[262] A letter written in August 1948 to the Freeland League from Brons' replacement tersely states: "After due and profound consideration, the Staten—pending the total clarification of the general international situation—prefer to suspend the discussions with your organization on immigration of Jews into Surinam."[263] Such total clarification was long in coming to the hypocritical Dutch government, which only formally recognized Israel in January 1950. The Freeland League pleaded with Prime Minister Drees to intervene with the Staten, but Drees claimed that the colonial parliament had acted independently and that "it is not possible to influence the decision taken."[264]

In New York, the disappointed *Fraylandistn* took comfort in Thomas Mann's public support for the Saramacca scheme as a way to provide a measure of justice to Europe's Jewish remnant. "For many months now I have been concerned with this new possibility," Mann wrote. "I have acquainted myself with the living conditions in Surinam. The Surinam project is the first that points in the direction of fulfilling our moral obligations. I am utterly convinced that every right-thinking person should support this project, morally and materially."[265] Mann's unequivocal support had no discernible impact. Other powerful figures tried to intercede more practically on the Freeland League's behalf. The International Ladies Garment Workers Union (ILGWU), under boss David Dubinsky, had contributed ten thousand dollars to the Commission of Experts' survey of Saramacca thanks to Steinberg's connections with the influential union leader. The ILGWU did not take kindly to the fact that its investment had evaporated, and Jay Lovestone, the ILGWU's director of international labor relations and a CIA operative, distrusted Israel's relationship with the Soviet Union and its bloc countries.[266] Lovestone wrote to request—in vain—that the Staten reconsider its decision.[267] The cold warrior's fellow CIA informant and unionist Irving Brown met with Sassen, the Dutch U.N. representative, to discuss the suspension of negotiations as well. Steinberg was apprised of the meeting, during the course of which Sassen charged that "the Netherlands Government influenced to a large degree the decision taken by the Staten in view of the overall international situation, and more concretely in view of the situation in Israel."[268]

While Israelis fought to defend their newborn state through force of arms, the Freelanders sent emissaries to Paramaribo in March 1949 to press the League's claims regarding the legality of the April 1947 agreement signed with Brons, and to prepare the groundwork for a propaganda campaign to revive the Saramacca plan.[269] The delegation was warned that Paramaribo's Jewish community had been "'taken over' by Zionists," including the new rabbi and a prominent businessman.[270] This was to be the last gasp for the Saramacca Plan, which had become another lost territorialist cause. Steinberg, however, was unwilling to admit defeat. He maintained contact with individuals and governmental figures in his effort to restart the project into the 1950s. As late as 1955, Steinberg approached Suriname's prime minister, Dr. Johan

Ferrier—author Cynthia McLeod's father—about the scheme. Ferrier politely promised that his government would study the issue, an empty gesture that served as a coda to the Saramacca Plan.[271] Steinberg was to remain a Moses without a promised land, and Suriname a promised land deferred. According to Dr. Alexander Heldring, a former Dutch diplomat who has written the definitive history of the episode, Suriname has to this day "never transformed the 'suspension' into a formal 'discontinuance.'"[272]

The Freeland League continued to publish dreamy reports on settlement in Suriname, on the proposed creation of a finance bank for colonization there,[273] and on Suriname's own struggle for independence.[274] Later, they turned their attention to settlement ideas in Latin America, proposing new ventures in Uruguay,[275] Costa Rica,[276] Chile,[277] Nicaragua,[278] and Ecuador.[279] None of these visions escaped from the black newsprint of *Freeland* magazine. In November 1956, Steinberg's devoted daughter Ada, editor of *Freeland*, succumbed to illness at the age of thirty-nine. Less than two months later, her father suffered a fatal heart attack.[280] The man who had given hope to so many died of grief for his favorite child, the daughter who had followed in his ideological footsteps.[281]

Steinberg was eulogized as a modern-day Herzl who "labored to attain his goal, but did not live to see its fruition."[282] To another devoted follower, he "was of the line of Jewish prophets."[283] Psychologist Erich Fromm praised his dear friend for his faith—faith "in ideas and in visions in spite of the fact that they do not yet exist, and in ideas in spite of the fact that they do not yet have power."[284] The *Fraylandistn* remained loyal to Steinberg's ideals after his death, though the pages of *Freeland* increasingly featured bitter denunciations of Israeli policy and the Jewish state's treatment of its Arab citizens. Steinberg was not hostile to Zionism himself, though he was a critic of the *yishuv*'s militarism and its rejection of Diaspora life, especially its denigration of Yiddish. Thanks in part to the triumphs of Zionism, a history of victors, Steinberg today is forgotten by all but his descendants, a handful of academics, and members of the Freeland League's current incarnation, the apolitical League for Yiddish.

True, the vigorous and far-sighted Steinberg failed to establish a toehold on even the most meager slice of earth. He failed in this mission both before the Holocaust, and during the height of the genocide, and after, when hundreds of thousands of survivors languished in camps. He failed to bring Jews to the Kimberley. He failed to bring them to Tasmania. He failed to bring them to Saramacca. His immediate family were among the few displaced persons Steinberg ever managed to resettle. Steinberg's legacy may indeed be one of failure, but it is the scope of his ambitions, and his sense of the peril and promise of the future that remain compelling. He endures as a Cassandra figure, gifted—or cursed—to foresee the dangers that lay ahead for world Jewry. In one prescient article from 1946, Steinberg divined that Israel's establishment would "force upon the Jewish people a new historic yoke—the yoke of struggle against the Mohammedan world."[285] "This," he warned, "is the future."[286] Steinberg's grim prediction of things to come, unlike Herzl's utopian dream of coexistence, has sadly come to pass.

Epilogue

Go to Uganda

In the summer of 2013, bullying wall posters appeared overnight across Jerusalem's fervently orthodox—*haredi*—neighborhoods. This was nothing out of the ordinary. These broadsides, known as *pashkvilim*, are a familiar part of the landscape of *haredi* life. Hastily pasted on walls along busy streets to communicate their messages to passersby, *pashkvilim* are ephemera, destined to be defaced or covered over. They are typically printed in stark black lettering against a white background, and often take the form of admonitions against such dangers as the Internet, immodest dress, or lax Sabbath observance. But these particular *pashkvilim* were notable because they demanded that Prime Minister Benjamin Netanyahu "go to Uganda" as his "adored leader," Theodor Herzl, had proposed more than a century earlier.[1] The Uganda *pashkvilim* testify to the extent to which some *haredi* factions hold onto the memory of the affair in their polemics, even as the episode has been downplayed as a curiosity in standard accounts of Zionism.[2] For many in the *haredi* community, this chapter of Zionist history serves as proof that Herzl was a false messiah, and his followers nothing but a godless troupe of troublemakers with little connection to the wellspring of Jewish tradition.

The anonymous *haredi* spokesmen behind the Uganda posters may be shaky on historical detail and their aims anathema to the vast majority of Israelis, yet they do have a point, at least in part. Herzl and his allies, some of whom were religious, were indeed willing to accept Great Britain's proposal for an East African "New Palestine" if for none other than tactical reasons. The leaders of the major territorialist movements that arose after Herzl's death, the ITO and the Freeland League, believed themselves to be the true heirs to his ambitions and political pragmatism. Like Mordecai Noah and Leon Pinsker before him, the humanistic brand of Zionism Herzl first endorsed in *Der Judenstaat* (1896) advocated the rise of a benevolent Jewish enterprise either in the New World, or in the ancient world—in Palestine.[3] Herzl's "proposal of a modern solution of the Jewish question,"[4] though colonialist by twenty-first-century standards, was in keeping with the liberal tenets of his era.

Certain aspects of the multiethnic and mutualist "New Society" Herzl depicted several years later in *Altneuland* (1902) remain estimable today, though more than a whiff of paternalism emanates from the novel. The utopian travelogue features opera-loving, German-speaking Jews who prosper in a *Mitteleuropean* Middle East. Moments of dramatic tension are few, and to contemporary readers, often laughable. At one point, visitors to the Old-New Land of Palestine find themselves in the "desperate predicament of accompanying ladies to the theater" without the proper attire: white gloves.[5] These urbane Jews live side by side with obliging Arabs in a demilitarized region where ecumenical tolerance reigns. The indigenous Arab residents are vocally indebted to the recent European immigrants for having brought the tools and culture of the Western world to their benighted backwater.

Despite the surface amity, whispered fears that Jewish power will breed "millennial terrorism" resound.[6] *Altneuland* conjures a nightmarish vision of Jewish nationalism in one of its central plotlines, which follows the political campaign of a demagogue whose platform calls for the expulsion of non-Jews from the New Society. The villain, Rabbi Geyer, may be read as a composite of Herzl's enemies, especially traditionalist rabbinic leaders in Europe. Geyer goes on to suffer defeat at the polls, thus freeing the New Society to develop in peace and harmony as a commonwealth for all its citizens, though it remains a particular showcase for Jewish industry and ingenuity.

The Old-New Land is meant not only to provide an answer to the Jewish question, however. Herzl's heroic technocrats aim to solve the

"Negro problem" as well.[7] "The depths of that problem," one founding father of the New Society explains, "only a Jew can understand. . . . That is why I am working to open up Africa."[8] Even as his own people remained in precarious exile, Herzl propounded a redemptive mission to free black men and women from bondage. It remains a remarkable twist of fate that just a year after *Altneuland* appeared in print, Herzl's closest friends and advisors found themselves pressing for a Jewish exodus to an African Zion.

The formal rejection of the British East African proposal allowed the Zionist Organization to fully territorialize the memory of the biblical land of Israel to suit the movement's modern, secular goals of nation-building.[9] The aftermath of the Uganda affair thus cemented Palestino-centric Zionism as normative, and assured the ascendency of the practical Zionists and their infiltration methods as championed by Herzl's adversary, Menachem Ussishkin. Yet territorialist proposals continued to exert their hold upon Jewish and non-Jewish thinkers for decades. The abandonment of humanitarian relief as a primary Zionist aim after the Seventh Zionist Congress (1905) directly contributed to the formation of the ITO. To Zangwill and his supporters, the Uasin Gishu Plateau of western Kenya, and later the Benguela Plateau of Angola, appeared more conducive to rescue and mass settlement than Palestine for reasons of agricultural fertility, political expediency, and population density.

Mainstream Zionism, meanwhile, largely discounted the demographics of Ottoman Palestine. Zangwill refused to do so, and called attention as early as 1904 to the significant obstacles on the road to creating a Jewish enclave in the midst of what was then Arab-dominated land. Zionist leaders believed that the Arabs could be mollified, that advancements in agronomy would make the land more productive, and that Ottoman opposition could be circumvented. Post-Ugandan Zionism therefore assured its followers of the ability to overcome physical and human geography. By contrast, the ITOists were convinced that geography constrained the limits of the possible. Transcendental thinking thus marked post-Ugandan Zionism, whereas ITOism remained bound to a kind of environmental determinism. The ITO's scientific expeditions to Cyrenaica and Angola demonstrate the movement's reliance on field work, expert opinion, and objective data to determine the promise of the various lands then considered for colonization. Notwithstanding the imperialist assumptions that underlay the ITO's many proposals, Zangwill's brand of territorialism emerged first and foremost as a humanitarian mission. The organization's professed goals of Jewish rescue and mass relocation bolstered its prestige, particularly in the Pale of Settlement.

Freeland League leaders between the wars not only drew inspiration from Zangwill's ITO, they also borrowed the organization's evidence-based approach to Jewish colonization and hoped to duplicate its early popularity on the *yidishe gas*.[10] They absorbed as well the apocalypticism implicit in the ITO's forecast for European Jewry. In the 1930s, prominent *Fraylandistn* like Melech Ravitch and Isaac Nachman Steinberg, as well as others in their orbit, like Nathan Birnbaum and Alfred Döblin, followed Zangwill in endorsing a territorialist variant of what has been termed "catastrophic Zionism."[11] The phrase refers to those Zionists who predicted an imminent end for Diaspora Jewry. Consequently, those identified with catastrophic Zionism strove for the immediate establishment of a Jewish safe haven in the biblical land of Israel. The *Fraylandistn*, however, believed that *any* port in the coming storm would suffice; they therefore may be said to have promulgated "catastrophic territorialism."

Territorialism, whether that of Noah, the "Ugandists," the ITOists, or the *Fraylandistn*, shifted according to historical context and the political sensibilities of its individual proponents. Each period—from the age of industrial and political revolutions of the early nineteenth century, to the imperialism of the fin-de-siècle, to the bellicose irredentism of the interwar period, and on to the traumatic Holocaust era of cataclysm and national rebirth—fostered its own brand of territorialism that reflected prevailing conceptions of the modern world and the place of Jewry within it. The problem of Jewish homelessness remained constant; responses to the consequences of homelessness were variable. Territorialism's political mutability tempted many Jewish luminaries over the years, including Sholem Aleichem, Eliezer Ben-Yehuda, Yosef Chaim Brenner, Jakob Lestschinsky, and perhaps to some degree even Ze'ev Jabotinsky. The fact that representatives of the Zionist Organization and its partners felt the need to gather intelligence about, undermine, and attack ITO and Freeland League projects the world over demonstrates territorialism's lure as much as it does the insecurity of Palestinocentric Zionism.

Leaders of the two rival groups accused one another of utopianism, but in fact both wedded visionary desires to *realpolitik*. Like Zionism, territorialism attracted adherents through force of its claim to an earthly necessity—the establishment of Jewish autonomy—combined with an appeal to the transcendent—the creation of a better world. Zionism and territorialism each attempted in its own way to right—and to rewrite—history by securing the Jewish future. Explicit revisions of the past therefore played a central role in territorialist rhetoric. Territorialists demonstrated a perennial fascination with the supposed Jewish origins of indigenous peoples, and the indigeneity of Jews in lands proposed for settlement. The identification of American Indians as members of the lost tribes, a view advanced by Noah and his Christian restorationist allies, linked the fate of native peoples whose lands had been usurped to the Jews, who had been exiled from their ancestral land. Later, some of the more fanciful proponents of "Ugandism" saw the Great Rift Valley as a geographical extension of greater Israel, and thereby sought to bolster territorialist claims to portions of British East Africa. Antisemites and philosemites alike considered the Malagasy to be remnants of the ancient Israelites, a belief that helped set the stage for interwar plans to colonize Madagascar. Melech Ravitch and I. N. Steinberg reveal a sensitivity toward the plight of Australian Aborigines in their works, though neither author went so far as to conflate their autochthony with Jewish origins. Steinberg and the *Fraylandistn* subsequently highlighted the long history of Jewish settlement in Suriname to legitimate their schemes for colonization in Saramacca. In territorialist discourse, the identification of Jews *qua* native peoples emerged as a cautionary tale that allowed them to demonstrate the vulnerability of the stateless to the storms of modern nationalism. Imagined indigeneity also presented an incipient nation with a compelling convergence between land and people: an ethnoscape.[12]

Like their territorialist counterparts, Zionist ideologues sought to reconstruct an idealized ethnoscape. Perhaps these parallel projects of the imagination help to explain why authors, journalists, playwrights, and poets were so crucial to the formulation, dissemination, and dramatization of both territorialist and Zionist ideologies. Literary language is fundamentally *counter*factual; it represents possible worlds rather than a description of a real state of affairs. Literature's figurative language employs the creative potential latent in everyday language in order to open a horizon of new possibilities.[13] Gifted men and women marshal the incantatory power of words to vitalize the imaginary and render phantasms substantial. Noah, Herzl, Zangwill, Döblin, Melech Ravitch, and Steinberg all possessed this galvanic talent. Nonetheless, the idealized futures they conjured never came to pass. If anything, it is their darker speculations that haunt our present.

Steinberg's jeremiad "Down with War!", published in the midst of his negotiations for parcels of land in Suriname, blames the Zionist leadership for having neglected the rights and welfare of the Arab residents of Mandate Palestine. As a consequence, Steinberg predicted a long and bloody war between Palestine's Jews and "the Arabs and their Moslem allies."[14] To some, his warnings may seem prophetic. Others may dismiss his doomsaying as weak-kneed capitulation. Regardless, it is clear that the State of Israel remains embattled within and without, as any daily paper or nightly news broadcast reveals. The ongoing conflict was not foreordained, however. No sequence of historical events ever is, for things could always have turned out otherwise. Inevitability is a chimera, a product of organizing contingencies into a narrative that elides the haphazardness of existence. This book has aspired to chart the accidents of history—hesitations, false starts, and miscarried hopes—in order to allow readers to recover a sense of the "fluid context" of the past.[15] I realize that in doing so my work has produced a competing and at times provocative counternarrative to traditional Zionist historiography. By training and temperament, historians tend to focus on accomplished facts. Perhaps because of my background in literary scholarship, I have concentrated instead on acts of the geopolitical imagination.

Though defunct as a political ideology, territorialism continues to infuse the world of Jewish arts and letters. This cultural interest in territorialism in the twenty-first century, like the movement's periodic popularity throughout the first half of the twentieth century, has been catalyzed by existential fears concerning Jewish survival. Israel's battered international reputation, the perception of a resurgent global antisemitism, the stalemate in peace negotiations, recurrent terror attacks, the spread of exterminationist rhetoric, and the shadow cast by a potentially nuclear Iran all combine to challenge the cherished notion that the Jewish state can secure Jewish existence. Catastrophic territorialism emerged as a political response to Jewish powerlessness; today, cultural expressions of territorialism reflect disquiet over Jewish power and its limits. So long as Israel remains threatened or is viewed as a threat, we can expect further explorations of territorialism's legacy.

For readers in the diaspora, Michael Chabon's award-winning novel *The Yiddish Policemen's Union* (2007) offers the most conspicuous example of a territorialist Zion. His alternate history depicts a Jewish micronation in Sitka, Alaska, a fantasy that derives from an abortive proposal supported by the Freeland League in the 1940s.[16] Yet even Chabon's very American fiction reflects anxieties over Jewish power. The novel imagines the destruction of the State of Israel shortly after its founding, and one of its subplots concerns a Jewish paramilitary group's effort to bomb the Dome of the Rock to avenge that loss. Israeli author Nava Semel's *Isra Isle* (2005) presents a complementary what-if scenario. Her novel features a parallel world in which the development of Mordecai Noah's prosperous and tranquil American Jewish homeland of Ararat has supplanted memory of the biblical land of Israel. Other significant contemporary Israeli authors have examined territorialist dreams in recent years, including Eshkol Nevo in *Neuland* (2011) and Yoav Avni in *Herzl Amar* (*Herzl Says* [2011]). Nevo's conscious appropriation of *Altneuland* portrays a utopian commune in Argentina, the eponymous "new land," founded by an Israeli who improves upon Herzl's reveries. Avni's novel recalls the bitter struggle over the "Uganda" plan in its illustration of what might have happened had a Jewish state arisen in East Africa.

Visual art has similarly incubated surrogate visions of Jewish sovereignty—or its loss. A joint Canadian-American project, "Mapping Ararat," utilizes augmented reality technologies and produces artifacts of material culture to resurrect Noah's failed city-state on Grand Island in the virtual world.[17] Celebrated Israeli video artist Yael Bartana made headlines with her "Polish Trilogy" (2007, 2009, 2011), a series of films that follows the machinations of the quasi-territorialist "Jewish

Renaissance Movement in Poland" (JRMP). The JRMP's manifesto invites three million Jews to return "[n]ot to Uganda . . . or to Madagascar, not even to Palestine," but to the Polish "land of our fathers" as a response to "these times of crisis, when faith has been exhausted and old utopias have failed."[18] Another Israeli-born artist, Michael Blum, imagines the expulsion of Jews from Israel in his installation *Exodus 2048* (2008). In Blum's account of the future, a "New State of Israel" rises in Uganda after Palestinians overrun the Jewish homeland.[19] In 2012, the Israeli Center for Digital Art curated a group exhibition, *Whither?*, whose title echoes the oft-repeated Jewish lament. In addition to work by Bartana and the "Mapping Ararat" project, the Center for Digital Art showcased more than a dozen artists whose works were selected in part because they present "the question of Jewish existence as a current problem that remains unsolved."[20] The subversion of Herzl's proposed "modern solution of the Jewish question" could hardly be clearer.

Many people, of course, consider the creation of a politically independent Jewish entity in parts of the biblical land of Israel to have solved this question and to have vindicated mainstream Zionist ideology. Indeed, general opinion as well as much historiography treat the creation of Israel as a "happy ending"[21] to Jewish travails. One result of this teleological view is to efface the victory of Zionism over formidable ideological and popular opposition. My fascination with territorialist authors and thinkers does not stem from a set of rigid political convictions. Nor am I ignorant of, or morbidly preoccupied with, the State of Israel's flaws. I remain, as I began, a partisan of the imagination.

For six years, my research led me to the quiet of archives and into the orbit of strangers the world over, and plunged me into the often remote regions of each of the proposed settlements this book has detailed. As the anonymous *pashkvilim* exhorted, I have gone to "Uganda." And I have gone to Grand Island, Angola, Madagascar, Tasmania, and Suriname. By following in the footsteps of those who explored these locales, I have learned that the ideals and aspirations that exist in people's minds—their mental topography, so to speak—is as important, perhaps more so, than the physical lay of the land. This is a lesson that the territorialists learned only belatedly. Theodor Herzl, whose affinity with territorialism this book makes clear, noted that "[h]ome is the acknowledged connection with the thought and feeling of a national community. The emphasis is on 'acknowledged'; without this acknowledgement there can be no home."[22] Neither Africa, Australia, North America, nor South America were in the end acknowledged as Jewish homes. The mythopoesis of Israel ultimately proved more potent a nationalist force than any other territory. Of all the many promised lands, only one today is real.

ACKNOWLEDGMENTS

This book could absolutely not have been written without the support and wise counsel of two important people in my life. First, thanks to my wife, Jessica Cohen, my first reader and most trusted advisor, whose patience while I traipsed around the world and then wrote and rewrote this book deserves all my gratitude. Her thoughts and deeds help make this a better world for me, for our daughter, Talia, and for many others. Second, thanks to my good friend and travel partner, Michael B. Kollins. To merely call Mike a friend does not adequately pay compliment to his generosity of spirit, his encouragement, and his boundless energy. Even when he wasn't sure what I was doing, or why I was doing it, he walked by my side. Well, typically he walked ahead of me, except, now that I think about it, when that dog sunk its teeth into my leg on the way down to the Suriname River. At least he got me to the hospital for rabies shots. We traveled tens of thousands of miles together and I'd do it all again with him. Mike is a mensch, and I am fortunate to call him a friend. For photographs, videos, and more on our travels, visit www.AdamRovner.com.

My excellent editor, Jennifer Hammer, believed in this project and has helped me bring it to fruition. I thank her for taking this risk.

Many others contributed to my work in ways both large and small. Their kindnesses have helped me think and write better. I am grateful to: the anonymous reviewers of my manuscript, Laura Almagor, Gur Alroey for sharing materials and for his superb scholarship, Alexandra Aparício, Nick Arvin, Ian Balmer and Kim Kaufmann for logistics in southwest Tassie, Eitan Bar-Yosef, Barbara (Joan) Beck, Gunnar Berg, Magnus Brechtken, Abe Brennan, Booker C. and Rufus C., Melissa Campbell, Mariana Candido, Vicki Caron, Sarah Carroll for telling me to get out there and do it, Adam Castle and Tracey Kennair (and Charlotte and Emma), Michael Chabon, Joe Charleson for logistics in Kenya, Robert Clark, my in-laws Ruth Cohen z"l and Stanley Cohen z"l for their wisdom and generosity—they fought for unpopular causes and are much missed, Charlotte Crow, Dimitri da Gama Rose, Horatius and Fernanda da Gama Rose for superb hospitality in Nairobi, Karel and Joyce Dawson, Kathy DiCenzo, Connor Duffy, Lilly Duym, Udi Edelman, George Eltman for his expert editorial eye, Nathan Englander for believing I should do this, Janet Fenton, Shai Fierst, Bayden Findlay, Richard Flanagan and Majda for great conversation and liquor, Howard Freeman, Aida Freudenthal, Dan Friedman, Michael Gawenda, Herzl and Rachel Genussov, Michal Genussov, Leon Gettler, Patricia Gillet, Nonna Gorilovskaya, Batya Graber, Constance Grady, John Grehan, Susan Gubar, Deborah Harris for having faith in my work, Todd Hasak-Lowy, Erez Heiman, Alexander Heldring, Vincent Homolka, Peter Isaacson, Eric Jennings, James Kamau, Louis Kaplan, Samuel Kassow, Stephen Katz, Dubi Kaufman, David Kretzmer for always making us welcome in Jerusalem, Bernard Leake, Monique Leblois, Donald Lewis, Robyn Lewis, Angela Lynkushka, Portia and Sats Machancoses, Domenica Macheda, Anne McCall, Cynthia McLeod, João Medina, Amitai Mendelsohn, Breon Mitchell, Margaret Morris, Joe Mozingo, Jessica Munns, Kevin Murray, Nolan Navarre, São Neto, Nga Nguyen, Ron Ofer, Mark Paskowitz for camaraderie in Madagascar, the staff of the Penrose Library and especially Michelle Kyner, Karen Pomer, Mark Raider, Solofo Rajoharisoa, Brian Ritchie and Varuni Kulasekera, Guido Robles, Meri-Jane Rochelson, Hilary Rubinstein, Rochelle Rubinstein, my brother Matthew Rovner and my parents Neil and Nina Rovner for their support, Lyndall Ryan, Jonathan Sarna, Melissa Schiff, Jeff Schulte, Tom Segev, Bill Seiner, Nava Semel, Tuvik and Hagit Shlonsky, David Shneer for his friendship and unflagging support, Sarah Shoemaker, Sam Shuman, Rabbi Daniel Siegel, Esther Siegel, Shefa Siegel, Clive Sinclair, Ariel Snapiri, Rob Socket for reading this far, Josh Sohn for reading a bit farther, Leo Steinberg z"l, Hanan and Jude Suissa (and Lia and Yonatan) for vacating their bedrooms in London, Adam Sutcliffe, Carla Tonini, Bill Untiedt, Nadia Valman, Michiel van Kempen, Sandy Vinnick, Richard Wafula, David Walsh, Amanda Weaver for cartography, Bruce Weber for cheerleading, Robert Weisbord, Brett Werb, Paul Wesson, the late Charles Wilson, Vanessa Yacoob, and Sheva Zucker. A special thanks to my many wonderful friends in Seattle who are like family, to my former colleagues in the Department of Comparative Literature and Languages as well as Bernie Firestone and Herman Berliner of Hofstra University, to the committees of the University of Denver Faculty Research Fund and Professional Research Opportunities for Faculty Grant, and to my current colleagues in the Department of English and the Center for Jewish Studies, as well as the administration of the University of Denver for their continued support.

Excerpts from this book previously appeared in different form:
"Portuguese Palestine: How a British Author Nearly Created a Jewish State in Angola." *History Today.* (December 2012): 27–33.
"Promised Lands: Alfred Döblin as a Territorialist Ideologue." *Ma'arav: Art, Culture, Media.* (April 2012). (Online in English and Hebrew.)
"Madagascar: An Almost Jewish Homeland." *Moment.* (May/June 2009): 43–48.
"In Suriname: Shake a Family Tree, a Jew Falls Out." *Forward.* 22 May 2009: 14.

NOTES

INTRODUCTION

1. Details of this scene are recalled by Tchernichovsky's friend Avraham Broides in *Pgishot u'Dvarim.* p. 91.
2. Klausner. *Shaul Tchernichovsky.* p. 187.
3. Ibid., pp. 186–187.
4. Author's translation of Tchernichovsky's "Omrim: Yeshnah Eretz" as it appears in Harshav, ed. *Shirat ha'Tkhiya ha'Ivrit.* pp. 190–192. I am grateful to Gur Alroey, whose excellent study of the ITO, *Mikhapsey Moledet,* first called my attention to the significance of this poem for my topic.
5. Klausner. *Shaul Tchernichovsky.* p. 248.
6. Tchernichovsky. "In Place of a Letter." p. 26.
7. Ibid.
8. Benjamin Nelson qtd. in Goodman. *Growing Up Absurd.* p. 216.
9. My understanding of the role of space/place is influenced by Mann. *Space and Place in Jewish Studies.*
10. The phrase is drawn from Alfred Lord Tennyson's "In Memoriam A.H.H."
11. Cf. Vital. "The Afflictions of the Jews and the Afflictions of Zionism." pp. 120, 128.
12. I draw on the distinction between fundamental vs. operative ideology as developed by Seliger. "Fundamental and Operative Ideology." Especially pp. 327–328. Shimoni's *The Zionist Ideology* makes regular use of this distinction.
13. Schama. *Landscape and Memory.* p. 24.
14. The phrase has been widely used since the appearance of Homi Bhabha's edited essay collection of the same name.
15. The best history of Israel Zangwill's Jewish Territorial Organization is Alroey's *Mikhapsey Moledet.* A comprehensive, but often polemical history of the Freeland League by Astour, *Geshikhte fun der Frayland-Lige,* appeared in two volumes in Yiddish. Because of the strident anti-Zionist tone of Astour's book, I have preferred to locate the source documents he refers to wherever possible. Binyamini's *Medinot L'Yehudim* borrowed much from Astour's earlier history. There are additional scholarly works devoted to aspects of each particular plan I discuss; these are noted within the relevant chapters.
16. Smith. *The Ethnic Origins of Nations.* pp. 157–170.
17. The term and concept are from Anderson. *Imagined Communities.*
18. The term appears in Lewin's essay "Agudism."

19. Cf. similar conclusions reached by Rabinovitch. "Diaspora, Nation, and Messiah." pp. xv–xvi.
20. The phrase is borrowed from Arendt. "Truth and Politics." p. 243.
21. Smith defines the term in *Chosen Peoples*. p. 136. See also references to Zionism in Smith, pp. 207–213.
22. The source of the acronym is a cause of confusion. Rochelson notes that the shift from the acronym "JTO" to the easier-to-pronounce "ITO" was due to another official name of Zangwill's organization, the "International Territorial Organization." See *A Jew in the Public Arena*. p. 268, n. 1. The genesis of the name is also discussed in Alroey's *Mikhapsey Moledet* where he notes that the organization was originally to be the "Jüden Territorial Volks Organization" (JTVO). Later the name was finalized as the "Jewish Territorial Organization" (JTO). See pp. 83–84.

CHAPTER 1. NOAH'S ARK ON THE NIAGARA

1. Rock. *Haven of Liberty*. p. 93. See also Weinryb. "Noah's Ararat Jewish State in its Historical Setting." p. 179.
2. Thomas. *Reminiscences of the Last Sixty Five Years Commencing with the Battle of Lexington*. p. 58.
3. Noah. *Discourse Delivered at the Consecration* [*Discourse*]. p.19.
4. Ibid., p. 22.
5. Ibid., p. 30.
6. Ibid., p. 31.
7. Weinryb. "Yesodot haTzionut v'Toldoteha." p. 78.
8. For details on Noah's early life, see Sarna. *Jacksonian Jew*. pp. 1–14.
9. Noah's correspondence with Department of State (1811), qtd. in Sarna. *Jacksonian Jew*. p. 15.
10. Letter Monroe to Noah. 25 Apr. 1815. Reprinted in *Correspondence and Documents Relative to the Attempt to Negotiate for the Release of the American Captives at Algiers* [*Correspondence*]. p. 82.
11. Fascinating details of Noah's secret mission to rescue captives taken by Barbary powers and the fallout from the affair may be found in Sarna. *Jacksonian Jew*. pp. 16–21, 26–28.
12. See Noah. *Correspondence*.
13. Ibid., p. 126.
14. Ibid.
15. Noah. *She Would Be a Soldier*. p. 58.
16. Noah. Preface to *She Would Be a Soldier*. p. 26.
17. Noah. *Travels in England, France, Spain, and the Barbary States* [*Travels*]. p. 366.
18. Ibid., p. 381.
19. Ibid., pp. xxv–xxvi.
20. Ibid., p. 56.
21. Ibid.

22. Noah. *Discourse*. p. 43.

23. See Hague. *William Wilberforce*. p. 468.

24. Articles ran 22, 23, 25, and 27 Oct. 1817 in *National Advocate*, all p. 2.

25. See Parkes. "Lewis Way and His Times." pp. 189–190.

26. Lewis. *The Origins of Christian Zionism*. pp. 53–60.

27. See Stirling. *Ways of Yesterday*. pp.134–136.

28. Ibid., p. 135.

29. See portrait by James Leakey in Stirling. *Ways of Yesterday*. facing page 83.

30. "The Conversion of the Jews." *Church Quarterly Review*. p. 195.

31. Kohler. *Jewish Rights at the Congresses of Vienna and Aix-La-Chapelle* [*Jewish Rights*]. p. 87–88.

32. Stirling. *Ways of Yesterday*. pp. 149–150, 159.

33. "Journey of the Rev. Messrs. Way, Cox, and Solomon." *Missionary Register*. p. 507; Letter L. Way to Mary Way. 9 July 1818. [HLS MS 85 29/5/47].

34. "Journey of the Rev. Messrs. Way, Cox, and Solomon." *Missionary Register*. p. 507.

35. In Way's memorandum of his third interview he advocates a gradual emancipation. 11 Oct. 1818 [HLS MS 85 29/4/1]; Stirling. *Ways of Yesterday*. pp. 146–149.

36. Poem to B. N. Solomon. [HLS MS 85 29/5/23].

37. Letter B. N. Solomon to Mary Way. 5–17 Apr. 1818. [HLS MS 85 29/5/39].

38. Letter B. N. Solomon to Mary Way. n.d. [HLS MS 85 29/5/29].

39. Letter L. Way to Mary Way. 6 Nov. 1817. [HLS MS 85 29/5/16].

40. See Kohler. *Jewish Rights*. p. 84; Parkes. "Lewis Way and His Times." p. 196; Rey. *Alexander I*. pp. 302–305.

41. The dates of these meetings as memorandized by Way are 3 Jan. 1818, 18 May 1818, 11 Oct. 1818, and 15 Nov. 1818. [HLS MS 85 29/4/1].

42. Qtd. in Kohler. *Jewish Rights*. p. 88.

43. Memorandum of first interview. 3 Jan. 1818. According to Way, Alexander could hear him only on his right side. [HLS MS 85 29/4/1].

44. See memorandum of first interview. 3 Jan. 1818. [HLS MS 85 29/4/1].

45. Memorandum of second interview in Crimea. 18 May 1818. [HLS MS 85 29/4/1]; See also Kohler. *Jewish Rights*. p. 86.

46. Parkes. "Reverend Way and His Times." pp. 196–197.

47. Memorandum of third interview. 11 Oct. 1818. [HLS MS 85 29/4/1].

48. Way. *Mémoires sur l'état Israélites*. p. 11; Kohler. *Jewish Rights*. pp. 55–56.

49. Letter L. Way to Mary Way. 1 Dec. 1818. [HLS MS 85 29/5/77].

50. Ibid.

51. Noah. *Discourse*. p. 41.

52. Noah. *Travels*. p. 241.

53. Ibid. Noah singles out Grégoire's good works for mention in his *Discourse*. p. 41.

54. See Grégoire. *Enquiry Concerning the Intellectual and Moral Faculties, and Literature of Negroes*. p. i. For mention of Grandville Sharpe, a major force behind Freetown, and Wilberforce see "Dedication." pp. ii–iii.

55. "Paul Cuffee." Reprinted in *National Advocate*. 25 Oct. 1817. p. 2.

56. See editions of 16 Sept. 1818. p. 2; 17 Nov. 1818. p. 2; 2 Dec. 1818. p. 2.

57. Reprinted in Way. *Mémoires sur l'état Israélites*. p. 79.

58. Stirling. *Ways of Yesterday*. p. 192.

59. "England." *Koblenzer Anzeiger*. 2 July 1819. p. 1.

60. Ibid.

61. Ibid.

62. Ibid.

63. Several articles on Way's work appear in various European publications. These clippings are pasted into the pages of his personal copy of *Mémoires sur l'état Israélites*. [HLS MS 85 29/4/1]. Previous scholarly identification of Way as having been involved in Noah's 1819 project on the basis of the *Koblenzer Anzeiger* article should be treated with skepticism. See Gelber. "Mordecai Emanuel Noah." pp. 384–386. Later historians base their discussions of this episode on Gelber.

64. Rohrbacher. "The 'Hep Hep' Riots of 1819." pp. 22–23.

65. Ibid., pp. 31–33.

66. Gans, Moser, Zunz, et. al. "The Society for the Culture and Science of the Jews: Statutes." p. 213.

67. Meyer. *The Origins of the Modern Jew*. pp. 171–173; Reissner. "Heinrich Heine to Eduard Gans: 'Quand Même.'" p. 3. [LBI AR 4147, box 1 folder 3].

68. Hauptman. *Conspiracy of Interests*. pp. 137–138.

69. Ibid., p. 137.

70. *Albany Daily Advertiser*. 20 Jan. 1820. Reprinted in "The Jews." *North-Carolina Gazette*. 4 Feb. 1820. p. 1.

71. Ibid.

72. Ibid.

73. Ibid.

74. Ibid.

75. Ibid.

76. Ibid.

77. Ibid.

78. Sarna. *Jacksonian Jew*. p. 69; Shalev. "'Revive, Renew, and Reestablish.'" pp. 12–14; Diner. *A Time For Gathering*. pp. 40–42.

79. Cone. "New Matters Relating to Mordecai M. Noah." p. 132.

80. *Albany Daily Advertiser*. 20 Jan. 1820. Reprinted in "The Jews." *North-Carolina Gazette*. 4 Feb. 1820. p. 1.

81. Qtd. in Cone. "New Matters Relating to Mordecai M. Noah." p. 132.

82. Ibid., p. 133.

83. Noah. "Grand Island." *National Advocate*. 6 Mar. 1820. p. 2.

84. Noah. "Letter to the Editors." *Albany Daily Advertiser*. 11 Feb. 1820. p. 2. The Latin phrase was already an antisemitic slogan at this time. See Katz. "A State Within a State."

85. Noah. "Letter to the Editors." *Albany Daily Advertiser*. 11 Feb. 1820. p. 2.

86. Noah. "Grand Island." *National Advocate*. 6 Mar. 1820. p. 2.

87. Noah. "Letter to the Editors." *Albany Daily Advertiser*. 11 Feb. 1820. p. 2.

88. See letter Noah to J. Q. Adams. 24 July 1820. In Blau and Baron. *The Jews of the United States*. p. 886 [document 311] and p. 889 [document 312]. In the latter, Noah mentions Vienna, the Hague, and Denmark as potential diplomatic posts.

89. Adams. *Memoirs of John Quincy Adams*. 7 Sept. 1820. p. 173.

90. *The First Report of the American Society for Meliorating the Condition of the Jews*. p. 26.

91. Goldman. *God's Sacred Tongue*. pp. 95–98.

92. Adams. *Memoirs of John Quincy Adams*. 7 Sept. 1820. p. 173.

93. "Aus Nordamerika." *Sulamith*. p. 283–284.

94. Meyer. *The Origins of the Modern Jew*. p. 179.

95. Reissner. "'Ganstown, U.S.A.'" pp. 22–23.

96. Ibid., p. 22.

97. Ibid., p. 24.

98. Letter E. Gans and L. Zunz to Noah. 1 Jan. 1822. Reprinted in Oppenheim. "Notes." *American Jewish Historical Society Publications*. V. 20. p. 148.

99. Ibid.

100. Ibid. Note too that Noah's ideas received support from *Verein* member Eliezer Sinai Kirschbaum, who published a tractate in 1822 that touted Noah's plans. See Weinryb. "Noah's Ararat Jewish State in its Historical Setting." pp. 183–184; Malachi. "Mkorot Ivri'im l'Ararat' shel Mordecai Emanuel Noah." pp. 83–84.

101. Reprinted [document 71] in Schappes. *A Documentary History of the Jews in the United States*. pp. 157–160.

102. Ibid., p. 158.

103. Ibid.

104. See reports in "Department of State." *National Advocate*. 12 July 1822. p. 4.

105. "Surveyor General's Office" [notice]. *National Advocate*. 28 Apr. 1825. p. 3.

106. "Sale of Grand Island." Reprinted in *Daily National Intelligencer*. 13 June 1825. p. 2.

107. The figure appears in Sarna. *Jacksonian Jew*. p. 65. It is derived from Allen's account in "Founding of the City of Ararat" p. 313. Contemporary newspapers estimated the cost to have been $20,000, see "Sale of Grand Island." Reprinted in *Daily National Intelligencer*. 13 June 1825. p. 2.

108. "Sale of Grand Island." Reprinted in *Daily National Intelligencer*. 13 June 1825. p. 2.

109. "Major Noah" [notice]. *American Sentinel* (CT). 29 June 1825. p. 3.

110. Allen. "Founding of the City of Ararat." p. 314.

111. "From Our Correspondent." *New-York Spectator*. 27 Sept. 1825. p. 4.

112. "Corner Stone of a City on Grand Island Laid at Buffalo." *Gazette* (Black Rock, NY). 20 Sept. 1825. p 1.

113. Ibid.

114. Ibid.

115. See Allen's description of Noah. "Founding of the City of Ararat." p. 310.

116. See report in *Buffalo Patriot, Extra* (20 Sept. 1825) reprinted in Allen. "Founding of the City of Ararat." p. 316. Also reprinted in Schuldiner and Kleinfeld. "Ararat Proclamation and Speech." p. 105. The text of the "Ararat Proclamation" in Allen differs slightly from that in Schuldiner and Kleinfeld.

117. "Corner Stone of a City on Grand Island Laid at Buffalo." *Gazette* (Black Rock, NY). 20 Sept. 1825. p 1.

118. See report in *Buffalo Patriot, Extra* reprinted in Allen. "Founding of the City of Ararat." p. 317. Also in Schuldiner and Kleinfeld. "Ararat Proclamation and Speech." p. 107.

119. "Corner Stone of a City on Grand Island Laid at Buffalo." *Gazette* (Black Rock, NY). 20 Sept. 1825. p 1.

120. See report in *Buffalo Patriot, Extra* reprinted in Allen. "Founding of the City of Ararat." p. 316. Also in Schuldiner and Kleinfeld. "Ararat Proclamation and Speech." p. 106.

121. Ibid.

122. Sarna. *Jacksonian Jew*. p. 66.

123. Van Schaack. "Reminiscences of a Four Years Residence on the Niagara Frontier, 1823 to 1827." MS. [BECHS A00–464].

124. Part of the inscription on the Ararat Cornerstone held at BECHS. The inscription is recorded in numerous reports on the ceremony, including Allen. "Founding of the City of Ararat." p. 317. The text of the "Ararat Proclamation" qtd. in Allen is reprinted in Schuldiner and Kleinfeld in "Ararat Proclamation and Speech." p. 106. This more readily available text does not include this wording.

125. See report in *Buffalo Patriot, Extra* reprinted in Allen. "Founding of the City of Ararat." p. 317. Also in Schuldiner and Kleinfeld "Ararat Proclamation and Speech." p. 106.

126. See report in *Buffalo Patriot, Extra* reprinted in Allen. "Founding of the City of Ararat." p. 317. Also in Schuldiner and Kleinfeld. "Ararat Proclamation and Speech." pp. 106–107.

127. See report in *Buffalo Patriot, Extra* reprinted in Allen. "Founding of the City of Ararat." p. 316. Also in Schuldiner and Kleinfeld. "Ararat Proclamation and Speech." p. 106.

128. "Corner Stone of a City on Grand Island Laid at Buffalo." *Gazette* (Black Rock, NY). 20 Sept. 1825. p 1.

129. See report in *Buffalo Patriot, Extra* reprinted in Allen. "Founding of the City of Ararat." p. 319. Also in Schuldiner and Kleinfeld. "Ararat Proclamation and Speech." p. 109.

130. See report in *Buffalo Patriot, Extra* reprinted in Allen. "Founding of the City of Ararat." p. 318. Also in Schuldiner and Kleinfeld. "Ararat Proclamation and Speech." p. 107.

131. See report in *Buffalo Patriot, Extra* reprinted in Allen. "Founding of the City of Ararat." p. 319. Also in Schuldiner and Kleinfeld. "Ararat Proclamation and Speech." p. 108.

132. "Prepatory Arrangements" in appendix to Colden. *Memoir Prepared at the Request of the Committee of the Common Council of the City of New York.* p. 126.

133. See report in *Buffalo Patriot, Extra* reprinted in Allen. "Founding of the City of Ararat." p. 319. Also in Schuldiner and Kleinfeld. "Ararat Proclamation and Speech." p. 108.

134. See report in *Buffalo Patriot, Extra* reprinted in Allen. "Founding of the City of Ararat." pp. 319–20. Also in Schuldiner and Kleinfeld. "Ararat Proclamation and Speech." p. 109.

135. See report in *Buffalo Patriot, Extra* reprinted in Allen. "Founding of the City of Ararat." pp. 320–21. Also in Schuldiner and Kleinfeld. "Ararat Proclamation and Speech." p. 109–110.

136. See report in *Buffalo Patriot, Extra* reprinted in Allen. "Founding of the City of Ararat." pp. 321. Also in Schuldiner and Kleinfeld. "Ararat Proclamation and Speech." p. 110.

137. See memorandum of first interview 3 Jan. 1818 in which he speculates that Asian tribes from Siberia that may have crossed to North America might still reveal traces of Jewish customs. [HLS MS 85 29/4/1].

138. See report in *Buffalo Patriot, Extra* reprinted in Allen. "Founding of the City of Ararat." pp. 321. Also in Schuldiner and Kleinfeld. "Ararat Proclamation and Speech." p. 110. See also Noah to Adams. 24 July 1820 reprinted in Blau and Baron. pp. 885–890. Noah had thought of organizing "emigration Societies" (p. 889) as early as 1820 when he sought a federal appointment as a chargé d'affaires in Europe from Adams.

139. Gans was baptized 12 Dec. 1825. See Reissner. "Heinrich Heine to Eduard Gans." p. 4.

140. Heine was baptized 28 June 1825. See Ibid.

141. See report in *Buffalo Patriot, Extra* reprinted in Allen. "Founding of the City of Ararat." pp. 322. Also in Schuldiner and Kleinfeld. "Ararat Proclamation and Speech." p. 111.

142. In Schuldiner and Kleinfeld. "Ararat Proclamation and Speech." p. 111.

143. Ibid., p. 112.

144. Ibid.

145. Ibid., p. 117.

146. Ibid., p. 114.

147. Ibid.

148. Ibid., p. 112.

149. Ibid.

150. Ibid., p. 113.

151. Ibid., p. 114.

152. Ibid., p. 115.
153. Ibid., p. 124.
154. Ibid., p. 114.
155. "City of Refuge" reprinted from *New-York Commercial Advertiser* in *Carolina Observer* (NC). 6 Oct. 1825. p. 2.
156. "Advertisement" reprinted from *New York American* in *Carolina Observer* (NC). 6 Oct. 1825. p. 2.
157. [No headline] "The ceremony of the foundation . . . " reprinted from *Richmond Enquirer* in *Carolina Observer* (NC). 6 Oct. 1825. p. 2.
158. Ibid.
159. [No headline] "We have given . . . " reprinted from *Newburyport Herald* in *Statesman* (NH). 10 Oct. 1825. p. 2.
160. "Proclamation to the Red Skins." *Missouri Republican.* 28 Nov. 1825. p. 2.
161. Colden. *Memoir Prepared at the Request of the Committee of the Common Council of the City of New York.* p. 88.
162. Stone. "Narrative of the Festivities Observed in Honour of the Completion of the Grand Erie Canal." p. 313.
163. Van Schaack. "Reminiscences of a Four Years Residence on the Niagara Frontier, 1823 to 1827." MS. [BECHS A00–464].
164. [No headline] "We have given . . . " *Morning Chronicle* (London). 29 Oct. 1825. p. 3.
165. Qtd. in Reissner. "Heinrich Heine to Eduard Gans." p. 7.
166. Gelber. "Mordecai Emanuel Noah." p. 394, n. 15.
167. Cologna. "Au Redacteur." *Journal des Debats.* 18 Nov. 1825. p. 2.; Translation in "Re-assemblage of the Jews." *Evening Post* (NY). 12 Jan. 1826. p. 2.
168. Ibid.
169. Jeitteles. "Hadashim m'Karov Ba'oo." *Bikkure ha-Ittim.* (1826). p. 45. Further mockery of Noah in relation to *Esther* is found in his footnotes, especially nn. 2, 4.
170. Ibid., p. 45, n. 6.
171. Ibid., p. 47, n. 8.
172. Letter Noah to E. Simon. 22 Oct. 1825. Reprinted in Kohn. "Mordecai Manuel Noah's Ararat Project and the Missionaries." p. 183.
173. Farrar. *Recollections of Seventy Years.* p. 232.
174. Ibid., pp. 232–233. For Simon's involvement in colonization schemes for Jewish-Christians see Blau and Baron. "Committee Report, 1824" [Doc. 254]; Simon and Jadowinsky. "Letter of Protest, 1825" [Doc. 255] in *The Jews of the United States.* pp. 738–746.
175. Farrar. *Recollections of Seventy Years.* pp. 234–235.
176. Letter Noah to E. Simon. 22 Oct. 1825. Reprinted in Kohn. "Mordecai Manuel Noah's Ararat Project and the Missionaries." p. 183.
177. Sarna. *Jacksonian Jew.* p. 157.
178. Catlin qtd. in Noah. *Evidences.* pp. 29–30.

179. Ibid., p. 35.
180. Ibid., p. 36.
181. Ibid., p. 37.
182. Ibid.
183. Ibid., p. 38.
184. Ibid., p. 39.
185. Ibid.
186. See description of venue in "Celebration of Washington's Birth–Day." *London Illustrated News.* 29 Mar. 1845. p. 194. Accompanying illustration on p. 193.
187. Noah. *Discourse on the Restoration.* p. 10.
188. Ibid., p. iii.
189. Ibid., p. 10.
190. Ibid., pp. 10–11.
191. Ibid., p. 34.
192. Ibid., p. 35.
193. Ibid., p. 39.
194. Ibid., p. 38.
195. Ibid., p. 35.
196. Ibid., p. 37.
197. Ibid.
198. Ibid., p. 50.
199. Ibid.
200. Ibid.
201. Poe. "Restoration of the Jews." *Evening Mirror* (NY). 16 Jan. 1845. p. 2. [unsigned, attributed to Poe.].
202. Ibid.
203. "A Romance That May Become a Reality." *Spectator.* 5 July 1845. p. 638.
204. Trowbridge. *My Own Story.* p. 98.
205. Noah. "Address Delivered at the Hebrew Synagogue." p. 158.
206. Ibid., p. 159.
207. Sarna interviewed 9 Jan. 2008.
208. See Allen. "Founding of the City of Ararat." pp. 324–326; Sarna. *Jacksonian Jew.* pp. 74–75.
209. Allen. "Founding of the City of Ararat." p. 325.
210. Orr. *Pictorial Guide to the Falls of Niagara.* p. 232.
211. Allen. "Founding of the City of Ararat." p. 326.
212. Zangwill. "The Territorial Solution of the Jewish Problem." p. 279.
213. Chabon. Correspondence with author. 5 Jan. 2008.
214. Kohler. "Some Early American Zionist Projects." p. 84. Kohler states that "the idea of a Jewish State, wherever to be located, is the important element" of Zionism. p. 75.
215. "Das Project zur Gründung eines Judenstaates aus dem Jahre 1825." *Die Welt.* No. 42. 19 Oct. 1900. p. 6; Loewe. "Ararat." *Die Welt.* No. 5. 31 Jan. 1902.

216. Raisin. *Mordecai Manuel Noah*. p. 28.

217. Sokolov. *History of Zionism*. V. 1. pp. 135–136.

218. Netanyahu. "Israel Zangwill." p. 163.

219. Gelber. "Mordecai Emanuel Noah." pp. 385, 413.

220. Malachi. "Mkorot Ivri'im l'Ararat." p. 84.

221. Astour. *Geshikhte fun der Frayland-Lige*. V. 1. p. 7.

222. Katz. "l'Birur haMusag 'Mivasrei haTzionut.'" p. 272.

223. Shimoni. *The Zionist Ideology*. p. 63.

224. Weinryb. "Yesodot haTzionut." p. 71.

225. Such as Rabbi Zvi Hirsch Kalischer and Moses Hess.

226. J. Fraenkel qtd. in Leftwich. *Israel Zangwill*. p. 181.

CHAPTER 2. GREETINGS FROM THE PROMISED LAND

1. Herzl. *Diaries* [*Diaries*]. Vol. I. 13 June 1895. pp. 133–34; Herzl. *The Jewish State*. pp. 29–30.

2. Herzl. *Diaries*. Vol. III. Entries for 2–8 Nov. 1899. pp. 882–885.; *Diaries*. Vol. III. 4 Jan. 1901. pp. 1023–1024; *Diaries*. Vol. IV. Entries for 5–10 July 1902. pp. 1294–1296.

3. Herzl. *Diaries*. Vol. III. 29 Dec. 1899. p. 899; *Diaries*. Vol. IV. Letter Herzl to Lord Rothschild. 12 July 1902. pp. 1302–1303; *Diaries*. Vol. IV. 28 July 1902. pp. 1320–1321; *Diaries*. Vol. IV. Letter Herzl to Holo Al-Abed Izzet Pasha. 4 June 1903. p. 1503.

4. Herzl. *Diaries*. Vol. IV. 13 May 1903. p. 1487; *Diaries*. Vol. IV. 26 May 1903. pp. 1499–1500. Herzl believed that Mozambique would chiefly be of use as a bargaining chip with England.

5. Herzl. *Diaries*. Vol. IV. 5–10 July 1902. pp. 1294–1296; *Diaries*. Vol. IV. 23 Oct. 1902. pp. 1362–1363; *Diaries*. Vol. IV. Letter Herzl to J. Chamberlain. 26 Jan. 1903. pp. 1398–1399; *Diaries*. Vol. IV. Letter Herzl to Jacob Schiff. 10 Apr. 1904. p. 1620; *Diaries*. Vol. IV. 29 Apr. 1904. Letter Herzl to Lord Rothschild. 29 Apr. 1904. p. 1621.

6. "The Basle Program." p. 21.

7. Herzl. *Old-New Land*. p. 165.

8. Weisbord. *African Zion: The Attempt to Establish a Jewish Colony in the East African Protectorate, 1903–1905*.

9. Both David Wolffsohn and Otto Warburg voted in favor of exploring the British offer of land in East Africa at the Sixth Zionist Congress. *Protokoll VI*. pp. 224–225. See also Warburg's somewhat optimistic article in *Ost und West*.

10. Letter Nordau to Herzl. 17 July 1903. In Heymann. *The Uganda Controversy*. Vol. II. p. 122.

11. *Protokoll VI*. p. 71.

12. Stanley. *Through the Dark Continent*.

13. Herzl. *The Jewish State*. Spring 1895. p. 4.

14. Herzl. *Diaries*. Vol. I. Spring 1895. p. 4.

15. Ibid.

16. Ibid., 12 June 1895. p. 91.

17. Letter H. Rider Haggard to Israel Zangwill. "Letters and the ITO." p. 638.

18. Hertzka. "Author's Preface." *Freeland*. p. 24.

19. Ibid., p. 80.

20. Ibid., p. 390.

21. "Freeland" [review]. *Saturday Review*. 10 Oct. 1891. p. 424.

22. See German original: Hertzka. *Freiland*. p. 675.

23. Hertzka. *Freeland*. p. 493.

24. This English formulation is actually a translation of the passage as it appears in the Hebrew version of Herzl's novel.

25. [No headline]. *Illustrated London News*. 3 Mar. 1894. p. 253.

26. Hardinge. *A Diplomatist in the East*. p. 145.

27. Letter Capt. Dugmore to A. Hardinge, Lamu. 26 June 1894. [CZA A87/263].

28. Letter Capt. Dugmore to A. Hardinge on "Freeland Detrimentals," Lamu. 27 June 1894. [CZA A87/263].

29. Letter Capt. Dugmore to Sir. L. Mathews, Lamu, 27 June 1894. [CZA A87/263].

30. Hardinge. *A Diplomatist in the East*. p. 145.

31. Ibid.

32. Ibid.

33. Herzl. *The Jewish State*. p. 7.

34. Ibid.

35. Ibid.

36. Zangwill. "Two Dreamers of the Ghetto." p. 120.

37. Herzl. *The Jewish State*. p. 8.

38. Ibid., p. 30.

39. Statistics drawn from Bronner, et al. "Argentina." p. 429.

40. Statistics drawn from Alfassi, Itzhak, et al. "Land of Israel: Aliyah and Absorption." p. 334.

41. Pinsker. *Auto-Emancipation*. p. 32.

42. Ibid., pp. 8–9.

43. Ibid., p. 30.

44. See Menes. "The *Am Oylom* Movement." pp. 9–33.

45. Herzl's "A Solution to the Jewish Question" appeared in *Jewish Chronicle*. 17 Jan. 1896. pp. 12–13.

46. Herzl. *Diaries*. Vol. I. 17 Nov. 1895. p. 273.

47. Letter Nordau to Zangwill. 17 Nov. 1895. [CZA A120/509].

48. Ibid.

49. Herzl. *Diaries*. Vol. I. 26 Nov. 1895. p. 276.

50. Rochelson. *A Jew in the Public Arena*. pp. 9–10.

51. Zangwill. "Zionism." p. 504.

52. Herzl worked with both Zangwill and Leopold Jacob Greenberg to set up a meeting with banking magnate Lord Rothschild (*Diaries*. Vol. III. 26 Nov.

1900. p. 994; 9 Feb. 1901. pp. 1063–1064). Rothschild, in turn, offered to broker a meeting between Herzl and Chamberlain (*Diaries*. Vol. IV. 10 July 1902. pp. 1296–1297), but when that fell through (*Diaries*. Vol. IV. 5 Aug. 1902. pp. 1344–1345), Herzl worked with Greenberg to arrange a conference with Chamberlain (*Diaries*. Vol. IV. 22 Sept. 1902. pp. 1352–1355), which first occurred 22 Oct. 1902 (*Diaries*. Vol. IV. p. 1360).

53. Herzl. *Diaries*. Vol. IV. 22 Oct. 1902. p. 1360.

54. Marsh. *Joseph Chamberlain*. pp. 123, 160.

55. Chamberlain to Landsdowne. "Notes on Mombasa and East African Protectorate." 2 Jan. 1903. p. 12. [TNA FO 2/722].

56. See Ransom. "Translator's Note." In Hertzka. *Freeland*. p. 7.

57. See Quinalt. "John Bright and Joseph Chamberlain." pp. 623, 636.

58. Herzl. *Diaries*. Vol. IV. 24 Apr. 1903. p. 1473.

59. Ibid.

60. The confusion is compounded by the fact that the Uganda Protectorate encompassed the region that later become the separately administered East African Protectorate—the "Kenya Colony"—until 1902.

61. Chamberlain to Landsdowne. "Notes on Mombasa and East African Protectorate." 2 Jan. 1903. [TNA FO 2/722]. See also Matson. "The Zionist Offer." p.1. ms. [KNA MSS 10/1].

62. Hardy. *The Iron Snake*.

63. The creation of the Anglo-Palestine Company—Zionism's central bank—was modeled on that of the Imperial British East Africa Company, the commercial entity that had originally administered Kenya under charter from Queen Victoria. See Sokolow. Vol. II. p. xlvii.

64. *Protokoll VI*. p. 215.

65. Chamberlain to Landsdowne. "Notes on Mombasa and East African Protectorate." 2 Jan. 1903. [TNA FO 2/722].

66. See Herzl's assessment of Chamberlain in *Diaries*. Vol. IV. 23 Oct. 1902. p. 1361.

67. For Chamberlain's support of the railway see Weisbord. pp. 123–124.

68. "Mr. Chamberlain in the East–End." *Times* (London). 16 Dec. 1904, p. 8.

69. Ibid.

70. Ibid.

71. Ibid.

72. Ibid.

73. Herzl. *Diaries*. Vol. IV. 24 Apr. 1903. p. 1473.

74. Telegram Greenberg to Herzl. 18 Aug. 1903. In Heymann. *The Uganda Controversy*. Vol. I. p. 98.

75. Greenberg and Joseph Chamberlain, draft agreement. 13 July 1903. [CZA A87/36].

76. See Rabinowicz. pp. 78–79; Weisbord. p. 70.

77. Herzl. *Diaries*. Vol. IV. 22 Aug. 1903. p. 1547.

78. Ibid.

79. The figure of 592 is given in *Protokoll VI*. p. 122. Vital writes that it is "virtually certain that at least 611 delegates showed up at Basel." p. 480.

80. *Protokoll VI*. p. 3.

81. Zangwill. "Zionism and Territorialism." p. 645.

82. Lipsky. "Sixth International Zionist Congress." p. 201.

83. *Protokoll VI*. p. 6.

84. Ibid., pp. 6–8.

85. Herzl. "Opening Address." p. 227. In *Protokoll VI*. p. 8.

86. *Protokoll VI*. p. 9.

87. Greenberg and Joseph Chamberlain, draft agreement. 13 July 1903. p. 6, clause (N). [CZA A87/365].

88. Herzl. "Opening Address." p. 66. In *Protokoll VI*. p. 9.

89. *Protokoll VI*. p. 215.

90. Weisbord. pp. 172–173. Sir Charles Eliot, commissioner for the East African Protectorate, had proposed the territory of "Gwas Ngishu" two months earlier in an internal document. He reasoned the region would "ensure a very considerable addition to the traffic of the Uganda Railway." Eliot to Lord Landsdowne. 4 Nov. 1903. p. 49. [CZA A87/365]. See also Weisbord. p. 102.

91. *Protokoll VI*. p. 216.

92. Ibid.

93. Letter Herzl to Nordau. 23 Dec. 1903. In Heymann. *The Uganda Controversy*. Vol. II. p. 194. See also Heymann's discussion in Vol. II. p. 48. In addition to Heymann, Almog, Alroey (2011), and Luz all relate the instrumental aspects of Herzl's support for settlement in Palestine.

94. Herzl. *Diaries*. Vol. IV. 31 Aug. 1903. pp. 1547–1548.

95. Ibid., p. 1548.

96. Reuven Breinin. "Sikha im ha'Dr. Herzl." *HaZofeh*. 1 Sept. 1903. p. 827. Reprinted in Heymann. "Herzl v'Tzioney Rusia." p. 74.

97. Moshe N. Syrkin. "Sikha im ha'Dr. Herzl." *HaZfira*. 7 Sept. 1903. p. 3. Reprinted in Heymann. "Herzl v'Tzioney Rusia." p. 78.

98. Recorded in *Protokoll VI*. pp. 62–72.

99. Letter Nordau to Herzl. 17 July 1903. In Heymann. *The Uganda Controversy*. Vol. II. p. 123.

100. Zangwill. "Zionism and Charitable Institutions." p. 180. This is the text of Zangwill's address, which is not recorded in the official stenographic record because he spoke in English. See *Protokoll VI*. p. 125.

101. Wilbusch. *haMassa l'Uganda*. p. 42. Weizmann also mentioned this "fantastic map." See "On the Concept of an 'Overnight Shelter.'" 8–10 Nov. 1903 in Weizmann. *The Letters and Papers of Chaim Weizmann*. Vol. I. Ser. B. p. 43.

102. "Was Gibt's Denn Neues: Zum Attentate gegen Dr. Nordau." *Illustriertes Wiener Extrablatt*. 22 Dec. 1903. p. 3. Reprinted in Heyman. Vol. II. p. 192.

103. Letter Ussishkin to Ben–Zion Mossensohn. 20 Dec. 1903. In Heymann. "Herzl v'Tzioney Rusia." p. 84.

104. Klausner. *Menahem Ussischkin*. p. 65; Goldstein. *Ussishkin—Biographia*. Vol. I. p. 168.

105. Letter Ussishkin to Yehoshua Barzilai–Eisenstadt. 5 Apr. 1904. In Heymann. *The Uganda Controversy*. Vol. II. p. 282.

106. See descriptions in Herzl. *Old–New Land*. Book II. Chapters 2–3.

107. Heymann. *The Uganda Controversy*. Vol. II. pp. 10–11.

108. *Protokoll VI*. p. 209.

109. Ibid., p. 211.

110. Ibid., p. 221.

111. Ibid., pp. 224–225.

112. *Protokoll VI*. pp. 226.

113. Weizmann. "Rallying the Forces of Opposition." Sept. 1903. Weizmann. *The Letters and Papers of Chaim Weizmann*. Vol. I. Ser. B. p. 36.

114. *Protokoll VI*. p. 225.

115. Ibid., p. 226.

116. As Vital demonstrates, 62.4 percent of all votes cast supported the creation of a commission and only 37.6 percent of votes cast opposed the resolution. However, only 50.6 percent of all those present who *could* vote supported the resolution, while 30.5 percent opposed it. The distinction between those who could vote and those who did so owes to Herzl's executive decision that all thirty-four members of the Greater Actions Committee abstain. See Vital. Table 6. p. 487.

117. Letter Reines to Herzl. 9 Dec. 1903. In Heymann. *The Uganda Controversy*. Vol. II. p. 180.

118. *Protokoll VI*. pp. 224–226. Of the twenty-eight religious leaders or rabbinical students identified in the *Protokoll* rolls, twenty-one voted *ja*, seven *nein*. Some of these delegates were not identified with orthodoxy as such, though Shimoni identifies that the majority of *Mizrahi* delegates did vote to send the Commission. *The Zionist Ideology*. p. 337.

119. See Shimoni's cogent analysis in *The Zionist Ideology*. pp. 335–338. See also Luz. *Parallels Meet*. pp. 257–282.

120. Alroey. *Mikhapsey Moledet*. p. 162. Alroey quotes from a letter from Reines to Zangwill to support this assertion.

121. *Protokoll VI*. p. 230.

122. Lipsky. "Sixth International Zionist Congress." p. 209.

123. *Protokoll VI*. p. 340. See also Zangwill's account in "Zionism and Territorialism." p. 649.

124. *Protokoll VI*. p. 340.

125. Lipsky. "Sixth International Zionist Congress." p. 212.

126. Herzl. *Diaries*. Vol. IV. 31 Aug. 1903. p. 1547.

127. Ibid.

128. Ussishkin to delegates of Sixth Zionist Congress. 16 Oct. 1903. In Heymann. *The Uganda Controversy*. Vol. II. pp. 140–141.

129. Goldstein. *Ussishkin—Biographia*. Vol. I. p. 169.

130. Lipsky. "Sixth International Zionist Congress." p. 209.

131. "Un Attentat Sioniste." *Archives Israelites*. Vol. 64. 1903. p. 412.

132. "Attentat contre M. Max Nordau." *Le Gaulois*. 20 Dec. 1903. p. 2.

133. Brésil. "Attentat contre le Dr. Max Nordau" *Le Figaro*. 20 Dec. 1903. p. 2.

134. Slousch. "haHitnakshut b'Nefesh Nordau." *HaZfira*. 25 Dec. 1903. p. 2.

135. "Un Attentat Sioniste." *Archives Israelites*. Vol. 64. 1903. p. 412.

136. Ibid. See also Ben–Simha. "b'Khutz l'Artzeinu." *HaMelitz*. 29 Dec. 1903. p. 2.

137. "Attentat contre M. Max Nordau." *Le Gaulois*. 20 Dec. 1903. p. 2.

138. R—n. Telegram from 20 Dec. printed under correspondence "Hitnakshut b'Nefesh Nordau." 23 Dec. 1903. *HaZfira*. p. 2.

139. Slousch. "haHitnakshut b'Nefesh Nordau." *HaZfira*. 25 Dec. 1903. p. 2.

140. Nordau to Herzl. 20 December 1903 in Heymann. *The Uganda Controversy*. Vol. II. p. 188. See also "Un Attentat Sioniste." *Archives Israelites*. Vol. 64. 1903. p. 413. A slightly different formulation is presented in Slousch. "haHitnakshut b'Nefesh Nordau." *HaZfira*. 25 Dec. 1903. p. 2.

141. Ben-Simha. "b'Khutz l'Artzeinu." *HaMelitz*. 29 Dec. 1903. p. 2. A different report has the bullet grazing his cheek, though this does not seem to have been the case. See this version in "Attempt on Dr. Max Nordau." *Times* (London). 21 Dec. 1903. p. 5.

142. "Attempt on Dr. Max Nordau." *Times* (London). 21 Dec. 1903. p. 5.

143. Ben-Simha. "b'Khutz l'Artzeinu." *HaMelitz*. 29 Dec. 1903. p. 2.

144. Ibid.

145. "Attempt on Dr. Max Nordau." *Times* (London). 21 Dec. 1903. p. 5.

146. Brésil. "Attentat contre le Dr. Max Nordau." *Le Figaro*. 20 Dec. 1903. p. 2; "Attentat contre M. Max Nordau." *Le Gaulois*. 20 Dec. 1903. p. 2; "Un Drame Dans Un Bal." *Le Matin*. 20 Dec. 1903. p. 3; Ben-David. "Hitnakshut b'Nefesh Nordau." *HaZfira*. 23 Dec. 1903. p. 2.

147. "Attentat contre M. Max Nordau." *Le Gaulois*. 20 Dec. 1903. p. 2.

148. Preserved in [CZA A119/129]. See telegram from Joe Cowen 22. Dec. 1903.

149. Letter Nordau to Herzl. 20 Dec. 1903. In Heymann. *The Uganda Controversy*. Vol. II. p. 188.

150. "Attempt on Dr. Max Nordau." *Times* (London). 21 Dec. 1903. p. 5. According to another report, he was a medical student. See Slousch. "haHitnakshut b'Nefesh Nordau." *HaZfira*. 25 Dec. 1903. p. 2.

151. "The Attempt to Kill Nordau." *New York Times*. 22 Dec. 1903. p. 5.

152. Ibid.

153. Letter Herzl to Nordau. 23 Dec. 1903. In Heymann. *The Uganda Controversy*. Vol. II. pp. 194–196.

154. Slousch. "haHitnakshut b'Nefesh Nordau." *HaZfira*. 25 Dec. 1903. p. 2; "Hitnakshut b'Nefesh Max Nordau." *HaZman*. 22 Dec. 1903. p. 7; "Attentant L'eumi." 28 Dec. 1903. *Habazeleth*. p. 4.

155. Letter Herzl to Nordau. 23 Dec. 1903. In Heymann. *The Uganda Controversy*. Vol. II. p. 196.

156. Slousch. "haHitnakshut b'Nefesh Nordau." *HaZfira*. 25 Dec. 1903. p. 2; Ben–Simha. "b'Khutz l'Artzeinu." *HaMelitz*. 29 Dec. 1903. p. 2.

157. NBD. "Hitnakshut b'Nefesh Nordau" 28 Dec. 1903. *HaZfira*. p. 3; Slousch. "haHitnakshut b'Nefesh Nordau." *HaZfira*. 25 Dec. 1903. p. 2.

158. See Ushisskin's "Open Letter." 16 Oct. 1903. In Heymann. *The Uganda Controversy*. Vol. II. pp. 140–141.

159. Weisbord. *African Zion* pp. 198–199; Heymann. *The Uganda Controversy*. Vol. II. pp. 16, 19.

160. Johnston. "The Zionists and East Africa." *Times* (London). 1 Sept. 1903. p. 4.

161. Wolf. "Lord Landsdowne and the Zionists." *Times* (London). 28 Aug. 1903. p. 5.

162. Johnston. "The Zionists and East Africa." *Times* (London). 1 Sept. 1903. p. 4.

163. Ibid.

164. Johnston. *The Uganda Protectorate*. Vol. I. p. 270.

165. Ibid.

166. Ibid., Plate IV. "Density of Native Population and European Settlements."

167. "The Threatened Jewish Invasion." *African Standard*. 5 Sept. 1903. p. 5.

168. "More Jewganda Jewdrops." *African Standard*. 17 Oct. 1903. p. 2; "Is It to Be Jewganda?" *African Standard*. 17 Oct. 1903. p. 4; "Jewganda." *African Standard*. 17 Oct. 1903. p. 8; "Uganda or Jewganda." *African Standard*. 12 Dec. 1903. p. 2; "To Palestine via Jewganda." *African Standard*. 28 May 1904. p. 6. See also Matson. "The Zionist Offer." p. 8; Weisbord. *African Zion*. pp. 88–94.

169. Letter. *African Standard*. 10 Oct. 1903. p. 2.

170. "More Jewganda Jewdrops, or Petticoat Lane Pars." *African Standard*. 17 Oct. 1903. p. 2.

171. "The Halfway House to Palestine." *African Standard*. 26 Sept. 1903. p. 4.

172. "Indignation in Nairobi." *African Standard*. 5 Sept. 1903. p. 5.

173. "The Advent of the Undesireable." *African Standard*. 12 Dec. 1903. p. 2; "The Zionist Scheme." *African Standard*. 21 Jan. 1905. p. 6.

174. Ahad Ha'am. "haBokhim." p. 338.

175. Ibid., p. 340.

176. See Alroey. *Mikhapsey Moledet*. pp. 148–155.

177. Borochov. "l'She'aylat Tzion v'Teritoria." p. 20.

178. Ibid., p. 27.

179. Ibid., pp. 70–71.

180. Ibid., p. 23.

181. Ibid., p. 103.

182. Ibid., p. 132–133.

183. Ibid.

184. Ibid., p. 148.

185. Ibid.

186. Ibid., p. 153.

187. Rabbi Moshe Rosenblatt, a *Mizrahi* Zionist and Jewish leader from Kiev, claims to have "converted" Sholem Aleichem to territorialism after Herzl's death. See

Rosenblatt's letter to Zangwill. 6 Dec. 1905, reprinted in Alroey. *Bread to Eat*. pp. 143–147.

188. Sholem Aleichem. "Doctors in Consultation." pp. 132–134.
189. Ibid., p. 133.
190. Ibid., p. 135.
191. Ibid., p. 137.
192. Sholem Aleichem. "Ugandaade." p. 154–155.
193. Ibid., p. 158.
194. "haTayara haTzionit." *Hashkafa*. 30 Dec. 1904. p. 1.
195. Ben–Yehuda. *haMedinah haYehudit*. p. 9.
196. Ibid., p. 16.
197. Ibid., pp. 19–20.
198. Ibid., p. 23.
199. Ibid., p. 24.
200. Ibid., p. 31.
201. Ibid., p. 42.
202. Ibid.
203. Borochov. "l'She'aylat Tzion v'Teritoria." p. 77.
204. Alroey. *Mekhapsey Moledet*. pp. 181–188.
205. Ibid., pp. 188–198.
206. Zangwill. "Zionism." p. 500.
207. Ibid., p. 510.
208. Ibid., p. 507.
209. Ibid.
210. Ibid.
211. Ibid., pp. 508–509.
212. Zangwill. "Land of Refuge" p. 239; "Be Fruitful." p. 15.
213. Zangwill. "Zionism." p. 509.
214. Zangwill. *The East African Question*. p. 35.
215. Zangwill. "The East Africa Offer." This is a slightly revised version of *The East African Question*. p. 213.
216. Zangwill. *The East African Question*. p. 18.
217. See Shimoni. *The Zionist Ideology*. pp. 92–93.
218. Zangwill. *The East African Question*. p. 55.
219. Frederic S. Franklin qtd. "And 1950." *Jewish Chronicle*. p. 8.
220. See Alroey's analysis of East Africa as compared to Palestine. *Mekhapsey Moledet*. pp. 72–73.
221. Weisbord. *African Zion*. pp. 203–204.
222. Johnston. *The Uganda Protectorate*. Vol. I. p. 270.
223. "haTayara haTzionit." *Hashkafa*. 13 Jan. 1905. p. 1. Weisbord identifies this donor as Mrs. E. A. Gordon. *African Zion*. pp. 203–204.
224. Letter Johnston to Greenberg. 29 Sept. 1904. Reprinted in "Jewganda: The Proposed Jewish Settlement in East Africa." *African Standard*. 12 Nov. 1904. p. 4.

225. Ibid.
226. See Johnston. *The Life and Letters of Sir Harry Johnston*. pp. 289–290.
227. "The Proposed Jewish Settlement in East Africa." *Times*. 7 Dec. 1904. p. 11.
228. Ibid.
229. Ben-Yehuda. "haTayara haTzionit." *Hashkafa*. 30 Dec. 1904. p. 1.
230. "haExpeditzia l'Uganda." *HaZfira*. 18. Dec. 1904. p. 1.
231. Ben-Yehuda. "haTayara haTzionit." *Hashkafa*. 30 Dec. 1904. p. 1; Saposnik. *Becoming Hebrew*. pp. 57–58. See also Klausner's telling defense against this charge in *Menahem Ussischkin*. p. 71.
232. Klausner. *Menahem Ussischkin*. p. 70. See also Goldstein. *Ussishkin—Biografia*. Vol. I. p. 184.
233. Pepper. "ha'Im Ussishkin Yipol Shaynit, Gam b'Bira?" 20 Sept. 2007. http://www.haaretz.co.il/hasite/spages/905545.html.
234. *Report on the Work of the Commission Sent Out to Examine the Territory Offered by H. M. Government to the Zionist Organization for the Purposes of a Jewish Settlement in British East Africa* [*Report*]. p. 57.
235. Ibid.
236. See Wilbuschewitz's "Palestinian Temporary Resident Card." [CZA A355/1].
237. List of materials to be taken on expedition. [CZA A12/72].
238. Wilbuschewitz's "Laisser-Passer." [CZA A355/1].
239. Wilbusch. *haMassa l'Uganda*. p. 45.
240. Ibid., p. 21.
241. Ibid., p. 23.
242. Ibid., p. 42.
243. Ibid.
244. Ibid.
245. *Report*. 24 Dec. 1904–13 Jan. 1905. p. 57.
246. Warburg. "Einiges Ueber Die Zionistische Ostafrika-Expedition." *Ost und West* (Mar. 1905): p. 159.
247. Wilbusch. *haMassa l'Uganda*. p. 43.
248. Ibid., pp. 43–44.
249. List of materials to be taken on expedition. [CZA A12/72].
250. *Report*. p. 57.
251. Gibbons. "British East African Plateau and its Economic Conditions." p. 243.
252. Wilbusch. *haMassa l'Uganda*. p. 43.
253. Ibid., pp. 43–44.
254. *Report*. p. 15.
255. Ibid.
256. Zangwill. *The East African Question*. p. 49.
257. Wilbusch. *haMassa l'Uganda*. p. 90.
258. Ibid., p. 23.
259. Wilbusch. "Aussichten der Industrie in Palästina." [CZA 355/211].
260. Wilbusch. *haMassa l'Uganda*. p. 24.

261. Ibid., p. 30.
262. Ibid., p. 29.
263. Ibid., p. 34.
264. Letter Greenberg to Otto Warburg. 7 Nov. 1904. [CZA A12/72].
265. Wilbusch. *haMassa l'Uganda*. p. 42. See also Wilbusch's handwritten note describing the "great impression" his report on Palestine made on Warburg. [CZA 355/211].
266. *Report*. p. 4.
267. Letter Greenberg to Warburg. 12 Dec. 1904 [CZA A12/72].
268. Postcard Wilbusch to Warburg. 13 Jan. 1905 reproduced in Warburg. pp. 155–156.
269. *Report*. 18 Jan. 1905. p. 58.
270. Wilbusch. *haMassa l'Uganda*. p. 60.
271. Ibid., p. 68.
272. Ibid., p. 64.
273. Ibid., p. 51.
274. Ibid., p. 52.
275. *Report*. p. 21.
276. Ibid., p. 20.
277. Ibid., 28 Jan. 1905. p. 59.
278. *Report*. p. 60; Wilbusch. *haMassa l'Uganda*. p. 67.
279. *Report*. 30 Jan. 1905. p. 60. Mount Sirgoit is called "Mt. Sirgoi" in his field notes.
280. Wilbusch. *haMassa l'Uganda*. p. 68.
281. *Report*. 30 Jan. 1905. p. 60.
282. *Report*. 1 Feb. 1905. p. 60.
283. *Report*. 2 Feb. 1905. p. 60; 8 Feb. 1905. p. 62.
284. *Report*. 3 Feb. 1905. p. 61.
285. *Report*. 18 Feb. 1905. p. 64; Wilbusch. *haMassa l'Uganda*. p. 64.
286. Wilbusch. *haMassa l'Uganda*. p. 73.
287. *Report*. 3 Feb. 1905. p. 61.
288. Wilbusch. *haMassa l'Uganda*. p. 73.
289. *Report*. 7 Feb. 1905. p. 62.
290. *Report*. 8–9 Feb. 1905. p. 62.
291. Wilbusch. *haMassa l'Uganda*. p. 91.
292. Ibid., p. 75.
293. Ibid., p. 78.
294. The German version of Wilbusch's report bears this designation. [CZA A355/50].
295. *Report*. 14 Feb. 1905. p. 63.
296. *Report*. pp. 63–65; Alroey. "Journey to New Palestine." p. 41.
297. *haMassa l'Uganda*. pp. 87–92.
298. Ibid., p. 81.
299. Ibid.
300. Ibid., p. 65.

301. Wilbusch. *haMassa l'Uganda*. p. 92.
302. "Return of Major Gibbons from East Africa." *Times* (London). 31 Mar. 1905. p. 11.
303. *Report*. p. 56.
304. Ibid., p. 90.
305. Ibid., p. 73.
306. Ibid., p. 90.
307. Warburg. "Einiges Ueber Die Zionistische Ostafrika–Expedition." p. 152.
308. Ibid., p. 154.
309. Ibid.
310. Ibid., p. 162.
311. Book of Numbers 13:32. The connection between this passage and the expedition's report has been made before. See "Hartza'at haTayara l'Mizrakh Africa." *Hashkafa*. 30 June 1905. p. 2; Margolis. "The Year 5665." p. 248; Bar–Yosef. "Spying Out the Land." pp. 183–200.
312. *Report*. 28 Feb. 1905. p. 65.
313. Letter Ussishkin to Chaim Katzenelson. 2 Apr. 1905. Emphasis in Hebrew original. [CZA AK25/1].
314. Letters Ussishkin to Wilbuschewitz. 24 Apr. and 7 May 1905. [CZA A355/131] (Russian; trans. Larissa Kulinich).
315. Ibid.
316. Ibid.
317. Ibid.
318. Weisbord. *African Zion*. p. 208; Wilbusch. *haMassa l'Uganda*. p. 49. There was support for a Jewish colony in East Africa from South African Zionist officials. See S. Goldreich's letter of 24 Oct. 1903. [CZA A143/15].
319. *Report*. 17 Jan. 1905. p. 58; Wilbusch. *haMassa l'Uganda*. pp. 47–49.
320. Wilbusch. *haMassa l'Uganda*. p. 52.
321. Schechtman. *Rebel and Statesman*. p. 89.
322. Rubinstein. "Greenberg, Leopold Jacob (1861–1931)." http://0-www.oxforddnb.com.bianca.penlib.du.edu/view/article/70402 (2004).
323. Arthur Hardinge. 10 June 1912. [TNA FO 367/291].
324. Balfour. "Balfour Declaration." 2 Nov. 1917. p. 29.

CHAPTER 3. ANGOLAN ZION

1. Yaffe. *Tzion b'Basle*. p. 281.
2. Ibid.
3. *Stenographisches Protokoll der Verhandlungen des VII Zionisten–Kongresses* [*Protokoll VII*]. pp. 37–38.
4. Ibid., p. 45.
5. Ibid., p. 46.
6. Ibid., p. 69.

7. "Mr. Zangwill on the Future of Zionism." *Jewish Chronicle*. 14 July 1905. pp. 14–15.

8. *Protokoll VII*. p. 70.

9. Noah. *Discourse on the Restoration*. p. 50.

10. *Protokoll VII*. p. 72.

11. Ibid.

12. Ibid., p. 75.

13. Ibid., p. 132.

14. Ibid., pp. 133–134.

15. Emphasis mine. *The Jewish Colonial Trust, Limited, Memorandum and Articles of Association*. p. 1.

16. See legal judgment of Justice H. T. Eve. 4 May 1908. *The Law Journal Reports for the Year 1908*. pp. 629–637.

17. *Protokoll VII*. p. 134.

18. Ibid.

19. N. B. D. "haCongress Shel ha'Teritoriali'im." p. 2.

20. *Protokoll VII*. p. 135.

21. Ibid.

22. See Alroey's description. *Mikhapsey Moledet*. p. 75.

23. Syrkin qtd. in N. B. D. "haCongress Shel ha'Teritoriali'im." p. 2.

24. Ibid.

25. Ibid.

26. Ibid.

27. *Protokoll VII*. p. 305.

28. Qtd. in letter from Ussishkin to Zangwill. 6 Jan. 1907. [CZA A36/225].

29. This notation appears on an English translation of a postcard sent by Usshishkin to Zangwill regarding the affair. [CZA A36/225].

30. Alroey. *Mikhapsey Moledet*. p. 88.

31. Ibid.

32. Ibid., pp. 89, 111.

33. Ibid., pp. 121, 136.

34. Ibid., pp. 98–99.

35. Ibid., p. 120, n. 103.

36. Zangwill. "Land of Refuge." p. 246.

37. Zangwill. "Jewish Colonial Trust." pp. 264–265.

38. Zangwill. "Territorialism as Practical Politics." p. 311.

39. *Protokoll VII*. p. 92.

40. Kleinman. "haKongress haUgandi." *HaZman*. 3 Aug. 1905. p. 2.

41. Zangwill. *The East African Question*. p. 31.

42. Zangwill. "Territorialism as Practical Politics." p. 314.

43. Ibid.

44. Zangwill. *The Voice of Jerusalem*. pp. 108–115.

45. Zangwill. *The East African Question.* pp. 31–32.

46. This is the figure Zangwill notes in "Territorialism as Practical Politics." p. 314.

47. Zangwill. "Territorialism as Practical Politics." pp. 310–311.

48. See Alroey's conclusions in *Mikhapsey Moledet.* pp. 195–198.

49. Ben-Yehuda. "haSakh haKol." *Hashkafa* 18 Aug. 1905. p.1.

50. Ibid.

51. Ibid., p. 2.

52. Brenner. "m'Tokh haPinkas." p. 130.

53. Ibid.

54. Brenner. "Mikhtav l'Rusya." p. 13.

55. Ibid.

56. Ibid.

57. Zangwill. "The Jewish Territorial Organisation." *Jewish Chronicle.* 5 Aug. 1905. p. 17.

58. Ibid.

59. Ibid.

60. Ibid.

61. Ibid.

62. Ibid.

63. Herzl. "Programm." p. 1. See also Fraenkel. "Mathias Acher's Fight for the 'Crown of Zion.'" p. 122.

64. Cf. Alroey's conclusions in *Mikhapsey Moledet.* p. 294.

65. Letter Zangwill to J. W. Gregory. 23 Nov. 1905. [CZA A120/39].

66. Leake. *The Life and Work of Professor J. W. Gregory.* p. 19.

67. Ibid., p. 126.

68. Zangwill. "British East Africa: Supplementary Note by the President of the ITO." p. 1. A thorough survey of the ITO's various plans appears in Marmor's two-part article "haMasa u'Matan" and Alroey's *Mikhapsey Moledet.* pp. 199–244. My presentation is partly based on their work and draws as well from confidential reports on various territories published exclusively for ITO membership.

69. Hart et. al. "Canada: Report to the Council of the Jewish Territorial Organisation"; Zangwill. "Canada: Supplementary Note by the President of the ITO."

70. Langdon and Salaman. "Australia: Report to the Council of the Jewish Territorial Organization"; Zangwill. "Supplementary Note by the President of the ITO [to Australia Report]."

71. Wingate. "Mesopotamia: Report to the Council of the Jewish Territorial Organization." 1907; Zangwill. "Supplementary Notes [to Wingate's Report]." c. 1907. For Herzl's support see Herzl. *Diaries.* Vol. III. 29 Dec. 1899. p. 899; *Diaries.* Vol. IV. Letter Herzl to Lord Rothschild. 12 July 1902. pp. 1302–1303; *Diaries.* Vol. IV. 28 July 1902. pp. 1320–1321; *Diaries.* Vol. IV. Letter Herzl to Holo Al-Abed Izzet Pasha. 4 June 1903. p. 1503.

72. Zangwill. "Supplementary Notes [to Wingate's Report]." c. 1907. p. 26.

73. Zangwill. "Be Fruitful and Multiply." p. 10.
74. Zangwill. "Mr. Zangwill on the Future of Zionism." *Jewish Chronicle*. 14 July 1905. p. 14.
75. Zangwill. "Preface, Historical and Political." p. viii.
76. Ibid.
77. Ibid.
78. Ibid.
79. Ibid., p. vii.
80. Ibid., p. viii.
81. *Protokoll VII*. p. 89.
82. Ibid.
83. Slousch. "Jews and Judaism in Ancient Cyrenaica." p. 51.
84. Ibid. (italics in original).
85. Zangwill. "Preface, Historical and Political." p. ix.
86. Gregory. *Report on the Work of the Commission* [Cyrenaica]. pp. 2–5.
87. Ibid., p. 13.
88. Ibid.
89. See Sakolski. "Nevada and Idaho: Report to the Council of the Jewish Territorial Organization."
90. Ibid., p. 5.
91. Eder. "Report to the Council of the ITO on the possibility of Settlements in the Republics of Bolivia, Colombia, and Brazil." pp. 6–23. Eder also traveled to Cyrenaica as part of the ITO Commission.
92. Abrahams. "Paraguay: Report to the Council of the Jewish Territorial Organization."
93. Spielmann. "Rhodesia: Report to the Council of the Jewish Territorial Organization."
94. Zangwill. "A Land of Refuge." p. 243.
95. For more on the origins of the Galveston plan, see Cohen. *Jacob H. Schiff*. pp. 159–168; Best. "Jacob H. Schiff's Galveston Movement"; Marinbach. *Galveston*, especially pp. 1–20.
96. On the friction between them, see Best. "Jacob H. Schiff's Galveston Movement." pp. 52–54.
97. Best. "Jacob H. Schiff's Galveston Movement." pp. 45–46, 50; Cohen. *Jacob H. Schiff*. pp. 162–167; Marinbach. *Galveston*. pp. 9–10.
98. Alroey. *haMehapekha haShkayta*. table 22, p. 230.
99. Zangwill. *The Melting Pot*. p. 155.
100. Ibid., p. 185.
101. Letter H. H. Johnston to Zangwill. 29 Jan. 1914. [CZA A120/409].
102. Letter Zangwill to Roosevelt. 25 Aug. 1908. [CZA A120/559] .
103. Qtd. in "Mr. Zangwill in Town." *Jewish Exponent* (Philadelphia). 16 Oct. 1908. p. 2.
104. Letter Roosevelt to Zangwill. Qtd. in Nahshon. "*The Melting Pot*: Introductory Essay." p. 242.

105. Zangwill. "Afterword [to *The Melting Pot*]." p. 199.

106. Zangwill. "What is the ITO?" p. 233.

107. "Jewish Territorial Organisation/Fourth Anniversary." *Jewish Chronicle*. 14 May 1909. p. 14.

108. "Helsingfors Conference." *The Jew in the Modern World*. p. 555.

109. Ussishkin was absent from the conference that drafted this statement. See Vital. *Zionism*. p. 467.

110. See table qtd. in Shafir. "Zionist Immigration and Colonization in Palestine until 1948." *Cambridge Survey of World Migration*. p. 407. Vital suggests that only about two thousand of this total were motivated by an adherence to Zionist ideology. See *Zionism*. p. 385.

111. Almog. "Role of Religious Values in the Second Aliyah." p. 238.

112. Kaniel estimates the rate between forty and fifty percent. "Memadai haYeridah min haAretz b'Tkufat haAliyah haRishona v'haShniyah (1882–1914)." p. 130.

113. Alroey. *haMahapekha haShkayta*. p. 230.

114. All those named were affiliated with the ITO during the Angola plan discussions. See letter from Zangwill to Rothschild. 1 Nov. 1912. [CZA A120/69].

115. Letter Zangwill to A. Bensaúde. 30 Oct. 1912. [CZA A36/73].

116. Letter M. Spielmann to Zangwill. 10 Dec. 1907. [CZA A36/73].

117. Ibid.

118. Ibid.

119. Ibid.

120. Letter Zangwill to M. Spielmann. 16 Dec. 1907. [CZA A36/73].

121. Letter M. I. Cohen to Zangwill. 3 June 1911. [CZA A36/73].

122. Letter Zangwill to M. I. Cohen. 12 July 1911. [CZA A36/73].

123. Letter Zangwill to H. H. Johnston. 15 Oct. 1917. Here Zangwill reiterates his opposition to colonial exploitation. [CZA A120/409].

124. On his thinking about race, see Rochelson. *A Jew in the Public Arena*. pp. 157–167.

125. Zangwill. "Mr. Morel and the Congo." p. 283.

126. Description from Zitron. "Reshimot Min haKonferencia haITOit." *HaZman*. 9 July 1912. p. 2.

127. Composite of biographical details drawn from Descamps. *Le Portugal*. p. 443; Zitron. "Reshimot Min haKonferencia haITOit." *HaZman*. 9 July 1912. p. 2.

128. Terló. "Projecto de Colonização." p. 41.

129. Terló to ITO. 6 Mar. 1912. Published in "Khalifat Mikhtavim b'Dvar Hatza'at Angola." *HaZman*. 15 May 1912. p. 2.

130. Ibid.

131. Letter ITO to W. Terló. 31 Mar. 1912. [CZA A36/46].

132. Letter Zangwill to W. Terló. 19 Apr. 1912. [CZA A120/571].

133. See Teitel. *Aus meiner Lebensarbeit*. pp. 121–122.

134. Letter W. Terló to Zionist Central Bureau. 23 Jan. 1912. [CZA Z3/971].

135. Ibid.

136. Letter Zionist Central Bureau to Terló. 1 Feb. 1912. [CZA Z3/971].

137. Terló qtd. in "A Colonisação Dos Judeus." *O Seculo*. n.d. n. p. [CZA Z3/971].

138. Ibid.

139. Ibid.

140. Diário Câmara dos Deputados. Session 49 (8 Feb. 1912), p. 5. Nearly complete transcripts of parliamentary debates are available at http://debates.parlamento. pt/. All citations to debates in the Chamber of Deputies and Senate refer to this online archive.

141. Ibid.

142. Diário Câmara dos Deputados. Session 78 (19 Mar. 1912), p. 13.

143. Terló. "Projecto de Colonização." p. 41.

144. Letter Terló to Zionist Central Bureau. 23 Apr. 1912. [CZA Z3/971].

145. Letter Terló to Zionist Central Bureau. 23–24 Apr. 1912 [CZA Z3/971].

146. Letter Terló to Zionist Central Bureau. 24 Apr. 1912 [CZA Z3/971].

147. This issue is treated in Medina and Barromi. "The Jewish Colonization Project in Angola." pp. 3–5. See also the debates related to these bills in parliament, Diário Câmara dos Deputados. Session 78 (19 Mar. 1912).

148. Letter Zionist Central Bureau to Terló. 30 Apr. 1912. [CZA Z3/971].

149. Letter Zionist Central Bureau to Terló. 17 June 1912. [CZA Z3/971].

150. Ibid.

151. Teitel. *Aus meiner Lebensarbeit*. p. 122; Kruk. *Takhat Diglan*. p. 156.

152. Ibid.

153. Teitel. *Aus meiner Lebensarbeit*. p. 123; Kruk. *Takhat Diglan*. p. 156.

154. Teitel. *Aus meiner Lebensarbeit*. p. 123.

155. Ibid., pp. 124–125.

156. Ibid., pp. 126–127.

157. Ibid., p. 128.

158. Ibid., p. 130.

159. Teitel. *Aus meiner Lebensarbeit*. p. 130; Kruk. *Takhat Diglan*. p. 157.

160. Biographical details in Medina and Barromi. "The Jewish Colonization Project in Angola." p. 2.

161. Teitel. *Aus meiner Lebensarbeit*. p. 132.

162. Ibid., p. 134.

163. Letter Teitel published in "Al Davar Hatza'at Angola." *HaZman*. 19 June 1912. p. 2.

164. Teitel. *Aus meiner Lebensarbeit*. pp. 133–134.

165. The document preserved is almost certainly from Teitel though no authorship is attributed. The date of the memo accords with that of Teitel's stay in Lisbon and his recollection of his dispatch in his memoirs. Memorandum to ITO [regarding Angola]. 16 May 1912. [CZA A36/73].

166. Ibid.

167. Ibid.

168. Letter Teitel published in "Al Davar Hatza'at Angola." *HaZman*. 19 June 1912. p. 2.

169. Letter Emanuel, Round, Nathan [solicitors] to Zangwill. 21 May 1912. [CZA A36/33/3].
170. Terló. "Projecto de Colonização." p. 43.
171. Diário Câmara dos Deputados. Session 112 (17 May 1912), p. 4.
172. Ibid.
173. Diário Câmara dos Deputados. Session 113 (18 May 1912), p. 30.
174. Ibid.
175. Diário Câmara dos Deputados. Session 115 (21 May 1912), p. 17.
176. Diário Câmara dos Deputados. Session 119 (25 May 1912), p. 9.
177. Diário Câmara dos Deputados. Session 130 (8 June 1912), p. 15.
178. Photograph in Ilustração Portuguesa. 10 June 1912. p. 759.
179. Report A. Hardinge to E. Grey. 3 June 1912. [TNA FO 367/291].
180. Ibid.
181. Ibid.
182. Minutes A. Hardinge. 10 June 1912. [TNA FO 367/291],
183. Report A. Hardinge to E. Grey. 3 June 1912. [TNA FO 367/291].
184. See Lichnowsky. "My Mission to London." pp. 15–16.
185. See Langhorne. "Anglo–German Negotiations Concerning the Future of the Portuguese Colonies, 1911–1914"; Vincent–Smith. "The Anglo–German Negotiations Over the Portuguese Colonies in Africa, 1911–1914."
186. Zangwill's reasoning is explicit in Report A. Hardinge to E. Grey. 3 June 1912. [TNA FO 367/291].
187. Translated copy of "The Bill." 20 June 1912. [CZA A36/73]. For notification of passage, see Diário Câmara dos Deputados. Session 139 (20 June 1912), p. 9.
188. "The Bill." 20 June 1912. Articles 7, 8. [CZA A36/73].
189. Ibid., Art. 2.
190. Ibid., Art. 1, Clauses 1–2.
191. Ibid., Arts. 1 and 10.
192. "haPratim Al Davar Hatza'at Angola b'Parliament haPortugali." HaZman. 25 June 1912. p. 1.
193. Sokolov. "Eretz Yisrael v'Angola." HaZfira. 25 July 1912. pp. 1–2.
194. "Ito Conference Speech." Jewish Chronicle. 5 July 1912. pp. 21–22.
195. "Angola is Offered for Zionist Colony." New York Times. 28 June 1912. p. 8.
196. "haVe'ida haTeritoriali'im b'Vienna." HaZfira. 1 July 1912. p. 2.
197. Detail from "Ito Conference Speech." Jewish Chronicle. 5 July 1912. p. 22.
198. "haVe'ida haTeritoriali'im b'Vienna." HaZfira. 1 July 1912. p. 2.
199. "haVe'ida Shel haTeritoriali'im b'Vienna." HaZfira. 30 June 1912. p. 2.
200. Zitron. "Ptikhat haKonferentzia haITO'it." HaZman. 2 July 1912. p. 3.
201. Zitron. "haKonferentzia haITO'it." HaZman. 5 July 1912. pp. 2–3.
202. Zitron. "Reshimot Min ha'Konferenzia haITO'it." HaZman. 9 July 1912. p. 2.
203. Letter Rhodesian colonist to Zangwill. 23 Aug. 1912. [CZA A20/135].
204. Zangwill. "Introduction, Historical and Political." p. ix.
205. Ibid.

206. Ibid., p. x. And see Appendix A, letter from H. H. Johnston in the same *Report* [Angola]. pp. 39–40.

207. Zangwill. "Introduction, Historical and Political." p. x. This reproduced text is identical to the original telegram of June 1912. [CZA A36/73].

208. Ibid.

209. Diário Câmara dos Deputados. Session 155 (2 July 1912), p. 2.

210. Nascimento. *A Colonisação do planalto de Benguella*. p. 155.

211. Ibid., p. 158.

212. Report A. Hardinge to E. Grey. 2 July 1912. [TNA FO 367/291].

213. "Ito Conference Speech." *Jewish Chronicle*. 5 July 1912. p. 22.

214. Reported in letter Zangwill to J. D'Almada. 19 July 1912. [CZA A120/64].

215. Letter Zangwill to J. D'Almada. 19 July 1912. [CZA A120/64].

216. Leake. *The Life and Work of Professor J. W. Gregory*. p. 136.

217. Ibid., p. 5.

218. Ibid., p. 135.

219. Ibid., p. 26.

220. Letter J. W. Gregory to Harris. 17 July 1912. [TNA FO 367/291].

221. Letter J. W. Gregory to W. Langley. 22 July 1912. [TNA FO 367/291].

222. Ibid.

223. Letter W. Langley to J. W. Gregory. 25 July 1912. [TNA FO 367/291].

224. Satre. *Chocolate on Trial*. Especially pp. 197–205.

225. John. "A New Slavery?" pp. 34–35.

226. Letter Zangwill to H. Auerbach. 23 July 1912. [CZA A36/22].

227. Letter Zangwill to A. Bensaúde. 25 Aug. 1912. [CZA A36/73].

228. Letter Zangwill to Bensaúde. 11 July 1912. [CZA A120/386]. See also Zangwill's negative assessment of Terló in letter to Bensaúde. 5 Aug. 1912. [CZA A120/386].

229. Bastos is identified as the author in the installment "Colonização Judaica." *Jornal de Benguela*. Vol. I. No. 5. 31 July 1912. p. 2.

230. Bastos. "Colonização Judaica." *Jornal de Benguela*. Vol. I. No. 6. 7 Aug. 1912. p. 2.

231. Ibid., Vol. II. No. 35. 27 Aug. 1913. p. 6.

232. Ibid., Vol. I. No. 9. 28 Aug. 1912. p. 2.

233. Dias. *Benguela*. p. 46.

234. Gregory. *Report on the Work of the Commission* [Angola]. p. 7.

235. Ibid., p. 8.

236. Ibid., p. 10.

237. Ibid., p. 11.

238. Gregory to Zangwill. "Preliminary Report on Visit to Angola, 1912." 3 Oct. 1912. [CZA A36/73].

239. Gregory. *Report on the Work of the Commission* [Angola]. p. 7.

240. Letter Gregory to Zangwill. 21 May 1913. [CZA A36/73].

241. Martin. "Report Upon the Highlands." p. 34.

242. Ibid., p. 35.

243. Gregory. *Report on the Work of the Commission* [Angola]. pp. 18, 22.

244. Ibid., p. 22.

245. Ibid.

246. Ibid.

247. Ibid., p. 24.

248. Ibid., p. 25.

249. Ibid.

250. Ibid.

251. Ibid., p. 29.

252. Ibid.

253. Gregory to Zangwill. "Preliminary Report on Visit to Angola, 1912." 3 Oct. 1912. [CZA A36/73].

254. Notes of Meeting. 22 Oct 1912. [CZA A142/185].

255. Letter Zangwill to L. Rothschild. 1 Nov. 1912. [CZA A36/138].

256. Letter Zangwill to L. Rothschild. 24 Oct. 1912. [CZA A120/69].

257. Letter Zangwill to L. Rothschild. 1 Nov. 1912. [CZA A120/69].

258. Letter M. Nathan to Zangwill. 4 May 1913. [CZA A36/204].

259. See references to resignation in file [CZA A120/58].

260. "ITOism: Brilliant Address by Mr. Israel Zangwill." *Jewish Chronicle*. 4 Apr. 1913. p. 25.

261. Ibid. p. 26.

262. Ibid., p. 119.

263. Ibid., pp. 119–127.

264. Ibid., p. 120.

265. Ibid., pp. 124–125. Emphasis in published translation.

266. Zangwill. "Introduction, Historical and Political." p. ix. He quotes here the text of a speech he gave at the ITO Conference in 1912.

267. Letter Zangwill to Bensaúde. 4 June 1913. [CZA A36/73].

268. "Os Israelitas no planalto de Benguella." *A Capital*. n.d. p.1. [CZA A36/73]. This article appears to be from July or Aug. 1913.

269. Ibid.

270. Diário Do Senado. Session 91 (1 May 1913), pp. 19–21.

271. Diário Do Senado. Session 124 (11 June 1913), p. 16.

272. Diário Do Senado. Session 129 (16 June 1913), p. 12.

273. Diário Do Senado. Session 100 (14 May 1913), p. 20.

274. Diário Do Senado. Session 123 (9 June 1913), p. 14.

275. Ibid., p. 17.

276. Diário Do Senado. Session 91 (1 May 1913), pp. 20–21; Diário Do Senado. Session 124 (11 June 1913), p. 15.

277. Diário Do Senado. Session 126 (12 June 1913), pp. 13–14.

278. Ibid., p. 14.

279. Diário Do Senado. Session 127 (13 June 1913), p. 5.

280. Ibid.

281. Letter Zangwill to Bensaúde. 24 June 1913. [CZA A36/73].

282. Diário do Senado. Session 144 (29 June 1913), p. 78. See also Medina and Barromi. "The Jewish Colonization Project in Angola." pp. 14–15.

283. "Sikha Im Zangwill, She'aylat Angola." *HaZfira*. 22 Aug. 1913. p. 2.

284. "Sikha Im haProfessor Gregory b'Dvar Angola." *HaZfira*. 4 Aug. 1913. p. 3.

285. Letter Zangwill to Bensaúde. 24 Aug. 1913. [CZA A36/73].

286. Letter Bensaúde to Zangwill. 13 Sept. 1913. [CZA A36/204].

287. "The Ito Angola Scheme." *Jewish Chronicle*. 12 Sept. 1913. p. 33.

288. Zangwill expressed these frustrations in his address to the ITO's London Council. 5 Oct. 1913. [CZA A36/46].

289. Medina and Barromi. "The Jewish Colonization Project in Angola." p. 15.

290. Zangwill's address to London Council. 5 Oct. 1913. [CZA A36/46].

291. Ibid.

292. Ibid.

293. Ibid.

294. Letter H. Kisch, n.d., responding to Zangwill's letter of 8 Oct. 1913. [CZA A36/46].

295. Letter Sebag-Montefiore to Zangwill. 10 Oct. 1913. [CZA A36/46].

296. Zangwill's address to London Council. 5 Oct. 1913. [CZA A36/46].

297. Memorandum by the President (Zangwill) to the London ITO Council. 22 Nov. 1913. [CZA A36/46].

298. Ibid. Emphasis in original.

299. Letters Zangwill to Ginsburg. 22 Mar. 1914 and 15 Apr. 1914. [CZA A36/204].

300. Letter Bensaúde to Zangwill. 22 July 1914. Emphasis in original. [CZA A36/204].

301. Letter Zangwill to Gregory. 22 Apr. 1915. [CZA A120/39].

302. Zangwill. *The Voice of Jerusalem*. pp. 81–86. These pages quote the text of a speech Zangwill gave on 3 Dec. 1917 in celebration of the Balfour Declaration.

303. Letter Zangwill to Churchill. 6 Dec. 1918. [CZA A120/307].

304. Ibid.

305. Zangwill. "The Territorial Solution of the Jewish Question (II)." p. 736.

306. Zangwill. *The Voice of Jerusalem*. p. 294.

307. Gregory qtd. in "Suggested Homes for Zionism." *Glasgow Herald*. 16 Mar. 1920. p. 9. Italics mine.

308. Ibid.

309. Rochelson. *A Jew in the Public Arena*. p. 220.

310. "ITO Presentation Album on the Closure of the Organisation." July 1925. [HLS MS 294].

311. Rochelson. *A Jew in the Public Arena*. p. 221.

312. H. Cohen qtd. in Leftwich. *Israel Zangwill*. p. 177.

313. See Netanyahu. "Israel Zangwill." pp. 144–183.

CHAPTER 4. THE LOST JEWISH CONTINENT

1. Oppenheimer. "Merchavia." p. 28.

2. Ibid.

3. Ibid.

4. Ibid., p. 29.

5. "Enthusiastic Reception for Franz Oppenheimer." p. 88.

6. See "The Life Work of Franz Oppenheimer." pp. 12–13.

7. Ibid., p. 12.

8. Oppenheimer [1890] qtd. in McElligott. *The German Urban Experience 1900–1945*. pp. 65–66.

9. 18 Jan. 1903. Herzl. *Diaries*. Vol. IV. p. 1393. For the relationship between Herzl and Oppenheimer, see Oppenheimer. "Merchavia." Preface; Penslar. *Zionism and Technocracy*. pp. 52–59.

10. Heyman. *The Uganda Controversy*. Vol. I. p. 24. See Oppenheimer's address to the Congress, *Protokoll VI*. pp. 182–195.

11. "Does Peru Hold Out Hope of Jewish Settlement?" Jewish Telegraphic Agency. 19 Feb. 1931.

12. Letter Einstein to Max Warburg. 5 Aug. 1930. Reprinted in Jerome, ed. *Einstein on Israel and Zionism*. p. 91.

13. Letter Einstein to ICA. 28 Nov. 1930. Reprinted in Jerome, ed. *Einstein on Israel and Zionism*. p. 93.

14. "Does Peru Hold Out Hope of Jewish Settlement?" Jewish Telegraphic Agency. 19 Feb. 1931.

15. Ibid.

16. Astour. *Geshikhte fun der Frayland-Lige*. Vol. I. pp. 34–35.

17. Ibid., pp. 81–82. Dr. Josef Kruk, a socialist and territorialist activist who worked closely with Israel Zangwill and his ITO project, later became involved with the Freeland League. He claimed in his autobiography to have suggested the "Freeland" name. Kruk. *Takhat Diglan*. p. 446.

18. In English, see Kagedan. *Soviet Zion*; Srebrnik. *Jerusalem on the Amur*; Srebrnik. *Dreams of Nationhood*; Weinberg. *Stalin's Forgotten Zion*.

19. Shneer. "Zion Without Zionism."

20. Zangwill. "Rosy Russia." p. 366.

21. Zangwill. "Siberia as a Jewish State." p. 13.

22. Ibid.

23. Leftwich. *Israel Zangwill*. p. 161.

24. The 1906 date appears in "Colonization Projects, Jewish." p. 153. A partial handwritten, untitled and undated manuscript by Zangwill reads: "One of these solutions was offered to me the other day by Prince Kropotkin, who thinks that Russia . . . organized on the Federal principle . . . would become the seat of a Jewish autonomy." [CZA A120/135].

25. Belolutskaia. "Kropotkin, Petr Alekseevitch." pp. 1134–1135.

26. Leftwich. *Israel Zangwill*. pp. 216–217.

27. Zhitlowski. "Der Teritorialism." p. 26.

28. Minutes of Freeland meeting in London. 6 Jan. 1936. [CZA A330/14].

29. Astour. "Thirty Years of Birobidzhan." p. 8.

30. Ibid.

31. "Constitution of the Freeland League for Jewish Territorial Colonization." n.d. Shaechter Papers. [YIVO RG 682/300]. This English version probably dates from 1938.

32. Freeland League leaders and supporters had affiliations with numerous political parties and movements. Some were drawn from the Zionist-Socialists (S.S.) of prerevolutionary Russia, or from the peasant-oriented Soviet Left Socialist Revolutionaries (L-SRs), and others were attracted to the movement from folkist, diaspora nationalist, Bolshevik, internationalist, and other backgrounds.

33. Minutes of Freeland meeting in London (date illegible). The suggestion was made by Creech Jones, MP, and reported by British Freeland League Chair, Joseph Leftwich. [CZA A330/14].

34. Letter (likely from I. N. Steinberg) to Polish Freeland League. Aug. 1934. Steinberg Papers. [YIVO RG 366/12].

35. Zhitlowski and Ben-Adir published in *Frayland*. No. 1–2 (Sept.–Oct. 1934). Lestschinsky and Ravitch appeared in *Frayland*. No. 3–4 (Nov.–Dec. 1934).

36. "Berlin Food Rioters Attack and Beat Jews." *New York Times*. 6 Nov. 1923. p. 2.

37. Döblin qtd. in Graber. "Editor's Introduction." p. xii.

38. See Huguet. "Alfred Döblin et le Judaisme." pp. 66–68; Jelavich. *Berlin Alexanderplatz*. pp. 6–7.

39. Graber. "Editor's Introduction." p. xii; Huguet. "Alfred Döblin et le Judaisme." pp. 66–68; Müller-Salget. "Döblin and Judaism." p. 235.

40. Graber. "Editor's Introduction." p. xii.

41. Ibid., p. ix.

42. Döblin. *Journey to Poland*. p. 50.

43. Ibid.

44. Ibid., p. 102.

45. Ibid., p. 255.

46. Huguet. "Alfred Döblin et le Judaisme." pp. 68–69.

47. See Kruk. *Takhat Diglan*. p. 448.

48. *Jüdische Erneuerung* (1933) and *Flucht und Sammlung des Judenvolkes* (1935).

49. Döblin. "Jews Renew Yourselves." p. 80. (Excerpt from *Jüdische Erneuerung*.)

50. Ibid., p. 83.

51. Ibid., p. 84.

52. Ibid.

53. Döblin. *Briefe*. p. 181. Letter to Elvira and Arthur Rosin. 4 July 1933. See also Kruk's recollection of the hold the Angola plan had on Döblin. *Takhat Diglan*. p. 448.

54. Döblin. "Jews Renew Yourselves." p. 87.

55. Ibid.

56. Huguet. "Alfred Döblin et le Judaisme." p. 84; Müller-Salget. "Döblin and Judaism." p. 238.

57. See also Döblin. "I Am Not a Hitler Jew!" pp. 308–311.

58. London's *Dos Fraye Vort* (*The Free Word*) first published an excerpt of Döblin's musings on territorialism in September 1933. See Huguet. "Alfred Döblin et le Judaisme." p. 82.

59. Döblin. *Briefe*. pp. 207–208. Letter to Thomas Mann. 23 May 1935; Huguet. "Alfred Döblin et le Judaisme." p. 83.

60. This is the English title that Astour gives the article, entitled, "Gzar–Din un Veg fun di Merav Yidn." See Astour. "Alfred Döblin (1879–1957)." *Freeland*. Vol. XI. No. 2 (41) (July–Sept. 1958): 11–12.

61. Döblin. "Gzar–Din un Veg fun di Merav Yidn." *Frayland*. No. 1–2 (Sept.–Oct. 1934): 44–45.

62. Ibid., p. 48.

63. Ibid.

64. Ibid.

65. Ibid., p. 49.

66. Döblin's correspondence includes numerous letters to Birnbaum from 1934–1935. See *Briefe* II. Following Birnbaum's death in the Netherlands in 1937, Döblin wrote a eulogy for him. See Huguet p. 89. For more see Olson's intellectual biography *Nathan Birnbaum and Jewish Modernity*. Although excellent overall, Olson's book makes no mention of Birnbaum's influence on or collaboration with Freeland League leaders.

67. Jankowksy. *The Jews and Minority Rights*. p. 63.

68. The earliest usage of the term appears to be in Birnbaum. "Die Ziele der jüdisch–nationalen Bestrebungen. Eine Artikelserie. II." *Selbst–Emancipation*. No. 4. 16 May 1890. p. 1.

69. Birnbaum. "Methodisches zur Palästinafrage." p. 207. See also Doron. *Haguto haTzionit Shel Natan Birnbaum*. pp. 146–149.

70. Wistrich. *Laboratory for World Destruction*. p. 138.

71. Birnbaum. "Methodisches zur Palästinafrage." p. 208. On this early usage of "Palestinian," see also Doron. *Haguto haTzionit Shel Natan Birnbaum*. p. 147.

72. Olson. *Nathan Birnbaum and Jewish Modernity*. esp. pp. 244–246, 290–291.

73. See Huguet. "Alfred Döblin et le Judaisme." pp. 88–95.

74. Döblin. "Gzar-Din un Veg fun di Merav Yidn." p. 49.

75. Döblin. "Teritorialism un Naye-Yehuda." p. 18.

76. Ibid., p. 20.

77. Ibid.

78. Ibid., p. 23.

79. Ibid., p. 24.

80. Ibid., p. 20.

81. Ibid., p. 24.

82. Ibid.

83. Ibid.

84. Ibid.

85. Ibid.

86. Ibid., p. 25.

87. The publication details are: 17 Nov. 1933: pp. 3–4, 11; 24 Nov. 1933: p. 4; 8 Dec. 1933: pp.1–2; 22 Dec. 1933: pp. 4, 15; 5 Jan. 1934: pp. 6–7; 12 Jan. 1934: pp. 3–4; 26 Jan. 1934: pp. 5–6; 8 Feb. 1934: pp. 5–6; 28 Feb. 1934: pp. 11–12.

88. Döblin. "l'Korei Ivrit." *Turim.* 8 Dec. 1933. p. 1.

89. Döblin. "Tkhiya Yehudit (part 8)." *Turim.* 8 Feb. 1934. p. 5.

90. Müller-Salget. "Döblin and Judaism." p. 238.

91. Döblin. "Informations–Bulletin No. 1." In Horch. p. 373.

92. Döblin. *Briefe.* pp. 205–208. Letter to Thomas Mann. 23 May 1935.

93. Döblin. "Ziel und Charakter der Freiland-Bewegung."

94. Huguet. "Alfred Döblin et le Judaisme." p. 95.

95. See list in "Realist Attitude to the Jewish Problem." *Jewish Chronicle.* 26 July 1935. p. 42.

96. Ibid., pp. 36, 42.

97. Chanoch. "Mikhtav m'London." *Davar.* 9 Aug. 1935. p. 2.

98. Döblin. "Ziel und Charakter der Freiland–Bewegung." p. 315.

99. Ibid., p. 319.

100. Ibid., p. 321.

101. Ibid., p. 318.

102. Ibid., p. 321.

103. Ibid., p. 322.

104. Ibid.

105. "Tribute to Israel Zangwill." *Jewish Daily Post.* 23 July 1935. n.p. [HLS MS 294 18/3/2].

106. See invitation card for the closing session. [HLS MS 294 18/3/2].

107. Qtd. in *Jewish Chronicle.* 26 July 1935. pp. 36, 42.

108. Qtd. in *South African Jewish Chronicle.* 21 June 1935. p. 483.

109. Müller-Salget. "Döblin and Judaism." pp. 238–239.

110. Letter Brutzkus to J. Leftwich. 1 Mar. 1937. [CZA A330/14].

111. Huguet. "Alfred Döblin et le Judaisme." p. 97.

112. Astour. *Geshikhte fun der Frayland Lige.* Vol. I. pp. 238–246.

113. Huguet. "Alfred Döblin et le Judaisme." p. 98.

114. Ibid., pp. 105–108. Döblin converted in November 1941 but kept it a secret until July 1947, in part because of the sensitivities of his Jewish friends.

115. Astour. *Geshikhte fun der Frayland Lige.* Vol. I. pp. 184–187. Astour indicates that this joint commission was controlled by the Freeland League Central Executive Committee.

116. Ibid., p. 186.

117. See undated agenda. Steinberg Papers. [YIVO RG 366/31]. See also Astour. *Geshikhte fun der Frayland Lige.* Vol. I. p. 186.

118. Döblin. *Briefe.* pp. 216–217. Letter to Peter Döblin. 18 Sept. 1937.

119. Astour. *Geshikhte fun der Frayland Lige*. Vol. I. p. 184.

120. Letter J. Doubossarsky to Freeland League (Warsaw). 6 May 1937. p. 2. Steinberg Papers. [YIVO RG 366/31].

121. See translation of original letter in the J. Leftwich Papers [CZA A330/14]. See also "Settlement Possibilities in French Colonies." *Jewish Chronicle*. 16 Apr. 1937. pp. 24–25. This episode is noted briefly in Brechtken. *Madagaskar für die Juden*. pp. 102–103.

122. J. Leftwich Papers. [CZA A330/14].

123. Alter. "Madagaskar." p. 2.

124. Bash. "Gender and Survival: A Jewish Family in Occupied France, 1940–1944." p. 302.

125. Astour. *Geshikhte fun der Frayland Lige*. Vol. I. p. 191.

126. See "Possibilities of Land Settlement in the French Colonies, America Joint Distribution Committee, European Executive Office, Paris. Sept. 1938." Letter M. Moutet to Freeland League–EMCOL. 19 Jan. 1937. Reproduced in this document, henceforth referred to as "Possibilities of Land Settlement in French Colonies." [AN AJ43/43]. Special thanks to Vicki Caron for helping me track down this source. See also Astour. *Geshikhte fun der Frayland Lige*. Vol. II. p. 812, n. 2. Rosenthal referred to Moutet as his "friend and adviser" in *The Pearl Hunter*. p. 128.

   According to a press account written by the French correspondent for the Hebrew newspaper *Davar*, the Freeland League–EMCOL alerted Moutet to Jewish suffering in Eastern Europe thanks to the intervention of noted French author René Maran. *Davar*'s correspondent claims to have spoken with Moutet himself about the genesis of the Minister's involvement in the plan. See N. Herman. "Hatzarat Moutet." *Davar*. 1 Mar. 1937. p. 2. I have found no corresponding sources that document Maran's intercession with Moutet, though Maran was certainly acquainted with Moutet and publicly praised him. See Maran. *Afrique Équatoriale*. pp. 75, 82.

127. "A propos d'un project d'établissement d'israélites dans les colonies françaises." *Le Petit Parisien*. 16 Jan. 1937. p. 2. See also the report "Government Offers Jews Colonial Territory." *The American Hebrew*. 29 Jan. 1937. p. 822.

128. "A propos d'un project d'établissement d'israélites dans les colonies françaises." *Le Petit Parisien*. 16 Jan. 1937. p. 2.

129. "Possibilities of Land Settlement in French Colonies." Letter M. Moutet to Freeland League–EMCOL. 19 Jan. 1937. [AN AJ43/43].

130. Herman. "Hatzarat Moutet." *Davar*. 1 Mar. 1937. p. 2.

131. P. Bouteille. "Statement Regarding Project for Jewish Colonization in the French Colonies." Reproduced in "Possibilities of Land Settlement in French Colonies." [AN AJ43/43]

132. Ibid.

133. "A propos d'un project d'établissement d'israélites dans les colonies françaises." *Le Petit Parisien*. 16 Jan. 1937. p. 2.

134. Moutet. "Re: Project of Jewish Colonization in Certain French Possessions."
     Reproduced in "Possibilities of Land Settlement in French Colonies." [AN
     AJ43/43].

135. Weinbaum. *A Marriage of Convenience*. p. 7.

136. Bauer. *My Brother's Keeper*. p. 193. According to Bauer, Beck discussed transfer-
     ring up to six hundred thousand Jews in six years to Madagascar.

137. British Ambassador Hugh Kennard described in official dispatches the Jewish
     situation in Poland and Polish efforts to drive the Jews out. Kennard to Foreign
     Secretary Anthony Eden. 11 May 1937. [TNA FO 371/20763; C 3699/765/55].

138. Zack. "Ups and Downs of a Daily." p. 74.

139. Schechtman. *The Life and Times of Vladimir Jabotinsky: Fighter and Prophet*. p.
     338.

140. Letter V. Jabotinsky to J. Beck. 21 June 1936. [BJ 1/26/2/1A].

141. Weinbaum. *A Marriage of Convenience*. p. 22.

142. Jabotinsky. "The Max Nordau Plan." *The Jewish War Front*. pp. 188–211.

143. Shechtman. *The Life and Times of Vladimir Jabotinsky: Fighter and Prophet*. p. 26.

144. Ibid., p. 27.

145. Ibid., p. 28.

146. Jabotinsky. *Atlas*. Key to Maps 28–29.

147. Weinbaum. *A Marriage of Convenience*. p. 45.

148. Schechtman. *The Life and Times of Vladimir Jabotinsky: Fighter and Prophet*. pp.
     354–355.

149. Letter Weizmann to Shertok. 18 Oct. 1936. In Weizmann. *Letters and Papers of
     Chaim Weizmann*. Vol. XVII. p. 364.

150. Report H. Kennard to Anthony Eden. 11 May 1937. [TNA FO 371/20763; C
     3699/765/55]

151. "Ende einer Illusion." *Judische Rundschau*. 31 Dec. 1937. p. 2.

152. Jabotinsky. "Evacuating a Ruin." *The Jewish War Front*. pp. 114–115.

153. Letter Jabotinsky to Robert Briscoe. 1 Jan. 1938. [BJ 28/2/1A].

154. Jabotinsky. "Two State Projects Outside of Palestine." *The Jewish War Front*. p.
     152.

155. Ibid., p. 142.

156. Telegram Goldmann to Wise. 4 Oct. 1936. WJC Papers. [WL A15/File 3 France
     36–37]

157. Ibid.

158. Goldmann qtd. in Tonini. *Operation Madagascar*. p. 11. Special thanks to
     Carla Tonini for providing me with her unpublished translation of her
     monograph.

159. Goldmann qtd. in Salomone. "Le Pouvoir Colonial et Les Communautes Etran-
     geres a Madagascar 1896–1939." p. 222.

160. Telegram Goldmann to S. Wise. 4 Oct. 1936. WJC Papers. [WL A15/File 3
     France 36–37].

161. Letter Dr. Bernhard Kahn and Dr. J. Rosen to Charles J. Liebman. 12 June 1937. In "Possibilities of Land Settlement in French Colonies." [AN AJ43/43]. Rosen was the director of the Agro-Joint, a famous agronomist, and a supporter of mass settlement in Birobidzhan. See also Caron. *Uneasy Asylum*. pp. 144–146.

162. Letter Dr. Bernhard Kahn and Dr. J. Rosen to Charles J. Liebman. 12 June 1937. In "Possibilities of Land Settlement in French Colonies." [AN AJ43/43].

163. Summary of "Previous Efforts on Behalf of Jewish Settlements in French Colonies." In "Possibilities of Land Settlement in French Colonies." [AN AJ43/43].

164. Letter Weizmann to Shertock. 18 Oct. 1936. In *Letters and Papers of Chaim Weizmann*. Vol. XVII. p. 364; "Madagascar Scheme Announced." *Jewish Chronicle*. 31 Dec. 1937. p. 23.

165. For a thorough study of the prehistory of the Madagascar Plan see Jennings. "Writing Madagascar Back into the Madagascar Plan."

166. Defoe. *The History of the Pyrates*. p. 9.

167. Defoe and Drury. *Madagascar*. p. viii. The attribution of this document to Defoe is contested.

168. Ibid., pp. x–xi.

169. Peters. *The Eldorado of the Ancients*.

170. Keane. *The Gold of Ophir*.

171. Ibid., p. 155.

172. Ibid., p. 65.

173. See Jennings. "Writing Madagascar Back into the Madagascar Plan."

174. Catane. "Abraham Schrameck." p. 167.

175. Jennings. "Writing Madagascar Back into the Madagascar Plan." p. 187. Lagarde's theories exerted influence on the Nazi leadership.

176. Ibid., p. 209.

177. Tonini. "The Polish Plan for a Jewish Settlement in Madagascar 1936–1939." p. 472; Zack. "Ups and Downs of a Daily." p. 73.

178. See Mazor. *The Vanished City*. p. 9.

179. See Yaari. "Zionist Labour Dailies." p. 127.

180. Reproduced in Werb and Milewski. "From 'Madagaskar' to Sachsenhausen." p. 274 fig. 2 for newspaper (5 Mar. 1938) advertisement for the play.

181. Piotrowski, M. "Zycie Codzienne Na Madagaskarze." n.p. Image provided courtesy of Bret Werb.

182. Werb and Milewski. "From 'Madagaskar' to Sachsenhausen." p. 275.

183. Reprinted in Olivier. "Madagascar—Terre d'Asile?" p. 198.

184. Arcand. "Jewish Problem Solved: Madagascar a National Jewish Home." *World Monthly*. p. 114.

185. "Territorial Tremens." *Jewish Frontier* (1937): 5. [CZA A330/270].

186. Lepecki. *Madagaskar; kraj, ludzie, kolonizacja* [*Madagaskar*]. p. 5.

187. Astour. *Geshikhte fun der Frayland Lige*. Vol. I. pp. 205–207.

188. Letter J. Doubossarsky. 18 May 1937. Steinberg Papers. [YIVO RG 366/31].

189. Ibid.

190. "Freeland" Bulletin #1 (Warsaw). 15 May 1937. Steinberg Papers. [YIVO RG 366/12].

191. Ibid.

192. Lepecki. *Madagaskar*. p. 6.

193. Gauthier. "Nous sommes prêts à toutes les collaborations pacifiques dans nos colonies." *Le Petit Parisien*. 11 May 1937. p. 3.

194. Lepecki. *Madagaskar*. p. 6.

195. Ibid., p. 11.

196. Alter. "Memoire (Madagascar)." p. 1. [YIVO 245.5 HIC EN Europe F29].

197. See photo opposite p. 208 in Lepecki. *Madagaskar*.

198. Ibid., p. 11.

199. Ibid., photo opposite p. 16.

200. Tonini. *Operation Madagascar*. p. 54.

201. Lepecki. *Madagaskar*. p. 7; Alter. "Memoire (Madagascar)." p. 1. [YIVO 245.5 HIC EN Europe F29].

202. Bradt. *Madagascar*. p. 206.

203. For their itinerary, see Lepecki. *Madagaskar*. pp. 8–9.

204. Qtd. in ibid., p. 296.

205. Ibid., p. 11.

206. Ibid.

207. Ibid.

208. Ibid., p. 12.

209. Figures, provided by Lepecki, are quoted in a dispatch from H. Kennard to A. Eden. 28 Dec. 1937. [TNA FO 371/20763; C 8957/765/55]. These approximate figures also reported in "Al Efsharut Hagira Yehudit l'Madagascar." *Davar*. 22 Feb. 1938. p. 8.

210. "Schemes of Land Settlement in Madagascar." p. 1. In "Possibilities of Land Settlement in French Colonies." [AN AJ43/43].

211. Ibid., p. 2.

212. Ibid.

213. Ibid., p. 3.

214. Ibid.

215. Ibid., p. 4.

216. Dyk qtd. in Hevesi. "Madagascar" [Division of Migration and Colonization Report No. 1]. p. 20.

217. Ibid., p. 21.

218. See undated letter from Dyk to Ruppin about his travels in Madagascar and Ruppin's response. 9 Jan. 1938. [CZA A107/843].

219. Report H. Kennard to A. Eden. 28 Dec. 1937. [TNA FO 371/20763; C 8957/765/55].

220. Alter. "Madagaskar." p. 2.

221. Ibid.

222. Ibid.

223. Ibid., p. 3.

224. Ibid.

225. According to Hevesi in "Madagascar." p. 30.

226. Alter. "Madagaskar." pp. 2–3.

227. Alter. "Memoire (Madagascar)." p. 1. [YIVO 245.5 HIC EN Europe F29].

228. See "The Madagascar Scheme." *Jewish Chronicle*. 23 July 1937. p.18.

229. Qtd. in Salomone. "Le Pouvoir Colonial et Les Communautes Etrangeres a Madagascar 1896–1939." p. 226.

230. Ibid., p. 1196.

231. "The Madagascar Scheme." *Jewish Chronicle*. 23 July 1937. p.18.

232. Olivier. "Madagascar—Terre d'Asile?"

233. Ibid., p. 197.

234. Ibid., p. 198.

235. Ibid.

236. Ibid.

237. Ibid.

238. Alpern. "Biro-Bidzhan, Madagaskar, Naye Caledonia." p. 3.

239. Tonini. *Operation Madagascar*. pp. 67, 74.

240. Report H. Kennard to A. Eden. 28 Dec. 1937. [TNA FO 371/20763; C 8957/765/55].

241. "Polish Jews for Madagascar." *Manchester Guardian*. 31 Dec. 1937. n.p. In Kennard–Eden correspondence file [TNA FO 371/20763].

242. Letter Ormsby-Gore to Lord Halifax. 26 Apr. 1938. [TNA FO 371/21876.E2570].

243. Ibid.

244. Ibid.

245. "Settling the Refugees." *Times* (London). 3 Dec. 1938. p. 11.

246. "Vichy Government Arrests Jewish Social Workers; Brutzkus Still Held." Jewish Telegraphic Agency. 6 Dec. 1940.

247. Bru. "Doeblin's Life and Work from His Correspondence." p. 13. He killed himself in June 1940.

248. Beyer. "Menachem Birnbaum." p. 714.

249. Friedman. "The Lublin Reservation and the Madagascar Plan." p. 49.

250. "For a Jewish 'Reservation.'" *New York Times*. 8 Feb. 1939. p. 17.

251. Friedman. "The Lublin Reservation and the Madagascar Plan." p. 49.

252. "For a Jewish 'Reservation.'" *New York Times*. 8 Feb. 1939. p. 17.

253. See Yahil. "Madagascar—Phantom of a Solution for the Jewish Question," especially pp. 324–325. Further details of Himmler's and Hitler's advocacy of the plan can be found in "Hitler's Support for Plans to Deport Four Million Jews to Madagascar," Irving vs. Lipstadt Defense Document. http://www.hdot.org/trial/defense/pl1/12.

254. Rademacher. "The Madagascar Plan." In *Documents on the Holocaust*. p. 217.

255. Diary entry for 20 June 1940 qtd. in Yahil. "Madagascar." p. 325.

256. Rademacher. "The Madagascar Plan." In *Documents on the Holocaust*. p. 217.

257. Ibid.

258. Arendt. *Eichmann in Jerusalem*. pp. 74–79. See also transcripts of the Trial of Adolf Eichmann, State of Israel, Ministry of Justice. Session 77 (22 June 1961); Session 91 (11 July 1961); Session 92 (11 July 1961). Quote from statement of accused, Session 90 (10 July 1961).

259. Jansen. *Het Madagascarplan*. p. 531.

260. Trial of Adolf Eichmann. Session 91 (11 July 1961).

261. Ibid.

262. See Yahil. "Madagascar," p. 326.

263. See Jansen. *Het Madagascarplan*. pp. 529–534.

264. Testimony of Adolf Leschnitzer recorded by Dr. Ball-Kaduri. Dec. 1959. [YV 01/256].

265. Jennings. "Writing Madagascar Back into the Madagascar Plan." p. 188.

266. See Rademacher. "The Madagascar Plan." In *Documents on the Holocaust*. p. 217.

267. Defoe. *The History of the Pyrates*. p. 45.

268. See Grehan. *The Forgotten Invasion*. Chapter 4.

269. Letter British military chaplain to Genussow family. 23 Dec. 1945. Reprinted in *U'veLibam—Ahavat Elohim v'Adam*. p. 43.

270. Letter I. Genussow to family. 24 June 1944. Reprinted in *U'veLibam—Ahavat Elohim v'Adam*. p. 48.

CHAPTER 5. NEW JERUSALEM, DOWN UNDER

1. Melech Ravitch. *Iber Oystralye*. p. 42. Special thanks to Clive Sinclair for providing me with a translation he commissioned from Vincent Homolka of this work. Many of the direct translations are Homolka's, though page citations refer to the original Yiddish.

2. Description and photographic reproduction in Sinclair. "The Kimberley Fantasy." p. 39.

3. Ravitch. *Iber Oystralye*. p. 71.

4. Ibid., p. 72.

5. Ravitch. *Sefer haMa'asiyot Shel Hayai*. pp. 498–499.

6. Ravitch. "An Idea oder an Ideal, a Teritorye oder Teritoryes."

7. Bergner. p. 70. Ravitch tells a different version of how he came to travel to Australia. *Sefer haMa'asiyot Shel Hayai*. p. 443.

8. Ravitch. *Australian Jewish Almanac*. "Foreword." n.p.

9. Ravitch. "Through Central Australia to the Northern Territory." p. 218.

10. Ravitch. "An Idea oder an Ideal, a Teritorye oder Teritoryes." p. 55.

11. Photograph in Ravitch. *Iber Oystrayle*. p. 107.

12. Ibid., p. 102.

13. Ravitch. "Through Central Australia to the Northern Territory." p. 218.

14. Ravitch qtd. in "Jews Settle in North: Polish Writer's Idea." p. 17.

15. Ravitch. *Iber Oystralye*. p. 104.

16. Ibid., p. 105.

17. Ibid., p. 103.
18. Ibid., pp. 104–110.
19. Ravitch traveled through Australia between August 1933 and April 1934. See M. Teichman's introduction to *Iber Oystralye*. p. 3.
20. Ravitch. "An Idea oder an Ideal, a Teritorye oder Teritoryes." p. 58.
21. Even Josef Kruk, who attended the organizational Freeland League conference in London (1935) seemed to have been unaware of Ravitch's interest in Australia. See *Takhat Diglan Shel Shalosh Mahapekhot*. p. 463.
22. Cohen. *Sefer, Sofer v'Iton*. p. 255.
23. Ibid.
24. Ravitch. *Iber Oystralye*. p. 103.
25. Ravitch. *Kantinentn un Okeanen*. pp. 175–178. Date of 1933 supplied in Ravitch. "Aborigines." *haMnudim al haDalim*. p. 96.
26. Bergner. *Ikar Shakhakhti*. 102.
27. Ravitch. *Iber Oystralye*. p. 89.
28. "Poles Continue Talks." p. 12.
29. A representative of the South Australian government approached Zangwill's ITO in November 1906 asking whether Jewish emigration "now taking place to British East Africa" could be diverted to Australia's Northern Territory. Document reproduced in Marmor. Supplement to "haMasa u'Matan [Part II]." p. 205. Marmor "haMasa uMatan [Part I]" also notes Zangwill's meeting with Prime Minister Alfred Deakin (1907) [p. 134] and Western Australia's premier, Sir Newton Moore (1910) [p. 138]. See also Zangwill. "Mr. Chamberlain and Zionism." p. 9.
30. Arthur. "Australia for the I.T.O." *Hebrew Standard*. 29 June 1906. n.p. [CZA A36/89].
31. See letter Arthur to Zangwill. 27 Nov. 1906. [CZA A36/89].
32. Advertisement. *The Times*. 24 May 1910. p. 30.
33. Letter Zangwill to N. Moore. 24 May 1910. [CZA A36/89].
34. Letter N. Moore to Zangwill. 21 June 1911. [CZA A36/89].
35. Minutes of Freeland meeting. 6 Jan. 1936. [CZA A330/14].
36. Steinberg and Melville. "Report on the Kimberleys." [TNA DO 35/1140].
37. The area under consideration straddled both Western Australia and the Northern Territory administrative units. The majority of the territory, 5,262,080 acres, was within the boundaries of the Northern Territory, with 1.7 million acres in Western Australia. See "Memorandum on the Durack Properties and the Northern Portion of Western Australia and the Northern Territories." p. 1. Addendum prepared by "Mr. Wise" to letter from Geo. W. Miles to I. N. Steinberg. 20 July 1938. Steinberg Papers. [YIVO RG 366/870]. See also *Toward Peace and Equity*. p. 80.
38. Letter M. P. Durack to Steinberg. 26 Oct. 1938. Steinberg Papers. [YIVO RG 366/300].
39. Ibid.

40. "Memorandum on the Durack Properties and the Northern Portion of Western Australia and the Northern Territories." p. 1. Addendum prepared by "Mr. Wise" to letter from Geo. W. Miles to Steinberg. 20 July 1938. Steinberg Papers. [YIVO RG 366/870]. The figure of 180,000 pounds sterling is taken from the letter itself.

41. Minutes of Freeland meeting. 6 Jan. 1936. [CZA A330/14].

42. "Memorandum Prepared by the Freeland League for Jewish Territorial Colonisation for the Consideration of the Delegates at the International Refugees Conference at Evian." p. 3.

43. "Memorandum on the Durack Properties and the Northern Portion of Western Australia and the Northern Territories." p. 2. Addendum prepared by "Mr. Wise" to letter from Geo. W. Miles to Steinberg. 20 July 1938. Steinberg Papers. [YIVO RG 366/870].

44. "A propos d'un project d'établissement d'israélites dans les colonies françaises." *Le Petit Parisien*. 16 Jan. 1937. p. 2.

45. Letter L. G. Montefiore to Jewish Board of Deputies. 23 Mar. 1937. [LMA ACC 3121/B4/JC30].

46. "The Urgent Need of Jewry." Masthead. n.p.

47. For more on the nature of these meetings see Gettler. *An Unpromised Land*. pp. 54–59.

48. For Weizmann's reluctance to attend and the discouragement he received from the U.S. see *The Letters and Papers of Chaim Weizmann*. V.2, series B. p. 314 n. 5. See Kohavi on Ussishkin's opposition. "The Zionist Executive and the Distress of the Jews in Germany and Austria, up to the Outbreak of World War II." p. 103.

49. Weizmann. "Palestine's Role in the Solution of the Jewish Problem." p. 326.

50. "Memorandum Prepared by the Freeland League for Jewish Territorial Colonisation for the Consideration of the Delegates at the International Refugees Conference at Evian." p. 3.

51. Steinberg. *Australia—The Unpromised Land*. p. 12.

52. See Steinberg. "The Three Roads." pp. 2–3. Also Steinberg. *Australia—The Unpromised Land*. pp. 12–13.

53. Steinberg was elected to the Executive Committee of Great Britain's "League for Territorial Colonisation." See minutes of Freeland meeting. 29 July 1935. His role in the International Council is noted in the minutes of the Freeland meeting. 6 Jan. 1936. [CZA A330/14].

54. Letter Steinberg to Ben–Adir. 30 Mar. 1942. Ben–Adir Papers. [YIVO RG 394/2].

55. Steinberg. *Australia—The Unpromised Land*. p. 108.

56. Jabotinsky. *The Jewish War Front*. p. 143.

57. Ibid., p. 144.

58. State of New York, County of Bronx court document. 10 Mar. 1947. Steinberg Papers [YIVO 366/883]

59. Ibid.

60. Barbara Joan Beck interviewed 6 Dec. 2009.

61. Leo Steinberg interviewed 14 Jan. 2010.

62. Fromm. "Dr. I. N. Steinberg." p. 4. Fromm was on the editorial board of *Freeland* and active in the organization.

63. Angell. "Your Future . . . Our Future." pp. 3–4; Mann. "Letter to Steinberg 18 Sept. 1945." p. 19; Mann. "I Believe in Freeland." p. 8. Angell accompanied Steinberg to the British Embassy in Washington, D.C., to deliver a memorandum on a Jewish settlement in Australia. See "Settlement of Jews in the Dominions." [TNA DO 34/1140].

64. Fruchtbaum. "Tribute to Dr. I. N. Steinberg." p. 2.

65. Rapaport. "I. N. Steinberg." p. 15. See also Enav. *b'Sa'arat haHayim*. p. 53.

66. *Die Lehre vom Verbrechen im Talmud. Eine juristisch–dogmatische Studie*. Diss. Heidelberg, 1910.

67. Enav. *b'Sa'arat haHayim*. p. 20. Steinberg ultimately did not participate in the trial.

68. Leo Steinberg interviewed 14 Jan. 2010.

69. Ibid.

70. Steinberg. "The Biography of Dr. I. Steinberg (Berlin)." n.d. n.p. Steinberg Papers. [YIVO 366/880].

71. Ibid.

72. Steinberg. "Letter to the Interdepartmental Visa Review Committee, Department of State, Washington, DC." 19 June 1944. p. 2. Steinberg Papers. [YIVO 366/883].

73. See Ravitch's reminiscence in Bar. *The Jewish Press That Was*. p. 206.

74. Steinberg. "The Biography of Dr. I. Steinberg (Berlin)." n.d. n.p. Steinberg Papers. [YIVO 366/880].

75. Steinberg. *The Thorny Path*. p. 22–23.

76. Ibid.

77. Ibid., p. 47.

78. The play appears in Yiddish in Melech Ravitch, ed. *I. N. Steinberg Gedenk-Bukh*. pp. 451–505.

79. Schniederman. "Di Ufirung fun 'Mochnatschow' in Barcelona in Miten fun Birger–Krig." pp. 507–508. See also Steinberg's obituary in *Jewish Chronicle* (London). 3 Jan. 1957. Reprinted in *Freeland*. Vol. X. No.1 (Jan.–Mar. 1957): 11. Emma Goldman asked Steinberg to assist the producer of the play in Barcelona after he and his wife were forced to flee Spain for Paris. Letter E. Goldman to I. N. Steinberg. 7 Mar. 1939. Steinberg Papers. [YIVO RG 366/248].

80. Reminiscence of Steinberg's granddaughter, Esther Siegel. Correspondence with author. 24 June 2011.

81. Ibid.

82. The Yiddish journal Steinberg edited, *Dos Fraye Vort*, based in London, was advertised in the first issues of *Frayland*.

83. Huguet. "Alfred Döblin et le Judaisme." p. 82. Döblin and Steinberg corresponded both before and after World War II. See Döblin. *Briefe II.* for their correspondence.

84. See Cohen. *Sefer, Sofer v'Iton.* p. 247. For excerpts of this speech, see D. Charney. "Oprufen nokh dem Parizer P.E.N.-Kongres." pp. 437–439.

85. Charney. "Oyf a P.E.N–Kongres in Pariz." p. 430.

86. Recollection of Charney in "Oyf a P.E.N–Kongres in Pariz." p. 429.

87. Minutes of Freeland meeting. 29 July 1935. [CZA A330/14].

88. Minutes of Freeland meeting. 23 Sept. 1935. [CZA A330/14].

89. Unsigned letter from London to Central Committee (Warsaw). 27 Jan. 1939. Steinberg Papers. [YIVO RG 366/870].

90. Steinberg. *Australia—The Unpromised Land.* p. 13.

91. Ibid., p. 17.

92. Ibid.

93. Ibid., p. 19.

94. Ibid.

95. Ibid.

96. Ibid.

97. Reproduced in Gettler. *An Unpromised Land.* p. 71.

98. Steinberg. *Australia—The Unpromised Land.* p. 18–19.

99. Ibid., p. 119.

100. Ibid., pp. 119–120.

101. Ibid., p. 146. See also Steinberg and Melville. "Report on the Kimberleys" [TNA DO 35/1140]. The "Report on the Kimberleys" was submitted 29 Aug. 1939.

102. Steinberg and Melville. "Report on the Kimberleys." p. 9. [TNA DO 35/1140].

103. Ibid., p. 7.

104. Ibid., p. 10.

105. Jenkins ("Refugee Settlement in Australia," p. 120) reports that Steinberg publicized the figure of fifty thousand refugees. In a memorandum to Western Australia's premier, Willcock, Steinberg suggested a figure of seventy-five thousand refugees. See Gettler. *An Unpromised Land.* p. 79.

106. Gettler. *An Unpromised Land.* pp. 80–84. See also Jenkins. "Refugee Settlement in Australia." p. 121; *Toward Peace and Equity.* pp. 80–81.

107. Gettler. *An Unpromised Land.* p. 87.

108. Barbara Joan Beck interviewed 6 Dec. 2009.

109. Letter C. Isaacson to Steinberg. n.d. Steinberg Papers. [YIVO RG 366/703].

110. Letter C. Isaacson to Steinberg. 18 July 1940. Steinberg Papers. [YIVO RG 366/703].

111. Letter C. Isaacson to Steinberg. 7 June 1942. pp. 4, 6. Steinberg Papers. [YIVO RG 366/703].

112. Letter C. Isaacson to Steinberg. 3 Mar. 1940. Steinberg Papers. [YIVO RG 366/703].

113. Steinberg. *Australia—The Unpromised Land*. p. 123.

114. Ibid., p. 122.

115. "Memorandum on the Durack Properties and the Northern Portion of Western Australia and the Northern Territories." p. 4. Addendum prepared by "Mr. Wise" to letter from Geo. W. Miles to I. N. Steinberg .20 July 1938. Steinberg Papers. [YIVO RG 366/870].

116. Steinberg. *Australia—The Unpromised Land*. p. 122.

117. See Metcalf. "Utopian Communal Experiments in Tasmania." Special thanks to Richard Flanagan for bringing this source to my attention.

118. Bateson. *The Convict Ships*. p. 202.

119. Ibid., p. 74.

120. From a convict ballad cited in Hughes. *The Fatal Shore*. p. 368.

121. http://www.abs.gov.au/Ausstats/abs@.nsf/7d12b0f6763c78caca257061001cc588/e743fe07252b0081ca256c3200241879!OpenDocument.

122. Plomley. "Prelude." In *Friendly Mission*. p. 14.

123. Robinson stood five-foot-seven. Ellis. *Trucanini*. p. 15.

124. Ibid.

125. Portrait of George Augustus Robinson, 1840, by Benjamin Duterrau. Oil on canvas. Reproduced in Plomley. *Friendly Mission*. Frontispiece. n.p.

126. Plomley. "Prelude." p. 13.

127. George Augustus Robinson [GAR]. 16 Mar. 1829. In Plomley. *Friendly Mission*. p. 51.

128. Ibid., p. 52.

129. Ibid., 15 Nov. 1830. p. 310.

130. Ibid.

131. Ibid., n.d. p. 52.

132. Ibid., 18 May 1831. p. 390.

133. Ibid., 29 Mar. 1832. p. 629.

134. Plomley. "Prelude." *Friendly Mission*. p. 26.

135. Hughes. *The Fatal Shore*. p. 414, n. 75.

136. GAR. 11 Oct 1829. In Plomley. *Friendly Mission*. p. 91.

137. Ibid., n.d. p. 52.

138. Ibid., 10 Mar. 1830. p. 155.

139. Ibid.

140. Ibid., 18 Mar. 1830. p. 163.

141. Drawing of Towterer by William Buelow Gould reproduced in Plomley. *Friendly Mission*. p. 710.

142. Boyce reconstructs Robinson's deceptions and self–deceptions. *Van Diemen's Land*. pp. 295–313.

143. GAR. 18 Mar. 1830. In Plomley. *Friendly Mission*. p. 164.

144. Plomley. "Aftermath." *Friendly Mission*. p. 968.

145. GAR. 21 Mar. 1837. In Plomley. "Aftermath." *Friendly Mission*. p. 968.

146. Ellis notes that two other women, Betty and Sukey, outlived Trugernanna, though they had relocated from Tasmania. *Trucanini*. p. 149.

147. Ibid., p. 116.
148. See Lehrer. "Repopulating Jewish Poland—In Wood."
149. Photograph held by State Library of Victoria. [SLV MS 8789, MSB 436].
150. Holroyd. "Parker, Frank Critchley (1862 – 1944)." pp. 136–137.
151. R.E.S. "Refugees as Pioneers." pp. 73–74.
152. Ibid., p. 74.
153. Ibid. Emphasis in original.
154. Letter C. Isaacson to Steinberg. 7 June 1942. p. 2. Steinberg Papers. [YIVO RG 366/703].
155. Ibid.
156. Letter C. Isaacson to Steinberg. 17 June 1942. n.p. Steinberg Papers. [YIVO RG 366/703].
157. Baldwin worked for the Parker family until Kathleen Parker's death in 1971. Correspondence 15 May 2011 with Bayden Findlay, Baldwin's great–grandson.
158. Letter C. Isaacson to Steinberg. 7 June 1942. p. 2.
159. *The Corian*. Dec. 1927. p. 127. [GGSA].
160. Letter C. Isaacson to Steinberg. 7 June 1942. p. 2–3.
161. Parker, Critchley. "An Australian in Lapland." p. 6.
162. "La Mabelleion: Modern by Circumstance." pp. 24–25.
163. Dr. Charles Wilson, former owner of "La Mabelleion" (later renamed "Wildfell"), interviewed 4 Dec. 2009.
164. Parker, F. C. *Tasmania*. p. 42.
165. Steinberg. *Australia—The Unpromised Land*. p. 123.
166. Ibid., p. 124.
167. Ibid., p. 123.
168. Letter Cosgrove to C. Parker. 1 May 1940. [TAHO PD1/1/641 File 55].
169. Steinberg. *Australia—The Unpromised Land*. p. 124.
170. Ibid., p. 129.
171. Letter C. Isaacson to Steinberg. 24 (date unclear) Aug. 1940. Steinberg Papers. [YIVO RG 366/703].
172. Steinberg. *Australia—The Unpromised Land*. p. 125.
173. Ibid., p. 126.
174. Ibid.
175. Letter E. Parkes to C. Parker. 5 Nov. 1940. [TAHO PD1/1/641 File 55].
176. Steinberg. *Australia—The Unpromised Land*. p. 129.
177. Ibid., p. 130.
178. Ibid.
179. Ibid.
180. Ibid., p. 133.
181. Ibid., p. 134.
182. Ibid., pp. 131–132.
183. Letter C. Parker to Steinberg. 29 Dec. 1940. p. 2. Steinberg Papers. [YIVO RG 366/807].
184. Steinberg. *Australia—The Unpromised Land*. p. 133.

185. Ibid. See also Letter C. Parker to Steinberg. 29 Dec. 1940. p. 1. Steinberg Papers. [YIVO RG 366/807].
186. Steinberg. *Australia—The Unpromised Land.* pp. 133–34.
187. Letter C. Parker to Steinberg. 29 Dec. 1940. p. 1–2. [YIVO RG 366/807].
188. E. Parkes. Memorandum "Freeland League – Settlement of Migrants." 21 Jan 1941. p. 2. [TAHO PD1/1/641 File 55].
189. Steinberg. *Australia—The Unpromised Land.* p. 140.
190. Ibid., p. 128.
191. Ibid., p. 135.
192. Letter Colin Pitt. 15 Jan. 1941. Steinberg Papers. [YIVO RG 366/807].
193. Ibid.
194. Letter Cosgrove to Steinberg. 21 Jan. 1941. p. "G." [TAHO PD1/1/641 File 55].
195. Steinberg. *Australia—The Unpromised Land.* p. 139.
196. Ellis concludes that only the skull can be identified as Trugernanna's with assurance. *Trucanini.* pp. 167–172. These remains were ultimately cremated and spread at sea according to Trugernanna's request.
197. Photograph reproduced in Ellis. *Trucanini.* p. 157.
198. Steinberg. *Australia—The Unpromised Land.* p. 140.
199. Many letters, pamphlets, and other ephemera related to these speaking engagements have been preserved. Steinberg Papers. [YIVO RG 366/762–783].
200. Barbara Joan Beck interviewed 6 Dec. 2009.
201. Letter C. Isaacson to Steinberg. 29 June 1942. p. 2. Steinberg Papers. [YIVO RG 366/703].
202. Letter C. Isaacson to Steinberg. 17 July 1942. p. 2. Steinberg Papers. [YIVO RG 366/703].
203. Letter C. Isaacson to Steinberg. 29 June 1942. p. 2. Steinberg Papers. [YIVO RG 366/703].
204. Letter C. Isaacson to Steinberg. 7 June 1942. p. 4. Steinberg Papers. [YIVO RG 366/703].
205. Ibid., p. 3.
206. Ibid., p. 4.
207. Ibid.
208. Transcription of diary of Critchley Parker Jr., inscription. n.p. [SLV MS 14052, Box 4128/8].

   Critchley's diary was given to Isaacson by his mother after his death and at Critchley's express request. In an undated letter [SLV Australian Jewish Historical Society MS 9352A; Series 100 Box 3] Kathleen Parker notes that several pages were cut from the diary because of letters he had written to friends. After Isaacson's death, the diary came into the possession of her son, Peter Isaacson. Photocopies of the diary and photographs of its cover were deposited in the State Library of Victoria in the collection of the Australian Jewish Historical Society. A transcription of the diary was also prepared. The original diary has since been lost, though the photocopies and transcription remain. The

photocopied diary and transcription are unfortunately incomplete when compared against one another, thus I differentiate between copies of the diary itself
[Diary] and the transcription [Transcription]. Moreover, the page numbering of
the Diary is inconsistent and I have indicated this with a (?) next to the number.
I have tried to clarify as much as possible.

209. Letter C. Isaacson to Steinberg. 7 June 1942. p. 5. Steinberg Papers. [YIVO RG
366/703].

210. Diary. n.d. p. 4. [SLV MS 9352A; Series 100 Box 3].

211. Letter to C. Isaacson in Diary. n.d. p. 3(?). [SLV MS 9352A; Series 100 Box 3].

212. Ibid.

213. Letter to C. Isaacson in Diary. 28 Mar. 1942. n.p. [SLV MS 9352A; Series 100 Box
3].

214. GAR. 13 Mar. 1830. In Plomley. *Friendly Mission*. p. 159.

215. In a letter (9 Apr. 1942) excised from his diary by Kathleen Parker and sent to
a bushwalking friend, Miss Gwladys Morris, Critchley writes that he took "14
days provisions" with him. Critchley's hand-written provisions list indicates
the stores for either "16" or "8" days. I have used the "16 days" provisions list.
Readers may assume these figures are therefore a bit higher than the two weeks
(fourteen days' worth) of stores he noted that he actually brought with him.
[TMAGC R2007.46.2].

216. Diary. 8 Apr. 1942. n.p. [SLV MS 9352A; Series 100 Box 3].

217. Transcription. 29 Mar. 1942. n.p. [SLV MS 14052, Box 4128/8].

218. Ibid.

219. Ibid.

220. Ibid.

221. Letter to C. Isaacson in Diary. 8 Apr. 1942. p. 1. [SLV MS 9352A; Series 100
Box 3].

222. Ibid.

223. Ibid.

224. Ibid., p. 2.

225. Ibid.

226. Ibid.

227. Letter C. Parker to G. Morris. 9 Apr. 1942. n.p. [TMAGC R2007.46.1].

228. Letter to C. Isaacson in Diary. 8 Apr. 1942. p. 2. [SLV MS 9352A; Series 100
Box 3].

229. Ibid.

230. Ibid., pp. 2–3.

231. Diary. n.d. p. 10. [SLV MS 9352A; Series 100 Box 3].

232. Letter to C. Isaacson in Diary. 12 Apr. 1942. In this letter he notes that his "considerations on Jewish settlement" followed this letter and so readers can assume
that the date for all of his "considerations" on the settlement are from 12 Apr.
1942, or soon thereafter though I list them as n.d. below since this is not explicit
in the Diary. [SLV MS 9352A; Series 100 Box 3].

233. Diary. n.d. p. 19. [SLV MS 9352A; Series 100 Box 3].

234. Ibid.

235. Ibid., p. 22.

236. Parker, F. C. *Tasmania*. p. 124.

237. Diary. n.d. p. 3. [SLV MS 9352A; Series 100 Box 3].

238. Ibid., p. 7.

239. Ibid., p. 13.

240. Transcription. n.d. n.p. [SLV MS 14052, Box 4128/8].

241. Ibid.

242. Diary. n.d. p. 16. [SLV MS 9352A; Series 100 Box 3].

243. Ibid., pp. 16–17.

244. Ibid., p. 17.

245. Ibid. This generosity is particularly notable given the ongoing war in the Pacific and the threat of Japanese invasion.

246. Ibid.

247. Ibid., p. 24.

248. Ibid., p. 23.

249. Ibid.

250. Letter C. Isaacson to Steinberg. 7 June 1942. p. 3. Steinberg Papers. [YIVO RG 366/703]. As an eighteen-year-old student at Geelong Grammar School, Critchley demonstrated his interest in the ancient world in an article he wrote entitled "Archaeology" for a school publication. The article appeared in a bound journal published with support of his father. The journal was called, with appropriate wistfulness, *If*. [GGSA].

251. Diary. n.d. p. 14. [SLV MS 9352A; Series 100 Box 3].

252. Ibid., p. 15.

253. Ibid., p. 19.

254. Ibid., p. 7.

255. Ibid., p. 9.

256. Ibid., p. 10.

257. Ibid., pp. 11–12.

258. Ibid., p. 10.

259. Ibid., p. 11.

260. Ibid., p. 12.

261. Ibid., p. 13.

262. Ibid., p. 20.

263. Ibid., pp. 19–20.

264. Ibid., p. 20.

265. Letter to C. Isaacson in Transcript. 8 Apr. 1942. n.p. [SLV MS 14052, Box 4128/8].

266. GAR. 11 Feb. 1830. In Plomley. *Friendly Mission*. p. 148.

267. Ibid., 3 Mar. 1830. p. 153.

268. Ibid., 5 Mar. 1830. p. 154.

269. Letter to C. Isaacson in Diary. 8 Apr. 1942. p. 3. [SLV MS 9352A; Series 100 Box 3].

270. Ibid.

271. Letter to C. Isaacson in Transcript. n.d. (likely 8 Apr. 1942) n.p. [SLV MS 14052, Box 4128/8].

272. Letter to Steinberg in Diary. 9 Apr. 1942. n.p. [SLV MS 9352A; Series 100 Box 3].

273. Letter to C. Isaacson in Diary. 21 Apr. 1942. n.p. [SLV MS 9352A; Series 100 Box 3].

274. Letter to C. Isaacson in Diary. n.d. (likely 8 Apr. 1942). n.p. [SLV MS 9352A; Series 100 Box 3].

275. See Murray. "The Promised Land." p. 2. Special thanks to Kevin Murray for discussing his views with me.

276. Letter to C. Isaacson in Diary. 12 Apr. 1942. n.p. [SLV MS 9352A; Series 100 Box 3].

277. Rubinstein. "Critchley Parker (1911–42)." p. 66.

278. Qtd. in letter from C. Isaacson to Steinberg. 7 June 1942. p. 1. Steinberg Papers. [YIVO RG 366/703].

279. Letter C. Isaacson to Steinberg. 7 June 1942. p. 1. Steinberg Papers. [YIVO RG 366/703].

280. Letter C. Isaacson to Steinberg. 17 June 1942. n.p. Steinberg Papers. [YIVO RG 366/703].

281. Letter C. Isaacson to Steinberg. 17 July 1942. p. 2. Steinberg Papers. [YIVO RG 366/703].

282. Letter Steinberg to C. Isaacson. 5 June 1942. n.p. Steinberg Papers. [YIVO RG 366/703].

283. "Hiker's Tragic End." p. 2.

284. Fenton, Janet. http://www.kitezh.com/haven/fenton.htm. Fenton is the granddaughter of Charles King and niece of Clyde Clayton.

285. Story related to the author by Richard Flanagan, interviewed 8 Dec. 2009.

286. "Formal Parts of Inquisition." 26 Oct. 1942. [AOT SC195/1/103/18637].

287. Steinberg. *Australia—The Unpromised Land.* p. 145.

288. Ibid.

289. Ibid.

290. "Israel Honours Elder for Defying Nazis." p. 4.

291. See Rubinstein. "Critchley Parker (1911–42)." p. 56. Though there is no memorial to his sacrifice, a Critchley Parker, Jr. forest does exist near the site of his former home in Upper Beaconsfield, Victoria.

292. Barbara Joan Beck interviewed 6 Dec. 2009; Peter Isaacson interviewed 16 Dec. 2009.

293. Barbara Joan Beck interviewed 6 Dec. 2009.

294. Letter C. Isaacson to Steinberg. 7 June 1942. p. 5. Steinberg Papers. [YIVO RG 366/703].

295. Letter C. Isaacson to Steinberg. 26 Aug. 1943. p. 3. Steinberg Papers. [YIVO RG 366/703].

296. Peter Isaacson interviewed 16 Dec. 2009.
297. Letter C. Isaacson to Steinberg. 1 Jan. 1952. n.p. Steinberg Papers. [YIVO RG 366/703].
298. Ibid.
299. Letter C. Isaacson to Steinberg. 5 Sept. 1951. n.p. Steinberg Papers. [YIVO RG 366/703].
300. Letter C. Isaacson to Steinberg. 1 Jan. 1952. n.p. Steinberg Papers. [YIVO RG 366/703].
301. Letter Steinberg to E. Parkes. 16 Oct. 1942. Steinberg Papers. [YIVO RG 366/728].
302. Letter Cosgrove to Steinberg. 22 Mar. 1943; Letter Cosgrove to Steinberg 5 Apr. 1944; Letter Cosgrove to Steinberg 13 Aug. 1945. Steinberg Papers. [YIVO RG 366/807]. An additional letter from Cosgrove's agent general indicates that he considered a mass Jewish settlement in Tasmania as late as 1946. Letter C. James to Steinberg. 3 May 1946. Steinberg Papers. [YIVO RG 366/496].
303. Confidential Department of State letter (1 July 1943) including telegram (28 June 1943) listing passengers aboard the ship. A handwritten notice across the telegram reads: "search underlined names." Steinberg's name is one of those underlined. (Information released by US Department of State Office of Information Programs and Services.)
304. Confidential letter Col. L. R. Forney (Military Intelligence Service) to J. Edgar Hoover. 3 July 1943.
305. Confidential letter Dept. of State to James C. Strickland (FBI) 1 July 1943.
306. Report on Steinberg from G. H. Kyd (FBI) to Special Agent in Charge (SAC). 7 July 1943. p. 2.
307. Ibid., p. 1.
308. Letter S. Wise to A. M. Warren (Dept. of State). 6 Jan. 1941. Steinberg Papers. [YIVO RG366/883].
309. Report on Steinberg in memorandum from D. Milton Ladd (FBI assistant director of Domestic Intelligence Division) to Director. 2 July 1945. n.p.
310. Dates of rejection were 3 Nov. 1941 and 20 July 1942. See Report on Steinberg in memorandum from D. Milton Ladd to Director. 2 July 1945. n.p.
311. Report on Steinberg in memorandum from D. Milton Ladd to Director. 2 July 1945. n.p.
312. Memorandum D. Milton Ladd to Director. 2 July 1945. n.p.
313. Report on Steinberg in memorandum from D. Milton Ladd to Director. 2 July 1945. n.p.
314. This is clear from the report on Steinberg included in the memorandum from D. Milton Ladd to Director. 2 July 1945. n.p.
315. Report G. H. Kyd (FBI) to Special Agent in Charge (SAC). 7 July 1943. p. 1. In the report on Steinberg in the memorandum from D. Milton Ladd to Director, Steinberg is said to have "been attached to the staff of a German General who was the Chief of German Espionage against Russia." 2 July 1945. n.p.

316. Report on Steinberg in memorandum from D. Milton Ladd to Director. 2 July 1945. n.p.

317. Letter Melvina Thompson to June Burn (Magazine Digest Publishing). 23 Aug. 1943. [FDR: Eleanor Roosevelt Papers; Series 170: Appointments, "B", 1943 (Box 1207)].

318. Letter M. Thompson (for E. Roosevelt) to Welles. 23 Aug. 1943. Eleanor Roosevelt Papers. [FDR Series 70 (Box 400)].

319. His date of entrance is given as 9 Sept. 1943. See Report on Steinberg in memorandum from D. Milton Ladd to Director. 2 July 1945. n.p.

320. Report on Steinberg in memorandum from D. Milton Ladd to Director. 2 July 1945. n.p.

321. FBI case file report (File No. 100–51033 AHD). p. 2.

322. Steinberg applied 21 Mar. 1944. Report on Steinberg in memorandum from D. Milton Ladd to Director. 2 July 1945. n.p.

323. Letter Steinberg to Interdepartmental Visa Review Committee. 19 June 1944. p. 2. Steinberg Papers. [YIVO RG 366/883].

324. Report on Steinberg in memorandum from D. Milton Ladd to Director. 2 July 1945. n.p.

325. Ibid.

326. FBI case file report (File No. 100-51033 AHD). pp. 2, 4.

327. Ibid., p. 4.

328. "We Aim . . . " *Freeland*. Vol. 1, No. 1. (Dec. 1944). n.p.

329. Leo Steinberg interviewed 5 Jan. 2010.

330. See point 2 in the "Memorandum of The Freeland League to The Delegations at San Francisco (May 1945)." Reprinted in *Freeland*. Vol. 1. No. 4 (June 1945): p. 5.

331. Steinberg. "The Place of Freeland in Jewish Life." p. 6.

332. Letter N. Goldmann on behalf of Silverman. 12 May 1944. [CZA Z5/687].

333. Letter I. Silverman to Editor. *Jewish Forum* (Oct. 1956): p. 143.

334. Silverman. "What I Learned about Kimberley." p. 12.

335. Ibid.

336. Goodman. "On the Kimberley Project." p. 28.

337. Letter Cosgrove to Mr. L. Fink. 4 Dec. 1945. Steinberg Papers. [YIVO RG 366/807].

CHAPTER 6. WELCOME TO THE JUNGLE

1. See points 16–18 in the "Memorandum of The Freeland League to The Delegations at San Francisco (May 1945)." Reprinted in *Freeland*. Vol. 1. No. 4 (June 1945): p. 7.

2. Ibid., p. 6.

3. Ibid.

4. Ibid., p. 5.

5. Ibid., p. 8.

6. Ibid.

7. Leftwich. *Israel Zangwill.* p. 221. This information is corroborated by a long report on Suriname present in Zangwill's ITO papers. [CZA A36/84].

8. See undated agenda of Paris Freeland conference, Steinberg Papers. [YIVO RG 366/31]. See also Astour. *Geshikhte fun der Frayland Lige.* Vol. I. pp. 185–186.

9. "A propos d'un projet d'établissement d'israélites dans les colonies françaises." *Le Petit Parisien.* 16 Jan. 1937. p. 2.

10. Steinberg letter. 27 Mar. 1938. Qtd. in Astour. *Geshikhte fun der Frayland Lige.* Vol. I. p. 250.

11. Nasaw. *The Patriarch.* p. 361.

12. "Emergency Parley of World Refugee Body Convoked as London Ponders Plan to Settle Guiana." Jewish Telegraphic Agency. 17 Nov. 1938. n.p; Kuhn. "Would Aid 700,000." *New York Times.* 16 Nov. 1938. p. 1. For Kennedy's motivations, beliefs, and actions, see Nasaw. *The Patriarch.* pp. 350–370. For Kennedy's assessment of the situation post–*Kristallnacht*, see also Sherman. *Island Refuge.* p. 173. Feingold, however, believes that the idea originated in the British Foreign Office. "Roosevelt and the Resettlement Question." p. 304.

13. Nasaw. *The Patriarch.* pp. 361–362.

14. "US Opinion Shocked." *Times* (London). 16 Nov. 1938. p. 14.

15. Ibid.

16. Ibid.

17. Earl of Selborne qtd. in Kuhn. "Quick Action Seen." *New York Times.* 17 Nov. 1938. p. 10.

18. "400 Toizener Plitim Kayn Amerika?" *Haynt.* 17 Nov. 1938. p. 1.

19. Ibid.

20. "Proposed Havens Rich in Resources." *New York Times.* 22 Nov. 1938. p. 9.

21. Kuhn. "World Searched for Havens." 20 Nov. 1938. p. 68.

22. Ibid.

23. "Text of the Statement by Chamberlain." *New York Times.* 22 Nov. 1938. p. 8.

24. Ibid.

25. Kuhn. "Tanganyika is Open." *New York Times.* 22 Nov. 1938. p. 1.

26. Ibid., p. 9.

27. Sherman. *Island Refuge.* pp. 184–188.

28. Kuhn. "Would Aid 700,000." *New York Times.* 16 Nov. 1938. p. 1; Kuhn. "Quick Action Seen." *New York Times.* 17 Nov. 1938. p. 1.

29. Sherman. *Island Refuge.* p. 207, n. 105.

30. Smith. *American Empire.* pp. 297, 305.

31. Astour. *Geshikhte fun der Frayland Lige.* Vol. II. p. 867, n. 173.

32. O. Lattimore qtd. in Smith. *American Empire.* p. 309. For Bowman's obstructionism see also pp. 310–311.

33. [Unidentified communication] S. Welles to Roosevelt. 12 Jan. 1939. Qtd. in Sherman. *Island Refuge.* p. 206. See also Feingold. "Roosevelt and the Resettlement Question." p. 290.

34. Cable Roosevelt to Chamberlain. 14 Jan. 1939. Qtd. in Feingold. "Roosevelt and the Resettlement Question." p. 290.

35. Sherman. *Island Refuge.* pp. 206–207; Feingold. "Roosevelt and the Resettlement Question." pp. 290–292.

36. Kenya Settlement Committee Report qtd. in Sherman. *Island Refuge.* p. 192.

37. Weizmann. "Statement of Jew Refugees." *Times* (London). 23 Jan. 1939. p. 13.

38. Ibid.

39. Ibid.

40. Steinberg. "Jewish Colonisation Outside Palestine." *Jewish Chronicle.* 27 Jan. 1939. p. 22.

41. Ibid.

42. Ibid.

43. "French Guiana Settlement." *Jewish Chronicle.* 27 Jan. 1939. p. 22.

44. For the American initiative see "British Guiana and Refugees." *Times* (London). 4 Feb. 1939. p. 11.

45. See terms in *Report of the British Guiana Refugee Commission.* pp. 3–4. For further details, see also Sherman. *Island Refuge.* p. 208; "British Guiana and Refugees." *Times* (London). 4 Feb. 1939. p. 11.

46. List of expedition personnel in *Report of the British Guiana Refugee Commission.* p. 3. For Rosen's support of Madagascar, see letter to Charles J. Liebman from Dr. Bernhard Kahn and Dr. J. Rosen. 12 June 1937. In "Possibilities of Land Settlement in French Colonies." [AN AJ43/43].

47. *Report of the British Guiana Refugee Commission.* p. 3.

48. Ibid., p. 4.

49. Ibid., pp. 6–7.

50. Ibid., p. 7.

51. Ibid., p. 11.

52. Ibid., p. 16.

53. Sherman. *Island Refuge.* p. 231, n. 27.

54. Ibid., pp. 231–232.

55. Ibid., p. 233.

56. Letter Polish Central Committee to Ada Steinberg. 24 May 1939. Qtd. in Astour. *Geshikhte fun der Frayland Lige.* Vol. I. pp. 387–388.

57. Lestschinsky "Tsi Kon Men Gefinen a Land far Hunderter Toizenter Yidn?" 2 July 1939. Qtd. in Astour. *Geshikhte fun der Frayland Lige.* Vol. I. p. 390.

58. Ibid.

59. Feingold. "Roosevelt and the Resettlement Question." pp. 308–311.

60. "Het Bezoek van de delegatie van de Freeland League." *Teroenga.* May 1947. p. 1.

61. Ibid.

62. Hartsinck. *Beschryving van Guyane of de Wilde Kust in Zuid-America.*

63. Roos. "Additional Notes on the History of the Jews in Surinam," pp. 127–129.

64. Nassy, ed. *Historical Essay on the Colony of Surinam [Historical Essay].* p. 141.

65. Cohen. *Jews in Another Environment.* pp. 22–24.
66. The title of a manuscript found in the British Museum [Egerton mss. 2395] cited by Kohler in "Some Early American Zionist Projects," p. 91. This document may possibly be a Dutch, not an English, grant.
67. Nassy, ed. *Historical Essay.* p. 60.
68. Ibid.
69. Cohen. *Jews in Another Environment.* p. 148.
70. Nassy, ed. *Historical Essay.* p. 60.
71. Cohen. *Jews in Another Environment.* p. 301, n. 6.
72. Nassy, ed. *Historical Essay.* p. 149.
73. Ben-Ur. "Still Life." p. 44.
74. Friedman. *Jews and the American Slave Trade.* p. 67.
75. Voltaire. *Candide.* p. 86.
76. Nassy, ed. *Historical Essay.* p. 57.
77. See documents XIII–XV collected in Nassy, ed. *Historical Essay.* pp. 200–207.
78. Dr. Alan Singer of Shearith Israel. Personal correspondence. 9 Feb. 2010.
79. Noah. *The Evidences of the American Indians Being the Descendants of the Lost Tribes of Israel.* p. 27.
80. Stedman. *Narrative, of a five years' expedition.* Vol. I. p. 76.
81. Ibid., p. 292.
82. Ibid., p. 264.
83. Nassy, ed. *Historical Essay.* p. 67.
84. Ibid., p. 68.
85. Cynthia McLeod interviewed 3 Dec. 2008.
86. Cohen. *Jews in Another Environment.* p. 154.
87. Cynthia McLeod interviewed 3 Dec. 2008.
88. Ibid.
89. Detail supplied by Shai Fierst, who lived among the Ndjuka. Personal correspondence. 16 Nov. 2009.
90. Gerke. "Preface." p. iii. The Society was also known as "Jew–Col."
91. Ibid.
92. "Jews Would Shift Million Families." *New York Times.* 30 Nov. 1938. p. 15.
93. Letter Steinberg to Wolf. 9 Dec 1938. Steinberg Papers. [YIVO RG/490].
94. Letter W. Ritmeester (IRCS) to Steinberg. 28 May 1940. Steinberg Papers. [YIVO RG/490].
95. "Jews Would Shift Million Families." *New York Times.* 30 Nov. 1938. p. 15.
96. Ibid.
97. "Zionists Object to Plan." *New York Times.* 1 Dec. 1938. p. 12.
98. "Jews Would Shift Million Families." *New York Times.* 30 Nov. 1938. p. 15.
99. "Zionists Object to Plan." *New York Times.* 1 Dec. 1938. p. 12.
100. Mussert. *United States of Guiana.* p. 5. Special thanks to Alexander Heldring for providing this document.
101. Ibid., p. 6.

102. Ibid.
103. J. W. Albarda qtd. in ibid., p. 17.
104. Postcard Dyk to Ruppin. 30 Apr. 1939. [CZA A107/843].
105. "Dr. Solomon Dyk." *New York Times*. 25 May 1944. p. 21.
106. "Vichy Government Arrests Jewish Social Workers; Brutzkus Still Held." Jewish Telegraphic Agency. 6 Dec 1940. n.p.
107. Gafner. "Shlomo (Solomon) Dyk: B." http://www.buchach.org/book/dik.htm.
108. "Dr. Solomon Dyk." *New York Times*. 25 May 1944. p. 21.
109. Gerke. "Preface." p. iv.
110. Vink. "Over De Mogelijkheid Van Kolonisatie Van Blanken in Suriname." p. 675.
111. Swellengrebel. *Health of White Settlers in Surinam*. p. 62.
112. Ibid., p. 19.
113. Ibid., pp. 30–32.
114. Ibid., pp. 40–42.
115. Ibid., p. 66.
116. Ibid., p. 23.
117. Ibid., p. 106.
118. Ibid., pp. 112–113.
119. Ibid., p. 111.
120. Letter Steinberg to Swellengrebel. 3 June 1948. Steinberg Papers. [YIVO RG366/630].
121. Karen Pomer, Van Leeuwen's granddaughter, interviewed 5 Nov. 2012.
122. Ibid.
123. Correspondence with Karen Pomer. 4 Nov. 2012.
124. Ibid.; Interview with Pomer. 5 Nov. 2012.
125. Heldring. *Het Saramacca Project*. p. 72.
126. His eldest child remained with him until escaping on the eve of the Nazi invasion of the Netherlands in 1940.
127. Correspondence with Karen Pomer. 4 Nov. 2012.
128. Ibid.
129. Heldring. *Het Saramacca Project*. p. 72.
130. Letter Van Leeuwen to Brons. 25 June 1946. Shaechter Papers. [YIVO RG 682/819].
131. Letter Steinberg to Brons. 22 Apr. 1946. Steinberg Papers. [YIVO RG366/611].
132. Heldring. *Het Saramacca Project*. pp. 65–66.
133. Raptschinsky qtd. in ibid., p. 66.
134. Heldring. *Het Saramacca Project*. p. 66.
135. Ibid.
136. Astour. *Geshikhte fun der Frayland-Lige*. Vol. II. p. 562.
137. Freeland League for Jewish Territorial Colonization, Statement by Dr. I. N. Steinberg. p. 2. [TNA DO 35/1140].
138. Ibid. p. 7.
139. Ibid.

140. Letter Steinberg to Brons. 22 Mar. 1946. Steinberg Papers. [YIVO RG366/611].

141. Letter Brons to Steinberg. 18 Apr. 1946. Shaechter Papers. [YIVO RG 682/496].

142. Ibid.

143. Radiogram Saul Goodman and Henri van Leeuwen to Steinberg. Steinberg Papers.[YIVO RG366/611].

144. Note Brons to Steinberg. n.d. Steinberg Papers. [YIVO RG366/611].

145. Minutes of the meeting at the Department of Overseas Parts of the Kingdom, the Hague. 2 May 1946. Steinberg Papers. [YIVO RG366/611].

146. Letter S. Goodman and Steinberg to Dutch Minister of Overseas Territories. 22 Nov. 1946. Steinberg Papers. [YIVO RG 366/612].

147. Heldring. *Het Saramacca Project*. p. 76.

148. Raptchinsky. "Marginal Notes." n.d. Schaechter Papers. [YIVO RG 682/803].

149. Minutes of the meeting at the Department of Overseas Parts of the Kingdom, the Hague. 2 May 1946. Steinberg Papers. [YIVO RG366/611].

150. Confidential memorandum attached to letter 22 Nov. 1946 from Saul Goodman and Steinberg to Minister of Overseas Territories. Steinberg Papers. [YIVO RG 366/612].

151. See Raptschinsky. "The Guianas Are the Territory." *Freeland*. Vol. II No. 5 (Sept./ Oct. 1946). pp. 5–7, 19.

152. Memorandum to Dutch Government from Freeland League. 22 Nov. 1946. p. 2. Steinberg Papers. [YIVO RG366/612].

153. Ibid.

154. Letter Staten to Brons. 14 Feb. 1947. Steinberg Papers. [YIVO RG366/614].

155. "The Debate in the Staten on the Jewish Colonization Project 27 June 1947." p. 5.

156. Ibid., pp. 5–7, 16.

157. Telegram Brons to Steinberg. 25 Feb. 1947. Their correspondence indicates that Steinberg floated the figure of fifty thousand refugees, while Brons wanted a maximum of ten thousand. Steinberg Papers. [YIVO RG366/614].

158. "Surinam Talks Planned." *New York Times*. 22 Feb. 1947. p. 4.

159. Redaction of "letters from Europe." 9 Apr. 1947. Steinberg Papers. [YIVO RG366/615].

160. Letter I. Kaczerginsky to Freeland League. 22 Dec. 1947. Shaechter Papers. [YIVO RG 682/621].

161. Letter Mordekhe Schaechter (Vienna) to Freeland League. 27 Feb. 1948. Steinberg Papers. [YIVO RG366/626].

162. "Resolutions of the First Freeland Conference of the D.P. Camps Held in Upper-Austria on Oct. 5th 1947." p. 2.

163. "Het Bezoek van de delegatie van de Freeland League." *Teroenga*. May 1947. p. 1.

164. "Freeland League Expedition to Surinam." [YIVO VM 220].

165. Ibid., title cards.

166. "Joint Statement of the Last Session of the Governmental Advisory Commission of Surinam and the Delegation of the Freeland League." 19–20 Apr. 1947. Shaechter Papers. [YIVO RG 682/306].

167. Fruchtbaum notes that de Groot was Jewish. "Where Else Could Jews Have Gone?" p. 90.

168. "Het Bezoek van de delegatie van de Freeland League." *Teroenga*. May 1947. p. 1.

169. Ibid.

170. Ibid., p. 3.

171. Ibid., p. 2.

172. Letter and memorandum of agreement from Brons to Freeland League. Steinberg Papers. [YIVO RG366/615].

173. Ibid.

174. "Haven for Homeless Is Offered by Dutch." *New York Times*. 25 Apr. 1947. p. 6.

175. Letter Dr. M. de Groot to Freeland League. 2 June 1947. Steinberg Papers. [YIVO RG366/617].

176. Telegram H. Samson to Steinberg. 28 June 1947. Steinberg Papers. [YIVO RG366/617].

177. Official letter from Brons. 21 July 1947. Steinberg Papers. [YIVO RG 366/618]. This figure is reconfirmed in a later letter from office of Gouvernements Secretaire to Freeland League. 4 Dec. 1947. Copy in *Preliminary Report on the Possibilities of Jewish Colonization in Surinam* (Paramaribo). 1948. n.p.

178. Letter Brons to de Groot. 21 July 1947. Shaechter Papers. [YIVO RG 682/306].

179. Ibid.

180. Letter B. [unknown] to Freeland League. Steinberg Papers. [YIVO RG366/618].

181. Letter W.C.H. Indiaan Pache to Freeland League. 25 Aug. 1947. Steinberg Papers. [YIVO RG366/619].

182. L. E. Thijm poem. n.d. Schaechter Papers. [YIVO RG 682/805].

183. L. E. Thijm poem. n.d. Schaechter Papers. [YIVO RG 682/805]. Special thanks to Cynthia McLeod who translated from Sranan-Tongo.

184. Letter H. Samson to Steinberg. 29 Nov. 1948. Schaechter Papers. [YIVO RG 682/813].

185. Telegram Steinberg. 14 July 1947. Steinberg Papers. [YIVO RG366/618].

186. Letter Steinberg to de Groot. 26 Sept. 1947. Steinberg Papers. [YIVO RG366/620].

187. Text of speech by Sassen before U.N. General Assembly. 26 Nov. 1947. Shaechter Papers. [YIVO RG 682/306].

188. See list of Freeland League Committee Members in Los Angeles. Oct.–Dec. 1947. Shaechter Papers. [YIVO RG 682/566].

189. *Preliminary Report*. p. 3.

190. A. S. Fisher was a civil engineer. Ray C. Roberts was a "soil correlator" in the U.S. Department of Agriculture. Atherton Lee had been the director of a tropical experimental station in Puerto Rico. George Giglioli was a physician who advocated the use of DDT in Guyana to combat malarial mosquitos.

191. See group photo. Shaechter Papers. [YIVO RG 682/560].

192. Menu for "Scientific Dinner at Samson's in Paramaribo." 3 Jan. 1948. Steinberg Papers. [YIVO RG366/624].

193. Doctor's report Paramaribo. 28 Jan. 1948. Steinberg Papers. [YIVO RG366/624].
194. *Preliminary Report.* p. 2.
195. Total area proposed indicated in *Preliminary Report.* p. 56. An earlier document notes that the area to be settled would first be 50,000 hectares, followed by an additional 250,000. Letter Brons to Freeland League. 19 Feb. 1948. Shaechter Papers. [YIVO RG 682/306].
196. Ibid.
197. Map of proposed settlements. Shaechter Papers. [YIVO RG 682/811].
198. Ibid.
199. *Preliminary Report.* p. 58.
200. Ibid., p. 95.
201. Ibid., p. 79.
202. A. Lee to Steinberg. "Estimated Community Elements for the Surinam Settlement Project." pp. 1–3. n. d. Steinberg Papers. [YIVO RG366/625].
203. Ibid., p. 2.
204. *Preliminary Report.* p. 110.
205. Ibid., p. 123.
206. Ibid., p.139
207. Ibid., p. 4.
208. Untitled document from American Jewish Committee. n.d. Shaechter Papers. [YIVO RG 682/561].
209. "The FAO and the Commission's Report." pp.16–17.
210. "Financial Estimates for Jewish Settlement in Surinam." Schaechter Papers. [YIVO RG 682/535]. It appears that this document was prepared by N. Weyl and A. Lee in Apr. 1948. See telegram S. Goodman to A. Fisher. 5 Apr. 1948. Schaechter Papers. [YIVO RG 682/524].
211. "Financial Estimates for Jewish Settlement in Surinam." p. 1. Schaechter Papers. [YIVO RG 682/535].
212. Ibid., p. 3.
213. Ibid., p. 17.
214. Ibid., p. 8.
215. Ibid., pp. 9–11.
216. Ibid., pp. 11–12.
217. Ibid., pp. 14–15.
218. Ibid., pp. 4–6.
219. Ibid., p. 8.
220. Ibid., pp. 26–27.
221. Interview with C. McLeod 3 Dec. 2008.
222. Yaffe. "All–Jewish Colony in Surinam Sought." *PM.* 11 Jan. 1948. p. 4.
223. "Erets Jisraël." *Teroenga.* Dec. 1947. p. 8.
224. "Nieuws van de Afdeling Suriname van de Freeland League." *Teroenga.* Feb. 1948. p. 3.
225. Letter Swellengrebel to Steinberg. 14 May 1948. Steinberg Papers. [YIVO RG366/629].

226. Letter M. Schaechter in Vienna to Freeland League. 15 May 1948. Steinberg Papers. [YIVO RG366/629].

227. Ibid.

228. Refugee–Freelanders in Austria qtd. in Steinberg. "The Place of Freeland Within Jewish Life." Address to Second Freeland Conference, New York. Oct. 1948. p. 4. Steinberg Papers. [YIVO RG366/635].

229. Steinberg. "The Place of Freeland Within Jewish Life." Address to Second Freeland Conference, New York, Oct. 1948. p. 4. Steinberg Papers [YIVO RG366/635].

230. "Who Will Go to Surinam." *Freeland*. Vol. IV. No. 2 (May/June 1948): p. 19.

231. "Rumanian Freeland Resolutions." p. 2.

232. Steinberg. "Statement." pp. 3–4. [TNA DO 35/1140].

233. Ibid.

234. Freeland League for Jewish Territorial Colonization/Statement by Dr. I. N. Steinberg and discussion before the Anglo–American Committee on Palestine. 14 Jan. 1946. p. 4. [TNA DO 35/1140].

235. Letter S. Wise to A. M. Warren, Chief, Visa Division, Dept. of State. 6 Jan. 1941. Steinberg Papers. [YIVO RG366/883].

236. Telegram S. Wise to Mrs. A. Silverman. 25 Mar. 1948. Qtd. in Astour. *Geshikhte fun der Frayland–Lige*. Vol. II. p. 718. Trans. Dr. Israel Zelitch for Alexander Heldring.

237. Silver. "Ida Camelhor Silverman." p. 274.

238. Photo in Morris. "Ida Silverman." p. 113.

239. Letter to Editor from Silverman. *Jewish Forum* (Oct. 1956): p. 3.

240. Astour. *Geshikhte fun der Frayland–Lige*. Vol. I. p. 543.

241. Letter to Editor from Silverman. *Jewish Forum* (Oct 1956): p. 3.

242. Ibid.

243. Telegram Silverman to Keren HaYesod officials 9 Mar. 1948. [CZA KH4/3415].

244. Letter to Editor from Silverman. *Jewish Forum* (Oct. 1956): p. 3.

245. Telegram S. Goodman to H. Samson. 13 Feb. 1948. Shaechter Papers. [YIVO RG 682/524].

246. "Left–Handed Zionism." pp. 8–10.

247. Letter to Editor from Silverman. *Jewish Forum* (Oct. 1956): p. 3.

248. Letter Silverman to Keren HaYesod officials. 27 Mar. 1948. [CZA KH4/3416].

249. Ibid.

250. Silverman. *Canadian Jewish Chronicle*. 7 May 1948. p. 7.

251. Ibid.

252. Ibid., p. 14.

253. Letter H. Samson to Steinberg. 2 May 1948. Steinberg Papers. [YIVO RG 366/629].

254. Letter de Groot to Steinberg. 1 May 1948. Shaechter Papers. [YIVO RG 682/306].

255. Letter Izak K[aczerginsky]. 21 May 1948. Shaechter Papers. [YIVO RG 682/561].

256. Letter I. Kaczerginsky and M. Shaechter to Mr. Montgomery (acting chief of PC IRO Area–Team, Linz). 7 Sept. 1948. Shaechter Papers. [YIVO RG 682/621].

257. Letter Steinberg to Hans Samson. 15 Sept. 1948. Steinberg Papers. [YIVO RG366/634].

258. "Resolutions Adopted by Conference." p. 10.

259. "A Call to the Jewish People by the Second Freeland Conference" (New York). Oct. 1948. Steinberg Papers. [YIVO RG366/635].

260. Letter Freeland League in Austria to Freeland League (New York). 15 May 1948. [YIVO RG 682/563].

261. Letter A. M. Fisher to Freeland League. 15 July 1948. Shaechter Papers. [YIVO RG 682/563]. It is not clear whether Fisher refers here to a particular Zionist group in Paramaribo or the U.S., or whether he is using the term generally.

262. Letter Raptschinsky to Freeland League 13, 16, 17 July (1948—the year is not dated but surrounding material and context makes this clear). Shaechter Papers. [YIVO RG 682/806].

263. Letter Dr. W. Huender to Freeland League. 14 Aug. 1948. Steinberg Papers. [YIVO RG366/633].

264. Letter Drees to Freeland League. 29 Nov. 1948. Schaechter Papers. [YIVO RG 682/306].

265. Mann. "I Believe in Freeland." p. 8.

266. Morgan. *A Covert Life.* pp. 271, 332.

267. Letter Lovestone. 18 Oct. 1948. Schaechter Papers. [YIVO RG 682/817]. For Lovestone's CIA work, see Morgan. *A Covert Life.* pp. 195–243.

268. According to a letter sent by Freeland League to Drees on 20 Jan. 1949, Brown and Sassen met in the Hague 15 Oct. 1948. Schaechter Papers. [YIVO RG 682/306].

269. See draft of "Instructions" for delegates. Schaechter Papers. [YIVO RG 682/806]. See also Heldring. *Het Saramacca Project.* pp. 272–274.

270. Draft of "Instructions" for delegates. p. 2. Schaechter Papers. [YIVO RG 682/806].

271. Letter Ferrier to Steinberg. 2 Feb. 1956, in response to Steinberg's letters of 3 Dec. 1955 and 21 Dec. 1955. Schaechter Papers. [YIVO RG 682/807].

272. Heldring. "The Saramacca Project." http://www.jewcy.com/post/saramacca_project.

273. Infield. "The Role of Cooperation in the Surinam Settlement." pp. 6–7; Gorski. "Finance Bank for Surinam." pp. 7–8

274. Siegel. "Suriname Among the Nations." p. 6.

275. Fruchtbaum. "Uruguay." pp. 4–5.

276. Fruchtbaum. "Costa Rica." pp. 9–11.

277. Fruchtbaum. "Chile: Land for Colonization." pp. 8–9.

278. Fruchtbaum. "Nicaragua." pp. 9–10.

279. Fruchtbaum. "Ecuador (Part I)." pp. 3–5; "Ecuador (Part II)." pp. 2–4.

280. "Isaac Steinberg, a Jewish Leader." *New York Times.* 3 Jan. 1957. p. 32.

281. Leo Steinberg interviewed 5 Jan. 2010.
282. Fruchtbaum. "Tribute to Dr. I. N. Steinberg." p. 2.
283. Zuckerman. "Dr. I. N. Steinberg." p. 6.
284. Fromm. "Dr. I. N. Steinberg." p. 4.
285. Steinberg. "Down With War!" p. 6.
286. Ibid.

EPILOGUE

1. Thanks to Ariel Snapiri for this image, and to filmmaker Ron Ofer for his insights into these *pashkvilim*.
2. For example, a controversial book by Shabtai Beit-Zvi, *Post-Ugandan Zionism on Trial*, is available in English translation on a website purporting to be affiliated with the extreme anti-Zionist Neturei Karta faction. Beit-Zvi's book offers a sharp critique of Zionist leaders and advances a polemical and conspiratorial view of history.
3. Herzl. *The Jewish State*. p. 30. See Pinsker on the question of Palestine or the New World. *Auto-Emancipation*. p. 30.
4. Subtitle of Herzl's *The Jewish State*.
5. Herzl. *Old New Land*. p. 114.
6. Ibid., p. 285.
7. Ibid., p. 193.
8. Ibid.
9. See Smith's formulation of the territorialization of memory in *Chosen Peoples*. p. 134.
10. See for example the large number of ITO agents in the Pale and the circulation figures of the ITO's Yiddish newspaper *Vohin?* (*Whither?*) in Alroey. *Bread to Eat and Clothes to Wear*. pp. 23–26.
11. Vital discusses the concept in *Zionism: The Formative Years*. pp. 470–475.
12. Smith. *Chosen Peoples*. p. 136.
13. My thoughts on literature and the utopian impulse result from numerous conversations with literary scholar Tuvia Shlonsky.
14. Steinberg. "Down with War!" p. 6.
15. Trevor-Roper. *History and Imagination*. p. 16.
16. Astour. *Geshikhte fun der Frayland–Lige*. Vol. I. pp. 391–393, 506–508. See also Eshkoli-Wagman. "Tokhniyot Teritoriyaliyot l'Fitron Metzukat haPlitim haYehudi'im 1938–1943."
17. See the "Mapping Ararat" website: http://www.mappingararat.com/.
18. Bartana. "The Jewish Renaissance Movement in Poland: A Manifesto." p. 126.
19. Winters. "Exodus 2048." *Image*. 15 Apr. 2009. Available at http://imagejournal.org/page/blog/exodus-2048.
20. Edelman et. al. "Where to?" p. 13.
21. Astour. *Geshikhte fun der Frayland–Lige*. Vol. I. p. VII. See also Alroey. *Mikhapsey Moledet*. pp. 3–4.
22. Herzl. "The Hunt in Bohemia." p. 171.

BIBLIOGRAPHY

RESEARCH COLLECTIONS CITED
Archive Nationales, Paris, France [AN]
Archive Office of Tasmania, Hobart, Australia [AOT]
Beit Jabotinsky, Tel Aviv, Israel [BJ]
Buffalo and Erie County Historical Society, Buffalo, NY [BECHS]
Central Zionist Archives, Jerusalem, Israel [CZA]
Franklin D. Roosevelt Presidential Library, Hyde Park, NY [FDR]
Geelong Grammar School Archives, Geelong, Australia [GGSA]
Hartley Library, University of Southampton, Southampton, England [HLS]
Kenyan National Archives, Nairobi, Kenya [KNA]
Leo Baeck Institute, Center for Jewish History, New York, NY [LBI]
London Metropolitan Archives, London, England [LMA]
The National Archives, London, England [TNA]
State Library of Victoria, Melbourne, Australia [SLV]
Tasmanian Archives and Heritage Office, Hobart, Australia [TAHO]
Tasmanian Museum and Art Gallery Collection, Hobart, Australia [TMAGC]
Weiner Library, London, England [WL]
Yad Vashem, Jerusalem, Israel [YV]
YIVO Institute for Jewish Research, Center for Jewish History, New York, NY [YIVO]

OTHER RESEARCH COLLECTIONS CONSULTED
American Jewish Committee Archives, New York and Jerusalem
Arquivo Histórico Nacional de Angola, Luanda, Angola
Nationaal Archief Surinam, Paramaribo, Suriname
Neve Shalom Synagogue Archives, Paramaribo, Suriname
University of Chicago–Ludwig Rosenberger Library of Judaica, Chicago

PUBLISHED SOURCES
"400 Toizener Plitim Kayn Amerika?" *Haynt* 17 Nov. 1938. p. 1. [Yiddish]
Adams, Charles Francis, ed. *Memoirs of John Quincy Adams* Vol. 5. Philadelphia: Lippincott, 1875.
"The Advent of the Undesirable." *African Standard* (Nairobi) 12 Dec. 1903. p. 2.
"Advertisement." *Carolina Observer* (North Carolina) 6 Oct. 1825. p. 2.
Ahad Ha'am. "haBokhim." *Kol Kitve Ahad Ha'am.* Jerusalem: Jewish Publishing House, 1947. pp. 337–341. [Hebrew]

"Al Davar Hatza'at Angola." *haZman* 19 June 1912. p. 2. [Hebrew]

"Al Efsharut Hagira Yehudit l'Madagascar." *Davar* 22 Feb. 1938. p. 8. [Hebrew]

Alfassi, Itzhak, et al. "Land of Israel: Aliyah and Absorption." In *Encyclopaedia Judaica*. Ed. Michael Berenbaum and Fred Skolnik. Vol. 10. 2d ed. Detroit: Macmillan Reference USA, 2007. pp. 329–373.

Allen, Lewis F. "Founding of the City of Ararat on Grand Island—by Mordecai M. Noah." *Publications of the Buffalo Historical Society*. Vol. I. Buffalo, NY, 1879 [1866]. pp. 305–328.

Almog, Shmuel. "Role of Religious Values in the Second Aliyah." *Zionism and Religion*. Hanover, NH: Brandeis UP, 1998. pp. 237–250.

———. *Zionism and History: The Rise of a New Jewish Consciousness*. New York: St. Martin's, 1987.

Alpern, A. "Biro-Bidzhan, Madagaskar, Naye Caledonia." *Haynt* 28 Feb. 1938. p. 3. [Yiddish]

Alroey, Gur. *Mikhapsey Moledet: haHistadrut haTeritorialistit haYehudit (ITO) u'Ma'avakah b'Tnua haTzionit b'Shanim 1905–1925*. Sde-Boker: Machon Ben-Gurion, 2011. [Hebrew]

———. *Bread to Eat and Clothes to Wear*. Detroit: Wayne State UP, 2011.

———. "Journey to New Palestine: The Zionist Expedition to East Africa and the Aftermath of the Uganda Debate." *Jewish Culture and History* 10.1 (Summer 2008): 23–58.

———. *haMehapekha haShkayta: haHagira haYehudit m'haEmpiria haRusit 1875–1924*. Jerusalem: Zalman Shazar Center for Jewish History, 2008. [Hebrew]

Alter, Leon. "Madagaskar." Trans. Mariusz Szajnert. *Epoka* 5.2 (105/Jan. 1937): 2–3. [Polish]

"And 1950." *Jewish Chronicle* (London) 14 Oct. 1904. pp. 8–9.

Anderson, Benedict. *Imagined Communities: Reflections on the Origin and Spread of Nationalism*. New York: Verso, 2006.

Angell, Norman. "Your Future . . . Our Future." *Freeland* I.2 (Feb. 1945): 3–4.

"Angola is Offered for Zionist Colony." *New York Times* 28 June 1912. p. 8.

"A propos d'un project d'établissement d'israélites dans les colonies françaises." *Le Petit Parisien* 16 Jan. 1937. p. 2. [French]

Arcand, Adrien. "Jewish Problem Solved: Madagascar a National Home." *World Monthly* 15 July 1938. Vol. I. No. 1. pp. 111–114.

Arendt, Hannah. "Truth and Politics." *Between Past and Future*. New York: Penguin, 1993. pp. 227–264.

———. *Eichmann in Jerusalem: A Report on the Banality of Evil*. New York: Penguin, 1992.

Arthur, Richard. "Australia for the I.T.O." *Hebrew Standard* 29 June 1906. n.p. [CZA A36/89].

Astour, Michael. *Geshikhte fun der Frayland-Lige*. Vols. I and II. New York: Freeland League, 1967. [Yiddish]

———. "Thirty Years of Birobidzhan." *Freeland* XII.1 (42/Apr.–June 1959): 8–9.

———. "Alfred Döblin (1879–1957)." *Freeland* XI.2 (41/July–Sept. 1958): 11–12.

"Attempt on Dr. Max Nordau." *Times* (London) 21 Dec. 1903. p. 5.

"The Attempt to Kill Nordau." *New York Times* 22 Dec. 1903. p. 5.

"Attentat contre M. Max Nordau." *Le Gaulois* 20 Dec. 1903. p. 2. [French]

"Attentant L'eumi." *Habazeleth* 28 Dec. 1903. p. 4. [Hebrew]

"Aus Nordamerika." *Sulamith* (1820): 283–284. [German]

Balfour, Lord James. "Balfour Declaration." In *Israel in the Middle East: Documents and Readings on Society, Politics and Foreign Relations, Pre-1948 to the Present.* Ed. Itamar Rabinovich and Jehuda Reinharz. Waltham, MA: Brandeis UP, 2008. p. 29.

Bar, Aryeh. Ed. *The Jewish Press That Was: Accounts, Evaluations and Memories of Jewish Papers in Pre-Holocaust Europe.* Jerusalem: Jerusalem Post Press, 1980.

Bartana, Yael. "The Jewish Renaissance Movement in Poland: A Manifesto." *And Europe Will Be Stunned.* London: Artangel, 2011.

Bar-Yosef, Eitan. "Spying Out the Land: The Zionist Expedition to East Africa, 1905." In *The "Jew" in Late-Victorian and Edwardian Culture: Between the East End and East Africa.* Ed. Nadia Valman and Eitan Bar-Yosef. New York: Palgrave Macmillan, 2009.

Bash, Françoise. "Gender and Survival: A Jewish Family in Occupied France, 1940–1944." *Feminist Studies* 32.2 (Summer 2006): 299–331.

"The Basle Program." In *Israel in the Middle East: Documents and Readings on Society, Politics and Foreign Relations, Pre-1948 to the Present.* Ed. Itamar Rabinovich and Jehuda Reinharz. Waltham, MA: Brandeis UP, 2008. p. 21.

Bastos, Augusto. "Colonização Judaica." *Jornal de Benguela* Vol. II. No. 35., 27 Aug. 1913. p. 6. [Portuguese]

———. "Colonização Judaica." *Jornal de Benguela* Vol. I. No. 9., 28 Aug. 1912. p. 2. [Portuguese]

———. "Colonização Judaica." *Jornal de Benguela* Vol. I. No. 6., 7 Aug. 1912. p. 2. [Portuguese]

———. "Colonização Judaica." *Jornal de Benguela* Vol. I. No. 5., 31 July 1912. p. 2. [Portuguese]

Bateson, Charles. *The Convict Ships: 1787–1868.* Sydney: Library of Australian History, 1983.

Bauer, Yehuda. *My Brother's Keeper: A History of the American Jewish Joint Distribution Committee 1929–1939.* Philadelphia: Jewish Publication Society, 1974.

Belolutskaia, Marina. "Kropotkin, Petr Alekseevitch." In *Encyclopedia of the Arctic.* Vol. 2. Ed. Mark Nuttall. New York: Routledge, 2005.

Ben-David, N. "Hitnakshut b'Nefesh Nordau." *haZfira* 23 Dec. 1903. p. 2. [Hebrew]

Ben-Simha, Avraham. "b'Khutz l'Artzeinu." *haMelitz* 29 Dec. 1903. p. 2. [Hebrew]

Ben-Ur, Aviva. "Still Life: Sephardi, Ashkenazi and West African Art and Form in Suriname's Jewish Cemeteries." *American Jewish History* 92.1 (Mar. 2004): 31–79.

Ben-Yehuda, Eliezer. "haSakh haKol." *Hashkafa* 18 Aug. 1905. pp. 1–2. [Hebrew]

———. *haMedinah haYehudit.* Warsaw: Erelstein, 1905. [Hebrew]

———. "haTayara haTzionit." *Hashkafa* 30 Dec. 1904. p. 1. [Hebrew]

Bergner, Yosl and Ruth Bondi. *Ikar Shakhakhti: Masa'ot u'Ma'asiyot.* Sifriyat Ma'ariv, 1996. [Hebrew]

"Berlin Food Rioters Attack and Beat Jews." *New York Times* 6 Nov. 1923. p. 2.

Best, Gary Dean. "Jacob H. Schiff's Galveston Movement: An Experiment in Immigrant Deflection, 1907–1914." *American Jewish Archives* 30.1 (Apr. 1978): 43–79.

Beyer, Sonja. "Menachem Birnbaum." In *Encyclopedia Judaica*. Vol. 3. 2d ed. Ed. Michael Berenbaum and Fred Skolnik. Detroit: Macmillan Reference USA, 2007. p. 714.

Binyamini, Eliahu. *Medinot l'Yehudim: Uganda, Birobidzhan v'Od 34 Tokhniyot*. Tel Aviv: HaKibbutz HaMeuchad, 1990. [Hebrew]

Birnbaum, Nathan. "Methodisches zur Palästinafrage." In *Ausgewählte Schriften zur Jüdischen Frage*. Vol. I. Czernowitz: Birnbaum and Kohut, 1910 [1903]. pp. 200–212. [German]

———. "Die Nationale Wiedergeburt des jüdischen Volkes in seinem Lande." In *Ausgewählte Schriften zur Jüdischen Frage*. Vol. I. Czernowitz: Birnbaum and Kohut, 1910 [1893]. pp. 3–21. [German]

———. "Die Ziele der jüdisch–nationalen Bestrebungen. Eine Artikelserie. II." *Selbst–Emancipation* 4.16 (May 1890): 1–2. [German]

Borochov, Ber. "l'She'aylat Tzion v'Teritoria." In *Ktavim*. Vol. 1. Ed. L. Levitah and D. Ben-Nahum. Tel Aviv: Hakibbutz Hameuchad, 1955. pp. 18–153. [Hebrew]

Boyce, James. *Van Diemen's Land*. Melbourne: Black Ink, 2009.

Bradt, Hilary. *Madagascar: The Bradt Travel Guide*. Guilford, CT: Globe Pequot Press. 2005.

Brechtken, Magnus. *Madagaskar für die Juden: antisemitische Idee und politische Praxis 1885–1945*. München: Oldenbourg, 1997. [German]

Breinin, Reuven. "Sikha im ha'Dr. Herzl." *haZofeh* 1 Sept. 1903. p. 827. Reprinted in Heymann. "Herzl v'Tzioney Rusia: Makhloket v'Haskama." *haTsiyonut* 3 (1973): 56–99. [Hebrew]

Brenner, Yosef Chaim. "m'Tokh haPinkas." *Kol Kitvei Y. C. Brenner*. Vol. 2. Tel Aviv: Hakibbutz Hameuchad, 1960 [1906]. pp. 127–155. [Hebrew]

———. "Mikhtav l'Rusia." *Kol Kitvei Y. C. Brenner*. Vol. 2. Tel Aviv: Hakkibutz Hameuchad, 1960 [1906]. pp. 12–13. [Hebrew]

Brésil, Léon. "Attentat contre le Dr. Max Nordau." *Le Figaro* 20 Dec. 1903. p. 2. [French]

"British Guiana and Refugees." *Times* (London) 4 Feb. 1939. p. 11.

Broides, Avraham. *Pgishot u'Dvarim*. Ramat–Gan, Israel: Massada, 1976. [Hebrew]

Bronner, Fred, et al. "Argentina." In *Encyclopaedia Judaica*. Ed. Michael Berenbaum and Fred Skolnik. Vol. 2. 2d ed. Detroit: Macmillan Reference USA, 2007. pp. 426–450.

Bru, Bernard. "Doeblin's Life and Work from His Correspondence." In *Contemporary Mathematics: Doeblin and Modern Probability*. Ed. Harry Cohn. Providence, RI: American Mathematical Society, 1993. pp. 1–64.

Caron, Vicki. *Uneasy Asylum: France and the Jewish Refugee Crisis, 1933–1942*. Stanford, CA: Stanford UP, 1998.

Catane, Shulamith. "Abraham Schrameck." In *Encyclopedia Judaica*. Vol. 18. 2d ed. Ed. Michael Berenbaum and Fred Skolnik. Detroit: Macmillan Reference USA, 2007. p. 167.

"Celebration of Washington's Birth–Day." *London Illustrated News* 29 Mar. 1845. p. 194.

"Khalifat Mikhtavim b'Dvar Hatza'at Angola." *haZman* 15 May 1912. p. 2. [Hebrew]

Chanoch, N. "Mikhtav m'London." *Davar* 9 Aug. 1935. p. 2. [Hebrew]

Charney, Daniel. "Oprufen nokh dem Parizer P.E.N.-Kongres." In *I. N. Steinberg Gedenk–Bukh.* Ed. Melech Ravitch. New York: I. N. Steinberg Book Committee, 1960 [1937]. pp. 431–441. [Yiddish]

———. "Oyf a P.E.N-Kongres in Pariz." In *I. N. Steinberg Gedenk–Bukh.* Ed. Melech Ravitch. New York: I. N. Steinberg Book Committee, 1960 [1937]. pp. 427–431. [Yiddish]

"City of Refuge." *Carolina Observer* (North Carolina) 6 Oct. 1825. p. 2.

Cohen, Naomi W. *Jacob H. Schiff: A Study in American Jewish Leadership.* Hanover, NH: Brandeis UP, 1999.

Cohen, Natan. *Sefer, Sofer v'Iton: Merkaz haTarbut haYehudit b'Varsha, 1918–1942.* Jerusalem: Hebrew University Magnes Press, 2003. [Hebrew]

Cohen, Robert. *Jews in Another Environment.* New York: E. J. Brill, 1991.

Colden, Cadwallader. *Memoir Prepared at the Request of the Committee of the Common Council of the City of New York and Presented to the Mayor of the City at the Celebration of the Completion of the New York Canals.* New York: Corporation of New York, 1825. pp. 3–98.

Cologna, Abraham de. "Au Redacteur." *Journal des débats* 18 Nov. 1825. pp. 2–3. [French]

"Colonization Projects, Jewish." In *Vallentine's Jewish Encyclopaedia.* Ed. Albert Hyamson and Dr. A. M. Silbermann. London: Shapiro, Vallentine & Co., 1938. pp. 152–153.

Cone, G. Herbert. "New Matter Relating to Mordecai M. Noah." *American Jewish Historical Society Publications* 11 (1903): 131–137.

"Conversion of the Jews." *Church Quarterly Review* 51 (Apr. 1888): 185–204.

The Corian (Dec. 1927): 127.

"Corner Stone of a City on Grand Island Laid at Buffalo." *Gazette* (Black Rock, NY). 20 Sept. 1825. p 1.

"Das Project zur Gründung eines Judenstaates aus dem Jahre 1825." *Die Welt.* No. 42. 19 Oct. 1900. p. 6. [German]

"The Debate in the Staten on the Jewish Colonization Project 27 June 1947." *Freeland* III.3 (Nov./Dec. 1947): 5–7, 16.

Defoe, Daniel. *The History of the Pyrates.* London: T. Warner, 1724.

Defoe, Daniel, and Robert Drury. *Madagascar: Or, Robert Drury's Journal, During Fifteen Years Captivity on that Island.* London: W. Meadows, 1729.

Descamps, Paul. *Le Portugal: La Vie Sociale Actuelle.* Paris: Firmin-Didot, 1935. [French]

Dias, António Augusto. *Benguela.* Cadernos Coloniais No. 43. Lisbon: Cosmos, n. d. [Portuguese]

Diner, Hasia. *A Time for Gathering: The Second Migration, 1820–1880.* Baltimore: Johns Hopkins UP, 1992.

Döblin, Alfred. *Briefe* [II]. Eds. Walter Muschg, Heinz Graber. Düsseldorf and Zürich: Walter-Verlag, 2001. [German]

———. "Ziel und Charakter der Freiland–Bewegung." Trans. Lee Chadeayne. In Horch. *Schriften zu jüdischen Fragen*. Solothurn: Walter-Verlag, 1995. pp. 312–322. [German]

———. *Briefe* [I]. Ed. Walter Muschg and Heinz Graber. Olten: Walter-Verlag, 1970. [German]

———. "Jews Renew Yourselves." *Menorah Journal* XXIII.1 (Apr.–June 1935): 80–87.

———. "I Am Not a Hitler Jew!" (June 1935) in Horch. *Schriften zu jüdischen Fragen*. Solothurn: Walter-Verlag, 1995. pp. 308–311.

———. "Informations–Bulletin No. 1" (April 1935) in *Schriften zu jüdischen Fragen*. Solothurn: Walter-Verlag, 1995. pp. 370–373.

———. "Teritorialism un Naye–Yehuda." Trans. Yankl Salant. *Frayland* 3–4 (Nov.–Dec. 1934): 14–25. [Yiddish]

———. "Gzar–Din un Veg fun di Merav Yidn." Trans. Yankl Salant. *Frayland* 1–2. (Sept.–Oct. 1934): 42–49.[Yiddish]

———. "Tkhiya Yehudit (part 8)." *Turim* 8 Feb. 1934. pp. 5–6. [Hebrew]

———. "l'Korei Ivrit." *Turim* 8 Dec. 1933. p. 1. [Hebrew]

———. *Journey to Poland*. Trans. Joachim Neugroschel. New York: Paragon, 1991 [1926].

"Does Peru Hold Out Hope of Jewish Settlement?: Dr. Julius Brutzkus Urges Careful Investigation." Jewish Telegraphic Agency. 19 Feb. 1931.

Doron, Yehoyakim. *Haguto haTzionit Shel Natan Birnbaum*. Jerusalem: haSifriyah haTzionit, 1988. [Hebrew]

"Dr. Solomon Dyk." *New York Times* 25 May 1944. p. 21.

Edelman, Udi, Eyal Danon, and Ran Kasmy–Ilan. "Where To?" [exhibition catalogue]. Trans. Naveh Frumer. Holon: Israeli Center for Digital Art, 2012. pp. 13–14.

Ellis, Vivienne Rae. *Trucanini: Queen or Traitor*. Canberra: Australian Institute of Aboriginal Studies, 1981.

"Emergency Parley of World Refugee Body Convoked as London Ponders Plan to Settle Guiana." Jewish Telegraphic Agency. 17 Nov. 1938. n.p.

Enav, Moshe (Weintraub). *b'Sa'arat haHayim: Dr. Yitzkhak Nakhman Steinberg, l'Dmuto u'l'Derekh Hayav*. Tel Aviv: Machberet L'sifrut, 1967. [Hebrew]

"Ende einer Illusion." *Judische Rundschau* 31 Dec. 1937. p. 2. [German]

"England." *Koblenzer Anzeiger* No. 27. 2 July 1819. p. 1. [German]

"Enthusiastic Reception for Franz Oppenheimer." *Maccabaean* XXIV.3 (Mar. 1914): 88.

"Erets Jisraël." *Teroenga* (Dec. 1947): 8. [Dutch]

Eskoli-Wagman, Hava. "Tokhniyot Teritorialiyot l'Fitron Metzukat haPlitim haYehudi'im 1938–1943." *Iyunim* 23 (2013): 488–522. [Hebrew]

"The FAO and the Commission's Report." *Freeland* IV.2 (May/June 1948): 16–17.

Farrar, Elizabeth W. R. [Mrs. John]. *Recollection of Seventy Years*. Boston: Ticknor and Fields, 1865.

Feingold, Henry. "Roosevelt and the Resettlement Question." In *The Nazi Holocaust: Bystanders to the Holocaust*. Vol. 1. Ed. Michael Marrus. Westport, CT: Meckler, 1989. pp. 271–329.

The First Report of the American Society for Meliorating the Condition of the Jews. New York: 1823.

"For a Jewish 'Reservation.'" *New York Times* 8 Feb. 1939. p. 17.

Fraenkel, Josef. "Mathias Acher's Fight for the 'Crown of Zion.'" *Jewish Social Studies* 16 (1954): 115–134.

"Freeland." *Saturday Review* 10 Oct. 1891. pp. 423–424.

Freeland Youth Group. "Objective Freeland: The Cross Examination of a Territorialist." New York: Freeland League, 1947.

Friedman, Philip. "The Lublin Reservation and the Madagascar Plan: Two Aspects of Nazi Jewish Policy During the Second World War." In *Roads to Extinction: Essays on the Holocaust*. Ed. Ada June Friedman. Philadelphia: Jewish Publication Society, 1980 [1953]. pp. 34–58.

Friedman, Saul S. *Jews and the American Slave Trade*. New Brunswick, NJ: Transaction, 1998.

Fromm, Erich. "Dr. I. N. Steinberg." *Freeland* X.1 (Jan.–Mar. 1957): 4.

Fruchtbaum, Lesser. M. "Where Else Could Jews Have Gone?" *Issues: A Publication of the American Council for Judaism* 21–22 (1967): 85–94.

———. "Tribute to Dr. I.N. Steinberg." *Freeland* X.1 (Jan–Mar. 1957): 2–3.

———. "Ecuador (Part II)." *Freeland* VIII.11 (June/July 1955): 2–4.

———. "Ecuador (Part I)." *Freeland* VIII.10 (Apr./May 1955): 3–5.

———. "Nicaragua." *Freeland* VII.3 (May/June 1953): 9–10.

———. "Chile—Land for Colonization." *Freeland* VII.1 (Jan./Feb. 1953): 8–9.

———. "Costa Rica." *Freeland* VI.5 (June–Aug. 1952): 9–11.

———. "Uruguay." *Freeland* VI.4 (April/May 1952): 4–5.

Gans, Eduard, Moses Moser, and Leopold Zunz. "The Society for the Culture and Science of the Jews: Statutes." Trans. J. Hessing and P. Mendes-Flohr. In *The Jew in the Modern World: A Documentary History*. Ed. P. Mendes-Flohr and J. Reinharz. New York: Oxford UP, 1995 [1822]. pp. 213–214.

Gauthier, Robert. "Nous sommes prêts à toutes les collaborations pacifiques dans nos colonies." *Le Petit Parisien* 11 May 1937. p. 3. [French]

Gelber, Natan. "Mordecai Emanuel Noah." *Sura* 3 (1957–1958): 379–413. [Hebrew]

Gerke, P. J. "Preface." *Health of White Settlers in Surinam*. Amsterdam: Colonial Institute at Amsterdam, 1940.

Gettler, Leon. *An Unpromised Land*. South Fremantle, Australia: Fremantle Arts Centre Press, 1993.

Gibbons, A. St. Hill. "British East African Plateau and its Economic Conditions." *Geographical Journal* XXVII (Jan.–June, 1906): 242–259.

Goldberg, Isaac. *Major Noah: American-Jewish Pioneer*. Whitefish, MT: Kessinger Publishing, 2005. [1936]

———. "Mr. Noah, American." *Menorah Journal* XXIV.3 (Oct.–Dec. 1936): 276–293.

Goldman, Shalom. *God's Sacred Tongue: Hebrew & the American Imagination.* Chapel Hill, NC: University of North Carolina Press, 2004.

Goldstein, Yossi. *Ussishkin—Biographia.* Vol. I. Jerusalem: Magnes Press, 1999. [Hebrew]

Goodman, Paul. *Growing Up Absurd: Problems of Youth in the Organized System.* New York: Random House, 1960.

Goodman, Saul. "On the Kimberley Project" [letter to the editor]. *Jewish Frontier* XII.5 (123/May 1945): 27–28.

Gorski, John. "Finance Bank for Surinam." *Freeland* V.1 (Jan./Feb. 1949): 7–8.

"Government Offers Jews Colonial Territory." *American Hebrew* 29 Jan. 1937. p. 822.

Graber, Heinz. "Editor's Introduction." *Journey to Poland.* Alfred Döblin. Trans. Joachim Neugroschel. New York: Paragon, 1991.

Grégoire, Henri. *Enquiry Concerning the Intellectual and Moral Faculties, and Literature of Negroes.* Trans. David Baillie Warden. Brooklyn, NY: Thomas Kirk, 1810.

Gregory, J. W. *Report on the Work of the Commission Sent Out by the Jewish Territorial Organization Under the Auspices of the Portuguese Government to Examine the Territory Proposed for the Purpose of a Jewish Settlement in Angola.* London: ITO Offices, 1913.

Grehan, John. *The Forgotten Invasion.* Storrington, UK: Historic Military Press, 2007.

"haExpeditzia l'Uganda." *haZfira* 18. Dec. 1904. p. 1. [Hebrew]

Hague, William. *William Wilberforce: The Life of the Great Anti-Slave Trade Campaigner.* New York: Harcourt, 2007.

"The Halfway House to Palestine." *African Standard* (Nairobi) 26 Sept. 1903. p. 4.

"haPratim Al Davar Hatza'at Angola b'Parliament haPortugali." *haZman* 25 June 1912. p. 1. [Hebrew]

Hardinge, Arthur H. *A Diplomatist in the East.* London: Jonathan Cape Ltd., 1928.

Hardy, Ronald. *The Iron Snake.* New York: Putnam's, 1965.

"Hartza'at haTayara l'Mizrakh Africa." *Hashkafa* 30 June 1905. p. 2. [Hebrew]

Hartsinck, Jan Jacob. *Beschryving van Guyane of de Wilde Kust in Zuid–America.* Amsterdam: 1770. [Dutch]

"haTayara haTzionit." *Hashkafa* 13 Jan. 1905. p. 1. [Hebrew]

Hauptman, Laurence. *Conspiracy of Interests: Iroquois Dispossession and the Rise of New York State.* Syracuse, NY: Syracuse UP, 1999.

"haVe'ida haTeritoriali'im b'Vienna." *haZfira* 1 July 1912. p. 1–2. [Hebrew]

"haVe'ida Shel haTeritoriali'im b'Vienna." *haZfira* 30 June 1912. p. 2. [Hebrew]

"Haven For Homeless Is Offered By Dutch." *New York Times* 25 Apr. 1947. p. 6.

Heldring, Alexander. *Het Saramacca Project: Een Plan Van Joodse Kolonisatie in Suriname.* Hilversum: Uitgeverij Verloren, 2011. [Dutch]

———. "The Saramacca Project." *Zeek: A Jewish Journal of Thought and Culture* 1 Apr. 2009. http://www.jewcy.com/post/saramacca_project.

"Helsingfors Conference." Trans. R. Weiss. In *The Jew in the Modern World: A Documentary History.* Eds. Paul Mendes-Flohr and Jehuda Reinharz. New York: Oxford UP, 1995. p. 555.

Herman, N. "Hatzarat Moutet." *Davar* 1 Mar. 1937. p. 2. [Hebrew]

Hertzka, Theodor. *Freeland: A Social Anticipation.* Trans. Arthur Ransom. Charleston, SC: Bibliobazaar, 2006.

———. *Freiland: Ein Sociales Zukunftsbild.* Leipzig: Von Dunder & Humboldt. 1890. [German]

Herzl, Theodor. *The Complete Diaries of Theodor Herzl.* Vols. I–V. Ed. Raphael Patai. Trans. Harry Zohn. New York: Herzl Press and Thomas Yoseloff, 1960 [1895–1904].

———. "Opening Address at the Sixth Zionist Congress." *Zionist Writings: Essays and Addresses.* Vol. II. Trans. Harry Zohn. New York: Herzl Press, 1975 [1903]. pp. 221–230.

———. *Old New Land (Altneuland).* Trans. Lotta Levensohn. Minneapolis: Filiquarian Publishing, 2007 [1902].

———. "The Hunt in Bohemia." In *Zionist Writings: Essays and Addresses.* Vol. I. Trans. Harry Zohn. New York: Herzl Press, 1973 [1897]. pp. 169–175.

———. "Programm." *Die Welt* Vol. 1, No. 1. 4 June 1897. p. 1.

———. *The Jewish State: An Attempt at a Modern Solution of the Jewish Question.* Trans. Sylvie D'Avigdor. London: Central Office of the Zionist Organisation, 1934 [1896].

"Het Bezoek van de delegatie van de Freeland League." Trans. Daniel Bugel-Shunra. *Teroenga* May 1947: 1–3. [Dutch]

Hevesi, Eugene. "Hitler's Plan for Madagascar." *Contemporary Jewish Record* (Aug. 1941): 6.

Heyman, Michael, Ed. *The Uganda Controversy.* Vol. II. Jerusalem: Hassifriya Haziyonit Publishing House, 1977.

———. "Herzl v'Tzioney Rusia: Makhloket v'Haskama." *haTsiyonut* 3 (1973): 56–99. [Hebrew]

———. *The Uganda Controversy.* Vol. I. Jerusalem: Israel Universities Press, 1970.

"Hiker's Tragic End." *The Mercury* (Hobart) 12 Sept. 1942. p.2.

"Hitnakshut b'Nefesh Max Nordau." *haZman* 22 Dec. 1903. p. 7. [Hebrew]

Holroyd, J. P. "Parker, Frank Critchley (1862 – 1944)." In *Australian Dictionary of Biography.* Volume 11. Melbourne: Melbourne UP, 1988.

Horch, Hans Otto, Ed. *Schriften zu jüdischen Fragen.* Solothurn: Walter-Verlag, 1995. [German]

Hughes, Robert. *The Fatal Shore.* New York: Knopf, 1987.

Huguet, Louis. "Alfred Döblin et le Judaisme." Annales de la Universite d'Abidjan. Série D, V. 9. (1976): pp. 47–115. [French]

"Indignation in Nairobi." *African Standard* (Nairobi) 5 Sept. 1903. p. 5.

Infield, Henrik F. "The Role of Cooperation in the Surinam Settlement." *Freeland* V..1 (Jan./ Feb. 1949): 6–7.

"Isaac Steinberg, a Jewish Leader." *New York Times* 3 Jan. 1957. p.32.

"Is it to be Jewganda?" *African Standard* (Nairobi) 17 Oct. 1903. p. 4.

"Israel Honours Elder for Defying Nazis." *Australian* 31 July 2010. p. 4.

"The Ito Angola Scheme." *Jewish Chronicle* (London) 12 Sept. 1913. pg. 33.

"Ito Conference Speech." *Jewish Chronicle* (London) 5 July 1912. pp. 21–22.

"ITOism: Brilliant Address by Mr. Israel Zangwill." *Jewish Chronicle* (London) 4 Apr. 1913. pp. 23–26.

Jabotinsky, Vladimir. *The Jewish War Front*. Westport, CT: Greenwood Press, 1975 [1940].

Jankowsky, Oscar. *The Jews and Minority Rights (1898–1919)*. New York: Columbia UP, 1933.

Jansen, Hans. *Het Madagascarplan: de voorgenomen deportatie van Europese joden naar Madagascar*. Den Haag: SDU, 1996. [Dutch and English]

Jeitteles, Judah. "Hadashim m'Karov Ba'oo." *Bikkure haIttim* (1826): 45–49. [Hebrew]

Jelavich, Peter. *Berlin Alexanderplatz: Radio, Film, and the Death of Weimar Culture*. Berkeley, CA: UC Press, 2006.

Jenkins, Shirley. "Refugee Settlement in Australia." *Far Eastern Survey* 13.13 (28 June 1944): 120–122.

Jennings, Eric T. "Writing Madagascar Back into the Madagascar Plan." *Holocaust and Genocide Studies* 21.2 (Fall 2007): 188–217.

Jerome, Fred, Ed. *Einstein on Israel and Zionism: His Provocative Ideas about the Middle East*. New York: St. Martin's: New York, 2009.

"Jewganda." *African Standard* (Nairobi) 17 Oct. 1903. p. 8.

"Jewganda: The Proposed Jewish Settlement in East Africa" [letter from Sir Harry Johnston to Leopold Greenberg]. *African Standard* (Nairobi) 12 Nov. 1904. p. 4.

Jewish Colonial Trust, Limited., Memorandum and Articles of Association. London: Chambers & Sons, Ltd. 20 March 1898.

"Jewish Territorial Organisation/Fourth Anniversary." *Jewish Chronicle* (London) 14 May 1909. pp. 14–17.

"The Jews." *North–Carolina Gazette* 4 Feb. 1820. p. 1.

"Jews Settle in North: Polish Writer's Idea." *Courier-Mail* (Brisbane) 18 Jan. 1934. p. 17.

"Jews Would Shift Million Families." *New York Times* 30 Nov. 1938. p. 15.

John, Angela. "A New Slavery?" *History Today* 52.6 (June 2002): 34–35.

Johnston, Alex. *The Life and Letters of Sir Harry Johnston*. New York: Jonathan Cape and Harrison Smith, 1929.

Johnston, Harry. "The Zionists and East Africa." *Times* (London) 1 Sept. 1903. p. 4.

———. *The Uganda Protectorate*. Vol. I. New York: Dodd, Mead, 1904 [1902].

"Journey of the Rev. Messrs. Way, Cox, and Solomon." *Missionary Register* (Dec. 1817): 507–508.

Kagedan, Allan Laine. *Soviet Zion: The Quest for a Russian Jewish Homeland*. New York: St. Martin's, 1994.

Kaniel, Yehoshua. "Memadei haYeridah min haAretz b'Tkufat haAliyah haRishona v'haShniyah (1882–1914)." *Katedra* 73 (Sept. 1994): 115–138. [Hebrew]

Karp, Abraham. *Mordecai Manuel Noah: The First American Jew*. New York: Yeshiva University Museum, 1987.

Katz, Jacob. "l'Birur haMusag 'Mivasrei haTzionut.'" *Leumiut Yehudit: Masot u'Mekhkarim*. Jerusalem: HaSifriah HaTzionit, 1979. [Hebrew]

———. *Leumiut Yehudit: Masot u'Mekhkarim*. Jerusalem: HaSifriah HaTzionit, 1979. [Hebrew]

———. "A State Within a State: The History of an Anti–Semitic Slogan." *Proceedings of the Israel Academy of Sciences and Humanities* IV.3 (1969): 1–30.

Keane, Augustus Henry. *The Gold of Ophir: Whence Brought and by Whom?* London: Edward Stanford, 1901.

Klausner, Yosef. *Shaul Tchernichovsky: haAdam v'haMeshorer*. Jerusalem: Hebrew University Press, 1947. [Hebrew]

———. *Menahem Ussischkin: His Life and Work*. New York: Scopus Publishing, 1942.

Kleinman, Moshe. "haKongress haUgandi." *haZman* 3 Aug. 1905. pp. 1–2. [Hebrew]

Kohavi, Arik. "The Zionist Executive and the Distress of the Jews in Germany and Austria, up to the Outbreak of World War II." In *Studies on the Holocaust Period*. Vol. III. Ed. Asher Cohen, Zvi Shner, and Leni Yahil. Tel Aviv: Hakibbutz Hameuchad, 1984. pp. 97–122. [Hebrew]

Kohler, Max. *Jewish Rights at the Congresses of Vienna (1814–15) and Aix–La–Chapelle (1818)*. New York: American Jewish Committee, 1918.

———. "Some Early American Zionist Projects." *American Jewish Historical Society Publications* 8 (1900): 75–118.

Kohn, S. Joshua. "Mordecai Manuel Noah's Ararat Project and the Missionaries." *American Jewish Historical Quarterly* 55.2 (Dec. 1965): 162–195.

Kruk, Josef. *Takhat Diglan Shel Shalosh Mahapekhot: Rusim, Polanim, Yehudim*. Vol. II. Trans. M. Halamish and Moshe Hurvitz. Tel Aviv: Mahbarot l'sifrut, 1970. [Hebrew]

Kuhn, Jr., Ferdinand. "Tanganyika is Open." *New York Times* 22 Nov. 1938. pp. 1, 9.

———. "World Searched for Havens." *New York Times* 20 Nov. 1938. p. 68.

———. "Quick Action Seen." *New York Times* 17 Nov. 1938. pp. 1, 10.

———. "Would Aid 700,000." *New York Times* 16 Nov. 1938. p. 1.

"La Mabelleion: Modern by Circumstance." *Australian Home Beautiful* 1 Jan. 1934. pp. 24–25.

Langhorne, Richard. "Anglo–German Negotiations Concerning the Future of the Portuguese Colonies, 1911–1914." *Historical Journal* 16.2 (June 1973): 361–387.

Law Journal Reports for the Year 1908: Cases Decided in the Chancery Division of the High Court of Justice. Vol. LXXVII. London: Law Journal Reports, 1908.

Leake, Bernard. *The Life and Work of Professor J. W. Gregory FRS: Geologist, Writer, and Explorer*. London: Geological Society, 2011.

"Left–Handed Zionism." *Freeland* IV.2 (May/June 1948): 8–10.

Leftwich, Joseph. *Israel Zangwill*. New York: Thomas Yoseloff, 1957.

Lehrer, Erica. "Repopulating Jewish Poland—In Wood." *Polin: Studies in Polish Jewry* 16 (2003): 335–355.

Lepecki, Mieczysław. *Madagaskar; kraj, ludzie, kolonizacja*. Warsaw: Roj, 1938. [Polish/French]

Lewin, Isaac. "Agudism." In *Struggle for Tomorrow: Modern Political Ideologies of the Jewish People*. Ed. Basil Vlavianos and Feliks Gross. New York: Arts, Inc., 1954. pp. 200–206.

Lewis, Donald. *The Origins of Christian Zionism: Lord Shaftesbury and Evangelical Support for a Jewish Homeland.* Cambridge: Cambridge UP, 2010.

Lichnowsky, Karl Max. "My Mission to London 1912–1914." New York: George Doran Company, 1918.

"The Life Work of Franz Oppenheimer." *Maccabaean* XXIV.1 (Jan. 1914): 12–15.

Lipsky, Abram. "Sixth International Zionist Congress." *Menorah* XXXV: 199–213.

Loewe, Heinrich. "Ararat." *Die Welt* No. 5. 31 Jan. 1902. pp. 8–10. [German]

Luz, Ehud. *Parallels Meet: Religion and Nationalism in the Early Zionist Movement (1882–1904).* Trans. Lenn Schramm. Philadelphia: Jewish Publication Society, 1988.

"The Madagascar Scheme." *Jewish Chronicle* (London) 23 July 1937. p. 18.

"Madagascar Scheme Announced." *Jewish Chronicle* (London) 31 Dec. 1937. p. 23.

Malachi, A. R. "Mkorot Ivri'im l'Ararat shel Mordecai Emanuel Noah." *Bitsaron* 41 (Dec. 1959): 78–89. [Hebrew]

Mann, Barbara. *Space and Place in Jewish Studies.* New Brunswick, NJ: Rutgers UP, 2012.

Mann, Thomas. "I Believe in Freeland." *Freeland* V.1 (Jan./Feb. 1949): 8.

———. "Letter to Steinberg." 18 Sept. 1945. In *Freeland* II.1 (Feb. 1946): 19.

Maran, René. *Afrique Équatoriale: française: terres et races d'avenir.* Paris: L'Imprimerie de Vaugirard, 1937. [French]

Margolis, Max L. "The Year 5665." *American Jewish Year Book 5666.* Ed. Cyrus Adler and Henrietta Szold. Philadelphia: Jewish Publication Society, 1905. pp. 229–271.

Marinbach, Bernard. *Galveston: Ellis Island of the West.* Albany: State University of New York Press, 1983.

Marmor, David Yitzhak. "haMasa uMatan haDiplomati shel haHistadrut haTeritorialistit haYehudit u'Misibot Kishlono" [part II]. *Tsiyon* 11.4 (Summer 1946): 173–208. [Hebrew]

———. "haMasa uMatan haDiplomati shel haHistadrut haTeritorialistit haYehudit u'Misibot Kishlono" [part I]. *Tsiyon* 11.1–3. (Fall 1945–Spring 1946): 109–140. [Hebrew]

Marrus, Michael R., and Robert O. Paxton. *Vichy France and the Jews.* New York: Basic Books, 1981.

Marsh, Peter T. *Joseph Chamberlain: Entrepreneur in Politics.* New Haven, CT: Yale UP, 1994.

Martin, Charles J. "Report Upon the Highlands of the Province of Benguella from the Point of View of the Public Health." *Report on the Work of the Commission* [Angola]. J. W. Gregory. London: ITO Offices, 1913. pp. 30–35.

Mazor, Michel. *The Vanished City.* Trans. David Jacobson. New York: Marsilio, 1993.

McElligott, Anthony. *The German Urban Experience 1900–1945: Modernity and Crisis.* New York: Routledge, 2001.

Medina, João, and Joel Barromi. "The Jewish Colonization Project in Angola." *Studies in Zionism* 12.1 (1991): 1–16.

Melech Ravitch. "Aborigines." In *haMnudim al haDalim: Mivkhar Shirim m'Yiddish.* Ed. Y. Har, E. D. Shapir, Y. Bergner, and O. Bergner. Tel Aviv: Keshev, 2007. pp. 93–96. [Hebrew]

——. *Sefer haMa'asiyot Shel Hayai*. Trans. Moshe Yungman. Tel Aviv: haHevrah haAmerikait-Yisraelit l'Molut, 1976. [Hebrew]

——, Ed. *I. N. Steinberg Gedenk-Bukh*. New York: I. N. Steinberg Book Committee, 1960. [Yiddish]

——. "Through Central-Australia to the Northern Territory." In *Australian Jewish Almanac*. Ed. Melech Ravitch. Melbourne: York Press, 1937. pp. 215–232. [Yiddish]

——. "Aboridgin—Untergang-Balad." *Kantinentn un Okeanen*. Warsaw: Literarisher-Bleter, 1937. pp. 175–178. [Yiddish]

——. *Iber Oystralye*. Ed. M. Teichman. Warsaw: Kinder-Frajnd, 1937. [Yiddish]. Unpublished translation by Vincent Homolka.

——. "An Idea oder an Ideal, a Teritorye oder Teritoryes." *Frayland* 3–4 (Nov.–Dec.1934): 55–61. [Yiddish]

"Memorandum of The Freeland League to The Delegations at San Francisco (May 1945)." *Freeland* 1.4. (June 1945): 5–8.

"Memorandum Prepared by the Freeland League for Jewish Territorial Colonisation for the Consideration of the Delegates at the International Refugees Conference at Evian." London: Freeland League, 1938.

Menes, Abraham. "The *Am Oylom* Movement." *YIVO Annual of Jewish Social Science* 4 (1949): 9–33.

Metcalf, Bill. "Utopian Communal Experiments in Tasmania: a litany of failure?" *Communal Societies* 28.1 (2008): 1–26.

Meyer, Michael. *The Origins of the Modern Jew: Jewish Identity and European Culture in Germany, 1749–1824*. Detroit: Wayne State UP, 1967.

"More Jewganda Jewdrops." *African Standard* (Nairobi) 17 Oct. 1903. p.2.

Morgan, Ted. *A Covert Life: Jay Lovestone—Communist, Anti-Communist, Spymaster*. New York: Random House, 1999.

Morris, Helen. "Ida Silverman: Nobody's Puppet." *Rhode Island Jewish Historical Notes* 8.2 (Nov. 1980): 109–129.

"Mr. Chamberlain in the East-End." *Times* (London) 16 Dec. 1904, p.8.

"Mr. Zangwill in Town." *Jewish Exponent* (Philadelphia) 16 Oct. 1908. p. 2.

"Mr. Zangwill on the Future of Zionism." *Jewish Chronicle* (London) 14 July 1905. pp. 12–15.

Müller-Salget, Klaus. "Döblin and Judaism." In *A Companion to the Works of Alfred Döblin*. Ed. Roland Dollinger, Wulf Köpke, and Heidi T. Tewarson. Rochester, NY: Camden House, 2004.

Murray, Kevin. "The Promised Land." *Age—Saturday Review* (Melbourne) 24 Jan. 2004. p. 2.

Mussert, Anton Adriaan. *United States of Guiana—The Jewish National Home*. n.p. 1939.

Nahshon, Edna. "*The Melting Pot*: Introductory Essay." *From the Ghetto to the Melting Pot: Israel Zangwill's Jewish Plays*. Detroit: Wayne State UP, 2006. pp. 211–263.

Nascimento, J. Pereira do. *A Colonisação do planalto de Benguella*. Lisbon: J. Rodriques, 1912. [Portuguese]

Nasaw, David. *The Patriarch: The Remarkable Life and Turbulent Times of Joseph P. Kennedy*. New York: Penguin, 2012.

Nassy, David de Isaac Cohen, ed. *Historical Essay on the Colony of Surinam*. Trans. Simon Cohen. Ed. Jacob Marcus and Stanley Chyet. New York: Ktav, 1974.

NBD. "haCongress Shel ha'Teritoriali'im." *haZfira* 6 Aug. 1905. p. 2. [Hebrew]

———. "Hitnakshut b'Nefesh Nordau." 28 Dec. 1903. *haZfira* p. 3. [Hebrew]

Netanyahu, Benzion. "Israel Zangwill" [1938]. *The Founding Fathers of Zionism*. Noble, OK: Balfour Books, 2012. pp. 144–183.

"Nieuws van de Afdeling Suriname van de Freeland League." Trans. Daniel Bugel-Shunra. *Teroenga* Feb. 1948: 3. [Dutch]

Noah, Mordecai Manuel. "Address Delivered at the Hebrew Synagogue" [1849]. In *The Selected Writings of Mordecai Noah*. Ed. Michael Schuldiner and Daniel J. Kleinfeld. Westport, CT: Greenwood Press, 1999. pp. 149–159.

———. *Discourse on the Restoration of the Jews*. New York: Harper & Brothers, 1845.

———. *The Evidences of the American Indians Being the Descendants of the Lost Tribes of Israel*. New York: James Van Norden, 1837.

———. "Ararat Proclamation and Speech" [1825]. In *The Selected Writings of Mordecai Noah*. Ed. Michael Schuldiner and Daniel J. Kleinfeld. Westport, CT: Greenwood Press, 1999. pp. 105–124.

———. "Remarks." *The National Advocate* 1 Dec. 1820. p. 1.

———. "Mordecai M. Noah to J. Q. Adams, 1820" [docs. 311– 312]. In *The Jews of the United States 1790–1840: A Documentary History*. Vol. 3. Ed. Joseph Blau and Salo Baron. pp. 885–890. New York: Columbia UP, 1963.

———. "Grand Island." *National Advocate* 6 Mar. 1820. p. 2.

———. "Letter to the Editors." *Albany Daily Advertiser* 11 Feb. 1820. p. 2.

———. *Travels in England, France, Spain, and the Barbary States*. New York: Kirk & Mercein, 1819.

———. *She Would Be a Soldier, or The Plains of Chippewa; an Historical Drama, in Three Acts* [1819]. In *The Selected Writings of Mordecai Noah*. Ed. Michael Schuldiner and Daniel J. Kleinfeld. Westport, CT: Greenwood Press, 1999. pp. 25–63.

———. *Discourse Delivered at the Consecration*. New York: C. S. Van Winkle, 1818.

———. *Correspondence and Documents Relative to the Attempt to Negotiate for the Release of the American Captives at Algiers*. Washington City: n.p., 1816.

Nordau, Max. *Max Nordau to His People: A Summons and a Challenge*. New York: Scopus Publishing Company, 1941.

Olivier, Marcel. "Madagascar—Terre D'Asile?" *L'Illustration* 19 Feb. 1938. pp. 197–198. [French]

Olson, Jess. *Nathan Birnbaum and Jewish Modernity: Architect of Zionism, Yiddishism, and Orthodoxy*. Palo Alto, CA: Stanford UP, 2013.

Oppenheim, Samuel. "Notes." *American Jewish Historical Society Publications* 20 (1911): 147–149.

Oppenheimer, Franz. *Merchavia: A Jewish Co-operative Settlement in Palestine*. New York: Jewish National Fund, 1914.

Orr, J. W. *Pictorial Guide to the Falls of Niagara*. Buffalo: Salisbury and Clapp, 1842.

Parker, Critchley. "An Australian in Lapland." *Mercury Week-End Magazine* (Hobart) 9 Dec. 1939. p. 6.

———. "Archaeology." *IF* (Dec. 1929): 17–18.

Parker, Frank Critchley. *Tasmania: Jewel of the Commonwealth*. Hobart: Industrial Australian and Mining Standard, 1937.

Parkes, James. "Lewis Way and His Times." *Transactions—The Jewish Historical Society of England* 20 (1959–1961): 189–201.

"Paul Cuffee." *National Advocate* 22, 25 Oct. 1817. p. 2.

Penslar, Derek. *Zionism and Technocracy: The Engineering of Jewish Settlement in Palestine, 1870–1918*. Bloomington: Indiana UP, 1991.

Peters, Carl. *The Eldorado of the Ancients*. New York: E. P. Dutton, 1902.

Pinsker, Leo. *Auto-Emancipation*. New York: Masada, 1935.

Piotrowski, M. "Zycie Codzienne Na Madagaskarze." Trans. Barbara Milewski. *Szpilki* No. 5. Vol. IV. 30 January 1938. n.p. [Polish]

Plomley, N. J. B., ed. *Friendly Mission: The Tasmanian Journals and Papers of George Augustus Robinson 1829–1834*. Launceston and Hobart: Queen Victoria Museum and Art Gallery and Quintus Publishing, 2008.

Poe, Edgar Allan. "Restoration of the Jews." *Evening Mirror* (New York) 16 Jan. 1845. p. 2.

"Poles Continue Talks." *New York Times* 9 Dec. 1937. p.12.

Popkin, Richard. "Mordecai Noah, the Abbé Grégoire and the Paris Sanhedrin." *Modern Judaism* 2.2 (May 1982): 131–148.

Preliminary Report on the Possibilities of Jewish Colonization in Surinam. Paramaribo: 1948.

"Prepatory Arrangements" [appendix]. In Cadwallader Colden. *Memoir Prepared at the Request of the Committee of the Common Council of the City of New York and Presented to the Mayor of the City at the Celebration of the Completion of the New York Canals*. New York: Corporation of New York, 1825. pp. 125–126.

"Proposed Havens Rich in Resources." *New York Times* 22 Nov. 1938. p. 9.

"The Proposed Jewish Settlement in East Africa." *Times* (London) 7 Dec. 1904. p. 11.

Quinalt, Roland. "John Bright and Joseph Chamberlain." *Historical Journal* 28.3 (Sept. 1985): 623–646.

Rabinovich, Itamar and Jehuda Reinharz, eds. *Israel in the Middle East: Documents and Readings on Society, Politics, and Foreign Relations, Pre-1948 to the Present*. Waltham, MA: Brandeis UP, 2008.

Rabinovitch, Simon. "Diaspora, Nation, and Messiah: An Introductory Essay." In *Jews and Diaspora Nationalism: Writings on Jewish Peoplehood in Europe and the United States*. Ed. Simon Rabinovitch. Waltham, MA: Brandeis UP, 2012. pp. xv–xxxi.

Rabinowicz, Oskar K. "New Light on the East Africa Scheme." In *The Rebirth of Israel: A Memorial Tribute to Paul Goodman*. Ed. Israel Cohen. Westport, CT: Hyperion Press, 1976. pp. 77–97.

Rademacher, Franz. "The Madagascar Plan: 3 July 1940." In *Documents on the Holocaust: selected sources on the destruction of the Jews of Germany and Austria, Poland,*

and the Soviet Union. Eds. Yitzhak Arad, Israel Gutman, and Abraham Margaliot. Lincoln: University of Nebraska Press, 1999. pp. 216–218.

Raisin, Max. *Mordecai Manuel Noah.* Warsaw: Achiasaf Society, 1905. [Hebrew]

Rapaport, I. "I. N. Steinberg." *Freeland* X.1 (Jan.–Mar. 1957): 15.

Raptschinsky, Boris. "The Guianas Are the Territory." *Freeland* II.5 (Sept./Oct. 1946): 5–7, 19.

"Realist Attitude to the Jewish Problem." *Jewish Chronicle* (London) 26 July 1935. p. 42.

"Re–assemblage of the Jews." *Evening Post* (New York) 12 Jan. 1826. p. 2.

Reissner, Hanns. "'Ganstown, U.S.A.—A German-Jewish Dream.'" *American Jewish Archives* V.14 (April 1962): 20–31.

Report of the British Guiana Refugee Commission to the Advisory Committee on Political Refugees appointed by the President of the United States of America. London: H. M. Stationery Office, 1939.

Report on the Work of the Commission Sent Out to Examine the Territory Offered by H.M. Government to the Zionist Organization for the Purposes of a Jewish Settlement in British East Africa. London: Wertheimer, Lea & Co., 1905.

R. E. S. "Refugees as Pioneers." *Industrial Australian and Mining Standard* 15 March 1940. pp. 73–74.

"Resolutions Adopted by Conference (1948)." *Freeland* V.1 (Jan./Feb. 1949): 10.

"Resolutions of the First Freeland Conference of the D.P. Camps Held in Upper-Austria on Oct. 5th 1947." *Freeland* III.3 (Nov./Dec. 1947): 2.

"Return of Major Gibbons from East Africa." *Times* (London). 31 Mar. 1905. p. 11.

Rey, Marie-Pierre. *Alexander I: The Tsar Who Defeated Napoleon.* Trans. Susan Emanuel. DeKalb, IL: Northern Illinois UP, 2012.

R—n, M. Printed under correspondence "Hitnakshut b'Nefesh Nordau." *haZfirah* 23 Dec. 1903. p. 2.

Rochelson, Meri–Jane. *A Jew in the Public Arena: The Career of Israel Zangwill.* Detroit: Wayne State UP, 2008.

Rock, Howard B., and Deborah Dash Moore, eds. *Haven of Liberty: New York Jews in the New World 1654–1865.* New York: NYU Press, 2012.

Rohrbacher, Stefan. "The 'Hep Hep' Riots of 1819: Anti–Jewish Ideology, Agitation, and Violence." *Exclusionary Violence: Antisemitic Riots in Modern German History.* Ed. C. Hoffmann, W. Bergmann, and H. Walser-Smith. Ann Arbor: University of Michigan Press, 2002. pp. 23–42.

"A Romance That May Become a Reality." *Spectator* 5 July 1845. p. 638.

Roos. J. S. "Additional Notes on the History of the Jews in Surinam." *Publications of the American Jewish Historical Society* 13 (1905): 127–136.

Rosenthal, Leonard. *The Pearl Hunter: An Autobiography.* Trans. Herma Briffault. New York: Henry Schuman, 1952.

Rubinstein, Hilary L. "Greenberg, Leopold Jacob (1861–1931)." *Oxford Dictionary of National Biography.* Oxford University Press, Sept. 2004. http://0www.oxforddnb. com.bianca.penlib.du.edu/view/article/70402.

———. "Critchley Parker (1911–42): Australian Martyr for Jewish Refugees." *Journal of the Australian Jewish Historical Society* XI.1 (1990): 56–67.

"Rumanian Freeland Resolutions (March 28–29)." *Freeland* IV.2 (May/June 1948): 2.

"Sale of Grand Island." Reprinted in *Daily National Intelligencer*. 13 June 1825. p. 2.

Salomone, Sophie Romeuf. "Le Pouvoir Colonial et Les Communautes Etrangeres a Madagascar 1896–1939." Thesis. Univ. de Lille III, 1990. [French]

Saposnik, Arieh Bruce. *Becoming Hebrew: The Creation of a Jewish National Culture in Ottoman Palestine*. New York: Oxford UP, 2008.

Sarna, Jonathan. *Jacksonian Jew: The Two Worlds of Mordecai Noah*. New York: Holmes & Meier, 1981.

Satre, Lowell. *Chocolate On Trial: Slavery, Politics, and the Ethics of Business*. Athens: Ohio UP, 2005.

Schama, Simon. *Landscape and Memory*. New York: Vintage Books, 1996.

Schappes, Morris, ed. *A Documentary History of the Jews in the United States 1654–1875*. New York: Schocken Books, 1971.

Schechtman, Joseph. *The Life and Times of Vladimir Jabotinsky: Fighter and Prophet: The Last Years*. New York: Eshel Books, 1986.

———. *Rebel and Statesman: The Vladimir Jabotinsky Story—the Early Years*. New York: Thomas Yoseloff, 1956.

Schniederman, Sh. L. "Di Ufirung fun 'Mochnatschow' in Barcelona in Miten fun Birger–Krig." In *I. N. Steinberg Gedenk–Bukh*. Ed. Melech Ravtich. New York: I. N. Steinberg Book Committee, 1960. pp. 506–511. [Yiddish]

Seliger, M. "Fundamental and Operative Ideology: The Two Principal Dimensions of Political Argumentation." *Policy Sciences* 1.3 (Fall 1970): 325–338.

"Settlement Possibilities in French Colonies." *Jewish Chronicle* (London) 16 Apr. 1937. pp. 24–25.

"Settling the Refugees." *Times* (London) 3 Dec. 1938. p. 11.

Shafir, Gershon. "Zionist Immigration and Colonization in Palestine until 1948." In *Cambridge Survey of World Migration*. Ed. Robin Cohen. New York: Cambridge UP, 1995. pp. 405–409.

Shalev, Eran. "'Revive, Renew, and Reestablish': Mordecai Noah's Ararat and the Limits of Biblical Imagination in the Early American Republic." *American Jewish Archives Journal* 62.1 (2010): 1–20.

Sherman, A.J. *Island Refuge: Britain and Refugees from the Third Reich 1933–1939*. Berkeley: University of California Press, 1973.

Shimoni, Gideon. *The Zionist Ideology*. Hanover, NH: Brandeis UP, 1995.

Shneer, David. "Zionism without Zion: The Weakness of the Birobidzhan Idea." *Jews in Eastern Europe* 3.49 (2002): 5–30.

Sholem Aleichem. *The Further Adventures of Menachem–Mendl*. Trans. Aliza Shevrin. Syracuse, NY: Syracuse UP, 2001 [1913].

———. "Ugandaade" [1903]. *Why Do the Jews Need a Land of Their Own?* Trans. Joseph Leftwich and Mordecai S. Chertoff. New York: Herzl Press, 1984. pp. 154–159.

———. "Doctors in Consultation" [1903]. *Why Do the Jews Need a Land of Their Own?* Trans. Joseph Leftwich and Mordecai S. Chertoff. New York: Herzl Press, 1984. pp. 131–138.

"Sikha Im haProfessor Gregory b'Dvar Angola." *haZfira* 4 Aug. 1913. p. 3. [Hebrew]

"Sikha Im Zangwill, She'aylat Angola." *haZfira* 22 Aug. 1913. p. 2. [Hebrew]

Siegel, Ada. "Suriname Among the Nations." *Freeland* IX.1 (Jan.–Feb. 1956): 6.

Silver, Arlene F. "Ida Camelhor Silverman: The Early Years." *Rhode island Jewish Historical Notes* 13.2 (Nov. 2000): 272–284.

Silverman, Mrs. Archibald (Ida). "Letter to the Editor." *Jewish Forum* (Oct. 1956): 143.

———. "The Surinam Nightmare." *Canadian Jewish Chronicle* 7 May 1948.pp. 7, 14.

———. "What I Learned about Kimberley." *Jewish Frontier* XII.3 (121/Mar. 1945): 10–12.

Simon, Erasmus, and Bernard Jadowinsky. "Letter of Protest, 1825" [doc. 255]. In *The Jews of the United States 1790–1840: A Documentary History.* Vol. 3. Ed. Joseph Blau and Salo Baron. New York: Columbia UP, 1963. pp. 743–746.

Sinclair, Clive. "The Kimberley Fantasy: An Alternative Zion." *Wasafiri* 24.1 (Mar. 2009): 34–44.

Slousch, Nahum. "Jews and Judaism in Ancient Cyrenaica." *Report on the Work of the Commission Sent Out by the Jewish Territorial Organization Under the Auspices of the Governor-General of Tripoli to Examine the Territory Proposed for the Purpose of a Jewish Settlement in Cyrenaica.* J. W. Gregory. London: ITO Offices, 1909. pp. 51–52.

———. "haHitnakshut b'Nefesh Nordau." *haZfira* 25 Dec. 1903. p. 2. [Hebrew]

Smith, Anthony. *Chosen Peoples.* New York: Oxford UP, 2003.

———. *The Ethnic Origins of Nations.* New York: Basil Blackwell, 1987.

Smith, Neil. *American Empire: Roosevelt's Geographer and the Prelude to Globalization.* Berkeley: UC Press, 2004.

Sokolow, Nahum. *History of Zionism 1600–1918.* Vols. I and II. London: Longmans, Green and Col., 1919.

———. "Eretz Yisrael v'Angola." *haZfira* 25 July 1912. pp. 1–2. [Hebrew]

Srebrnik, Henry. *Dreams of Nationhood: American Jewish Communists and the Soviet Birobidzhan Project, 1924–1951.* Boston: Academic Studies Press, 2010.

———. *Jerusalem on the Amur: Birobidzhan and the Canadian Jewish Communist Movement, 1924–1951.* Montreal and Kingston: McGill-Queen's UP, 2008.

Stanley, Henry Morgan. *Through the Dark Continent.* New York: Harper and Brothers, 1879.

Stedman, John Gabriel. *Narrative, of a five years' expedition; against the revolted negroes of Surinam, in Guiana, on the wild coast of South America; from the year 1772, to 1777.* Vols. I and II. London: J. Johnson and J. Edwards, 1796.

Steinberg, Isaac N. *Australia—An Unpromised Land.* London: V. Gollancz, 1948.

———. "The Place of 'Freeland' in Jewish Life" [1948]. Trans. Yankl Salant. *Afn Shvel* (Summer 2011): 5–9.

———. "End the War!" *Freeland* II.6 (Nov.–Dec. 1946): 5–7; 14–15.

———. "The Three Roads." *Freeland* I.1 (Dec. 1944): 2–3.

———. "Jewish Colonisation Outside Palestine." *Jewish Chronicle* (London) 27 Jan. 1939. p. 22.

———. *Du host gezigt, Mochnatschow!* [1929]. Trans. Y. Rappaport. Ed. Melech Ravtich. New York: I. N. Steinberg Book Committee, 1960. pp. 451–505. [Yiddish]

———. (M. Lewadin). "The Thorny Path (*Der Dornenweg*)." Trans. Shulamith Charney. Unpublished mss. 1989 [1927].

Stenographisches Protokoll der Verhandlungen des VI Zionisten-Kongresses in Basel. Wien: Verlag des Vereins "Eretz Israel," 1903. [German]

Stenographisches Protokoll der Verhandlungen des VII Zionisten-Kongresses. Berlin: Juedischer Verlag, 1905. [German]

Stirling, A. M. W. *The Ways of Yesterday: Being the Chronicles of the Way Family from 1307–1885.* London: Thornton Butterworth, 1930.

Stone, William L. "Narrative of the Festivities Observed in Honour of the Completion of the Grand Erie Canal" [appendix]. In Cadwallader Colden. *Memoir Prepared at the Request of the Committee of the Common Council of the City of New York and Presented to the Mayor of the City at the Celebration of the Completion of the New York Canals.* New York: Corporation of New York, 1825. pp. 293–321.

"Surveyor General's Office" [notice]. *National Advocate* 28 Apr. 1825. p. 3.

Swellengrebel, N. H., and E. Van Der Kuyp. *Health of White Settlers in Surinam.* Amsterdam: Colonial Institute at Amsterdam, 1940.

Tchernichovsky, Shaul. "Omrim: Yeshnah Eretz" [1923]. In *Shirat haTkhiya haIvrit.* Ed. Benyamin Harshav. Jerusalem: Mossad Bialik, 2000. pp. 190–192. [Hebrew]

———. "In Place of a Letter" [1906]. In *Hebrew Writers on Writing.* Ed. and Trans. Peter Cole. San Antonio, TX: Trinity UP, 2008. pp. 25–26.

Teitel, Jacob. *Aus meiner Lebensarbeit.* Trans. Dr. Elias Hurwicz. Frankfurt: I. Kauffmann, 1929. [German]

Terló, Wolf. "Projecto de Colonização Israelita no Planalto de Angola." *Boletim do Comite Israelita de Lisboa* 1 (Sept. 1912): 39–46. [Portuguese]

"Territorial Tremens." *Jewish Frontier* (1937): 5.

"Text of the Statement by Chamberlain." *New York Times* 22 Nov. 1938. p. 8.

Thomas, Ebenezer Smith. *Reminiscences of the Last Sixty-Five Years, Commencing with the Battle of Lexington.* Vol. 2. Hartford, CT: Case, Tiffany, and Burnham, 1840.

Tonini, Carla. "The Polish Plan for Jewish Settlement in Madagascar, 1936–1939." *Polin: Studies in Polish Jewry* V.19 (2006): 467–477.

———. *Operation Madagascar.* Unpublished English MS. translation of *Operazione Madagascar: La Questione ebraica in Polonia, 1918–1968.* Bologna: CLUEB, 1999. [Italian]

"To Palestine via Jewganda." *African Standard* (Nairobi) 28 May 1904. p. 6.

Toward Peace and Equity: Recommendations of the American Jewish Committee. New York: American Jewish Committee, 1946.

Trevor-Roper, H. R. *History and Imagination.* Oxford: Clarendon Press, 1980.

Trowbridge, John Townsend. *My Own Story: With Recollections of Noted Persons.* New York: Houghton, Mifflin, 1903.

"Uganda or Jewganda." *African Standard* (Nairobi) 12 Dec. 1903. p. 2.

"Un Attentat Sioniste." *Archives Israelites* 64 (1903): 412–413. [French]

"Un Drame Dans Un Bal." *Le Matin* 20 Dec. 1903. p. 3. [French]

"The Urgent Need of Jewry." London: Freeland League, 1935(?).

"US Opinion Shocked." *Times* (London) 16 Nov. 1938. p. 14.

U'velibam—Ahavat Elohim v'Adam. Nir David, Israel: Kibbutz Nir David, 1971. [Hebrew]

"Vichy Government Arrests Jewish Social Workers; Brutzkus Still Held." Jewish Telegraphic Agency. 6 Dec. 1940. n.p.

Vincent-Smith, J. D. "The Anglo-German Negotiations Over the Portuguese Colonies in Africa, 1911–1914." *Historical Journal* 17.3 (Sept. 1974): 620–629.

Vink, Dr. G. J. "Over De Mogelijkheid Van Kolonisatie Van Blanken in Suriname." *Tijdschrift van het Nederlandsch Aardrijkskundig Genootschap*. Leiden: E. J. Brill, 1941. pp. 675–692. [Dutch]

Vital, David. "The Afflictions of the Jews and the Afflictions of Zionism: The Meaning and Consequences of the 'Uganda' Controversy." In *Essential Papers on Zionism*. Ed. Jehuda Reinharz and Anita Shapira. New York: NYU Press, 1996. pp. 119–132.

———. *Zionism: The Formative Years*. New York: Oxford UP, 1982.

Voltaire. *Candide*. Trans. John Butt. New York: Penguin, 1947.

Warburg, Otto. "Einiges Ueber Die Zionistische Ostafrika–Expedition." Trans. Lee Chadeayne. *Ost und West* (Mar. 1905): 151–162. [German]

Way, Lewis. *Mémoires sur l'état Israélites*. Paris: Firmin Didot, 1819. [French]

Weinberg, Robert. *Stalin's Forgotten Zion: An Illustrated History, 1928–1996*. Berkeley: University of California Press, 1998.

Weinryb, Bernard (Dov). "Noah's Ararat Jewish State in its Historical Setting." *American Jewish Historical Society Publications* 43 (1953–54): 170–191.

———. "Yesodot haTzionut v'Toldoteha." *Tarbits* 7.A (1935): 69–112. [Hebrew]

Weisbord, Robert G. *African Zion: The Attempt to Establish a Jewish Colony in the East African Protectorate, 1903–1905*. Philadelphia: Jewish Publication Society, 1968.

Weizmann, Chaim. *The Letters and Papers of Chaim Weizmann*. Vol. I. Series B. Ed. Barnet Litvinoff. New Brunswick, NJ: Rutgers UP, 1983.

———. *The Letters and Papers of Chaim Weizmann*. Vol. II. Series B. Ed. Barnet Litvinoff. New Brunswick, NJ: Transaction Books, 1983.

———. "Letter to Moshe Shertok 18 Oct. 1936." *Letters and Papers of Chaim Weizmann*. Volume XVII. Series A. Gen. Ed. Barnet Litvinoff. Ed. Yemima Rosenthal. Jerusalem: Israel Universities Press, 1979. p. 364.

———. "Palestine's Role in the Solution of the Jewish Problem." *Foreign Affairs* 20.2 (Jan. 1942): 324–338.

"Statement of Jew Refugees." *Times* (London) 23 Jan. 1939. p. 13.

Werb, Bret and Barbara Milewski. "From 'Madagaskar' to Sachsenhausen.'" *Polin: Studies in Polish Jewry* 16 (Nov. 2003): 269–278.

"Who Will Go to Surinam." *Freeland* IV.2 (May–June 1948): 19.

Wilbusch, Nahum. *haMassa l'Uganda*. Jerusalem: Hasifria Hatziyonit, 1963. [Hebrew]

Winters, Bradford. "Exodus 2048." *Image*. 15 Apr. 2009. http://imagejournal.org/page/blog/exodus-2048.

Wistrich, Robert. *Laboratory for World Destruction: Germans and Jews in Central Europe*. Lincoln: University of Nebraska Press, 2007.

Wolf, Lucien. "Lord Landsdowne and the Zionists." *Times* (London) 28 Aug. 1903. p. 5.

Wolf, Simon. *Mordecai Manuel Noah: A Biographical Sketch*. Philadelphia: Levytype Company Publishers, 1897.

Yaari, Chaim. "Zionist Labour Dailies." In *The Jewish Press That Was: Accounts, Evaluations and Memories of Jewish Papers in pre-Holocaust Europe*. Ed. Aryeh Bar. Jerusalem: Jerusalem Post Press, 1980. pp. 122–132.

Yaffe, Leib. *Tzion b'Basel: Katavot al haCongressim haTzionim haRishonim (1897–1905)*. Jerusalem: n.p., 1967–68. [Hebrew]

Yaffe, Richard. "All-Jewish Colony in Surinam Sought." *PM* 11 Jan. 1948. p. 4.

Yahil, Leni. "Madagascar—Phantom of a Solution for the Jewish Question." In *Jews and Non-Jews in Eastern Europe, 1918–1945: The Case of Slovakia*. Ed. Bela Vago and George Lachmann Mosse. New York: Wiley, 1974. pp. 315–334.

Zack, Abraham. "Ups and Downs of a Daily." In *The Jewish Press That Was: Accounts, Evaluations and Memories of Jewish Papers in Pre-Holocaust Europe*. Ed. Aryeh Bar. Jerusalem: Jerusalem Post Press, 1980. pp. 65–78.

Zangwill, Israel. *The Voice of Jerusalem*. New York: Macmillan, 1921.

———. "The Territorial Solution of the Jewish Question (II)." *Fortnightly Review* 105.629 (May 1919): 732–741.

———. "Siberia as a Jewish State." *Jewish World* (London) 8 Aug. 1917. p. 13.

———. "Afterword [to *The Melting Pot*]." *The Melting Pot*. New York: Macmillan, 1917. pp. 199–216.

———. "Rosy Russia." *The War for the World*. New York: Macmillan, 1916. pp. 358–368.

———. "Mr. Chamberlain and Zionism; Mr. Zangwill's Work" (Letter to the Editor). *Times* (London) 11 July 1914. p. 9.

———. "Territorialism as Practical Politics" [1913]. *Speeches Articles and Letters of Israel Zangwill*. Ed. Maurice Simon. London: Soncino Press, 1937. pp. 309–328.

———. "Introduction, Historical and Political." *Report on the Work of the Commission Sent Out by the Jewish Territorial Organization Under the Auspices of the Portuguese Government to Examine the Territory Proposed for the Purpose of a Jewish Settlement in Angola*. J. W. Gregory. London: ITO Offices, 1913. vii–xiii.

———. "Zionism and Territorialism." *Fortnightly Review* 86.520 (Apr. 1910): 645–655.

———. "Mr. Morel and the Congo" [1910]. *The War for the World*. New York: Macmillan, 1916. pp. 278–286.

———. "Be Fruitful and Multiply." London: ITO Offices, 1909.

———. "Preface, Historical and Political." *Report on the Work of the Commission Sent Out by the Jewish Territorial Organization Under the Auspices of the Governor-General of Tripoli to Examine the Territory Proposed for the Purpose of a Jewish Settlement in Cyrenaica*. J. W. Gregory. London: ITO Offices, 1909. pp. v–xiii.

———. *The Melting Pot*. New York: Macmillan, 1917 [1908].

———. "Jewish Colonial Trust" [1908]. *Speeches Articles and Letters of Israel Zangwill.* Ed. Maurice Simon. London: Soncino Press, 1937. pp. 262–282.

———. "A Land of Refuge" [1907]. *Speeches Articles and Letters of Israel Zangwill.* Ed. Maurice Simon. London: Soncino Press, 1937. pp. 234–261.

———. "Letters and the ITO." *Fortnightly Review* 79.472 (Apr. 1906): 633–647.

———. "What is the ITO?" [1905]. *Speeches Articles and Letters of Israel Zangwill.* Ed. Maurice Simon. London: Soncino Press, 1937. pp. 231–234.

———. "The Jewish Territorial Organisation." *Jewish Chronicle* (London) 5 Aug. 1905. p. 17.

———. "Mr. Zangwill on the Future of Zionism." *Jewish Chronicle* (London) 14 July 1905. pp. 12–15.

———. "Two Dreamers of the Ghetto" [1904?]. *Speeches, Articles and Letters of Israel Zangwill.* London: Soncino Press, 1937. pp. 120–122.

———. *The East African Question: Zionism and England's Offer.* New York: Maccabaean Publishing Co., 1904.

———. "Zionism and Charitable Institutions" [1903]. *Speeches, Articles and Letters of Israel Zangwill.* London: Soncino Press, 1937. pp. 167–180.

———. "Zionism." *Contemporary Review* 76 (Oct. 1899): 500–511.

Zhitlowski, Chaim. "Der Teritorialism, Zeyne Kegner un Zeyne Videroyflebn." *Frayland* 1–2. (1934): 22–41. [Yiddish]

"The Zionist Scheme." *African Standard* (Nairobi) 21 Jan. 1905. p. 6.

"Zionists Object to Plan." *New York Times* 1 Dec. 1938. p. 12.

Zitron, S. L. "Reshimot Min haKonferentzia haITO'it." *haZman* 9 July 1912. p. 2. [Hebrew]

———. "haKonferentzia haITO'it." *haZman* 5 July 1912. pp. 2–3. [Hebrew]

———. "Ptikhat haKonferentzia haITO'it." *haZman* 2 July 1912. pp. 2–3. [Hebrew]

Zuckerman, W. "Dr. I.N. Steinberg." *Freeland* X.1 (Jan–Mar. 1957): 5–6.

INDEX

ABOUT THE AUTHOR

Adam Rovner is Associate Professor of English and Jewish Literature at the University of Denver. His articles, essays, translations, and interviews have appeared in numerous scholarly journals and general interest publications. Rovner's short documentary on Jewish territorialism, *No Land Without Heaven*, has been screened at exhibitions in New York, Paris, and Tel Aviv.